Sambrook Court:
The Letters of J. C. Lettsom at
the Medical Society of London

edited by

Christopher Lawrence and
Fiona A. Macdonald

The Wellcome Trust Centre for the History of Medicine at
University College London
Occasional Publication 3

ISBN 0-85484-083-4

Contents

Illustrations

Preface and Acknowledgements

The Medical Society of London contains a large if miscellaneous collection of letters from and to John Coakley Lettsom which we were invited to edit. Our first thanks are to the Society for the invitation. Ian Murray, Archivist of The Worshipful Company of Barbers, made the initial transcriptions of the vast bulk of the letters, and to him we are most grateful. The Medical Society of London kindly provided funds to assist Fiona Macdonald in her researches, without which monetary assistance this project would not have been possible. Professor Harold Cook, Director of the Wellcome Centre for the History of Medicine at University College London, also provided funds for the same purpose. At the Medical Society of London, the Registrar, Colonel Richard Kinsella-Bevan, and the Assistant Registrar, Mrs Betty Smallwood, were invaluable in their assistance. At the Wellcome Trust Library for the History and Understanding of Medicine, Richard Aspin and John Symons were of immense help in tracing the history of Lettsom material, and Richard Aspin in deciphering handwriting. At the Wellcome Trust Centre for the History of Medicine at UCL, Sir Christopher Booth read through many of the letters with us and offered many helpful suggestions. Vivian Nutton and Simone de Angelis assisted with the translations from the Latin, Paddy Ricard helped with some of the French text, Claudia Stein transcribed the German letters, Sharon Messenger dug out related manuscripts and Emma Ford assisted in the typing. Caroline Tonson-Rye's editorial skills, as ever, proved invaluable. We are also grateful to Janet Dudley for compiling the index.

v

1

Introduction

The Medical Society of London contains a rich archive of manuscript material pertaining to the Quaker physician John Coakley Lettsom (1744–1815). Lettsom has been the subject of two book-length biographies. First, the three-volume work by Thomas Joseph Pettigrew, which appeared in 1817 shortly after Lettsom's death.[1] The biographical section is rather brief, and for the most part the volumes consist of letters. The second biography, by James Johnston Abraham, was published in 1933.[2] The latter is detailed and invaluable but, infuriatingly, Abraham cites manuscript sources without indicating their whereabouts. Together these volumes render anything other than the briefest account of Lettsom's life unnecessary here. For anyone to whom Lettsom is a complete unknown, however, Abraham's opening words neatly summarize the doctor's world:

JOHN COAKLEY LETTSOM, the eighteenth century Quaker physician, philanthropist and man of letters, who met everyone worth meeting in the intimate London of his time, stands out amongst his contemporaries as the central figure in the medical history of the period.

On account of his enormous practice he moved freely in every grade of life, equally at home in the presence of the King, and in the fever-laden atmosphere of the City prisons. He was as familiar with the conditions in the insanitary tortuous alleys behind the main streets, where he worked for charity, as with the spacious elegance of the homes of the city magnates, from whom he made his living.[3]

We first present a brief life of Lettsom, touching especially on those aspects that shed light on the letters. We follow this with a summary of the history of the Medical Society of London, the source of all the material presented here. We discuss some of the puzzles associated with the dispersal of Lettsom's collection of manuscripts after his death, and then describe the

---

[1] Thomas Joseph Pettigrew, *Memoirs of the life and writings of the late John Coakley Lettsom, M.D., F.R.S.: with a selection from his correspondence*, 3 vols, London, printed by Nichols, Son, and Bentley, for Longman, Hurst, Rees, Orme and Brown, 1817.

[2] James Johnston Abraham, *Lettsom: his life, times, friends and descendants*, London, William Heinemann, 1933.

[3] Ibid., p. 1.

various collections in the Society and as far as possible the origins of the originals transcribed here.

John Coakley Lettsom was born on 22 November 1744, on Little Jost Van Dyke, one of the Virgin Islands (see Figure 1). His family were Quakers. When he was six years old he was sent to England to be educated. These early years are recorded in detail in his autobiography, transcribed and printed later in this volume. After schooling and an apprenticeship in Yorkshire to a surgeon-apothecary, Abraham Sutcliff, he became a pupil at St Thomas's Hospital in London.[4] It was in London that Lettsom, carrying a letter of introduction, met the renowned Quaker physician, John Fothergill. This was probably one of the most fortunate events in Lettsom's life. It was to allow him entry into the elevated circles in which Fothergill moved and eventually enabled him to take on Fothergill's mantle. No doubt he took over much of Fothergill's practice, first, perhaps, when the latter moved out of the City to Harpur Street in Bloomsbury in 1767 and then after his death in 1780. For example, Lettsom seems to have inherited Lady Huntingdon as a patient.[5]

In 1767 Lettsom briefly returned to the West Indies, to the island of Tortola, to take possession of a property left to him by his father. On his return, he entered the University of Edinburgh in 1768. He graduated MD at Leyden in June 1769. In 1770 as a licentiate of the Royal College of Physicians he commenced medical practice in the City of London. He married in the same year and thereby acquired a considerable fortune. For most of his active professional life he lived at Sambrook Court, Basinghall Street—hence our title, since nearly all the letters published here were sent to or emanated from Sambrook Court. Although living in the City, Lettsom bought a house at Grove Hill, Camberwell, a village south of the river. This he made into a country estate with a museum, library and botanical garden. Towards the close of his life pecuniary circumstances forced him to part with it.

He was extraordinarily active in the scientific, medical and philanthropic societies and circles of London. In 1770 he helped found the General Dispensary in Aldersgate Street. He assisted Thomas Cogan and William Hawes in founding the Royal Humane Society in 1774. He was the prime mover in the establishment of the Sea-Bathing Hospital in Margate in 1791. As these letters show, prison reform was a cause that occupied much of his time. He was a prolific author, not only on medical subjects but on botany,

---

[4] See the only letter from Lettsom to Sutcliff in the Society's possession, 14 May 1791, in the 'Letters from Lettsom' section. On Sutcliff, see Lettsom's own account in the 'Recollections or Reminiscences'.

[5] See R. Hingston Fox, *Dr. John Fothergill and his friends. Chapters in eighteenth century life*, London, Macmillan, 1919, p. 48, and the letters from Lady Anne Erskine, this volume, pp. 53–70.

agriculture, temperance and many other topics as well. He also wrote a memoir of his patron, John Fothergill.

In 1773 Lettsom along with nine others founded the Medical Society of London. It seems likely that Lettsom was the prime mover. The minutes of the first meeting are dated 19 May 1773, and five other members were proposed and accepted. The members included physicians, surgeons and apothecaries. Lettsom was then living in the City of London in Great Eastcheap, in the Parish of St Leonard's. It is possible that the first meeting was held in his house, although Abraham thought it more likely it was held at the house of Nathaniel Hulme in Mudiford Court, Fenchurch Street. Membership grew quickly, and at the end of 1773 a committee was viewing premises at Crane Court off Fleet Street, which the Society moved into and occupied until 1788.[6] At the Society's meetings, papers were read. The Society also gradually began to build a library. Lettsom instituted the Fothergillian Medal, to be awarded for an essay in medicine or natural history. It was first given in 1786 and seems to have been awarded six times, the last in 1803 to Edward Jenner. The present Fothergillian Medal was established by a bequest from Anthony Fothergill, a distant relation of John, in 1813.[7]

This picture of a flourishing young medical club belies the fact that the first years of the Society were deeply troubled: factionalism broke out, members were locked out of the Crane Court premises and the Minute Book was tampered with. Lettsom was elected President in 1775. Peace returned briefly until the Society was riven by an even more explosive episode in 1784. Worse was to come. In the meanwhile, in 1787, Lettsom gave the Society the freehold of No. 3 Bolt Court, Fleet Street, a gift, says Abraham, "which undoubtedly preserved [the Society]...from extinction on several occasions afterwards".[8] This building the Society inhabited from 1788 until 1850. In 1805, says Abraham, "the great split which nearly wrecked the Society began".[9] The rift centred on the presidency of James Sims who had managed to hold that position continuously since 1786. Secessionists formed themselves into a new organization, the Medical and Chirurgical Society. Lettsom resigned his seat on the Council of the Medical Society of London in 1806. Sims hung on until 1808 when he resigned the presidency. Lettsom was President 1809–10 and again in 1813–15.

---

[6] Abraham, op. cit., note 2 above, pp. 125, 392, n.3.

[7] See Christopher C. Booth, 'The Fothergillian Medals of the Medical Society of London', *Journal of the Royal College of Physicians of London*, 1981, **15**: 254–8.

[8] Abraham, op. cit., note 2 above, p. 392.

[9] Ibid., p. 395.

In the mid-nineteenth century the centre of medical practice shifted from the City to the West End. In consequence, the Society, based in Fleet Street, saw a decline in membership. The Westminster Medical Society had seen an even worse decline in numbers. It was absorbed into the Medical Society of London, which, in 1850, moved from Bolt Court to 33 George Street, Hanover Square, in the Oxford Street / Regent Street area. In that same year an annual lectureship, 'The Lettsomian' was founded. In April 1873 the Society moved to its current location at 11 Chandos Street, Cavendish Square, near Harley Street.

The unpublished Lettsom material in the Medical Society of London presented here is of two sorts. First, a transcription of the original manuscript of Lettsom's autobiography written by him, probably in 1804, and titled 'Recollections or Reminiscences'. Second, letters, almost all either to or from Lettsom but with a small number from and to Pettigrew, and others between members of the Lettsom family. These letters are to be found at the Society in fascicles or in one of four bound volumes. We have confined this publication to the material in the Society for the simple reason that Lettsom manuscript material is widely dispersed.

Ironically, the manuscripts in Lettsom's possession at his death seem to have suffered a similar fate to those of his patron John Fothergill. The latter's papers and manuscripts remained in the hands of his niece, Alice Chorley, until her death in 1828 "after which they seem to have been dispersed, sold or lost".[10] The dispersal of Lettsom's correspondence and other manuscript material after his death merits a full-scale historical enquiry. We have been unable to undertake this. Rather, here we indicate the little that is known. Unfortunately, the matter has not been made easier by various writers who have treated the history of the Lettsom papers as though no issues were involved.[11] Matters are in fact extremely murky.

Thomas Joseph Pettigrew (1791–1865), surgeon and antiquary, was, as we have noted, Lettsom's first biographer and a key player in this story. The son of a naval surgeon, William Pettigrew, Thomas began studying medicine as his father's assistant and was later apprenticed to John Taunton, Surgeon to the City and the Finsbury Dispensaries, who was a great friend of Lettsom.

---

[10] Fox, op. cit., note 5 above, p. 418. See however, *Chain of friendship: selected letters of Dr. John Fothergill of London, 1735–1780*, with introduction and notes by Betsy C. Corner and Christopher C. Booth, Cambridge, MA, Belknap Press, 1971.

[11] On the Lettsom manuscripts at the Society, see Robin Price, 'Lettsom's letters', *Transactions of the Medical Society of London*, 1971, **87**: 108–18; G. B. Woodd-Walker, 'The Society's Library', in Thomas Hunt (ed.), *The Medical Society of London, 1773–1973*, London, William Heinemann Medical Books, 1972, pp. 89–104; Charles Newman, 'Dr Lettsom's letters', *Transactions of the Medical Society of London*, 1974, **90**: 31–7. Unfortunately none of these papers treats of the dispersal of the manuscripts.

Lettsom first met Pettigrew when he was elected a fellow of the Medical Society of London in 1808, at the very young age of seventeen. He served as secretary of the Society (1813–18), thanks to Taunton's backing and much to the chagrin of some of the older fellows, who had proposed George Birkbeck. Pettigrew also became Secretary of the Royal Humane Society (1813–20) through Lettsom's influence. Here he made the acquaintance of the Duke of Kent, the father of the future Queen Victoria, and became his surgeon; this led to posts as surgeon and later librarian to his brother the Duke of Sussex. He was surgeon at various London hospitals throughout his career, but gave more time to his private practice from the 1840s. He was also involved with various other London societies: the City Philosophical Society, the Philosophical Society of London and the British Archaeological Society.[12]

In his will made in 1795, twenty years before he died, Lettsom decreed that all his manuscripts were to pass to his son John Miers Lettsom.[13] Tragically, John predeceased his father, dying in 1800. Lettsom's will was proved on 4 March 1816, and his sole executor was his son-in-law, Philip Elliot (husband of Mary Ann Lettsom). Pettigrew, however, says that his access to the papers was by way of John Elliot, Philip's brother, who was another son-in-law (husband of Eliza Lettsom). That Pettigrew had this access was no doubt true, but it was not the whole truth about how he acquired Lettsom material. Lettsom was scarcely dead when Pettigrew began writing to Lettsom's correspondents asking for material.[14] Pettigrew says the letters that he published were "selected from among many thousands".[15] Nothing approaching this quantity of letters has been identified as extant, even totalling those from all holdings. Some material seems to have sunk without trace. Pettigrew, for example, reproduced numerous letters from the Dorchester physician William Cuming. None of these have been discovered. The Bath physician Anthony Fothergill left his manuscripts to Lettsom with £1,000 for the editing and publishing of them. This was not done and the whereabouts of these materials is also unknown.[16] Some letters Pettigrew

---

[12] Warren R. Dawson, 'Thomas Joseph Pettigrew, F.R.C.S., F.R.S., F.S.A., (1791–1865)', *Medical Life*, 1931, **38**: 1–136; Abraham, op. cit., note 2 above, pp. 141, 399–400. The Pettigrew papers are currently held in the James Marshall and Marie-Louise Osborn Collection, in the Beinecke Rare Book and Manuscript Library at Yale University. The Wellcome Library in London also has significant holdings pertaining to both Pettigrew's medical and antiquarian activities.

[13] Abraham, op. cit., note 2 above, p. 485.

[14] See the letter from Joshua Dixon to Pettigrew in the Pettigrew section, this volume, p. 298.

[15] Pettigrew, op. cit., note 1 above, vol. 1, p. vii.

[16] Abraham, op. cit., note 2 above, p. 413. There are four Fothergill Letters at the Royal Society, London. A letterbook containing transcriptions of Fothergill's letters to a young doctor, James Woodforde, is in the library of the American Philosophical Society in Philadelphia. See Christopher Lawrence, Paul Lucier and Christopher C. Booth (eds), *"Take time by the forelock": The letters of Anthony Fothergill to James Woodforde 1789–1813, Medical History*, Supplement No. 17, London, Wellcome Institute for the History of Medicine, 1997.

returned to their authors. The Reverend Thomas Maurice wrote to Pettigrew that he had a "fear" of his letters to Lettsom "getting, hereafter, into improper hands, for I wrote to *him* with unbounded openness and freedom".[17] Pettigrew returned them.

The Society had its bound manuscript collection catalogued in the early 1930s.[18] No letters of any sort were catalogued although we know a volume of Lettsom letters had been donated to the Society in 1930 (see p. 10). All other Lettsom letters seem to have been acquired after this. Hingston Fox, John Fothergill's biographer, writing in 1919, says "Lettsom's medical and other papers were passed to Pettigrew and were ultimately dispersed in 1906, many being sold at auction".[19] There was an auction of Pettigrew material in 1905 but no manuscripts were described in the catalogue, although there were evidently some in the many job lots.[20] In fact, Lettsom material in the hands of the Pettigrew family began to be dispersed before this, as letters in the Society indicate. In 1902, Pettigrew's grandson (also T. J.) wrote to Joseph J. Green in Tunbridge Wells who was seeking a copy of Pettigrew's *Memoirs* and other things. Green was a Quaker and a minor author who seems to have been interested in Quaker genealogy.[21] Pettigrew wrote that one of his grandfather's daughters was still living and she had a copy of the *Memoirs* "& possibly more & she would also have any letters or manuscripts of Dr Lettsom that my grandfather may have had at the time of his death". Pettigrew promised to see her and to try to get the book or any letters or manuscripts, adding, "I shall be glad to let you have them".[22] Green already had some of Lettsom's letters in his possession, for later that same year Pettigrew wrote to him thanking him for sending the "24 letters written by my grandfather".[23] For reasons to do with his aunt's incapacity after an accident it was not until 5 March 1906 that Pettigrew could write to Green reporting he had

---

[17] Letter from T[homas] Maurice to [T. J.] Pettigrew, 19 Jan. [*c*.1816?] in a bound volume, labelled 'Dr John Coakley Lettsom 1744–1815' on the spine. Bequeathed to the Medical Society of London by Sir Thomas Colyer-Fergusson, Bart.

[18] Warren Dawson, *Manuscripta medica: a descriptive catalogue of the manuscripts in the library of the Medical Society of London*, London, published for the Medical Society of London by John Bale, Sons and Danielsson, 1932.

[19] Fox, op. cit., note 5 above, p. 117.

[20] *A catalogue of books and engraved portraits (formerly belonging to Thos. J. Pettigrew…which will be sold by auction by Messrs. Knight, Frank & Rutley…23rd of August, 1905.*

[21] Joseph Joshua Green (1854–1921). He was the author of, for instance, *Quaker Records, being a complete index to the 'Annual Monitor', 1813–1892*; he also wrote, *A few serious thoughts on the subject of war*, [Tunbridge Wells?], 1900. Green was described in this volume as clerk to the meeting, Friends' Meeting House, Grosvenor Park.

[22] Letter from T. J. Pettigrew to J. J. Green, 21 Sept. 1902, in Colyer-Fergusson, op. cit. note 17 above.

[23] Letter from T. J. Pettigrew to J. J. Green, 26 Oct. 1902, in ibid.

finally sent the book, adding, "Since doing so I am pleased to have got hold of a few more papers that may perhaps interest you...they consist of some Recollections and Reminiscences in manuscript".[24] Two years later, Pettigrew sent Green "The purchase by the Dr of a mulatto boy and girl".[25] This was a deed of purchase of two slaves whose freedom Lettsom bought when he returned to Tortola in 1767. This correspondence then ceases and nothing more is heard until 22 July 1918 when Green wrote to Thomas Colyer-Fergusson explaining that he had been invalided and was unable to undertake "much in the way of genealogical and literary work" and that he was "disposing of some of my literary treasures. Amongst them is my collection of Lettsom items". These included "letters, slave deed, recollections, letters of P[ettigrew] senior and junior". He wondered whether Colyer-Fergusson was inclined to purchase them.[26] A week later Green said the price was five guineas.[27] Colyer-Fergusson bought the material and the volume in which it is bound is described below.

One of the bound volumes at the Society is of uncertain provenance. The Report of the Library Committee for the Session 1969–70 notes "A collection of letters which came on to the market, written by and to Dr. Lettsom, comprising some 38 documents, have [*sic*] been purchased at a cost of £750".[28] The vendor is not stated. Geoffrey Woodd-Walker in 1972 reported that this "packet of letters and correspondence" had been acquired "on favourable terms" in February 1970 in spite of a counter-bid from Yale University.[29] On 5 May 1970 the Library Committee reported that the "Lettsom letters" of the Society were to be deposited with the Wellcome Library for safekeeping.[30] The collection was bound into a volume by the Wellcome Library's binder soon after receipt[31] and remained on deposit until 24 January 1984, when it was returned to the Medical Society. The volume actually contains 76 documents (not all are letters: there is a Deed of Covenant, for example, and not all are to and from Lettsom; several are addressed to Pettigrew). The most likely explanation for this discrepancy is that the figure 38 in the Library Committee minutes is a mistake and that it should have read "documents by some 38 correspondents". Searches in the records of the

---

[24] Letter from T. J. Pettigrew to J. J. Green, 5 March 1906, in ibid.

[25] Letter from T. J. Pettigrew to J. J. Green, 25 June 1908, in ibid.

[26] Letter from Joseph J. Green to Mr T. Colyer-Fergusson, 22 July 1918, in ibid.

[27] Letter from Joseph J. Green to Mr Colyer-Fergusson, 29 July 1918, in ibid.

[28] Medical Society of London, Library Committee Minutes, Oct. 1891 to Feb. 1988. Report of the Library Committee for the Session 1969–70.

[29] Woodd-Walker, op. cit., note 11 above.

[30] Minutes, op. cit., note 28 above, 5 May 1970.

[31] "A collection of letters on lone [*sic*] to Library bound (guarded)". Wellcome Library records: Staff reports: Binding: D. Theobald, June–August 1970.

Medical Society and of the Wellcome Trust have so far failed to throw any light on the provenance.

Each correspondent's letters in the collection are collocated, but there appears to be no overall arrangement, either chronological or alphabetical. The collection has been described by Price and by Woodd-Walker.[32] Woodd-Walker's rather anecdotal paper identified some of the letters to Lettsom as coming from Benjamin Rush, John Warren, Jedidiah Morse, David Ramsey, Dr Christian August Struve, Dr J. Vaughan, Dr B. Wilmer and Jonathan Stokes. He also identified two letters from James Sims of 1816, which he implied were written to Lettsom, yet of course Lettsom died the previous year and they are in fact to Pettigrew. He refers to letters from Lettsom to Pettigrew, Lady Anne Erskine and Dr Thornton.[33] His quotations are not entirely reliable. Some, probably all, the letters in this bound volume were known to Pettigrew, and we indicate these in the footnotes. They do not seem to have been known to Abraham, which is not surprising if they had been in private hands since the dispersal of Lettsom's papers.

The Lettsom correspondence at the Wellcome merits brief notice. Letters to Lettsom are said to have been acquired before 1923, possibly with papers of Pettigrew. These latter are stated to have been acquired before that date and "Some items were purchased at the Pettigrew sale, Knight, Frank & Rutley 23 Aug. 1905."[34] As we have noted, however, there are no manuscripts listed in the Pettigrew auction catalogue. There are however a number of Pettigrew manuscripts at the Wellcome Library, which all seem to have come from this sale, although the acquisition dates in the published catalogue vary between 1905 and 1906.[35] They were presumably contained in the numerous lots of unbound pamphlets, etc. Letters to Lettsom at the Wellcome have been catalogued and there are 91 items. Again some, probably all, of these were known to Pettigrew, who published a number of them in whole or in part.[36]

---

[32] See note 11 above.

[33] Woodd-Walker, op. cit., note 11 above.

[34] Richard Palmer (compiler), *Catalogue of western manuscripts in the Wellcome Library for the History and Understanding of Medicine: western manuscripts 5160–6244*, London, Wellcome Library for the History and Understanding of Medicine, 1999, MS 5370–72. A detailed listing of MSS 5370–71 is provided in a typescript handlist available in the Library: 'Handlist 8. List of minor collections of Western manuscripts', revised Sept. 1990, pp. 6–16.

[35] See S A J Moorat, *Catalogue of western manuscripts on medicine and science in the Wellcome Historical Medical Library: MSS written after 1650 A.D.*, 2 vols, London, Wellcome Institute of the History of Medicine, 1973, vol. 2, nos. 3666, 3721, 3860–3866, 3924, and 4595.

[36] Letters to Lettsom catalogued in Palmer ('Handlist', op. cit., note 34 above) that were published in Pettigrew have the catalogue numbers 5370/2, 5370/22 (correctly dated by Pettigrew as 1787 not 1781 as in the Wellcome handlist), 5370/43 (Pettigrew incorrectly has Liverpool not Edinburgh), 5370/44 (in part), 5370/53 (in part), 5370/69, 5370/74 and 5370/77.

Abraham had access to a large number of Lettsom's papers in the early 1930s although clearly not as many as Pettigrew. They were described by him as in the possession of Lettsom's great-great-grandson, John Hugh Armstrong Elliot of the Middle Temple. A bound volume presented to the Society by Elliot (item 4 below), however, contains only a small amount of material. Descendants of Elliot know of no other papers. But Abraham also used unbound Elliot letters that eventually came to the Society by way of Abraham's daughter (item 1 below).

Overall there is no particular coherence to either the fascicles or the bound collections in the Society and so we have taken the liberty of imposing an order upon them while indicating their origins. It would be customary to organize letters chronologically in order to reproduce the quotidian life of the subject in temporal form. We have taken the liberty of rejecting this custom and have grouped the letters by subject and by author. There are two main reasons for this. First, with a couple of minor exceptions, there are scarcely any letters in the Society to Lettsom to which there are replies or letters from Lettsom to which he received a reply. This merely reflects the fact that the correspondence at the Society is only a fraction of that which once existed, as described above. Second there are groups of letters that clearly relate to a single subject, the import of which would be lost were they to be dispersed in a chronological arrangement. This is particularly true of the family letters, the letters respecting charitable giving, the letters from James Neild relating to prisons, and the correspondence from Lettsom with regard to the affairs of the Royal Humane Society. Nearly all letters from Lettsom have been assigned their own section. Letters to Lettsom have been organized alphabetically and where more than one letter exists from a correspondent they have been placed in date order. Family letters have been separated, as have those to and from Pettigrew and a small number that seem to relate to Lettsom's charitable donations to individuals. Medical readers may be disappointed at the relative dearth of clinical and pathological material to be found here. Nevertheless, this absence is counterbalanced by the vast canvas these letters paint of the major place of medicine as an engine of social change in the American and European Enlightenment.

The following is a description of the originals in the Society with the conventions we have used to identify them.

1. Identified as [L]: Letters now bound in fascicles but that were loose in a box when first seen by us. Charles Newman said in 1974 that a box of letters was lent to the Society by Mrs Jill Martin, the daughter of James Johnston Abraham.[37] He gave no date. Whether the loose letters seen by us

---

[37] Newman, op. cit., note 11 above, pp. 32–3.

included letters given by Thomas Colyer-Fergusson cannot be ascertained. Some of the loose material was possibly acquired by Abraham from John Hugh Armstrong Elliot. Certainly the letters to Lettsom from Lady Anne Erskine are called by Abraham "Elliot MSS".[38] Where possible, using Newman and Abraham, we have indicated the provenance of individual letters or groups of letters.

2. Identified as [CF]: Letters in a bound volume, labelled 'Dr John Coakley Lettsom 1744–1815' on the spine. These were bequeathed to the Medical Society of London by Sir Thomas Colyer-Fergusson, Bart. Their history is described above. Colyer-Fergusson, who died in 1951, was the grandson of the surgeon Sir William Fergusson. Sir Thomas married Beatrice Max-Müller, Lettsom's great-great-granddaughter. The letters were forwarded to the Society by his daughter Mary, Viscountess Monckton of Brenchley.[39] Also bound in this volume is Lettsom's autobiography 'Recollections or Reminiscences'.

3. Identified as [S]: Letters in a bound volume described on the spine as 'Lettsom Letters presented by Herbert R. Spencer, 12 May 1930'. Herbert Ritchie Spencer qualified in medicine at University College, London, in 1883. In 1893 he was made professor of obstetric medicine there, retiring in 1925. He owned a unique library of early works on obstetrics. This volume contains 53 letters addressed to John Nichols or his son.[40]

4. Identified as [E]: Letters to and from Lettsom and other material in a bound volume, described on the spine as 'Lettsom Relics 1768–1810' presented by John Hugh Armstrong Elliot, in 1933.[41] Elliot, as noted, was Lettsom's great-great-grandson and then managing director of William Heinemann (Medical Books) Ltd.

5. Identified as [JCL]: A bound collection lettered 'Lettsom' in gold at the foot of the spine by the Wellcome binder and with a later handwritten paper label 'A collection of letters, to and from, John Coakley Lettsom'. This latter title also appears at the head of a typed description inside the front cover. Also inside the front cover is a Wellcome Library bookplate on which is typed 'Medical Society of London. Autograph letters'.

---

[38] Abraham, op. cit., note 2 above, p. 273.

[39] The Library Committee records the gift on 25 April 1952. Minutes, op. cit., note 28 above. A letter from Lady Monckton pasted into the volume, apologizing for the delay in sending it, is dated 9 Sept. to which a pencilled 1950 has been added. This is surely wrong and the date must be 1951.

[40] "A hearty vote of thanks to Dr. Herbert Spencer for his generosity in presenting 53 autograph letters of Dr. Lettsom". Minutes, op. cit. note 28 above, 9 March 1931.

[41] Printed *Report of the Medical Society of London*, 5 March 1934, pasted in Minutes, op. cit., note 28 above, records Elliot's donation of "Lettsom Relics, 1768–1810". He also donated Lettsom's diary for the year 1813–14.

Transcription Conventions

In this volume original spelling has been used throughout. All shortenings have been extended, except those for months of the year and shortened titles, such as Revd., which have been kept in the form given in the manuscripts. Crossings through have been included in the text only where it has not obscured the words and they remain fully legible. The presentation is as faithful to the original manuscripts as possible, except where meaning is thereby obscured. Where an author has used capital letters at the beginning of words, these have been retained, since eighteenth- and early nineteenth-century orthography was not yet standardized. However, in general, titles of proper names and book titles have been capitalized. Punctuation has been inserted where the sense requires it or where the authors have not used much punctuation themselves. The letters of the Archer family in Switzerland, William Archer and his wife, Betsy, for example, are written in almost a stream of consciousness style. In their letters, full stops appear, perhaps, only two or three times on a page. In these circumstances, punctuation has been introduced where it seems most appropriate, but it has not always been possible to say with certainty to which sentence an odd phrase belongs.

2

Recollections or Reminiscences

The following is a transcription of Lettsom's autobiography 'Recollections or Reminiscences'. This manuscript came to the Society from Sir Thomas Colyer-Fergusson, having previously been in the hands of the Pettigrew family and Joseph J. Green (see Introduction, pp. 6–7). It finishes with a note by Green stating; "This valuable manuscript was presented to me 5 March 1906 by T. J. Pettigrew" (the grandson of Lettsom's biographer). Green notes that the watermark of the paper is 1801, "but the doctor says he wrote it in his 60th year which will make it 1804". In effect, on page 2 of the manuscript, Lettsom states that he began collecting materials for the recollections in his sixtieth year. The recollections extend only until 1767 (when Lettsom was twenty-three), in which year he returned to Tortola to sort out family business. It is paginated 1–31 but there are no pages numbered 6 and 8. They are not missing, however. The verso of pages 5 and 7 are simply blank. The narrative proceeds without interruption. Pettigrew used the recollections, and they were cited verbatim, extensively, by Abraham, but the text is scattered through his volume and is not reproduced in its entirety. Abraham took liberties with Lettsom's spelling and punctuation. We have reproduced the autobiography here without alteration and indicated its original pagination. Most of the material not reproduced by Abraham deals with eighteenth-century life generally rather than its medical aspects. The curious story of the farmer and his child appears here for the first time (pp. 18–19 in the original). So much secondary material pertaining to the contents of this document can be found in Abraham that we have annotated it only very lightly.

Recollections or Reminiscences
[by Dr J. C. Lettsom][1]

I was so early sensible of the want of a good memory, that at my 15th year I availed myself of notes, and constructed tables to assist it; and by often

---

[1] Added by Joseph J. Green.

reverting to them, the impressions that I wished more particularly to retain, were rendered so strongly as rarely to elude recollection; and thus with moderate powers of mind I have been enabled to supply by industry and art, what nature had denied.

About the age of 22 years, I had collected memorials of many persons with whom I had been acquainted, which had gradually swelled to a very considerable volume: This was a favourite companion during part of a voyage to the West Indies in the year 1767. But before I had arrived at the place of my nativity, I was at one time so much indisposed, as to doubt of my recovery, and in this state of mind, I threw the volume into the ocean, to prevent it from falling into other hands. I have since very much regretted this loss which I endeavoured some years afterwards to repair by collecting such materials as necessary might recall, or subsequent connections afford. About the time of /2/ my 56th year, my travelling trunk containing nearly all my subsequent memoranda was stolen out of my carriage, which reduced me to my former misfortune; and I relinquished any similar attempt till after five years had elapsed, so that I was sixty years of age before I felt a desire renewed of collecting together any memorials of friends chiefly with whom I had passed a pleasing portion of my life, or with whom I had maintained a correspondence more or less interesting to my happiness.

However deficient my memory might have been, I well recollect transactions of my fifth year; and one of these is at this period, as vivid and impressive as any subsequent one of my life.

In the cluster of the Virgin islands in the West Indies, Tortola is the largest; of the small ones, my father Edward Lettsom was in possession of three where I was born on the 22nd of November 1744: these were Little Vandyke, 1744 Green Island and Sandy island; besides which he owned a sugar plantation in Cane Garden Bay, Tortola, an island, although only 24 miles long, and not exceeding four or five in breadth, appeared like a continent in contrast to the smaller islands or keys scattered around it.[2] My father's favorite residence was on Little Vandyke, where he cultivated cotton with the aid of about 50 slaves, whose humble cottages were situated on a declivity near his little mansion.

When any merchant ships arrived at Tortola, it was /3/ usual with the commanders or captains to hire small vessels called shallops, to trade with the small islands, from whence cotton and some little other produce were collected and conveyed to the harbour where the ships were stationed.

---

[2] Acccording to Abraham, Lettsom's birthplace is properly called Little Jost Van Dykes. James Johnston Abraham, *Lettsom: his life, times, friends and descendants*, London, William Heinemann, 1933, p. 8.

Figure 1: Engraving 'Scene in the Island of Little Van Dyke, near Tortola, with the house in which Dr. Lettsom was born'. Frontispiece of the Supplement to the *Gentleman's Magazine*, 1815, **85**: ii. (Wellcome Library, London.)

The whole product of these Islands, including Tortola, which raised and exported sugar, was at this time inconsiderable; and the consignments were then chiefly to Lancaster and Liverpool: At the former resided two brothers, Abraham and Hatton Rawlinson, who maintained an extensive mercantile connection with these islands.

At this time one of these vessels was commanded by William Lindo, who formed an intimacy with my parents. It was proposed to take me to Europe for education when I was about five years of age. I well remember that a tenderness impressed their minds so forcibly on the prospect of seperation, as to induce them to postpone the present scheme to the subsequent year when I was placed under the protection of the Captain with whom I arrived at Lancaster, where I was received by the Rawlinsons, to whose care I was consigned by my parents, the first I believe in these islands who possessed the fortitude and good sense to make a sacrifice of private feeling to promote the advantages of an infant. /4/At this period of my departure from the West Indies, not one equipage was kept in any of the Virgin islands. In our passage we made Dublin in Ireland, and here no object attracted my admiration more forcibly than the view of the carriages, and the velocity and the ease with which they were moved.

1749 æt. 5

1750 æt. 6

The ministry among Friends (Quakers) is voluntary and for which no stipend is raised or received. They exert themselves with great zeal and frequently under great inconveniences: They travel from considerable distances to visit meetings, and to inculcate their sentiments publicly, as well as to convey private advice. As they admit of no specific mode of education, to qualify themselves for the pious functions to which they devote themselves; they are rarely learned or possess oratorial powers; They conceive that the great leading principles of religion are obvious to every intellectual being and that plain truths may be explained and enforced by plain diction, without the ornaments of oratory.

On my introduction to the house of the Rawlinsons there was one of these ministers, who afforded an exception to most others of their Society, for the wonderful powers of elocution which he exhibited; and he was generally considered the most distinguished /5/ orator that ever issued from this society. This was Samuel Fothergill of Warrington the younger brother of the celebrated Dr John Fothergill of London.

Without explaining the impulsive influences of the mind, which excites sympathy, or generates antipathy, it happened that this great preacher noticed me with marked attention and affection. The Rawlinsons had a sister of the name of Barnes who resided about 2 miles from this town, near which was a school, under the direction of Gilbert Thompson, an unmarried man, whose sister kept his house; he was celebrated among the Society of Friends; Under his tuition I was placed, and lodged at the house of Barnes then a widow.

15

The affectionate Lindo, the faithful friend of my father, took me to this rural residence. The house was situated in the parish of Sankey, which gave name to a street in Warrington. Within about 200 yards of this residence, ran a stream of water, or brook, which emptied into the river ~~Ribble~~ and divides the parish of Sankey from Penketh in which parish the school was erected, and adjoining to it was a meeting for the Society, which was frequently visited by Samuel Fothergill. A common or heath, about a mile in diameter, intervened between the dwelling house and the school which was often enlivened with huntsmen and hounds. The number of boys at the school varied from 40 to 60; they were governed and instructed by the master and an usher, /7/ his nephew and namesake. I introduce these particulars of a place and its amusements, because they contributed to the preservation of health and invigoration of constitution. The vicinity of the brook afforded amusement and exertion, as it contained fish of different kinds; which are usually caught by forming two dams at a little distance from each other, and then laving out the water included between them, the enclosed fish were easily taken. Upon Penketh heath several holes had been formed, by digging out the sand and gravel for the public roads, these cavities filled with water and formed so many ponds; each boy claimed one of them which were made store ponds for the fish taken out of the brook; and I do not recollect that any of them was ever robbed or molested.

The common amusements of bird-nesting, nutting, sliding and the usual country sports occupied much of our leisure. Each boy was in possession of a Linnet, Goldfinch or Canary bird, which were uniformly hung up in cages in our eating and sitting parlour, for we had only one room besides bed chambers, and our noise and their melody, formed a compound sufficient to stun the ear, and confuse the head of any unaccustomed to such confused notes. There were at my time two linnets each possessing, from some unknown cause, a most cogent attachment to the other. They were birds of /9/ fine song, but never appeared so happy as when put into one cage. In fine weather they were frequently taken to Penketh common, and one or the other allowed to fly in the open air, for the space of nearly the whole day; that at liberty would mix with the wild linnets, but never could be enticed to fly beyond the call of that in the cage. When he was tired of his liberty, he would go into an open cage placed by his favourite. They were distinguished by the names of Robert and Henry; the former at length died, and Henry afterwards pined away and in a short space of time likewise died.

One of the most violent and gratifying species of amusements, which we occasionally enjoyed, was following the hounds and huntsmen; by habit in the period of age between 10 and 13 years, we had acquired such activity and fleetness as enabled us to keep up with the hounds; each boy was furnished with a long elastic pole, by the aid of which, hedges and ditches were surmounted and passed with an agility and spring that have since appeared to me equally surprizing and dangerous.

In summer our master encouraged bathing and swimming, but upon these occasions, he either attended himself, or his usher to prevent accidents.

Our most favourite books were Robin Hood, and Robinson Crusoe; the former was so enchanting, that every /10/ boy had learnt to repeat it from memory. This gave rise to bows and arrows, in the use of which we became very expert; parties of boys arranged themselves under different leaders, each of whom assumed the name of some popular character in the exploits of Robin Hood, whose orders were implicitly obeyed by his followers; these parties traversed different parts of Penketh heath, either to shoot at a dead mark, or oftener at birds in flight; in the latter case the leader of the band gave the word of command, and immediately every arrow flew towards the object pointed out; by this shower of arrows the birds were frequently arrested in their flight and brought to the ground.

These exercises and amusements, probably contributed to our health, for during 40 years that our master presided in this happy place, one death only had occurred in the whole school; this was in the case of Springett Penn, the son and heir of the Penns of Pensylvania, and it was said that he was in a consumptive state when he first entered the school.

The delight we had in perusing Robinson Crusoe might probably inflame some of the boys with a spirit of enterprise; we were within a mile of Sankey bridge on the road to Warrington, where several small /11/ vessels unloaded and took in their cargoes; some of these were Irish traders; we could step upon their decks from the side of the canal, and we often listened to the sailors with admiration; at length a party of the boys engaged with one of the captains to venture with him to Ireland, where the parents of one of the boys resided; to effect this purpose, apparel, and every necessary article that could be privately conveyed away, was collected, and secreted in an out-house, and although six individuals had engaged in this plot, it was conducted with inviolable secrecy; but on the evening preceding the intended elopement, some of the hidden articles were accidentally discovered, and thus the whole plan was immediately disconcerted, and no similar conspiracy was ever afterwards formed.

Our master never had more than one usher, whom I have already mentioned; he adopted, however, a plan which saved the expense of an additional usher, and probably promoted a better state of subordination. There were 3 boarding houses, his house, widow Barnes' and a third, and each received from 15 to 20 boys; in each house, a monitor was appointed, of the most steady and best informed of them, to each of whom he delegated a certain portion of /12/ authority, but not the power of chastizement; every breach of order committed under the monitor, was punished with more severity than if it had been under the master; this gave a degree of consequence to the monitor, and entailed general obedience, at the same time his responsibility was such as rendered him more guarded over his own conduct, for if any misdemeanour had been committed, in which he was a party, he alone was punished, and sometimes even deposed, and another substituted in his place; from this system resulted a discriminating sense of obedience, as well as of command and secured a subordination that pervaded the conduct of every school boy.

1756
æt. 13

About 2 years before the school was dissolved, Gilbert Thompson [the usher] went to Edinburgh, where he took the degree of doctor of medicine: during these 2 years, no usher was engaged, but the station was supplied by monitors, selected from the schoolboys; two were selected from our master's boarders, and I was invested with equal powers as a coadjutor; jealousies soon sprang up, though in some measure smothered by the motive of maintaining our station, divided as our power and influence necessarily must have been. The house of the master was situated at the distance of half a mile /13/ from the school; on one occasion the master did not appear in school at his usual hour, and to ascertain the cause, one of the monitors left the schoolroom to enquire the reason, that in case of absence we might be at liberty to hear the lessons ourselves. The first monitor not returning as soon as might be expected, the other likewise left the school to ascertain the cause of the detention; before the return of either, the master who had accidently come to school by a circuitous walk, arrived; and finding that both his monitors had deserted their post, deposed both of them, and I was constituted the sole monitor, which I held for nearly two years when the school was dissolved. The widow Barnes had a son settled in Liverpool, to whose house she retired and took me with her.

I had a distant relation in Tortola, named John Pickering whose two youngest sons Isaac and Josiah by his last wife were sent to the care of Samuel Fothergill who placed them at Penketh school, but on its dissolution they were removed to a school at Shelborne.

My removal to Liverpool must have taken place about the conclusion of my 14th year: the death of my father had recently been communicated to me; and soon afterwards I heard of the second marriage of /14/ my mother to Samuel Taine; that my Father's executor had neglected my property, and had disposed of the sugar plantation in Cane Garden Bay. No directions had been recently transmitted to direct my studies; it was, however, at length concluded that I should attend a seminary in Liverpool, to learn merchants'

1760 æt.
$15\frac{1}{2}$

accounts, preparatory to admission into a mercantile house; which plan was pursued till my 15th year when an event occurred which diverted me to another pursuit. John Pickering of Tortola already mentioned, had by his first wife a son named after himself, who on his return married the daughter of

Bezaliel Hodge of the same island. John Pickering [Junr.] visited England for curiosity and improvement; on his arrival at Liverpool he was met by Samuel Fothergill who always appeared to feel an interest in promoting my happiness, and who proposed to him to join in my guardianship. This being settled it was concluded to send me as an apprentice to Abraham Sutcliff a Surgeon and Apothecary, at Settle in Yorkshire. Alas! How unqualified was I for the medical profession! The little classical knowledge I had acquired at Penketh was dissipated during the time I spent in acquiring the mercantile routine; and thus prepared, I was to be qualified for the most important professional duties, and that in an obscure part of the country. Sutcliff was distantly related to [Samuel] Fothergill, and I do not /15/ doubt, but that the latter, now my guardian, and the arbiter of my studies, had entertained a favourable opinion of my new tutor, who proved happily for me, a man of no ordinary talents; he became a classical scholar, although self taught, and so attached was he to Latin, that he never would permit me to read an English book in his presence, and often would instruct me in his favourite language. About Hallifax, weaving is extensively encouraged: Sutcliff having no patrimony, received only twelve months instruction to spell and read a little English, when he was appointed to the loom, but the exertion of throwing the shuttle was too hard for his constitution to bear; he was asthmatic early in life, and he suffered so much in the chest from the mechanical exertion of weaving, as to be obliged to relinquish the employment. He had a distant relation in Kendal, of the name of Ecroyd, an eminent surgeon, to whom he applied for any species of servitude; at first he was engaged in carrying out medicines, and in cleaning the shop. In this town, a considerable school was conducted by Thomas Rebanks: young Sutcliff became acquainted with some of the school boys, from whom he borrowed books, and occasionally procured instruction. He left the loom about 16, and at 18, he had acquired so much /16/ Latin, as to enable him to read a præscription, which he also learned to compound, and at length was permitted to visit patients for his master; and having by his œconomy saved a little money, was allowed by him to visit Edinburgh to attend some of the classes; in summer he walked back again to his old station, and resumed his services to his indulgent master; for two or three subsequent winters he repeated his perambulations; and became not only a scholar, but a proficient in medical science; and with a view of exercising his abilities independently, he visited the town of Settle, and commenced his professional duties; in which he acquired so much celebrity, as to include in his attendance, an extent of at least 10 miles on every quarter from his residence, at the period of my introduction to him. This is a market town, but the church is situated at Gigleswick about two miles distant, and separated by the river Ribble. This church and a Free-school were under the care of Paley, father of the celebrated archdeacon.

1761 æt. 16

Sutcliff was in the possession of a spacious house, built under his own direction; in Society he was courted, and for his knowledge employed by the neighbouring gentry, and no less so /17/ on legal subjects. The Attornies consulted him as an oracle; in many difficult matters he was made the sole arbitrator; his knowledge of the law surprized me the more, as he had not I believe one law book in possession, for I had access to his library at all times: when opponents got involved in law suits, both parties would conclude that "we must go to Sutcliff to settle matters"; and I do not recollect that any decision of his was disputed.

Although he was weakly and asthmatic in the early part of his life, he enjoyed uninterrupted health, exposed as he frequently was to all the changes and inclemency of weather, passing over mountains bleak, and almost tractless, by night as well as by day. On my arrival, he possessed an amiable wife, the mother of two children, and her consideration and kindness added much to my comfort during the whole of my residence. About my second year I began to visit patients, and these were often numerous when my master was out of town or engaged by midwifery; but never having /18/ heard a lecture or seen any anatomical figure except a skeleton, I could not be qualified to discharge the functions imposed upon me. I had certainly read much, and had even dissected animals, whose parts I studied from books only; I found in my master's library, Keil's anatomy, Monro on the bones, Douglas on the muscles, and Winslow's anatomy: In medicine were some of Boerhave's works and Shaw's practice of physick. From the defect of memory, and the want of tables and plates, my anatomical knowledge occasioned me very considerable trouble; this induced me to construct tables of my own, to enable me the better to understand what I collected by reading.

In introducing my master's engagements in midwifery, a circumstance is recalled to mind which happened about this time. A farmer in easy circumstances, after having been married at least 10 years, without any prospect of having a child, and reflecting that if he should not increase his family, he possessed a sufficiency to live upon, /19/ concluded to dispose of the products of his farm at half the value, with an agreement on bond, that whenever he should have a child by his present wife, the purchaser should pay double the value of the goods received: on these conditions persons purchased with avidity, from the distant prospect of being afterwards called upon; at the 14th year after marriage my master delivered the farmer's wife of a child, whose fortune was hence rendered very considerable.

By the attention of my master, aided by my application, having recovered my Latin, I was anxious to acquire such a proficiency in the French language as would enable me to read an author. To effect this a party of my acquaintance of both sexes, united in expense to procure a French master from London; and by due application in three months we could read the language with facility, and both speak and write it so as to be understood. Soon afterwards I procured a few Greek books, and with Hackhouse's /20/ grammar acquired a little knowledge of this language also, but I could never overcome the early neglect of my classical education.

My most favourite study indeed, was Botany; to assist me in it, I borrowed Gerard's herbal: In my excursions in the vicinity of Settle I collected many good specimens of rare plants from which I made an Hortus Siccus: with other specimens I made impressions on paper, which resembled drawings, and may be done with very little trouble. For this purpose, some printer's ink, and a pair of printer's bosses or cushions, such as are used for laying the ink on types are necessary. After rubbing them with a little of the ink, lay the plant between them, and press them so as to give the plant sufficient colour, then remove it, and lay it on a sheet of paper, and give it a little pressure, in order to convey the impression of the plant to the paper, which maybe afterwards coloured according to nature. A piece of paper should be placed between /21/ the plant and the hand, to prevent the latter being dirtied by the ink.

When I was at Penketh school, I often visited a copper smelting house at Sankey, and at that early period took a delight in collecting specimens of these ores, as well as of variegated stones or pebbles which I found in my walks: when I was at Liverpool my attention was diverted to sea-weeds, some of which I still possess; but at Settle my mind was absorbed by botany, under my guide Gerard.

Thus my time glided smoothly away. My chief acquaintances were the Birkbecks, who rose to opulence from poverty; but who never abused, or disgraced their riches by pride, extravagance or want of charity. Mary Morris who afterwards married Dr. Knowles, and settled in London; at this first period of our acquaintance we occasionally interchanged pieces of poetry, in the construction of which she was much my superior; she excelled also in epistolary correspondence; /22/ and in conversation, there was a poignancy and sprightliness, which riveted attention and gratified every hearer. She was introduced to the king, and rewarded by him for her great ingenuity in needlework; she made an excellent likeness of the king in worsted, which is now in the palace. She was too careless in dress, sometimes to an unpleasant degree.

Deborah Barnett, then a pretty, lively, and interesting young person of sweet temper and pleasing manners, who afterwards married Darby of Colebrooke dale, famous for the manufactory of the iron bridge near his works. She became a very eminent preacher in the Society of Friends; although she was not a person of literary education, she was very eloquent in her extemporaneous delivery.

Mary Fothergill of Warrington, with whom I was acquainted when a schoolboy and with whom I maintained a pleasing correspondence, married

Watson of Waterford in Ireland, and likewise became a celebrated preacher; but I do not recollect that any /23/ of my male acquaintances, either at Settle, or among all my school fellows, having entered into the ministry. Women after the warmth of youth has subsided, are more disposed to devotional exercises than men; and probably were it equally encouraged, and honourable for them to assume this character, even in the established church, the number of female preachers, would exceed that of the men, as is the case of the Society of Friends.

I had now completed five years residence in Settle, under the parental superintendance of Sutcliff; and was about to emerge from a small market town, to enter the metropolis of England, without having a relation, or knowing a friend in it. Many good people in Settle advised me against my intended journey, in consequence of four apprentices from the same house, having died soon after their entrance into London; my guardians, however, saw no obstacles, and having recommended me to his brother Dr. John Fothergill, one of the most celebrated /24/ physicians in England, I arrived in London, and came into his presence in the summer of 1766.

1766 æt. 21½

I have observed that Sutcliff was often appointed by both parties, the sole arbitrator in many disputable cases. Alexander Fothergill was the eldest of the family. His daughter had married counter to his inclination, and she soon came to great distress, and on application to him for some relief, she was refused assistance; at length after her repeated importunities, the matter was referred to the decision of Sutcliff, who decreed that the parent should extend such a degree of relief, as such [*sic*] prevent abject want. When I departed from Settle, Sutcliff gave me a letter to Dr. Fothergill, which I imagined to be introductory to his acquaintance. I had another from his brother Samuel Fothergill, of a kind purely introductory.

On my arrival in London I delivered Dr Sutcliff's letter. I instantly perceived that the doctor was agitated, and somewhat irritated; and he spoke to me in such a warm manner on the subject of Sutcliff's interfering in the concerns of his family as alarmed me considerably on my first introduction. I assured the doctor that I was ignorant /25/ of the content of the letter, and had indeed conceived it to have been an introduction to him. The doctor was naturally warm and hasty in his temper, but his good sense had in a great measure subdued this disposition. I have, however, occasionally observed it, in my future acquaintance with him; in such instances he would quickly reflect upon such unguarded warmth, and an obliging placidity would supervene; and where he suspected that he had hurt the feelings of any individual, however, afterwards more disposed to serve them. After perusing Sutcliff's letter, he cast his eye upon his brother Samuel's and recalling to recollection his kind patronage of me, he became truly condescending, and this continued to the end of his life; he was more like a parent than a friend. I had access to him at all times, and usually breakfasted with him once a week as long as he lived.

I have remembered that my old usher Gilbert Thompson left Penketh school to study medicine at Edinburgh, where he graduated, and then came to London, but meeting with little encouragement he attended a boarding school at Tottenham as a writing master, and afterwards became a journeyman and shopman to Bevan an eminent chemist in London Street.[3] A little before my arrival /26/ in London, his uncle Gilbert Thompson of Penketh, died, and left the doctor an independent fortune of £4000; who had recently taken apartments in Gracechurch Street; in which I was also accommodated and thus again engaged the kind attention of my former usher. The distance was convenient for St Thomas' hospital, where I entered as a surgeon's dresser under Benjamin Cowell Esq. The other surgeons were Baker and Smith, men of no great eminence.[4]

The physicians were Akenside, Russell and Grieve.[5] I was early fond of poetry and had read the pleasures of imagination with admiration, and anticipated great pleasure in coming under the author's notice, for by a small premium, a surgeon's pupil was admitted to the practice of the physicians of the hospital.

Great was my disappointment in finding Akenside the most supercilious and unfeeling physician that I had then, or have since known. If the poor affrighted patients did not return a direct answer to his queries, he would often instantly discharge them from the hospital. He evinced a particular disgust to females & generally treated them with harshness. I /27/ was informed that this moroseness was occasioned by disappointment in love; but hapless must have been that female that should have been placed under his tyranny. I was inexpressibly shocked at an instance of his inhumanity exercised towards a patient in Abraham's ward, to whom he had ordered bark in boluses; who, in consequence of not being able to swallow them, so irritated Akenside as to order the sister of the ward to discharge him from the hospital, adding "he shall not die under my care". As the sister was removing him in obedience to the doctor, the patient expired.

---

[3] Thompson graduated at Edinburgh in 1758. Silvanus and Timothy Bevan had an apothecary's business in Plough Court. See *Plough Court; the story of a notable pharmacy 1715–1927*, compiled by Ernest Cripps, London, Allen and Hanburys Limited, 1927. The business was the direct precursor of the pharmaceutical company, Allen and Hanburys.

[4] The three surgeons at St Thomas's in Lettsom's time were Benjamin Cowell appointed in 1749, Thomas Baker appointed in 1739, and Thomas Smith appointed in 1760. See Abraham, op. cit., note 2 above, p. 36.

[5] See ibid., p. 39. All three were distinguished physicians. Mark Akenside was also a poet, Alexander Russell was an F.R.S., and James Grieve was a translator of Celsus.

One leg of Dr Akenside was considerably shorter than the other which was in some measure remedied by the aid of a false heel; he had a pale strumous countenance; but was always very neat and elegant in his dress; he wore a large white wig and carried a long sword. I never knew him to spit, nor would he suffer any pupil to spit in his presence. One of them once accidentally did so, who stood at some distance behind him. I was present; the doctor instantly span round /28/ on his artificial heel, and hastily to demand "who was the person that spat in his face"? Sometimes he would order some of the patients on his visiting days to precede him with brooms to clear the way, and prevent the patients from too nearly approaching him. On one of these occasions, Richard Chester one of the governors upbraided him for his cruel behaviour. "Know" said he, "thou art a servant of this charity."

The greatest pitch of anger, to which I ever saw him raised, was excited by Baker, the senior surgeon, by simply answering a question the doctor put to him respecting his son Thomas, who was liable to epileptic fits, and was thereby somewhat weakened in intellect. " To what study do you purpose to place Tom" said Akenside to Baker. "I find he is not capable of making a surgeon, so I have sent him to Edinburgh to make a physician of him". Akenside span round from Baker, with impetuosity and would not speak to him for a considerable time afterwards. Young Baker graduated at Edinburgh, and settled as a physician at St Albans, from whence he has since consulted me on account of his health.

/29/ Dr Russell was as condescending as Akenside was petulant. Akenside, however, would sometimes condescend to explain a case of disease to the pupils which always appeared sagacious, and in spite of his irritable temper, he was more followed than Russell by the pupils. Russell resided at No. 1 Church Court, Walbrook. Dr Fothergill lived there at 2 White Hart Court, Gracechurch Street.[6] On a visit of Russell to Fothergill when I was present, the latter observed, in playing on the numbers of their respective houses; "if thou art the first physician in London, I am the second".

Dr Grieve lived in the Charter house, to which, I think he was physician: he appeared to be an amiable unassuming scholar, and was the translator of Sydenham.[7]

As I was well aware that my pecuniary circumstances would not enable me to continue longer than twelve months in London, and consequently exclude me from the school of Edinburgh, I devoted my time incessantly to the hospital, and the lectures which London afforded: as a small gratuity admitted me to see the books of the physicians, and to accompany them

---

[6] In the City of London.

[7] Charterhouse was a school in the City for poor boys near St Bartholomew's Hospital.

through the wards I embraced /30/ as many opportunities as I possibly could to avail myself of these advantages. In the morning early, before any attendance was given, I usually visited many select patients, wrote out the symptoms, and afterwards examined the praescriptions of the physicians on some particular cases. I compared the writings and practice of authors, and by degrees I acquired some precision in anticipating both the practice and the remarks of the faculty. If I thought myself much at a loss, I repeated my visits to the hospital in the afternoon, and this not only confirmed the little knowledge I had acquired, but likewise gave me a frankness and ease of demeanor at the bedside. During all my attendance, however, no other pupil I believe adopted this system, which I found so highly interesting to my advancement: at the same time I continued to take notes of, and made reflections upon, what I saw, and thus acquired a method of investigation and decision which ever afterwards proved of the highest use in determining my medical conduct and practice, which untill my return from the West Indies, I never could claim the advantages of any other lectures than those afforded by a course of Midwifery and Anatomy; and my private /31/ clinical practice was a substitute for the rest.

This close applications to my studies, prevented me from cultivating much acquaintance. My most intimate friends at the time were Samuel Clarke, James Beesley and Richard Chester, all of whom were then of the Society of Friends.[8]

[J. C. Lettsom
Circa 1804][9]

---

[8] Samuel Clark was a printer and Richard Chester a merchant. James Beesley, like Lettsom a Quaker from Tortola, was a life-long friend and seemed to live a hand-to-mouth existence as an author and amanuensis. See Abraham, op. cit., note 2 above, pp. 47–8, 161.

[9] Added by Joseph J. Green.

3

Letters to Lettsom

These letters form a very miscellaneous collection. They are from a variety of correspondents, on a wide range of topics and over a long time period. They have been arranged alphabetically according to the surname of the sender and where there is more than one letter from a correspondent they have been placed in chronological order. Lord Shelburne became the Marquis of Lansdowne and all his letters and notes are collected under Shelburne. Incredibly, there are almost no letters from Lettsom in the Medical Society of London to these correspondents. The exceptions are a draft letter to Lady Ann Erskine and a draft note to the Marquis of Lansdowne. These have been included here rather than in the 'Letters from Lettsom' section.

[JCL]

Endorsed: From Mr. Banau,[1] Dec. 12 1790, Paris. answered.

Monsieur

Permettés, que je vous fasse l'hommage d'un exemplaire de mes ouvrages sur les fièvres putrides. J'ai beaucoup profité de vos lumières, de vos travaux, de vos découvertes. M. Derché, porteur de ma lettre, est un de mes amis, qui va passer quelque temps à Londres—pour faire connaitre ses talents—vous voudriès bien l'aider de vos conseils et lui rendre tous le service, qui dependront de vous j'espère que vous voudrès bien m' honorer d'une réponce.

je suis avec respect

Monsieur	Votre très humble
le 12 xbre 1789	et très obeissant servant
Rue savoie N°. 9 à Paris	Banau Ard.
	medecin ordre du roi

Monsieur Le Docteur Lettsom

---

[1] Jean Baptiste Banau (1746–1804). *Moyens propres à combattre les fièvres putrides et malignes et à préserver de leur contagion*, Yverdon, [s.n.], 1779.

1. [JCL]

Endorsed: From Dr. Barton,[2] Apr. 29 1810, Philadelphia. By Mr. Brick [*sic*]
35 Leicester Square

To Dr. Lettsom
London.
Handed by Mr. Breck.

Dear Sir,
This will be handed to you by Mr. Breck, a young gentleman of great merit,
whom I take the liberty of recommending to your attentions. He is the son of
one of our most respectable and opulent citizens, the late Mr. S. Breck of this
city. My young friend will, I doubt not, feel gratified by being introduced to the
acquaintance of some of your literary friends, in London. He will be able to tell
you every thing you may wish to hear concerning our progress in literature.
Let me know, when you write next, what progress the Medical Society
have made towards their new volume.[3]
I am, Dear Sir,
Yours, etc. very etc.
respectfully,
B. S. Barton

Philadelphia
April 28 1810

2. [JCL]

Endorsed: From Professor Barton, May 10 1811, Philadelphia. answered.

Dear Sir,
A few days ago, I wrote to you by my friend Mr. Charles Breck, whom I recommended to your attention. I now take the same liberty by Mr. James West,

---

[2] Benjamin Smith Barton (1766–1815), physician and naturalist, studied medicine at the
College of Philadelphia under William Shippen junior. In 1786, he travelled to Europe to study
at the University of Edinburgh and in London. He returned to Philadelphia in 1789 without a
medical degree and was appointed professor of natural history and botany at the College of
Philadelphia. When, in 1791, the College joined the University of the State of Pennsylvania to
form the University of Pennsylvania, Barton stayed in post, also becoming professor of materia
medica. In 1813, he followed Benjamin Rush as professor of the theory and practice of medicine. See William Shainline Middleton, 'Benjamin Smith Barton', *Annals of Medical History*,
New series, 1936, **8**: 7–91.
[3] *The Transactions of the Medical Society of London* took over from the *Memoirs of the
Medical Society of London* (1787–1805). The first part of the first volume of this new series was
published in 1810. The second part was not published until 1817. The other volumes in the series
were issued after an even greater interval in 1846, 1861 and 1862.

a young gentleman of much respectability and of talents, and the son of one of the most wealthy and respectable merchants. Mr. West feels anxious to form an acquaintance with some of the literary characters of your metropolis; and I am persuaded that he will ~~feel~~ attach a peculiar value to the acquaintance which he may form with you.

I am, Dear Sir, with sincere esteem, your obliged and affectionate friend, etc., B. S. Barton

Philadelphia
May 10th 1811

3. [JCL]

Endorsed: From Prof. Barton, Oct. 10 1811, Philadelphia

Dr. Lettsom
London

Honoured by Mr. E. D. Cushing

Dear Sir,
  This will be handed to you by my friend and pupil, Mr. E. Cushing, a young man of much merit, and the son of one of the most respectable families. He is in London for the purpose of completing his medical education. He will, doubtless, be much gratified by being made acquainted ~~to~~ with one of whom he has heard so much, and one so much respected as Dr. Lettsom.

I beg your attention to Mr. Cushing
With very great respect,
I remain,
Dear Sir,
Yours. etc.,
B. S. Barton

Philadelphia,
October 10 1811.

Cushing
15 St. Thomas' Street
Borough

1. [L]

Endorsed: From Dr. Blair,[4] June 8 1807, Panton Square.[5] answered.

Post paid
Doctor Lettsom Physician
Basinghall Street
City.

18 Panton Square
6th June 1807

Dear Doctor,

When I took the liberty to call, it was not merely a complimentary visit, but to ask your advice about a malady to which I have been subject, that of a kind of deliquium (with so cold feet that except in the ~~wa~~ hottest weather, I cannot keep them warm, without a fire, even with the warmest woollen socks and stockings, and thick shoes) with palpitations, which have indeed rather left me and shaking. I find my mouth soo parched when I awake. I was obliged to leave my Living in Norfolk, where I had the advice of more than one of the faculty, especially of Dr. McQueen, formerly of Norwich, lately of Westminster and now retired;[6] and Dr. Marshall of Lynn Regis, Norfolk, about 12 miles from my place.[7] Their prescriptions were somewhat opposite. The latter thought that I lived too abstemiously; and advised me rather to indulge, and prescribed vinum ferri,[8] with Ginger Tea,[9] bathing, and to wear flannel next my skin, which would in some measure transport me to my old habitation at Naples, or to Portugal. The former, that I should drink nothing but water, live on solids, but avoid a plethora, and bathe, especially my head, which I was to keep as scanty of hair as I could conveniently. As to Medicine,

---

⁴ According to Charles Newman, Robert Blair was a graduate of Pembroke College, Cambridge and had been a vicar in Norfolk and although he called himself D.D. "there is no evidence that he was entitled to it". Charles Newman, 'Dr. Lettsom's letters', *Transactions of the Medical Society of London*, 1974, **90**: 31–7.

⁵ Panton Square, St James's, later part of Arundel Street.

⁶ Malcolm MacQueen (1750–1829), M.D. (Edinburgh), practised in Norwich and Yarmouth, in Norfolk and in London. P. J. and R. V. Wallis, with the assistance of J. G. L. Burnby and the late T. D. Whittet, *Eighteenth-century medics (subscriptions, licences, apprenticeships)*, Newcastle Upon Tyne, Project for Historical Biobibliography, 1988, p. 387.

⁷ Wallis provides only a little more information: an initial for the first name, S. Marshall. Ibid., p. 395.

⁸ Iron wine, used as a tonic.

⁹ Ginger was used as a tonic to stimulate weak organs and, externally, as a rubefacient. As a stimulant, expectorant and astringent, it was traditionally used for colds and flu and in cases of rheumatism and arthritis. Ginger tea was made from sliced ginger root, over which boiling water was poured and left to stand for some minutes. For a decoction, it would be simmered.

29

he prescribed Cuprum Pills.[10] I was to have a glass of spring water at hand to drink, if seized in the night, or a certain mixture. I was on the edge of the grave with that complaint at my Living. Both ordered me to elsewhere.

I have received by much the most benefit from the prescription of Dr. MacQueen as to the mode of living; and if I pass as a proverb of temperance among my parishioners, scarcely anyone can indulge less. Yet I am as much troubled with cold feet that even at this season, if I sit two or three hours, a pair of thick woollen socks, two pair of worsted stockings, and the stoutest shoes, cannot keep them warm. Nothing but a fire or exercise, and many a pair have I burnt at my living in endeavouring to warm them. It borders on the marshes, and the place lies low. Though I drink nothing but water, and eat of the plainest food, my mouth is no less parched when I awake in the night.

I have thought of going to Lisbon against Winter.

Yours etc.

Robert Blair D.D.

P.S.

If you can spare a few moments to write your sentiments that I may not again especially hazard to disturbing you; it will add to my many obligations.

2. [L]

Endorsed: From Dr. Blair, Dec. 13 1807, Essex Street. answered.

Dear Doctor,

My experience of your goodness induces me to this liberty. I was seized yesterday with another deliquium in St. Bride's, which is a very large Church,[11] after coming from officiating at the altar, and about 8 days before, I should have mentioned, with a deliquium and in Bed after burying a corpse in the Churchyard there, when dark, by candle light, where I had to stand some time. I am better but I should be glad to know when you have a moment to spare me a line if I can officiate so, there, with safety.

yours much obliged etc.

Robert Blair D.D.

13 Essex Street
Strand
14th Dec[r] 1807

---

[10] Copper pills. Copper salts used in medicines acted as a violent emetic and stimulated the nervous system.

[11] St Bride's church is just off Fleet Street in London. It was known, because of this, as "the Printers' Church". It was rebuilt by Sir Christopher Wren in 1675 after the Great Fire of London.

3. [L]

Endorsed: From Dr. Blair, 59 Portland Place,[12] Jan. 12 1808. done.

to be sorted

59 Portland Place

Tuesday

Dear Doctor,
I must appear ungrateful after very kind attention. But I have been so occupied with the Tuition of a very interesting youth, of frank and extraordinly fortune for whom I have had the honour to be sought after, and whose family are particularly good to me, that I have not had time to see my best friends, among whom I take the liberty to thank you.

I found myself benefited by your prescription, and have given up the arduous Church duty which injured me.

I intend to introduce to you my Pupil. Her ladyship, his surviving Parent, will be happy to take a ride in Spring to see your beautiful place and is flattered by the hopes of my introducing her son to you, no less than himself.
Yours much obliged
Robert Blair D.D.

4. [L]

Endorsed: From Dr. Blair, 44 Great Titchfield Street,[13] July 16 1808. 2

44, Great Titchfield Street

15th July

Dear Doctor,
I take this liberty to say that my Friend, the East India Gentleman, whom I was to introduce to you, next Sunday Evening at Grove Hill[14] who I was

---

[12] Portland Place was built on the Cavendish-Harley estate in the London borough of St Marylebone. It was named after William Bentinck, second Duke of Portland (1709–1762).

[13] In West London, the street takes its name from a subsidiary title of the Bentinck family who were Marquesses of Titchfield as well as Dukes of Portland.

[14] Lettsom frequently held soirées and rural retreats for professionals at weekends. See the 'Letters from Lettsom' section, note 4.

not aware was engaged, will accompany me there Sunday Evening 24th, if not inconvenient for you.
Yours etc.
Robert Blair

5. [L]

Endorsed: From Dr. Blair, Oct. 24 1808, 44 Great Titchfield Street. done.

Dr. Lettsom Physician
Basinghall Street
City.

44, Great Tichfield St
23^d Octr 1808

Dear Doctor,
    I am sorry to inform you that the Marquis and Marchioness Yrujo,[15] their Catholic Majesties' late Representatives to the United States, with whom I was to have made you acquainted, set off yesterday morning for Spain. But the Marquis, whom I saw before his departure, and to whom I mentioned that wish, expects to be in this Country next Spring, when I promised myself that happiness.
    It having been very indulgent, I thought, in consequence of my knowledge of the languages, [truth?] and some diplomatic expediency, that I might be of use there. At this juncture it is not impossible, but I may visit it. I have had the honour of an audience of H.R.H. the Duke of York,[16] and some correspondence with the Secretary of State on the subject. Should I go, I shall be glad to know if I can be useful to you, or any of yours in that interesting Country.
    The Marquis, I find, knows some of your friends at, I mind, Philadelphia.

---

[15] Carlos Martinez, the Chevalier d'Yrujo or by this time, the Marquis of Yrujo, was the Envoy of Spain to the United States.
[16] Frederick Duke of York (1763–1827), Augustus, son of George III and Charlotte Sophia (daughter of Duke Charles Louis Frederick of Mecklenburg-Strelitz). He was married to Princess Frederica Charlotte of Prussia.

Excuse my hasty scrawl,
Yours etc.
Robert Blair. D.D.

6. [L]

Endorsed: From D[r]. Blair, July 24 1809, 44 Great Titchfield Street.
answered.

Post paid
Dr. Lettsom Physician
Basinghall Street
City.

44 Great Titchfield Street
Monday

Dear Doctor,
   I have transmitted your Letter of regret to Major Mor[r]ison. I had dined between the morning and afternoon labours, in the viney[ard] for it is a maxim of the Chevalier not to leave a matter of that importance to chance, and I suffer, if I exceed long two o'clock.
   The Major quite misunderstood; for as I have written to him, though you be hospitality itself, I should have thought that I wanting in respect both to you, and to him, had I taken the liberty—Mrs. Lettsom rather urged him, which should make you easy. I am sorry that he allowed his modesty so to beguile him, and as an old soldier, I wonder that he was ceremonious.
   He is an excellent man. He was the great favourite of Lord Lake, late Commander in Chief in India,[17] and had the providing of the whole of the British forces in India. Many a d-mn-d f—l has he been called for not availing himself. Had he not had very rare integrity, his fortune might have been immense. He was sought after, too, by Lord

---

[17] Lieutenant-General Viscount (Gerald) Lake (1744–1808), was commander-in-chief of the British army in India between 1801 and 1805, where he set about modernizing the army. In 1805, he was removed from his command.

Cornwallis.[18] Not a soul was invited to the Commander in Chief's, Lord Lake's, table but through him.

As he knows more from his greater experience, of military matters there, etc., than any other man, I was solicitous from your thirst for all knowledge, to bring you together. I was surprized to see my Friend so much on the jiggets,[19] which is now accounted for. He did not dine till he got to Gunnersbury.[20]

Yours etc.

Robert Blair

7. [L]

Endorsed: From Dr. Blair, June 2 1813, London. answered.

18 Duke St
Portland Chapel

June 2^d 1813

The Rev^d Dr. Blair felicitates his ancient, and zealous friend, Dr. Lettsom, on his acquisition that Dr. B. hears of, only differing from the mentiones about its amplitude;[21] because Dr. B. thinks that were it twenty thousand times, twenty thousand with a hundred thousand to pay the Taxes, the two ends could not meet, to make all those whom Dr. Lettsom wishes to make comfortable, and as comfortable as Dr. L. wishes them, though beef were a penny per pound here, and wine threehalpence per bottle, to render the sum virtually some millions per annum ergo to go as far.

---

[18] Charles Cornwallis (1738–1805), second Earl Cornwallis until 1793 when he was made Marquis Cornwallis. He served as governor-general of India between 1786 and 1793.

[19] A roasted joint of meat. A jigget of mutton was "the legg splatted and half part of the loyn together". Gervase Markham, *The English housewife*, London, Printed for Hannah Sawbridge, at the Sign of the Bible on Ludgate Hill, 1683, section on 'Roast meats and carbonadoes: To roast a Jigget of Mutton'.

[20] In the early nineteenth century, Gunnersbury in West London was the site for many a country mansion. In 1835, Nathan Rothschild of the famous Rothschild banking family bought Gunnersbury Park, where Gunnersbury House was built, a splendid Italian villa with wonderful gardens.

[21] This refers to the settlement, in Lettsom's favour, of the disputed will of his daughter-in-law, Ruth Lettsom, the late wife of his deceased son Pickering Lettsom. With the decision in his favour he came into a considerable fortune. See also note 69 below.

8. [L]

Endorsed: From Dr. Blair, June 6 1813, Duke Street. done.

18 Duke Street
Portland Chapel

June[22] 6th 1813

Dear Friend,

I received your Ticket of admission to Sir Christopher Hawkins, to the Philosophical Society the 15th, which, with that of your hours, at home, I enclosed to him, but found that he was unexpectedly called out of Town and that he is gone into Cornwal, whither they are transmitted to him. He will regret very much having been prevented attending.

The Friend who is to accompany me 8th to your Society, is George Gardner Esq. of Lincoln's Inn, Barrister, a Gentleman of superior abilities, of an elegant taste, an excellent Classic and mathematician; and of an excellent heart, whom a miserly Father has left perhaps too independent.

I thought that it might have been best to have left Mr. Goode to his own meditation. I have often seen it best to leave the Babe to come to himself. One of the members observed that the Gentleman would kick all the world before him. I thought that he was of the cloth, and then I descryed the spirit of Pope Hildebrand alias Gregory 7th.[23]

When nothing is more to the honour of a man when he has done wrong than to acknowledge it, and the noblest minds are unhappy till they have atoned for any injury they have done, it is a very silly mind that thinks such a depradation is not a very unseemly one.

I made a mistake; it was Mr. Taunton, the Father of the Truss Society,[24] that expressed his regret for allowing Mr. Goode to harangue, at the Annual Meeting, when the Company gave such indications of its not being agreeable.

Though innocently, and in my desire to give any information in my power towards instruction, I am extremely sorry at having been the cause of want of harmony, on the occasion in question.

---

[22] This is overwritten and may have been changed from July.

[23] Pope Gregory VII or Hildebrand (fl. 1025 d. 1085), meaning either "a bright flame" or "a brand of hell", according to how his achievements are seen, is regarded, by some, as one of the greatest of Roman pontiffs.

[24] John Taunton, founder of the London Truss Society, was a demonstrator at Guy's Hospital, London, under Henry Cline (1750–1827) and was, at this stage, also principal lecturer to the London Anatomical Society.

I remain,
yours much obliged
Robert Blair

9. [L]

Endorsed: From Dr. Blair, July 3 1813, Duke Street. answered.

18 Duke Street
Portland Chapel

July 3^d 1813

My Good Friend,
    I regretted that I could not be at the Philosophical Society Thursday
last, according to your kind invitation, but trust that I shall be able with
a Friend to attend your Lecture. Had I known that Sir Christopher Hawkins
was yet in Town, he should have been that Friend. As I find it would be
very agreeable to him, to hear your interesting discourse, and I know that you
will be happy to see him, if it be not encroaching on your number, and inconvenient to you to send it to me, I shall forward your Ticket of admission
to him.
I remain, my Dear Friend,
Yours
Robert Blair

10. [L]

Endorsed: From Rev. Dr. Blair, Aug. 18 1813, Duke Street. answered.

18 Duke Street
Portland Chapel
Augt. 18th 1813

Dear Friend,
    Mrs. Lettsom having requested to know when I should preach the next
Chesily Sermon and you, being Zeal itself wherever humanity is concerned,

I thought I should mention that Mr. Taunton, Father of the City of London Truss Society,[25] has prayed me, through the Rev[d]. William Parker, to preach next Sunday at St Anthony's, Watling Street, for the City Dispensary of which H.R.H. the Prince Regent is Patron,[26] saying I understand from the specimen he had, where in a small Church and from the handful of people, that it could only contain, who knew not 8 days before of my erection. I got for the Truss Society above three times the sum that the Rev[d] Henry White, a very popular, good and respectable man, got for them, in a church with six times the number at a bitter season and where himself is the favourite Lecturer that no man gets so much money on such occasions as I.

At a season when it might require the Apostle Paul to muster up a tolerable congregation, in the City, the application or opinion of me, is certainly very flattering, but I do not think that the choice of the time is doing justice to the Charity, or to me.

I will do, however, what I can; which is saying not a little, seeing ~~they~~ a miracle is expected from me in Norfolk, that is, to support on a Benefice from which I derive not the interest of that expended on my Education to qualify me for the pastoral office, or the amount of the wages of a Journeyman Tradesman, Buildings more extensive than those of the Episcopal Palace where the last Bishop, now Primate, ~~could not su~~ Dr. Manners Sutton, could not subsist on the United Revenues of the See of Norwich and of the Deanery of Windsor in Commendam, now minus, with the £40,000 per annum of Cantuarius.[27]

What is rather against it there are many of those structures, such works of supererogation, that it were a sinful waste of means to support them, though the benefice were the fattest in Christendom and as to the materials, architecture or antiquity, they have no more to recommend them than a Building in the sinks of St Giles or of Clerkenwell.[28]

You know yet more of what is going on in the world.

Yours,

Robert Blair

---

[25] The Truss Society had sermons preached in order to raise money for it. See, for example, Samuel Locke, D.D., 'A Sermon [on Acts xiv. 15, 16] preached...for the benefit of the City Truss Society', London, n.p., 1810.

[26] George Augustus Frederick (1762–1830), eldest son of George III and Charlotte Sophia, was the unpopular Prince Regent between 1811 and 1820.

[27] Charles Manners-Sutton (1755–1828), was appointed Bishop of Norwich in 1792 and, in 1805, Archbishop of Canterbury.

[28] At this time, some of the most notorious slums in London were situated around St Giles, to the north of Covent Garden.

[L]^29

Endorsed: From Mr. Blair, Mar. 29 1814, Great Russell Street. answered.

Dated March 29th 1813

Dear Sir,

I am obliged to you for the ticket and the [account?] of poor Mr. Malcolm's circumstances. I hope the motive which induces me to be kind "to oppressed authors and artists" is somewhat better than "classical" and of a higher order. My principles lead me to act in the way you recommend on multitudes of other occasions where the arts and liberal sciences are not concerned; but I am glad to find a few professional men disposed to do good from motives purely "classical" and human such as perhaps might have influenced Plato, Seneca or Cicero—I am in hopes Mr. Malcolm's limb will be saved and in some month's time become useful, but it is really a dreadful case of arthro[cace?].^30 Let me now say a word about the London Medical Society. I think I have done as much to promote the institution as anyone except yourself and Dr. Sims and although no thanks were given to me for the trouble I took in printing the catalogue of books,^31 nor any post of honour assigned me beyond what is conferred on several scores of other members. I have not deserted the Society with those who seceded at various times. Nevertheless, I do observe that it is ill-conducted, without harmony, without suitable discrimination, in a spirit of party and personality, mixing together men of discordant principles in the Council^32 and that the members consist more of drones and wasps than of working bees. In short, I see clearly that it is not much respected among the higher classes of our medical brethren; and am therefore persuaded that it will not do any good till its reputation is raised to a higher tone. I am even in despair about it and think it almost incapable of being repaired; so that unless you gravely examine its foundation and afford it a new basis, it can never flourish. The fact is, I do not at this moment know who are your new officers and council: but I know that if your officers do not add dignity and stamp intrinsic value on the institution it will not much honour them or serve the public by its longer existence. You find me to be ingenuous and candid; for it will not do to flatter the Society or

---

[29] This letter, beginning at "Let me now say…" is reproduced in James Johnston Abraham, *Lettsom: his life, times, friends and descendants*, London, William Heinemann, 1933, p. 404.

[30] A collection of matter or ulcer within the cavity of a bone.

[31] *Medical Society of London: catalogue of books*, London, printed by S. Gosnell, 1803.

[32] On these problems, see the Introduction to this volume, p. 3.

dissemble with you; nor have I said this much to any besides Dr. Pinckard[33] And Mr. Taunton.[34] Unless you get a little <u>private</u> talk with me, I had rather you would not disclose the contents of this note. W.B.[35] [William Blair]

Dr. Lettsom
Sambrook Court
Basinghall Street

PS. If you have any disposition to invite Dr. P. and Mr. T. on Tuesday Evening, to talk over the affairs of the Medical Society at your house, I could then meet you, but I believe on no other evening this whole week. But if you say "no, let it go on as it has", I must beg to dis[s]en[t][36] [t]o be in the list of members of my name from this time, because I have no confidence in its well-doing on your present plan. No men of science and reputation will join us;[37] we can do no good, nor publish any more volumes which are acceptable to the medical world. I think you must be convinced of this. W.B.

[JCL]

Endorsed: From Dr. Blane, Jan. 31 1803, Sackville St. done

Dear Doctor,

I have read your apology with much satisfaction and congratulate you on the great success with which you have repelled the Master of the reviews.[38] Accept my best thanks for favouring me with a copy of it.
Yours very sincerely,
Gilbert Blane

Sackville Street
31st Jan 1803

---

[33] George Pinckard, graduated M.D. at Leiden 1792. He was appointed physician to the forces in 1795 and accompanied Sir Ralph Abercromby to the West Indies. He eventually settled in London and established the Bloomsbury Dispensary. He was appointed President of the Medical Society of London in 1811.

[34] At the time, Taunton (see note 24 above) was vying with the surgeon, William Blair, to be the first surgeon President of the Medical Society. The Society asked Lettsom to take up the post again, as the only person acceptable to all contending factions. See Abraham op. cit., note 29 above, p. 403.

[35] William Blair (1766–1822), surgeon to the Lock Hospital and sometime lecturer at the Bloomsbury Dispensary, 62 Great Russell Street, fell out with Lettsom over the issue of surgeons being eligible for the office of President of the Medical Society. Blair felt it unjust that only physicians could be President. Abraham, ibid., pp. 163, 337.

[36] Manuscript holed.

[37] The affairs of the Medical Society of London were not running smoothly at this juncture. See the Introduction to this volume, p. 3, and Abraham, op. cit., note 29 above, pp. 424–5, 432.

[38] See 'Letters from Lettsom' section, notes 53 and 54.

[JCL]

Endorsed: From Dr. Cheston, July 12 1789, Gloucester. Answered

Dr. Lettsom

Gloucester July 12 1789

Dear Sir,
    The particular manner in which I have been circumstanced ever since I received your very kind and obliging information of the Honor conferr'd on me by the Medical Society,[39] has alone prevented my returning an earlier acknowledgement of it.
    Be assured, Sir, I feel the strongest Attachment to so excellent an Institution, and that my endeavours shall not be wanting, when a proper Opportunity offers, to second its Intention.
I am, Sir, with the most perfect Respect
Your much obliged and very faithful servant
R. B. Cheston

1. [JCL]

Endorsed: From Dr. Cleghorn,[40] Jan. 13 1784, Dublin. answered.

To
Dr. J. C. Lettsom
Physician in London

---

[39] Richard Brown Cheston, M.D., F.R.S., was recommended as a Corresponding Member on Monday 1 June 1789. Medical Society of London Council Minutes, 31 August 1773–5 to November 1821. Also on microfilm at the Wellcome Library, WMS/MF/4, Medical Society of London, Reel 1.
[40] George Cleghorn (1716–1789) studied physic and surgery for five years under Alexander Monro *primus* in Edinburgh and also had lodgings in his house. He was a close friend of John Fothergill, who was a student in Edinburgh at the same time. He was one of the first members of the Medical Society of Edinburgh, a society for students established in 1737. At the age of nineteen he was appointed surgeon to the 22nd Regiment of Foot, then stationed at Minorca. See his *Observations on the epidemical diseases in Minorca: from the year 1744 to 1749*, London, D. Wilson, 1751. He afterwards moved to Dublin and began practising there in 1751, eventually acquiring considerable estates in the county of Meath. In Dublin, he started a similar course to Hunter's, and was the first to establish a proper anatomical school in Ireland.

Dublin Jan.^{ry} 13 1784

My dear Sir,
I am much Obliged to you for your favours of December 21 which came to hand the 5th instant, and would have been acknowledged sooner had not a severe Cold confined me to my Chamber for three weeks past.

I should be wanting to myself, if I did not gratefully Embrace the Opportunity you offer of being handed down to Posterity among the number of Dr. Fothergill's chosen Friends. I need not tell you who ~~hath~~ hast perused our confidential Letters, that our Friendship was recognized sincere and permanent, and that the Vaccancy in my affections, occasioned by his Death, can never be filled up.

Ille meos, primus, qui me sibi iunxit Amores
Abstulit; ille habeat secum, servetque Sepulchro.[41]

I have directed Mr. Home, an Eminent Artist from London, to take a Drawing from my Portrait of the same size with that of our friend Peter Collinson in the second volume of your Edition of Fothergill's works.[42] If he finishes it this week agreable to his promise, you may Expect to receive it soon after this Letter.

In obedience to your Commands I have thrown together Anecdotes of my own Life in the inclosed paper which you may suppress, or publish in any form you please.

I am glad to find by your Letter that our mutual friend Dr. Cuming is wed.[43] When an opportunity offers, pray make my best wishes Acceptable to Him. Farewell my dear Sir, and believe me to be very sincerely
your most obliged humble servant
George Cleghorn

---

[41] "The man who was the first to unite with me, has taken my love away: may he keep it with him and preserve it in the grave." Virgil, *Aeneid*, 4, 2.8–9.

[42] John Fothergill, 'Some account of the late Peter Collinson, Fellow of the Royal Society, and of the Society of Antiquaries, in London, and of the Royal Societies of Berlin and Upsal. In a letter to a friend. Printed in the year 1769', in John Coakley Lettsom (ed.), *The works of John Fothergill*, 3 vols, London, printed for Charles Dilly, in the Poultry, 1783–84, vol. 2, engraving facing the title page between pp. 331 and 334.

[43] William Cuming of Dorchester (1714–88) was the son of Mr. James Cuming, an eminent Edinburgh merchant and Margaret Hepburn, daughter of an Edinburgh merchant. He began studying medicine at the age of seventeen at Edinburgh University. In 1735, he visited the Paris hospitals and improved his dissection and knowledge of anatomy. He went on to Leiden and then Rheims, where he took his M.D. He was a friend of Dr. John Fothergill, on whose recommendation he began to practise in Dorchester at the beginning of 1739.

P.S. This letter will be delivered to you by my friend Mr. Cockburn of the Guards, but I request you may acknowledge the receipt of it by Post.

2. [JCL]

Endorsed: From Dr. Cleghorn, Jan. 14 1784, Dublin. answered

To
Dr. Lettsom
with a small Box which Mr. Cockburn is requested to pack up so as that it may not be crushed, or exposed to much pressure.

Dublin Jan^{ry} 14 1784

My dear Sir,

As Mr. Cockburn was prevented from sailing yesterday by contrary winds, and Mr. Home hath sent me the drawing you desired, I take this Opportunity of transmitting it to you, together with this Letter, and brother of yesterday's date; all which Mr. Cockburn hath promised to have safely delivered into your Hands.

I have your Edition of Fothergill's work, two Octavo volumes printed 1783, but find no Anecdotes of my friend's Life contained in them. I presume you have printed them in a separate volume which I should be glad to see.[44]

Pray inform me by post if all comes safe, or if there is anything else on which I can serve you. I shall gladly embrace every Opportunity that offers of shewing my Regard to one who was so nearly connected with my two valuable Friends Peter Collinson and John Fothergill; and who has done Honour to his Profession by his assiduous Endeavours to render it more extremely useful to the Community. Adieu and believe me sincerely
Yours etc.
George Cleghorn

P.S. In the Dedication of Fothergill's Thesis[45] the Translator has committed an Error in calling Dr. Alston King's Physician. He was only Professor regius Botanicus in consequence of his being Keeper of the King's garden at

---

[44] Lettsom (ed.), op. cit. note 42 above, the third volume of this work was published later in 1784.

[45] John Fothergill, 'A medical inaugural dissertation: on the use of emetics' (1736) in ibid., vol. 1, section 2. It had originally been published in Latin by the Edinburgh College publisher: *Dissertatio medica inauguralis, de emeticorum usu in variis morbis tractandis*, Edinburgi, In aedibus Tho. Ruddimanni, 1736.

Holyrood House.[46] Dr. St Clair was Medicus Regis in 1736, and for many years afterwards.[47]

[JCL]

Endorsed: From Dr. Coke, Febr. 5 1801. New Chaple. answered.

My dear Sir,

I have received the three Folio volumes on the West Indies, for which I return you many thanks. If I can so manage my engagements as to drink tea with you, Sir, at Camberwell on a Sunday afternoon, I will with great pleasure embrace the opportunity. I shall return you those three Volumes in a short time, and three Volumes of Herrera, but the other three Volumes of Herrera I'll request the favour of you to leave with me for some months.

I'll also request the favour of you, Sir, to lend me <u>Lettres edifians et curieuses des Jesuits</u> and <u>Labat, Voyages aux Isles</u>. Shall I send for them? or will it be convenient to you, Sir, to send them to me?

I am, my dear Sir, with great respect,

Your much obliged and faithful friend

T. Coke

New Chapel, City-Road

Feb. 5 1801

[JCL]

Endorsed: From Dr. Combe,[48] May 19 1788, Bloomsbury

Dr. Lettsom

My Good Doctor,

The medals are not worth two pence more than weight which you know is very little, the silver not being worth three shillings an oz.

---

[46] Charles Alston (1683–1760) was an internationally renowned botanist who became professor of medicine and botany in Edinburgh 1738.

[47] Andrew Sinclair (or St. Clair) was professor of the institutes or theory of medicine at Edinburgh University, a post which he held between 1726 and 1747.

[48] Charles Combe senior, who succeeded to William Hunter's obstetric practice, was also a numismatist. See Abraham, op. cit., note 29 above, p. 127.

Yours most sincerely
Charles Combe

Bloomsbury Square
Wednesday morning

[JCL]

(44) Endorsed: from G. Costard, Nov. 29 1779, Twickenham. answered
Dc. 7. 79 (10)

Dear Sir,

It is now a Twelvemonth ago since I received the obliging Present of your
Book, for which I immediately returned you my best Thanks. What I said to
you then, relating to Esculapius[49] I forget, but I know it could be but little to
the Purpose. I have not lost sight of him at Times ever since, and pursued him
through all the Coins and Inscriptions I could come at, but I found they all
came too late to be of any service, so that I began to dispair of ever finding
him. I will not say I have now found him, but think I am nearer to him than
I was twelve months ago. For, meeting with a Quotation from Damascius in
Photius,[50] I began to think it might serve as a clue to conduct me through this
labyrinth. I will not trespass so much on your Time as to transcribe all that I
had collected on this subject. I shall only begin with what Damascius says
and observe that when I had formerly had minuted it down, I did not attend
to it enough, till lately meeting with the Passage in Reinesius,[51] which is this.
Ο εν Βηρυτω Ασκληπιος ουκ εστιν Ελλην, ουδε Αιγεπτιος, αλλα
τις επιχωριος Φοινιξ.[52] Upon which in his Note on Inscript. CXIV. he
judiciously observes, e Syrorum igitur Phoenicumve Lingua, Etymon

---

[49] Aesculapius, the Greek god of healing.

[50] Damascius (born *c.*AD 480) studied rhetoric in his native Damascus before going to
Alexandria to continue his education. He abandoned rhetoric for philosophy and became head
of the Athenian school, which he generally revitalised, some time in the first two decades of the
sixth century. Photius (?820–891), patriarch of Constantinople, produced a collection of extracts
and abridgements of ancient authors, *Bibliotheca* or *Myriobiblon*.

[51] Thomas Reinesius (1587–1667), but quote not found.

[52] "The Asclepius in Berytus…is neither Greek nor Egyptian, but rather a native
Phoenician". See Damascius, *Vita Isidori*, 302, cited in Emma J. Edelstein and Ludwig
Edelstein, *Asclepius: collection and interpretation of the testimonies*, Baltimore and London,
Johns Hopkins University Press, 1998, p. 423.

<u>Asclepis</u> petemus, rectius quam Graecorum.[53] So that, with regard to the Greeks, Asclepius was a Foreigner. And in that supposition I am farther confirm'd from two Passages in Pausanias.[54]

The Remains of the Phoenician Language are so very small that nothing can be expected from thence. But we may very well suppose that it had a near affinity with the Hebrew. And while I was thinking so, I accidentally opened my Hebrew Bible at Ezekiel 5.1. where the Prophet is order'd to take a sharp instrument[55] תער הגלבים LXX Ρομφαιαν οξειαν υπερ ξυρον κουρεως.

The word גלב <u>galab,</u> or in the Plural <u>galabim</u> is read nowhere in the Bible but in this Place. Our Translators render it <u>Barbers,</u> as it really seems to signifie, from the Circumstances of the Place, and all the other concurrent Versions. But I suspected that originally it might have had a more extensive signification, and comprehended <u>surgeons</u>. For in those early Times, you know, surgery made the principal Part of Physic. And with this agrees Macrobius,[56] and long before him Celsus, as I had formerly minuted down from him.[57]

As no hopes could be entertained from the Hebrew, my next Concern was to have Recourse to the Arabic; a language much more copious than the other, and of which there are larger Remains.

In this Language the verb جلب i.e. גלב, in its primary sense, signifies to <u>draw</u>. And from thence come many derivative senses, as may be seen in the Anthologia Veterum published by Schultens,[58] and likewise in the 4th Consensus of Hariri,[59] published by the same author.

---

[53] "And so we will look for the etymology of Aesclepius better in the language of the Syrians or Phoenicians than in that of the Greeks."

[54] Pausanias was a Greek traveller reputedly born in Lydia during the zenith of Roman rule. His most significant work was *Periegesis Hellados* (Description of Greece), a description, in ten books, of a tour of Greece begun in Attica between AD 143–161. Pausanias stated that "Asclepius" (Esculapius) raised several people from the dead, including Hippolytus.

[55] Ezekiel 5.1 in the authorized Bible of 1611 reads: "As for you, son of man, take a sharp sword and use it like a barber's razor, passing it over your head and beard. Then take a set of scales and divide the hair you have cut".

[56] Ambrosius Macrobius, Roman philosopher and writer in the fifth century AD.

[57] The Roman physician Aulus Cornelius Celsus (25 BC–AD 50) practised surgery in Imperial Rome.

[58] *Anthologia veterum Latinorum epigrammatum et poëmatum, sive catalecta poëtarum Latinorum*, 2 tom., Amstelaedami, 1759, 1773. Albert Schultens (1686–1750) was a Dutch orientalist who studied theology and Hebraic language at Gröningen and later learned Syriac, Chaldaic and Arabic. He accepted the chair of Oriental languages at the Academy of Franeker.

[59] *Haririi eloquentiae Arabicae principis tres priores consessus. E codice manuscripto bibliothecae Lugduno-Batavae pro specimine emissi. Ac notis illustrati ab Alberto Schultens. Arab. & Lat.*, Franequerae [Lugduni Batavorum (Leiden)], 1731.

From this primitive sense of <u>Drawing</u> I suspected might come another of <u>drawing a shin</u>, and so <u>closing</u>, and <u>healing</u> a wound. And upon turning to Golius & Castell's Lexicons,[60] to my great surprise, I found my conjecture right.

In this same language the word اسو as signifies medicus, chirurgus. And thence, by combining these two words, we have اسو جلب <u>asgleb</u>, or as B and P, are easily changed in the Pronunciation, the <u>Arabs</u> having no P in their Language, <u>Asclep</u> & Asclepi. And hence the Greeks, by adding their Termination ΟΣ, would very easily form the word ΑΣΚΛΕΠΙΟΣ or, with the Η, ΑΣΚΛΗΠΙΟΣ. The meaning of which will be medicus, cuticulas vulneribus obducendo insignis, or what is shorter, medicus vulneribus sanandis insignis.[61] So that Asclepius was, probably, a famous Phenician <u>surgeon,</u> before he was known to the Greeks.

I don't know whether anyone hath attempted to explain the word ΑΣΚΛΗΠΙΟΣ in the manner I have here done. But whether I am right in my Conjecture or not, I have had the satisfaction of shewing an attempt to oblige you, so far as it lies in my Power. For I imagined such a Communication as this would not be unacceptable.

I cannot close this Letter, however long it is already, without observing that Dr. Nussel hath very obligingly lent me a very fine <u>Arabic</u> ms. which is a kind of Dictionary of Eminent persons, in an Alphabetical Order. Under Asclepius, he says that his staff, round which the serpent is seen twined, was made of the Wood, or Plant الخطمى <u>Hatmai,</u> or <u>Hitmai,</u> which, according to Golius, signifies the <u>Althea</u>, commonly supposed to mean a kind of <u>wild mallows</u>.[62] And the Reason which he gives is, because this <u>hatmai</u> is "of a middle Temperature between Hot and Cold," and that, by this, Asclepius would recommend the like Equability in the Affairs of Life. Where this Author met with this Information that this Staff was of this Wood, I know not, but, considering the Symbolising Temper of those Times, it may not be improbable that some wood, in <u>particular,</u> was meant. And it is very certain that the <u>Arabs</u> met with Greek Authors, that are now <u>lost</u>, at least not known.

---

[60] *Lexicon heptaglotton: Hebraicum, Chaldaicum, Syriacum, Samaritanum, Aethiopicum, Arabicum, conjunctum, et Persicum, separatim*, Londini, Imprimebat Thomas Roycroft, sumptibus Roberti Scott, 1686.

[61] "Doctor, excellent at causing wounds to close up", or "A doctor excellent at healing wounds".

[62] *Althea officinalis* (Malvaceae) is native to the marshes of Europe. According to Pliny, "whoever swallows daily half a cyanthus [wine glass] of the juice of any one of them [the mallows] will be immune to all diseases" (Pliny, *Natural history*, Loeb ed., London, Heinemann, 1951, vol. 6, bk 20, p. 131). The root is the officinal part of the plant—it produces large amounts of mucilage, said to have soothing and healing properties. It was used in the treatment of irritations such a sore throats and ulcers.

I have only to add that, dipping into Erpinius' Grammar,[63] I found a Proverb which says, that the "<u>Barber</u> learns to shave on the orphan's head". The word for <u>Barber</u> here signifies likewise <u>Chirurgus</u>. And this will justifie me in supposing that word for <u>Barber</u> in Ezekiel, might signifie likewise a surgeon.

I am

Dear Sir

Your very Faithful

and obliged humble servant

G. Costard

Novr. 29 1779

[JCL]

Endorsed: Revd Thomas Dalton, Northwood, Isle of Wight, Mar. 15 1802. done

For

Dr. Lettsom

I send this line to my Nephew who is a Tea-Dealer in Wormwood Street near the Excise-Office and will convey it to you.

Northwood, Isle of Wight, Mar. 15th 1802

My good Friend,

I now gladly embrace the Opportunity of my Neighbour's going to town, which enables me to give you some account of the good Effects which I have experienced from your Prescription. But I should have written immediately on the Arrival of your kind Letter, if I had obey'd the first Impulse of my Mind, as I had much to say on the <u>political</u> part of it, which was so exactly consonant to my own Feelings. My opinions were grounded on a close Attention to the Transactions of the time, and they were abundantly confirmed by that masterly Pamphlet which was published by Mr. Erskine.[64]

---

[63] The Dutchman Thomas Erpenius (1584–1624) became the first professor of Persian, Arabic and other Eastern Languages at the University of Leiden in 1613. His most famous work *Grammatica Arabica* (an Arab grammar) was published in the same year. It was the standard text for two centuries and was reprinted in 1636, 1656, 1748, 1767 and 1796.

[64] Thomas Erskine (1750–1823), the youngest son of David Henry, tenth Earl of Buchan, was a lawyer and renowned defence advocate. Erskine was a prolific author and it is difficult to

You mention the insulting Dismission of Mons[r]. Chauvelin[65] which was there mentioned in your Letter, and which we all remember from the Papers of the Time to have been precisely such. The whole series of the conduct of our pious Administration was a Tissue of bare-faced Corruption and Imposition on the Country, while they affected to call their Efforts a War of Religion. When Pitt quitted the Helm, by the Association of Tierney and others, we were persuaded to believe that a <u>new</u> and <u>different</u> system was to be adopted, to ensure <u>Peace</u> to the country.[66] But what are we <u>now</u> to hope after what has so very recently happened in the House, relating to Mr. Robson? I may truly say he was insulted and worried for his Integrity and support of the Country-Interest; and even the <u>virtuous</u> Mr. Martin (not the Irishman) had ~~had~~ hardly the Courage to sustain his Cause, which was lost (on the motion for Papers to prove its being right) by 77 against two. What are we to hope after such Events as we are daily Witnesses to prove! One cannot avoid grudging such exorbitant Taxes devoted to ruin the Country!

I must now inform you that after a due Trial of you Prescription, I feel new Occasion to exclaim daily—"blessed be the man who invented these Pills."! They have litterally superseded their own use now for a <u>Time</u>, as they have quite renovated my spirits by bringing back that former Diarrhoea which I mentioned in my last Letter as my Remedy of Nature, after all my Langour & bad Symptoms. I have now therefore left off the medicines for a Time, and certainly mean to renew them whenever that ruinous Inactivity of my Bowels returns. I sometimes took only 1 of the Pills which answered extremely well, and the 2 pro re natâ. The liquid medicine no doubt has had a competent share in producing that Benefit of Health which I now so <u>exultingly</u> feel. But the Pills are a golden Panacea, which I must never omit for any long Time. O! that I had known this happy composition much sooner! I had something bilious in my Maladies for years. The Expulsion of this is Relief inexpressible!

---

identify the pamphlet referred to. Possibly: Thomas Erskine, *Brief thoughts, &c. on A view of the causes and consequences of the present war with France*, London, Printed for J. Owen; and Lee and Hurst [1797?], or *idem, Substance of the speech of the honourable Thomas Erskine in the House of Commons, on … the 3d February, 1800, on a motion for an address to the throne, approving of the refusal of ministers to treat with the French republic*, London, printed for J Debrett by A Wilson, [1800].

[65] Bernard-François Chauvelin (1766–1832), "Minister Plenipotentiary", was the French Republic's ambassador to England after the French Revolution. When France executed its king, he was ordered to leave England within eight days.

[66] William Pitt (1759–1806) fought a duel with George Tierney, a pro-reform Whig, on Putney Heath at three o'clock on 27 May 1798 over an argument which had occurred in Parliament two days previously. Pitt wanted to bring in a bill to suspend for a limited time the protection enjoyed by various people from being impressed into service of the navy. Tierney objected, and Pitt accused him of obstructing the defence of the country. At which point Tierney demanded satisfaction and the matter proceeded to a duel.

I believe you know Mrs. Nowell and her sister Close, who are my near Neighbours. The former is in Town with her son (a confidential Clerk in the Duke of York's office) but soon expected home. She was House-keeper to the Prince of Wales who gave her an Annuity; but he is bankrupt, and has withdrawn it, which depresses her much.[67]

I deem it right to ascertain the good effect of your medicines, and am ever your much obliged Friend

T. Dalton

PS
I admire your Paper made of Straw, which I hope will abundantly answer the Hopes of the ingenious Inventor, by a liberal Encouragement, when the com. Paper was become so immoderately dear by Taxes and War. There is a Petition of the Stationers, which is meant, I fear, to injure the Patentee, but he deserves the Favor of the Public more than they do!

1. [JCL]

Endorsed: From Dr. Dickson, July 27 1813, Whitehaven. answered.
Dr. Lettsom

Whitehaven, July 27 1813

My dear Friend,
I am fully assured that neither the Whitehaven Dispensary Report of the last year,[68] nor my reply to your kind and most affectionate Letter, has been received, and, therefore feel myself anxiously desirous that you should not be disappointed in the acceptance of this communication.

The public papers have announced a very considerable and well merited addition to your private fortune.[69] Sincere are my congratulations, and

---

[67] The Prince of Wales, later George IV, was constantly beset by personal debts. See also note 26 above.

[68] The Whitehaven Dispensary (or Kendal Dispensary) was established in 1783. Its services were available to the poor of Kendal and Kirkland who were unable to afford medicines and medical and surgical care. It has proved impossible to locate an extant copy of the annual report of the dispensary for this year.

[69] On 2 March 1813, a case of a disputed will was decided in Lettsom's favour. When his daughter-in-law, Ruth Lettsom (née Hodge and widow of the wealthy Caribbean planter William Payne Georges) died, she left her fortune to him (see note 21 above). See Abraham, op. cit., note 29 above, p. 455, and also note 88 in the 'Letters from Lettsom' section.

equally so the wish that the accumulation of wealth may effectually promote your real happiness; certainly convinced that a portion of it will be most judiciously applied to the relief of every species of distressful indigency. I have long omitted, in our Dispensary arrangements, attending to the peculiar objects of the Royal Humane Society. No remarkable occasion had occurred in these Northern parts, or in the adjacent country, to give me an opportunity of noticing them. The slight but sincere regard which I have paid to the subject in our last Dispensary Report will, however, evince my attachment to it, and the best interests of suffering humanity. I hope the diffusive application of the oxygenated muriatic acid gas,[70] proposed by my good friend Mr. Birley (a sail cloth manufacturer of opulence and respectability) in all cases of malignant contagion, will be highly efficacious, and aid the salutary operation of our usual prophylactics; perhaps superseding the necessity of many which have been long employed.

I have not anywhere, in the libraries of this County, met with the last year's Report of your laudable Institution. Your judicious plan of concenterating its various objects and only displaying those which were most interesting I am fully assured will be strictly adhered to, and I trust establish its future utility. You may rest assured that no opportunity will be omitted of transmitting to you any acceptable information. My last year's report and letter went to Mr. Fox at Mr. Steele's, Tower Hill.[71] Our booksellers are connected with Messrs. Longman and Co.[72] or Messrs. Richardson and Co., Royal Exchange, London,[73] and any package sent to them will be readily conveyed to me and <u>most gratefully</u> received. The friends of your society are here very numerous and highly respectable. To them I gratefully acknowledge a sense of obligation, which I shall be happy to repay by every means in my power.

We have now with us the best of good men, Lord Lonsdale,[74] who accepts every opportunity of effectually promoting the interests of this country. I wish my son Richard, at Queen's College, Oxford, or William, Merchant, Rodney Street, Liverpool, could be of any service to you.

---

[70] Muriatic acid is now identified as hydrochloric acid, and oxygenated muriatic acid (or oxymuriatic acid) as chlorine gas. It was so named because it was held to be a compound of oxygen and muriatic acid.

[71] Steel was a surgeon based at Tower Hill.

[72] In the early nineteenth century, the bookselling firm of Longman and Co., based at Paternoster Row in London, was one of the biggest publishing concerns in the metropolis.

[73] William Richardson, bookseller, was in 1794, based at 23 Cornhill and Royal Exchange, London. See Henry Kent, *Kent's Directory. For the year 1794*, London, R. and H. Causton, 1794.

[74] William Lowther (1757–1844), second Earl of Lonsdale, succeeded to the title in 1802 and was the main landowner in the Lake District.

Sincere in my wishes for the long continuance of your health and happiness,
I remain,
Your faithful friend
Joshua Dixon[75]

2. [JCL]
Endorsed: Dixon
Mr. Beaumont

Dr. Dixon presents his best compliments to Mr. Beaumont,[76] and hopes
the enclosed Report of the Whitehaven Dispensary will be acceptable.
Dr. D– exquisitely feels the solicitude, which the privation of the dearest
friends, and their invaluable correspondence, during a life of 72 years, has
occasioned, and sincerely deplores its inevitable necessity. To the late worthy
Treasurers of you justly stiled most Humane Society are due every attestation
of gratitude and regard. Their extensive beneficence and professional merits
long will be held in respectful remembrance. From them regularly were
received the Annual Reports of the Royal Humane Society for thirty years, and
the Directors of the Whitehaven Dispensary are perfectly sensible of the obligations, which those judicious communications have conferred. The measures
requisite, assiduously, to be employed, in cases of Suspended Animation, arising from accident or design, printed upon large sheets of paper, are distributed
where they may be useful; particularly in the Sea Ports of this Coast, and in the
vicinity of Lakes and Rivers. Dr. D– observes, with great satisfaction, that a
considerable period has elapsed since these instructions were necessary

Whitehaven, Aug. 1 1816.

[JCL]

Dr. Lettsom

My Dear Sir,
     Sir Claude and Lady de Crespigny do me the favor to dine with me at
St Margaret Hill tomorrow at 1/2 past 5 exactly. If your Engagements will

---

[75] Joshua Dixon, the Elder, M.D., F.R.S. (1745–1825), of Whitehaven. Dixon was an old
friend of Benjamin Rush of Philadelphia who had been a medical student in Edinburgh at the
same time as Dixon.
     [76] John Beaumont was one of Lettsom's longstanding contacts. In 1791, he was one of the
founding members of the General Sea-Bathing Hospital at Margate and, at the time, also
Treasurer of the Royal Humane Society.

admit of your joining the Party, your Company will confer a great Pleasure and Honor upon, my dear Sir,
your obliged and faithful servant
Philip Dodd.[77]

Camberwell, July 2nd

I beg my best Respects to Mrs. Lettsom

[JCL]

Dr. Lettsom
Basinghall Street

Epsom Friday

Sir,
  I am extremely sorry that it is impossible for me to have the pleasure of waiting upon you on Sunday, but I did not recollect the Whitsun Holidays at which time I have a previous engagement at my own house in the country. I regret extremely the disappointment to me, and I am,
Sir
with great esteem
your most obedient
Humble servant
Egremont[78]

[CF][79]

Primrose Street

Dear Sir,
  I thank you for the notes in your last favour, and will take care they shall hereafter be noticed. With regard to the Abingdon Collections, your letter

---

[77] Philip Dodd was possibly one of Lettsom's neighbours in Camberwell.

[78] George O'Brien Wyndham (1751–1837), third Earl of Egremont, son of Charles Wyndham, the second Earl, and Alicia Maria, daughter of George, second Baron Carpenter, succeeded to the peerage at the age of only twelve. The family seat was at Petworth in Sussex. In addition, in 1774, he inherited the Irish estates of his uncle, Percy Wyndham O'Brien, the Earl of Thomond.

[79] There is no adressee. It is highly likely, given the "kind respects to Mrs Gough", that this letter was not to Lettsom at all but to Richard Gough of Enfield. See 'Letters from Lettsom' section, Letter 21.

mentioned that they should be left at Mr. Nicholls's in the course of next week; if they could be sent per coach this, I should prefer it, as on Monday Morning I quit London. I promise 1. "not to alter their present arrangement. 2. to publish them at Mr. Nichols' Press. 3. That you shall be acquainted with every proceeding concerning them".

The List of Spital Sermons which I mean to use, consists of such as were published previous to the Restoration. All published since that time may be found in Cooke's Edition of Lettsome's, Preacher's Assistant.[80] If I mistake not, Dr. Holmes's 8th report is published. I think Mr. Gutch shewed it to me. I will make enquiry after a copy for you.

With kind respects to Mrs. Gough, I remain

Dear Sir

Yours etc.

Henry Ellis[81]

January 2 1798
11 o'Clock Evening.

P.S. Excuse me for not meeting you tomorrow morning at Mr. Nichols'. It is out of my power. Any commands at Oxford shall be carefully executed. Parcels conveyed etc.

1. [L]

Endorsed: From Lady Ann Erskine,[82] Dec. 28 1789, London. answered.

To
Do[ctor Lettsom][83]

Spa = Fields[84] Thursday night
Decr 27th: 1789

---

[80] John Cooke [Rector of Wentnor, Salop], *The preacher's assistant: (after the manner of Mr. Letsome) containing a series of the texts of sermons and discourses*, Oxford, printed for the editor, at the Clarendon-Press, 1783.

[81] Henry Ellis (1777–1869), later Sir Henry Ellis, was principal librarian at the British Museum.

[82] Lady Anne Erskine (1739–1804), daughter of the tenth Earl of Buchan and sister of Henry Erskine, Lord Advocate of Scotland, was Lady Huntingdon's companion and secretary of many years' standing. She moved, as a young age, to Bath in Somerset where she was converted to Methodism on attending worship at Lady Huntingdon's chapel. After her father died in 1767, she became increasingly involved with 'The Lady Huntingdon Connexion' (for which, see notes 84 and 85 below). Lettson always spelt her first name without the final "e".

[83] The manuscript is extensively torn.

[84] The Spa Fields Chapel was in Finsbury, London, near Lady Huntingdon's house. A large, circular building in imitation of the Pantheon in Rome, it was originally opened in May 1770 as

My Good Friend Doctor Lettsom will I know be concerned to hear how ill Lady Huntingdon has been.[85] Yesterday Evening she was suddenly taken with a violent fit of the stone which lasted with unabated suffering for more than seven hours, notwithstanding that La[u]danum and the other medicines she has been used to take on such occasions were given. The lateness of the hour and the terrible weather prevented her sending to you, and it pleased God about three o'clock in the morning the pain abated and she is now very easey. I may say quite easey and less affected by the consequences of the pain and Laudanam she took than could possible be expected. The violence of the pain was in the right kidney—in former attacks it used to be in the side of her belly. She has passed very little Gravel and no stone, but had a warning of this attack the day before in a dark tinge upon her water, which I wish she had attended to more than she did. She desires every best wish to you, and is always sensible of, and grateful for, all your kind attentions for her. I wished you to be informed of these particulars and hope we shall see you. ~~when~~

I am with much regard very sincerely your friend and obliged servant

A. A. Erskine

2. [L]

Endorsed: From Lady Erskine, Dec. 16 1790, London. done

To Doctor Lettsom

I am in some hopes of our Good Friend Doctor Lettsom calling here today, but lest you should not, I wish to inform you that this morning Lady Huntingdon spit a <u>very little</u> blood. It is so little that but for what happened

---

a place of amusement, but went bankrupt within a year. It was acquired some years later by Lady Huntingdon and, after conversion, opened as a place of worship on 5 July 1777.

[85] The Countess of Huntingdon (1707–1791), was Selina Shirley, daughter of Washington Shirley, second Earl of Ferrars, who married Theophilus, ninth Earl of Huntingdon in 1728. Her husband died suddenly, in 1746, at the age of fifty, when she was only thirty-nine years of age. She devoted the rest of her life to the Methodist movement, founding an evangelical Calvinist sect of Methodists called 'The Lady Huntingdon Connexion'. See Abraham, op. cit., note 29 above, pp. 273–5. Lady Huntingdon's personal papers are held in the Methodist Archives and Research Centre at John Rylands University Library of Manchester.

before I should not have troubled you with this information of it, as it was little more than a large streak, but fresh and florid in the colour, and lest it should be a presage of more to come, I wished you to know it. In other respects Lady Huntingdon is the same as when you saw her, only for these two days past she has complained of some pain in the left side of her breast like what she had before the last attack, but her breath is very free. She has suffered much pain from the stone in passing her water, and yesterday made some that was very bloody. She has been up twice or thrice since you saw her, and sat up about 3 hours each time and bore it as well as usual. She intended to have come into the dining room to day, but Mr. Dodd[86] wishes her to keep as still as possible and has recommended her to take the draught you first ordered for her, i.e. with the Sweet Spirit of Nitre in it, which she means to do. If there is any thing else you wish, I beg you will be so good as to let me know. Lady H: desires every kind wish to you and yours, and I beg you to accept of the same from
your faithful and obliged friend
A. A. Erskine

Spa = Fields
Dec^r: the 17th 1790

3. [L]

Endorsed: From Lady A. Erskine, Jan. 9. 1791, London. answered.

Doctor Lettsom
Basinghall Street

Dear Sir,
     Not having had the pleasure seeing you lately, I cannot forbear informing you particularly how Lady Huntingdon does, as for these three days past she has been far from being so well as when you saw her last. Her pain from the stone has been very great, [s]o much so that she seldom makes a drop of

---

[86] A Robert Dodd (b. 1770) was operating as an apothecary in Rosoman's Street (in Finsbury, just south-west of Islington) in 1790 and later in Marlborough Street (Kensington) in London. Wallis, op. cit., note 6 above, p. 168.

water without crying out. She complains likewise of a great fulness and distention of her stomach, particularly after taking any nourishment. This morning the fulness and distention has left her stomach and is all over her breast, but particularly the left side of it, and oppresses her breath very much, particularly on moving. She says it is not <u>pain</u> but <u>oppression</u>, and the thirst and dryness of her mouth and tongue is beyond expression—but her pulse continues good and there is no heat more than usual. Her sleep is likewise good and her appetite as usual, but she is low, and yesterday her water was pale. Today it is of its usual colour. She did not bear getting up so well, nor was able to sit up so long as usual on Friday, and yesterday did not get up at all, but is now up and bears it pretty well, but the oppression on her breath is very distressing indeed.

I have given you this account that you me [*recte* may] do as you see best. Our best wishes ever attend you and yours, and believe me to be ever very sincerely
your obliged and faithful Friend,
Anne Agnes Erskine

Spa = Fields
Sunday 1 o'clock
Jany the 9th: 1791

4. [L]

Endorsed: Lady A. Erskine, Jan. 22 1791, London. done

To Doctor Lettsom

The daily expectation I have been in of seeing you here, has prevented my writing to inform you particularly concerning Lady Huntingdon who has been for more than a week past considerably worse. She visibly loses her flesh, and is indeed I think now nearly as thin as she can be and says she feels she loses strength likewise, though she continues to take her usual degree of nourishment. I must therefore, My Good Doctor, beg you to come as from her love and regard for you she is always glad to see you, and her confidence in you prevents her using any Physical help but under your direction, and she has taken no medicine since you was here except a little Daffy's Elix[ir], and you may perhaps Judge from these Symptoms, which certainly appear unfavourable, that more may be necessary. In hopes of seeing you soon I will only add that I am always with much regard, My Good Doctor

your obliged and faithful Friend
A. A. Erskine

Spa = Fields
Jan^y: 22^d 1791

5. [L]

Endorsed: From Lady A. Erskine, May 25 1791, Spafields. answered.

To
Dr. Lettsom

I wish it was in my power to send you a better account of your Good Friend Lady Huntingdon, but she has had the spasm in her throat ever since 9 o'clock this morning and no appearance, as yet, of going off. This united with great pain from the stone, and excessive lowness, she bids me tell you is more than she well knows how to Grapple with. She will be glad to see you this Evening if you return home in time for it, or if not tomorrow morning. The pain in her left side has likewise for some days past been much worse than usual. Every best wish from her ever attends you and yours, with those of my Good Doctor.
your obliged friend
A. A. Erskine

Spa = Fields
May the 25th 1791
$\frac{1}{2}$ past seven

6. [JCL][87]

Endorsed: 93 P. 79

To Lady A. Erskine

---

[87] Fair copy of a draft letter to Lady Anne Erskine on the death of the Countess of Huntingdon The draft copy with crossings out immediately precedes the fair copy in JCL. This letter is also reproduced in T. J. Pettigrew, *Memoirs of the life and writings of the late John Coakley Lettsom, with a selection from his correspondence*, 3 vols, London, printed by Nichols, Son, and Bentley, for Longman, Hurst, Rees, Orme and Brown, 1817, vol. 2, pp. 382–4.

June 18th 1791

Dear Lady Ann,

I deeply sympathise with thee, and all the family in Christ, in the removal of that evangelic woman, so lately among us, the Countess of Huntingdon.[88] Your souls were so united and your affections so endeared together, that I cannot but feel in a particular manner on thy account; lest the mournful state of thy mind may undermine thy constitution, and endanger a life spent in mitigating the painful sufferings of body of our deceased friend whilst living. Her advanced age and debelitated frame had long prepared my mind for an event which has at length deprived the world of its brightest ornament. How often have we, when sitting by her sick bed, witnessed the faithful composure with which she has viewed this awful change. Not with the fearful prospect of doubt, not with the dreadful apprehension of the judgment of an offended Creator—hers was all peace within; a tranquility and chearfulness which conscious acceptance alone would convey. How often have we seen her, elevated above the earth and earthly things, uttering this language "My work is done, I have nothing to do but to go to my Heavenly Father".

Let us therefore, under a firm conviction of her felicity, endeavor to follow her, as she followed her Redeemer. Let us be thankful that she was preserved to advanced age, with the perfect exercise of her mental faculties; and that, under long and painful days and nights of sickness, she never repined; but appeared constantly animated with prayer and thankfulness for unutterable mercies she experienced. When I look back upon the past years of my attendance and connect with it the multitude of others whom my profession has introduc'd me to, I feel consolation in acknowledging that of all the daughters of affliction, she exhibited the greatest degree of Christian composure that ever I witnessed; and that submission to divine allotment, however severe and painful, which nothing but divine aid could inspire.

It was on the 12th of this month that our dear friend appeared more particularly indisposed, and afforded me those apprehensions of danger, which on the 17th finally terminated her bodily sufferings. I had on former occasions of her illness, observed, that when she expressed "an hope and desire to go to her Heavenly Father"; (for this was often her language) she usually added

---

[88] The Countess of Huntingdon had died on 17 June 1791, in her house at Spa Fields, London, at the age of eighty-four. Her body, clothed in the white silk suit that she had worn for the opening of the chapel in Goodman's Fields was placed, according to the directions in her will, in a plain manner within her husband's vault at Ashby-de-la-Zouche in Leicestershire.

some solicitudes upon her mind respecting her Children, as she spoke of her people in religious profession; adding "But I feel for the good of their souls". When under the utmost debility of body, she has continued this subject in animated and pious conservation, extending her views to all mankind, she has expressed a firm persuasion in the gradual and universal extension of virtue and religion. Wherever a fellow creature existed, so far her prayers extended. In her last illness I never heard her utter a desire to remain longer on earth. A little before she died, she repeatedly said, in a feeble voice "I shall go to my Father this night", adding, "Has God forgot to be gracious, or is there any end of his loving kindness?"

It was on this day she conversed a little on the subject of sending Missionaries to Otaheite in the South Seas;[89] in the pious hope of introducing Christianity among that mild but uninformed, race of people; indeed, her whole life seemed devoted to one great object, the glory of God, and the salvation of his creatures.

John Coakley Lettsom

~~June the 18th 1791~~

7. [L]

Endorsed: From Lady Erskine, July 11 1791, Spafields. done

To
Doctor Lettsom

My very highly Esteemed Friend

The bearer of this, Mr: Hyde, is a student in the College of our late very Dear and precious Friend.[90] He is ill, and very desirous of your advice, and I have taken the liberty from my knowledge of your love and respect to her memory to introduce him to you by this few lines, and any directions you are so good as to give him concerning his health will be punctually observed.

---

[89] Otaheite is Tahiti in the South Pacific or, as it was sometimes known, King George III Island. The first missionaries were sent to Tahiti and other South Seas islands by the London Missionary Society, established in 1795.

[90] Hyde could not be identified by us. It may, therefore, be, since this letter states that he was ill, that he died and did not finish his training. See Methodist Archives and Research Centre, John Rylands University Library of Manchester, 'The Methodist Archives biographical index'. This can also be found online at http://rylibweb.man.ac.uk. See also the list of 'Ministers and probationers who have died in their work' which appears at the back of the 1969 edition of *Ministers and probationers of the Methodist Church formerly Wesleyan, Primitive and United Methodist, ... together with an alphabetical list of deceased ministers*, London, Methodist Publishing House, 1890–1969, generally taken to be the fullest index of Methodist ministers.

I am inexpressibly low, but always very much
your faithful and much obliged friend
A. A. Erskine

Spa = Fields
July the 11th: 1791

8. [L]

Endorsed: From Lady A. Erskine, Apr. 12 1792, London. done

To
Doctor Lettsom
Basinghall Street

My Very Good Friend Doctor Lettsome will I am sure easily forgive me for
troubling him by a request which springs from my full conviction of his kind
heart remaining still the same to his Dear old friend who is gone,[91] his sor-
rowful friend who is left.[92] It is on this ground I take the liberty of begging
your advice to the bearer of this, the Revd. Mr. Attley,[93] how far the Waters
at Cheltenham (where he is now going) are likely to be of any use to him, or
for any further directions you may see fit to give him. I hope Mrs. Lettsom
and all your Family are well. Remember me very kindly to them and when
you have a leisure moment, look in on an old friend who will rejoice in an
opportunity of assuring you how much she remains,
Sincerely yours
A. A. Erskine

Spa = Fields
April 12 1792.

9. [L]

Endorsed: From Lady A. Erskine, June 25 1792, London. done

---

[91] See note 88 above.

[92] Lady Anne is referring to herself here.

[93] Presumably a Methodist minister. However, he does not appear in any of the lists of ministers, op. cit., note 90 above.

To
Dr. Lettsom
Favour of Mr. Wilson

Forgive me, my kind Friend, for troubling you so often, but the bearer of this, Mr. Wilson,[94] is very much indisposed and has a particular desire to receive your opinion concerning him. He is one of your late Friend's young Ministers[95] which will plead my excuse for sending him. I beg you to believe me and to be with sincere regard
your faithful and much obliged friend
A. A. Erskine

Spa = Fields
June 25th: 1792

My best wishes attends Mrs. Lettsom and all your family.

10. [L]

Endorsed: From Lady A. Erskine, Sept. 3 1792, Spa fields. answered.

To Dr. Lettsom
From Lady Ann Erskine

My very Worthy Friend,

I have just received you very kind message by Mr. Best,[96] which adds to the obligations I already feel myself under to you. The Fidelity, diligence and ability with which he acquitted himself in the situation of a private secretary to my late Dear Friend and yours for seven years; the regard she had for him, and his faithful attentions to me in matters of business since her decease, all conspire to make me ardently wish to serve him, as my situation does not admit of his continuance with me in the same character he held with her. Mr. Holt of Palsgrave Place, with whom Mr. Best served as a Clerk upwards

---

[94] Not identified.

[95] This refers to the itineracy or circuit ministry. Lady Huntingdon gave her friend and companion, Lady Anne, responsibility for organizing and running the itineracy, which provided young ministers for placement in various active circuits. There were home circuits, for instance, a Newcastle circuit and a Birmingham circuit, as well as circuits abroad, in the West Indies. There was also an Irish itineracy. Many exercised an active circuit ministry throughout their lives.

[96] Private secretary to the late Countess of Huntingdon. He had previously served Mr Holt of Palsgrave Place as a clerk for over eight years, as the text of the letter indicates.

of Eight years, receommended him in terms of the warmest commendation to Lady Huntingdon, and he has fully answered the character given of him, and in every matter of Trust either respecting money or business in which confidence was reposed in him, he acquitted himself with an exactness and uprightness that is highly to his honour, and I think I may venture to say, as far as it is possible for one person to answer for another, that he will do credit to any recommendation you may be so good as to favour him with.

It is very unreasonable, my Good friend, not to conclude this letter without further trespassing on your kindness, but I am requested to ask your advice on a subject, which, as the Father of a family yourself, will lead you to feel for a very worthy Father who has a son not so diligent and attentive to his studies as I hope yours will prove. It is Thomas Scutt Esqr. of Brighthelmstone,[97] Brother to Miss Scutt whom you have so often seen with our late Dear Friend. His youngest son wished to study Physic and Surgery, and for that purpose served his time with a principal person in that line of Brigh[th]elmstone. The youth is sensible and good-tempered, but has been led aside and in some things inconsiderate, is now conscious of it and wishes to pursue his studies, and his Father is desirous it should be at the College of Edinburgh.[98] Any counsel you can give me respecting the best method of his proceeding in this business, or any recommendation with the young man to persons in the Physical line there would much oblige me as well as your old Friend Miss Scutt and would be a real relief to the mind of Mr. Scutt, a Worthy and deserving man and a particular Friend of mine.

It requires all your long experienced kindness of heart to me to forgive me the liberty I take and the trouble I give you by this letter. Past instances of it lead me to hope for it now and that you will believe me to be with a real sense of your Friendship and high esteem of it.
Your Faithful and much Obliged Friend
A. A. Erskine

Spa = Fields
Sep[r] 3[d] 1792

---

[97] The Rev. Thomas Scutt of Brighthelmstone, Brighton, in Sussex. He married, in May 1807, Mary White, youngest daughter of Joseph White of Cheshire.
[98] Benjamin Scutt, later surgeon, M.D. (Edinburgh), of Brighton in Sussex. Wallis, op. cit., note 6 above, p. 530. Wallis, gives no information to whom he was apprenticed.

11. [L]

Endorsed: From Lady A. Erskine, Sept. 17 1792, Spafields. done

To
Doctor Lettsom
By Favour of Mr. West

Accept my thanks, my very kind friend, my best thanks, for your most friendly attention to my requests. The inclosed is the answer I have received from Mr. Scutt to your Queries concerning his son. Would it not add to the obligation If Dr. Duncan[99] could recommend the young man to a proper place for Lodging and boarding, and be an advantage to him to be in a sober good family. I write in much haste as Mr. Best, who is the bearer of this, is just going out. How joyful shall I be if you succeed for him.
My best wishes attend Mrs. Lettsom and your family.
I am ever your truly obliged Friend
A. A. Erskine

Spa = Fields
Sepr 17 1792

12. [L]

Endorsed: From Lady A. Erskine, Sept. 23 1792, London. done

To
Dr. Lettsom

My Very Kind Friend,
    I have received a letter from Brighthelmstone by which I find that Mr. Scutt is to pass through London on Monday next on his way to Edinburgh, but not

---

[99] Andrew Duncan senior (1744–1827), professor of the institutes of medicine at the University of Edinburgh (1790–1819, and afterwards conjointly with his son), was an esteemed physician with an extensive private practice.

to stop even so long as to call upon me at Spa = Fields which I am sorry for as I not only wished him to see you, but likewise to see him myself as he is the only one of his Father's family who is not personally known to me. If you have any Packet you wish to convey to Doctor Duncan by him and will be so good as to send it to me on Monday morning, I will not fail to send it to Mr. Scutt at John Shoebreds Esqr., Mark Lane, where he is to stop when he comes to town.

I have written to my Old Friend Doctor Duncan, not to add any weight to your recommendation which I am sensible nothing from me can do, but to mention Mr. Scutt's entire acquiescence in whatever the Doctor may think most proper for his son and his wish to remit to him quarterly (in whatever way he may direct), whatever expense is incurred. I sincerely wish the young man may do well for his Father's sake as well as his own. Permit me once more to return you my grateful acknowledgement for your goodness to my on this and every other occasion, and to assure you how much I am

your truly obliged and faithful friend

A. A. Erskine

Spa = Fields
Sepr 22^{d} 1792

13. [L]

Endorsed: From Lady A. Erskine, Oct. 21 1792, Spa Fields. answered.

To
Doctor Lettsom
By Favour of Mr: Robertson[100]

My Very Kind Friend,

I send you inclosed a letter which I have received from our good Friend Doctor Duncan. When you have at your leisure perused it, be so

---

[100] This might be William Robertson, formerly of the Wesleyan church, who commenced his ministry in 1800 and preached for the Connexion for six years until his death in 1806. However, this would mean that he spent at least eight years in training. See list of 'Ministers and probationers who have died in their work', op. cit., note 90 above.

good as to return it to me (by the Penny Post to save you the trouble of another mode of conveyance) as I may have occasion to refer to it. Mr. Scutt begs me to convey to you his grateful acknowledgements for your kind care for his son. The Bearer of this, Mr. Robertson, would be much indebted to you for your kind Counsel for the Complaint in his face. He is one of the students in the College of your late Dear Friend and mine. Forgive this intrusion on your kindness, accept my best wishes for you and yours and believe me to be, with a real sense of your many truly friendly attentions to me,
your faithful and much obliged Friend
A. A. Erskine

Spa = Fields
Octr: the 21 1792

14. [L]

Endorsed: From Lady A. Erskine, Febr. 24 1793, Spafields. answered.

To
Doctor Lettsom
By Favour of Mr. Best

My Very Kind Friend,
    The bearer of this, Mr. Best, will state to you the case of the poor young man who is the subject of it, and whose situation and the difficulties I am under on his account will, I flatter myself, be an apology for giving you this trouble. I have no doubt but you will recollect having often seen him in the family of our late dear friend. I brought him up from a Boy and I believe once spoke to you concerning his complaint, which originated from a fall, and has now I am informed terminated in an Ulcer in his Bladder. Your kind advice on this occasion and your sentiments of what hopes there is of his recovery will very much oblige me and add to the many favours you have already confered by your kind attentions on
Your faithful and Much obliged Friend
A. A. Erskine

Spa = Fields
Feb^y: the 24th
1793

15. [L]

Endorsed: From Lady A. Erskine, Febr. 26 1793, Spafields. answered.

To
Dr. Lettsom

My Very Kind Friend,
I return you my best thanks for the Letter of admission to the Dispensary,[101] and you will very much add to the favour by giving the bearer of it a few lines to Doctor Simms [*sic*][102] (which Mr. Best told me you was so good as to propose) as I fear the poor Young Man's case is a very bad one. He will wait your leisure for the letter, and will without fail attend Dr. Simms at the dispensary tomorrow morning. I beg you to believe that I am with much regard
Your greatly obliged
Friend
A. A. Erskine

Spa = Fields
Feb^y: the 26th: 1793

16. [L]

Endorsed: From Lady A. Erskine, June 10 1794, London. answered.

To Doctor Lettsom
Sambrook Court
Basinghall Street
By favour of the Rev^d. Edward Davies.[103]

My Much Esteemed Friend,
Relying on the many proofs of your Friendship and kind attention to me, I take the liberty of requesting your advice for the bearer of this, the Rev^d.

---

[101] The General Dispensary in Aldersgate Street. The Dispensary was the first charitable institution that Lettsom helped to found. He also wrote an early account of it: John Coakley Lettsom, *Medical memoirs of the General Dispensary in London, for part of the years 1773 and 1774*, London, E. and C. Dilly, 1774.

[102] James Sims (1741–1820) was appointed third physician at the Aldersgate Dispensary in 1774. At this time, he was also President of the Medical Society, a position that he held, following a revision of the rules in 1787 that made the President and his officers eligible for re-election, for the next twenty-one years. See Introduction to this volume, p. 3, and Abraham, op. cit., note 29 above, pp. 392–3.

[103] Davies does not appear in the list of 'Ministers and probationers who have died in their work', op. cit., note 90 above.

Mr. Edward Davies. He is a worthy Good Man, and one of our late excellent friend's ministers and still continues to labour with us. He is to leave London in the course of this week, and is desirous to receive from you before he goes any directions which you may think necessary for him to observe. I sometimes receive a visit from your Friend Mr. Blair by which means I have the pleasure to hear of your welfare which ever affords peculiar satisfaction to her who I hope you will believe to be with sincere regard,
your Faithful and much
obliged friend
A. A. Erskine

Spa = Fields
June 10th 1794

My best wishes wait on Mrs. Lettsom and your family.

17. [L]

Endorsed: From Lady A. Erskine, July 15 1794, London. answered.

To
Doctor Lettsom
Sambrook Court
Basinghall Street

By Favour of The Rev^d Mr. Nicklin[104]

My Much Esteemed Friend,

Will you permit me once more to trouble you for your kind advice to the bearer of this. He is a deserving young man, and one of our Ministers who has of late been considerably indisposed, and as he is about to leave London I am desirous of his receiving some directions from you concerning his health. I know your time is so much occupied that I will not detain you longer than to offer my best wishes to Mrs. Lettsom and your family and to assure you that I am with much regard,
your obliged and faithful friend
A. A. Erskine

Spa = Fields
July the 15:th 1794

---

[104] Nicklin does not appear in ibid.

18. [L]

Endorsed:

From Lady A. Erskine, Mar. 12 1795, London. answered

To
Doctor Lettsom
Sambrook Court
Basinghall Street

By Favour of Mr. Thomas Winter

My Kind and Worthy Friend I hope will excuse me for the intrusion of this letter at the request of its bearer Mr. Thomas Winter, one of our young men at Cheshunt College.[105] He has long been very subject to violent Headaches arising from a Complaint in his stomach, but the immediate cause of his wishing (and indeed of my wishing likewise) for your advice to him, is that last week he brought a considerable Quantity of blood, and has not been well since. He had prescribed for himself a Vomit of Tartar Emitic [*sic*] which very much relieved his head, and he took a second, he informs me, on Wednesday se'enight which seem'd to operate very well, but it was in the course of the same day he brought up the blood which he never did either before or since. Any directions you think needful to give him will be very punctually observed by him, for he is a very worthy Good young man.

I hope Mrs. Lettsom and your family are well. My best wishes ever attend them, and I beg you to believe that I am with much esteem
your much obliged Friend,
A. A. Erskine

Spa = Fields
March 12 1795

You will oblige me by sending me by the bearer a direction to your Friend Mr. Blair if he is still in London.

---

[105] Cheshunt College was established in Hertfordshire in 1792 with space for fourteen students. It took over from Trefecca College in Breconshire (1768–91). In 1905, the College moved to the University of Cambridge. See Edwin Welch (ed.), *Cheshunt College: the early years: a selection of records*, Hertfordshire record publications, vol. 6, Ware, Hertfordshire Record Society, 1990.

19. [L]

Endorsed: From Lady A. Erskine, April 5 1795, Spafields. done

To
Dr. Lettsom
Basinghall St
By Favour of Mr. John James[106]

Spa = Fields
Apr 6 1795

My Worthy and Esteemed Friend,
    The regard I have for the bearer of this, Mr. John James, who is a very excellent young man and one of the students at Lady Huntingdon's College, joined to my apprehensions that he is in a very precarious state of health, leads me to trouble you on his behalf, previous to his making a few weeks trial of his native air which is Pembrokeshire South Wales. He will carefully attend to any directions you are so good as to give him. I cannot make mention of the College without returning you thanks for your kindness to it which I was yesterday informed of.
    I beg my best wishes to Mrs. Lettsom and for your family, and to assure you that I am with much regard.
your obliged Friend
A. A. Erskine

20. [L]

Endorsed: From Lady Erskine, Dec. 8 1795, Spafields. done

To
Doctor Lettsom
Basinghall St.
By Favour of The Revd. Mr. Kirkman

---

[106] John James (1785–1832) was born in Liverpool into a Methodist family. He appears in the various lists, op. cit., note 90 above.

My Kind and Esteemed Friend,

I was sorry to hear you were indisposed, but till a very few days ago I was ignorant how very ill you had been. Give me leave by the bearer of this, The Revd. Mr. Kirkman, to enquire more particularly how you do, and to assure you how truly glad I am to find that the Lord has been pleased to raise you from your bed of sickness, and I hope will in his own good time restore you to your wonted health and strength, and with the additional blessing of a heart truly sensible of his late Mercy to you and yours in preserving you.

Mr. Kirkman, though with every appearance of health, is at not well [*sic*] and has very frequently requested me for a line of introduction to you which my fear of encroaching too much on your kind permission to me, has hitherto prevented me from giving him, but as he is at present considerably indisposed and has recently been much affected by the death of one his Children who suffered very much, I could not deny him, which I hope will plead my excuse with you.

With my best wishes for Mrs. Lettsom and all your family, I beg you to believe that I am with sincere regard your much obliged Friend

A. A. Erskine

Decr 8 1795

[JCL]

Endorsed: From Dr. Haygarth,[107] Sept. 10 1809, Bath. answered.

Bath Sept. 10 1809

My dear Sir,

A new edition of my clinical history of the Acute Rheumatism and Nodosity of the Joints will soon be wanted.[108] Being very desirous to

---

[107] John Haygarth (1740–1827) was physician to the Chester Royal Infirmary between 1767 and 1798 and regarded as an authority on contagious diseases. Amongst other things he published *An inquiry how to prevent the small-pox*, Chester, printed by J. Monk for J. Johnson, London, and P. Broster, Chester, 1784, and *A sketch of a plan to exterminate the casual small-pox from Great Britain*, London, printed for J. Johnson, 1793. See Francis M. Lobo, 'John Haygarth, smallpox and religious dissent in eighteenth-century England', in Andrew Cunningham and Roger French (eds), *The medical Enlightenment of the eighteenth century*, Cambridge and New York, Cambridge University Press, 1990, pp. 217–53.

[108] A new edition was eventually published in 1813. John Haygarth, *I. A clinical history of the acute rheumatism, or rheumatick fever. ... To explain the beneficial effects of the Peruvian bark,*

improve it as far as may be in my power, I have thought that the best method of accomplishing this ~~desirable~~? purpose would be to enquire among the most intelligent of my medical friends, in intensive practice, how far their experience confirmed, corrected, or confuted any of the conclusions which I had deduced from the facts that had fallen under my own observation.

The very general practical cautions of Professors and Authors never to administer Cinchona[109] in inflammatory diseases, will obviously suggest suspicions that it may do mischief in the Rheumatick Fever; so that it may be difficult to obtain, from even experience, impartial observations to determine this question. If you, or any of your acquaintance, have ventured to employ this remedy in such cases, may I request the favour of your information what are the circumstances in which it has been observed to do good or harm. I solicit your remarks as a private favour, so that you may communicate them without reserve. I shall never take the liberty to quote your authority without special permission.

Have you known Soda, Arsenic or any other remedy given with beneficial effects in Nodosity of the joints?

I have no wish to establish any particular doctrine or practice, but fairly to investigate the truth. For so important a purpose I hope that my medical Friends will excuse the liberty I take in soliciting their assistance, which will confer a great obligation on your very respectful and truly faithful friend,
John Haygarth

---

cinchona… II. A clinical history of the new nodosity of the joints, A new edition, with corrections, London, Richard Cruttwell [etc.], 1813.

[109] Europeans in South America discovered cinchona bark in the early seventeenth century. Peruvian bark, as it was also known, was agreed to be more effective than any remedies plied by European physicians for malarial fevers or agues. It began to be exported to Europe in the year 1631–2. The bark was strongly promoted by the Jesuit order, particularly Juan de Lugo and hence cinchona is also known as Jesuit's bark or powder. First advertised for sale in England in 1658, it was usually administered as a hot, bitter-tasting drink. It was determined in the nineteenth century to contain the alkaloid quinine.

[JCL]

Endorsed: From Dr. Hosack,[110] Nov. 22 [*sic*][111] 1809, New York. answered.

New York Nov[r]. 27th 1809

Dear Sir,

I received your letter by Dr. Mott[112] and thank you for the membership[113] which it announces. I shall occasionally send you some practical remarks derived from the bedside. My work on yellow fever[114] to which I devote every leisure hour, will yet for some time occupy my enclusive attention. I find it growing to a size I did not at first dream of—the mere History of the disease will alone occupy a volume—when that is out of hand I shall have more liberty to range in other departments. I have not yet received the books you have sent me by Dr. Mott. I shall get them in a few days. I inclose you a case I consider

---

[110] David Hosack (1769–1835) was an eminent New York physician. He was appointed to the chair of botany at Columbia in 1795 and later became professor of materia medica there. He established the Elgin Botanic Garden in New York City, publishing *Hortus Elginensis: or a catalogue of plants, indigenous and exotic, cultivated in the Elgin Botanic Garden*, New York, printed by T. and J. Swords, 1811, 2nd edn. enlarged. The first edition is extremely rare and we have found no publishing information for it. It probably appeared in 1806. Like most eminent botanists, he published his own nosology: *A system of practical nosology*, New York, C. S. Van Winkle, 1818. He also published a great deal on medicine, surgery and contagious diseases. He was one of the founders of Bellevue Hospital, a supporter of vaccination, and an early advocate of use of the stethoscope. See Christine Chapman Robbins, *David Hosack: citizen of New York*, Memoirs of the American Philosophical Society, 62, Philadelphia, American Philosophical Society, 1964.

[111] The endorsement reads 22, but is clearly a mistake for 27, which Hosack has written at the top of his letter.

[112] Valentine Mott (1785–1865) was the most renowned New York surgeon of his day. Born in New York of a Quaker family (of English extraction), he was a Quaker for more than half his lifetime. After graduating in medicine from Columbia in 1806, he went to England where he studied under Astley Cooper in London. In 1809, he started out in practice in New York. In the following year, he taught a private class in surgery and in 1811 he was appointed to the chair of surgery in the medical school at Columbia College. As well as publishing on surgery, he also published an account of his journeys in Europe and the Middle East: *Travels in Europe and the East*, New York, Harper and Brothers, 1842. Samuel David Gross, *Memoir of Valentine Mott, M.D.*, New York, D. Appleton and Co.; Philadelphia, Lindsay and Blakiston, 1868.

[113] There is no record of David Hosack's recommendation or admittance as a corresponding member of the Medical Society of London between Monday 30 January and Monday 18 December 1809. See Council Minutes, op. cit., note 39 above.

[114] Hosack contributed over twenty pages of additional observations relating to the outbreak of yellow fever in New York, in 1799, to William Currie, *A sketch of the rise and progress of the yellow fever…to which is added, a collection of facts and observations respecting the origin of the yellow fever in this country; and a review of the different modes of treating it by Dr. D. Hosack*, Philadelphia, printed by Budd and Bartram, 1800, pp. 89–112. In the year after he wrote this letter, Hosack published a work on yellow fever and expressed his hope to Lettsom that "the facts I have assembled will counteract the mischievous doctrines propagated by our friends Rush, and the editors of the *Medical Repository*, of the non-contagiousness of the disease, and its generation in the United States". See Abraham, op. cit., note 29 above, p. 375. We have found no extant copy of this work on yellow fever.

interesting—if you think so, address it as communicated to you and give it a place in your memoirs. I write by Mr. Brownell[115] whom I beg leave to introduce to you—he is appointed to teach chemistry in the College of Schenectedy in this state—but before he enters upon his duties he is desirous of the advantages which London affords thos who are in pursuit of that science. He is very particularly introduced to me by Col. Barclay the British Consul who speaks of Mr. Brownell in the highest terms. Be so good as to make him known to your liter[116] in chemistry—your patronage will be bestowed upon one very worthy of it. Mr. Duer has arrived and is very grateful to you, as also is
your friend and humble servant
David Hosack

Dr. J. C. Lettsom

[JCL]

Doctor Lettsom
Sambrook Court
Basinghall Street

My Dear Doctor
I shall certainly do myself the pleasure of dining with you on Friday. To pass an hour with and [*recte* an] old scientific friend, after a long absence, is one of the greatest pleasures I can enjoy.
Yours truly,
James Jay

Wednesday morning 18 September

[JCL]

Endorsed: From Dr. Kirkland,[117] Febr. 25 1788, Ashby. Answered Med Soc. Rec'd Mar. 14. Private Business to Dr. Lettsom

To Dr. Lettsom Physician

Ashby Feb: 25 1788

---

[115] Thomas Brownell was appointed to teach chemistry at the College of Schenectady in 1809. He also taught a course in mineralogy. Brownell was sent to Europe by the College to buy specimens, teaching apparatus and instructional aids.
[116] This word is at the edge of the letter and has probably been cut off.
[117] Thomas Kirkland (*c*.1722–98) of Ashby-de-la-Zouche in Leicestershire. Kirkland lived near coal mines and took a particular interest in skeletal injuries. He was a friend of

Dear Sir,

I am truly sorry my avocations have prevented an earlier opportunity of returning my sincere thanks to the Medical Society of London, for the honor I receive in being elected a member of their body; but I now beg, Sir, that you will please to make my most grateful acknowledgements to them, and assure them I entertain the highest sense of this mark of distinction. I have received their Diploma, and the first volume of their memoirs with great pleasure and regard, and I trust I shall use my endeavours to assist this well intended and well directed scheme of promoting medical knowledge.

Indeed I have now by me, almost finished, a commentary on Apoplectic and Paralytic affections, at first intended for your second volume, but I foresee it will amount to fifty pages or more, which I apprehend will be too long for the nature of your work.[118] Its object is to prove from facts, that opium and other sedatives are the general cure for recent palsies that will admit of relief: nor is this a hasty opinion just taken up, but traced from one instance to another for the space of fifteen or sixteen years. If the society will do me the honor of reading it, I will send it, and if it suits their intentions it will be very much at their service. I cannot say when it will be ready to be sent to London, though little more than a fair copy remains to be done, and I shall employ the first leisure time in finishing this business.

I am much obliged to you for the seeds of the Beta Hybrida[119] and I hope my connections will enable me to give you a good account of the services, which in this part of the kingdom is to be expected from its use. Sincerely wishing Heaven may assist your endeavours for the benefit of mankind, I am with great esteem

Dear Sir,
Your most humble servant,
Thomas Kirkland

I beg the society to accept my two volumes on medical chirurgery and my essay on child bed fevers, which I shall desire my publisher, Mr. Dawson, to

---

Dr. Robert Chessher of Hinkley in Leicestershire, who is generally regarded to be the first specialist orthopaedist in England. Kirkland and Chessher first met in around 1780. Roger T. Austin, *Robert Chessher of Hinckley, 1750–1831: first English orthopaedist*, Leicester, Leicestershire County Council, Libraries and Information Service, 1981, p. 14.

[118] Thomas Kirkland, *A commentary on apoplectic and paralytic affections. And on diseases connected with the subject*, London, W. Dawson, 1792.

[119] Too unspecific to be identified.

deliver as soon as he can get them bound.[120] The latter, I have discovered by accident, has undergone a second impression without my knowledge and has not in it those observations my subsequent experience has enabled me to make.[121] But this I hope to remedy.

Adieu

[JCL]

Fife House June 20th 1811

Lord Liverpool[122] presents his Compliments to Dr. Lettsom, and will be obliged to him to give the necessary Order for the Admission of Robert Bryon into the Sea Bathing Infirmary in the usual manner, as Lord L—has every reason to believe, from the enclosed note, that the child abovementioned is in every respect a fit object.

1. [JCL]

Endorsed: (60) From Dr. Livingston,[123] June 29 1789, Aberdeen. answered (28)

Dr. Lettsom
London

Aberdeen June 29th 1789

Sir,
    I had the Pleasure of receiving your very Polite and friendly Letter—and Esteem myself very much honoured by your kind Attention. Not thinking of

---

[120] Thomas Kirkland, *An inquiry into the present state of medical surgery*, 2 vols., London, J. Dodsley and William Dawson, 1783; *idem, A treatise on child-bed fevers, and on the methods of preventing them*, London, printed for R. Baldwin and W. Dawson, 1774.
    [121] There appear to be no copies of a second impression in any British or American medical libraries. All extant copies date from 1774.
    [122] Robert Banks Jenkinson, second Earl of Liverpool (1770–1828), was, at this stage in his career, the Secretary for War and the Colonies. He entered the House of Commons as a Tory M.P. in 1790. He served successively as a member of the Board of Control for India (1793–6), Master of the Royal Mint (1799–1801), Foreign Secretary (1801–4), Home Secretary (1804–6, 1807–9), Secretary for War and the Colonies (1809–12) and finally, as Prime Minister (1812–27).
    [123] William Livingstone (1760–1822), M.D., professor of medicine at Marischal College, Aberdeen. Livingstone was an unpopular choice of professor, foisted upon the college by David Murray, second Earl of Mansfield, who was elected Chancellor in 1793 and was an Englishman who served Pitt and Dundas. Livingstone was the nominee of the town council. Dr. George Skene was the choice of his fellow university colleagues. Skene complained that Livingstone was "besides absenting himself whenever he chuses to go Wrong in the Head, has never done any one Part of the little Duty formerly annexed to the Office". See Roger L. Emerson, *Professors,*

75

making a Report of the Chimney Sweeper's Case, I omitted to take down his name. I have, however, enclosed the particulars of his situation. You are pleased to mention if there be a Misnomer in the Diploma, that the name might be erased, and mine substituted. If I thought that it lay in Mr. Dilly's,[124] I would ask my friend Mr. Jopp, Partner in the Woolen Draper's business, No. 14 Fenchurch Street, with Mr. Irvine, to call for it.[125] He could transmit it, along with the Packet you was so good as mention. The Hay Crop, and Grain, has a very promising Appearance here, but in this Country we can neither boast of the Quantity, nor Quality, of our fruit, and such as there is, has been very much blasted by Cold Easterly Winds. There never was an Ague known to be generated in Aberdeen till the year 1775, when some new streets were built in a low swamp near the Quay.[126] The season when the Undertaking was first begun was uncommonly rainy and there were several of the Masons and Bricklayers, who had been Exposed to it as well as from the Nature of the Situation who came into the Infirmary with regular Tertians. By the Common treatment they recovered—and I believe since that Period there has not been an Instance known. The Inhabitants of that Part of the Town, as the Marsh was pretty well drained, I believe have not been more unhealthy than in any other district. There has been for some months past an Epidemic Dysenteria among the Inhabitants of a Fishing Town in this neighbourhood. It has proved fatal to numbers of them. As such a Disease could not be admitted into our Hospital, a temporary one has been fitted up for those that are worst,and the faculty here have given their Attendance by Rotation. In the first stage of the Complaint there are evident Indications for bleeding, and the Inflammatory Crust always covers the Coagulum. Repeated Purgatives of neutral salts next have been administred; and when the bowels seemed to be in an atonic state, starch Clysters combined with Tinct. Thebiac, a certain allowance of wine, and small doses of Tinct. e Kino,[127] I think, has been the Plan of Cure that has most Contributed to Recovery.

---

patronage and politics: the Aberdeen Universities in the eighteenth century, Aberdeen University Press, 1992, pp. 92, 128 n.59.

[124] Charles Dilly, bookseller in the Poultry in London. See 'Letters from Lettsom' section, note 21.

[125] Irvine and Jopp, Woollen drapers, 14 Fenchurch Street. See Henry Kent, *Kent's Directory. For the year 1794*, London, R. and H. Causton, 1794.

[126] A square bracket marks the beginning of this sentence and is closed towards the end of the letter after "Contributed to Recovery". Having dispensed with personal matters at the beginning of the letter, it probably denotes the main section that was read to the Medical Society.

[127] Tincture of opium, commonly known as liquid laudanum. Tincture of kino, mainly tannin, was often prescribed as an astringent.

Your Indulgence in Correspondence, will prompt me from time to time, to give you the trouble of perusing any Case that occurs here, which I think deviates from common occurrence. With much Respect, I am, Sir
Your Most Obliged and Faithful Humble Servant
William Livingston

2. [JCL]

Endorsed: From Dr. Livingston, Aug. 24 1790, Aberdeen. answered

Aberdeen August 24 1790

Dear Sir,
I had the Honour of receiving your most friendly letter of the 11th Current. The Medal,[128] (by which I think myself highly Honoured, and for which I would presume to ask you to present to the Humane Society my best thanks, for so Estimable a Premium) came safe to Hand. The Rational, and easy directions to prevent Canine Madness, cannot be too well known, and I shall have it published in our next County-Newspaper. There were two Instances some years ago, where a fair tryal of the Ormskirk Medicine[129] was made in our Hospital, but they fatally and too terribly misgave. You are so kind as to Express a wish that I should offer some remarks on the Angina Maligna,[130]

---

[128] The Humane Society's Fothergillian medal. See Introduction to this volume, p. 3.

[129] Advertisements for Hill's Genuine Ormskirk Medicine said that it "infallably cures the bite of a mad dog". In the 1770s, it was prepared by William Hill, Esq. and his nephews, Messrs William Hill and James Berry. But it had been made two generations earlier by Hill's grand-father, William Hill. An advertisement in the first edition of the *Shrewsbury Chronicle* in 1772 stated that it was sold at James Berry's apothecary's shop, Mountstreet, Berkeley Square, at 5s 3d a dose and nowhere else in London. Agents elsewhere in England were: M. Swinney in Birmingham, Mr. Plant in Litchfield and Tamworth, M. Jopson in Coventry, Mr. Clay in Warwick, Mrs. Thurstans in Wolverhampton, Mr. Smith in Newcastle-under-lime, Mr. Eddowes in Salop and T. Wood, printer and bookseller, opposite the Shambles on Pride-Hill, Shrewsbury. Prophylatic use of the medicine was suggested. But William Buchan said of it: "The Ormskirk medicine, as it is called, seems to me to consist chiefly of cinnibar. Though it is said to be infal-lible, as a preventive; yet I would not advise anyone to trust to it alone. Indeed it is ordered to be taken in a manner which gives it more the appearance of a charm than of a medicine. Surely if a medicine is to produce any change in the body, it must be taken for some considerable time, and in sufficient quantity". William Buchan, *Domestic medicine*, London, A. Strahan; T. Cadell in the Strand; and J. Balfour, and W. Creech, at Edinburgh, 11th edn., 1790, p. 485n.

[130] Angina maligna was a disease of the throat, nowadays usually identified as diphtheria. It was a favourite topic for discussion in medical theses. The disease had a fatality rate of about 70 per cent in children between the ages of three and five and was particularly prevalent in the 1790s. For a contemporary view, see John Clark, *Observations on fevers ... Together with a comparative view of that epidemic with the scarlet fever as described by authors, and the angina maligna*, London, The author and T. Cadell, 1792.

77

as it has prevailed here of late. I intend soon to avail myself of so kind a Proposal, and shall likewise trouble you with a detail of a Case, where there was more Injury, and more derangement of the Inner part of the skull, and of the Substance of the brain, than I ever remember to have heard or read of, when at the same time, the Animal functions should have at all Existed. The Bearer, Mr. McIntosh, is a young man who served his Apprenticeship to me, Recommended to me in the Strongest Manner, by every individual of the University here, for his Assiduity and Attention during the four years he was a Student and for particular Marks of Ingenuity he shewed in most Branches of Science that are taught here. To such Opportunities of Medical Improvement as we have here he gave Uncommon Attention. His situation in life is such that he cannot Afford the more finished parts of Medical Education; But as his Character was known to the Most Respectable of the Faculty here, they have given him Testimonials of their good Opinion of him. He goes to London without any fixed Plan in view, but if he was to become an Object of your well-known Benevolence in protecting Merit, and Ushering it into the world, I can Answer that he would not discredit such Goodness; nor fail in feeling the Warmest sense of Gratitude.

Allow me to have the Honour of Remaining with much Respect,
Dear Sir,
Your Mucht Obliged and Obedient Humble Servant,
William Livingston

Dr. Lettsome

[JCL]

Endorsed: From Dr. Morse,[131] Oct. 8 1812, Charlestown. answered Aug. 18 1813

Charleston Oct 8th 1812

My Worthy and Respected Friend,
    In the precarious state of intercourse between our countries, I improve [*recte* approve] with much satisfaction an opportunity which offers to send

---

[131] Jedidiah Morse (1761–1826) was a congregational minister in Charleston, Massachusetts, between 1789 and 1819. He helped found the New England Tract Society and was secretary of the Society Propagating the Gospel among Indians. He published geographical works and is sometimes described as "the father of American Geography".

direct to London, which however is so sudden as to allow me time only hastily to acknowledge my great obligation to you for your kind attentions and civilities to my dear son, who is in your city.[132] He informs us, with much grateful sensibility, of your goodness to him. Also for ~~the~~ your excellent and useful Report of the transactions of your Humane Society.

You will accept my thanks, also, for your kind partiality in proposing my name to the respectable Society at Preston, as an honorary member. This mark of your and their respect, I receive with grateful emotions, and as soon as the intercourse between our respective countries shall be again be opened, (which I hope will be soon) I shall transmit some of our most valuable literary productions for the use of that Society. In the mean time, will you do me the favor to present to its officers my respectful regards, and acceptance of the honor conferred by their appointment & my intention by the earliest conveyance to make them a more suitable acknowledgement.

I have only time to ask your acceptance of the enclosed discourse, which was composed in great haste, and is valuable only as it discloses my own views of the present war between our countries. Our prospects of a change of administration, who will be favorable to an equitable peace, continually brighten.[133] May the good Lord accomplish an event so desirable in his due time.
With great respect and affection
I am sincerely
your friend
J. Morse

1. [JCL][134]

(169)

Oct. 8 1807
~~Isle of Wight. House Industry.~~

(a draft)

---

[132] Samuel Morse (1791–1872) later devised the Morse code. He sailed to England in 1811 to study painting.

[133] America wanted to gain control of the Canadian territory that backed onto the Great Lakes and declared war on Britain and sent militia units into Canada on 18 June 1812.

[134] This letter from "When I was at the…" is reproduced in Pettigrew, op. cit., note 87 above, vol. 2, pp. 208–9.

Dr. Lettsom 12

~~My dear Friend,~~
~~I like this motto much better than the other, and should have been pleas'd if~~
~~Mr. Urban~~[135] ~~had given us Shrewsbury in the September magazine.~~[136] ~~My~~
~~present publication on Debtors has got as far as that prison,~~[137] ~~and till he has~~
~~printed off my Account I cannot extract from it what is necessary to appear~~
~~in that work~~.

When I was at the Isle of Wight last month ~~I think~~, by the printed account given me,[138] it appeared there were 4 farmers who had in the year 1805 paid the Penalty of Ten Pounds each rather than take an apprentice out of the House of Industry.[139] The great end therefore propos'd by the benevolent Mr. Howard is not answered and confirms me in Opinion that the food and lodging of these Children is so much better than any state of servitude will allow, that they become lazy and restless, and that if each parish maintained its own poor, and if relief where necessary was administered at <u>home</u>, less money would be expended and a hardy race of lads introduc'd, to whom labour and coarse diet would be familiar, leaving (with a sound Policy and true Humanity) Families to themselves, to make the most of their respective Exertions, to enjoy the entire Fruits of their own Industry, and to bring up their Children in their own hardy and laborious way. In this there would be no violence to the strongest attachments of our nature, and I believe it was the practice of the statesmen in Queen Elizabeth's reign to hold out every inducement to Families, ~~to be~~ <u>by affording them the means with proper</u>

---

[135] Sylvanus Urban was the fictitious editor of the *Gentleman's Magazine*. The pseudonym was chosen by Edward Cave (1691–1754), who founded the periodical in 1731. See Arthur Sherbo, *Letters to Mr. Urban of the Gentleman's Magazine, 1751–1811*, Lewiston, NY, Edwin Mellen Press, 1997.

[136] James Neild's account of Shrewsbury Gaol was not published until October. 'Mr. Neild's Remarks on Shrewsbury Gaol', *Gentleman's Magazine*, 1807, **77** (ii): 916–18. For Neild, see 'Letters from Lettsom' section, note 52.

[137] This is presumably Neild's *State of the prisons in England, Scotland, and Wales*, London, printed by John Nichols and Son, 1812, which was not published for another five years.

[138] This refers to either the House of Industry's (poor house) annual report or, perhaps, a contemporary account of it. The poor house was considered one of the most modern. See, for example, Henry Wansey, 'Thoughts on poor-houses, with a view to their general reform: particularly that of Salisbury, comparing it with the more improved ones of Shrewsbury, Isle of Wight, Hull, Boldre, etc. and deductions drawn, useful to other poor-houses', London, printed for T. Cadell, Jun. and W. Davies, 1801. See also, Johanna Jones, *The early years of the Isle of Wight House of Industry*, Shalfleet, Pinhorn, 1967.

[139] Building was begun on the House of Industry in Newport, Isle of Wight, around 1797. It opened for business in 1803, functioning as a workhouse, hospital, lunatic asylum and school for the poor of the island and was, reportedly, generally well liked by the inhabitants, apart from the stigma of being "assisted".

industry of feeding and clothing themselves. But I am getting into a wide field and into business I am not competent to—'tis easier to find fault than to suggest a remedy. I wish you would lend me Colquhoun on Mendicity[140] when you can spare it for a month any day you pass the property office Adieu, yours truly
James Neild

Chelsea 8th Oc[r]. 1807

2. [L]

Endorsed: From James Neild, Jan. 29 1809, Chelsea.[141]

Doctor Lettsom
Basinghall Street

with a parcel
Car-paid

Sunday 29 Jany 1809

My dear Friend,
    I sent the Letter you so obligingly enclosed—to my son[142]—but have neither seen or heard from him on the subject since—so how he relishes—or what his final determinations are, I know not.
    I have just receiv'd some potted Moor Game, and being of Opinion that it nearest approximates the Quintessence of Epicurism, send for Home consumption—or other disposal—as to you it seemeth good. I am excusing myself from our Committee next Wednesday,[143] but I had a disagreeable pull back about five days ago which confined me to my bedroom two days. At the

---

[140] Patrick Colquhoun, *A treatise on indigence*, London, printed for J. Hatchard, 1806.

[141] In the late eighteenth century, Chelsea was popular with those seeking a piece of the countryside in the town. However, it had grown and become more populous since the 1770s because of the Cadogan estate, land acquired by the Earl of Cadogan through his marriage, in 1771, to Elizabeth Sloane, daughter of the court physician and collector Sir Hans Sloane.

[142] Lettsom obtained a legal position in Barbados for James Neild's eldest son, William, in 1809. His letter to William was probably to do with his preparations on his behalf. William was in the West Indies by May 1809. See 'Letters from Lettsom' section, note 147.

[143] The Committee of the Society for the Discharge and Relief of Persons Imprisoned for Small Debts.

time I was seiz'd I was writing a Letter, and though I had not 20 Words to add was unable to finish it. However, am now as well as usual.
Believe me my dear friend,
your oblig'd and grateful
James Neild

3. [L]

Endorsed: From James Neild Esq., Febr. 9 1809, Chelsea

Doctor Lettsom
Sambrook Court
Basinghall Street

My dear friend,
     On Tuesday my son and I dined with Mr. Colquhoun who has written to Judge Robertson[144] and been most extremely friendly. I thank you kindly, my dear Sir, for your Introductory Letters and consider you on my Sheet Anchor. I am very busy on William's Account in financial matters, for I find varieties of Channels to exhaust my present and anticipate my next coming resources.
     Have you got an Inventory of your late dear son's Law Libr? For want of that I have been obliged [to or]der some books which I understood [w]ere absolutely necessary—for fear he might not meet with them there—I will eat a Chop or anything with you at 5 on Saturday.
Adieu yours ever gratefully
James Neild

Thursday
9 Feby 1809

4. [L]

Endorsed: From James Neild Esq., Mar. 13 1809, Chelsea. answered.

Doctor Lettsom

My dear Friend,
     You would have heard from me sooner but I have been in Buckinghamshire and whilst there had better health than usual, but I brought

---

[144] Possibly a judge in the West Indies who was being asked to act in William's interest.

home ~~with~~ a Cold so violent as to oblige me to send for my Apothecary and I have been little out of bed since.

The two Impressions intended for the King and Lord Romney[145] are thrown off upon too small paper.[146] I must beg you to let Mr. Graswell[147] have two sufficiently large for Royal Octavo,[148] and that as soon as you can. If you write to Mr. G—No. 7 Craven Street,[149] he may as well call at your house for them, for he gets them bound at the King's Binders.

Let me caution you, if you value your Plate, to let the Person who engraved it get the impression thrown off and desire he will superintend the Press during the operation.[150] I have bought the Experience, my Plate was absolutely spoil'd before one half the Impressions it ought to have yielded, were thrown off,[151] and yours is too nearly done to risque it. I did not know how it came about till I afterwards saw the Engraver and he told me the

---

[145] Charles Marsham, third Baron Romney of Romney (1744–1811) was elected M.P. for Maidstone (1768–74) and for Kent (1774–90). The family seat was at Mote Park in Maidstone. Lord Romney served as vice-president of the Society for the Encouragement of Arts, Manufactures and Commerce and of the Marine Society. He was doctor of laws and was made a fellow of the Royal Society in 1776. Lord Romney also had connections with the West Indies.

[146] The Wellcome Library is in possession of a made-up copy, in four volumes, of all seventy-seven of the prison letters written by James Neild and John Coakley Lettsom over a ten year period. Reference: Wellcome Library, EPB Hunt. /Let, vols 1-4. The letters were assembled by Lettsom with the apparent intention of publishing them as a separate work. These four volumes were intended to serve as a printer's copy. They include a prefatory letter from Lettsom to the editor, followed by a letter from Neild to Lettsom, an autograph letter from Neild and a manuscript index. It seems likely that Neild is here referring to two small impressions of this or a similar work that were printed for the king and Lord Romney and other "persons of the first position" as presentation copies, especially since he mentions an engraving of Newgate. Neild and Lettsom certainly did not jointly publish any other work in that year. All four volumes were sold at the auction of Lettsom's library by Leigh and Sotheby in 1816 (item 343 in the sale), for which see *A catalogue of the greater portion of the library of John Coakley Lettsom M.D.F.R.S. Removed from his Residence at Camberwell*, London, s.n. 1811. The Wellcome Library's copy of Leigh and Sotheby's catalogue, Reference: EPB Suppl. B/Let, has marginalia noting prices against some of these books, presumably the prices at which they sold.

[147] Mr Grasswell was secretary to the Society for the Discharge and Relief of Persons Imprisoned for Small Debts. *Leigh's new picture of London*, London, printed for Samuel Leigh, 1819.

[148] Royal Octavo was an imperial book size, measuring $10 \times 6\frac{1}{4}$ inches.

[149] The meetings of the Committee of the Society for the Discharge and Relief of Persons Imprisoned for Small Debts were held in Craven Street. It therefore seems likely that they were held in Mr Grasswell's home.

[150] Lettsom's own copy of the prison letters contains an engraved portrait of Lettsom, by Ridley after Medley, in 1800. See the four-volume collection of Neild's and Lettsom's letters on prisons held in Wellcome Library (note 146 above), vol. 4, opposite p. 1.

[151] Lettsom's own copy also has an engraved frontispiece portrait of Neild, engraved by Maddocks after de Wilde, published in 1806. Ibid., vol. 1, 1–22, frontispiece.

Copper plate printer, or very likely his <u>Boy</u>—had ruined it. Mr. Nichols[152] got those of Newgate done, and most sadly they are done, as well as the Paper being too thick, which causes the Book to open, and I know some Gentlemen have cut it out on that Account.

I have just had the Plate touch'd up and several new parts added for the 50 Royal Octavos, and I intend to have 50 Impressions thrown off at my own expense for them. Yours is a beautiful Engraving. Suppose you send me twenty Impressions for I do not see why any should be given of yours except to Persons of the first position.

Yours truly,

J. Neild

The most beautiful Engraving lies at the [---- o]f[153] of a stupid copper plate printer or an ignorant boy. The Engraver for his own Credit will see Justice done to his Work and he will take care to preserve a <u>Proof</u> of what it <u>was</u> when he delivered it.

5. [E]

Endorsed: From James Neild Esq., Mar. ~~Feby~~ 29 1809, Hanawell bookbinder

Dr. Lettsom
Sambrook Court
Basinghall street

Tuesday 28 March

My Dear Friend,

The bearer comes from the Philanthropic Society to receive what heads you wish to have put in, they have 62 Royal Octavo and 291 Demi Octavo[154]—so that if you propose to send 50 impressions [I w]ill[155] have the whole in the Royal Octavo.

---

[152] John Nichols, owner and editor of the *Gentleman's Magazine*. See 'Letters from Lettsom' section, p. 131.

[153] The top of the page has been cut, presumably when the letter was opened.

[154] Demi octavo or demy octavo was an imperial book size measuring $8\frac{3}{4} \times 5\frac{5}{8}$ inches.

[155] The manuscript is stained here, from application of the seal, and the words obscured.

If you intend to have more heads put in, be so good to write a note to Mr. Hanawell[156] when you have got them from the engravers and he will send for them
yours truly
J. Neild

Mr. Hanawel Book binder to the Philanthropic Society
St. George's Fields

6. [E]

Endorsed: From James Neild Esq., May 19 1809, Chelsea

Dr. Lettsom

My dear friend
I thank you kindly for the perusal of your Relation's Letter, it has however increased my uneasiness on my son's Account—for it appears Mr. Lettsom ~~In~~ has receiv'd you letter which I suppose must have been sent per packet when my son sailed ~~which~~ and is a demonstrative proof that I might have heard from him by the same conveyance but hitherto I have not heard one syllable either from or about him since he saild from Portsmouth.
yours truly
James Neild

Fryday Evening
19 May

7. [E]

Endorsed: from James Neild Esq., June 22 1809, Chelsea

Doctor Lettsom

My dear Friend,
I received a letter from my son dated Barbadoes. It just informs that he has had a pleasant Voyage, is in good health, and had drawn upon me for 65£. On

---

[156] Mr. Hanawell was bookbinder to the Philanthropic Society, a reformatory establishment founded in 1788 for the criminal poor to encourage industry and morality. It was established by Robert Young Esq. (who had the original idea), John Coakley Lettsom, the Hon. Robert Pusey, James Sims and the Duke of Leeds. Its sister Philanthropic Society in Mile End was instituted in 1803 for the discharge of persons confined for small debts. *Leigh's new picture of London*, printed for Samuel Leigh, 1819.

the 20th Instant I received another from him dated Tortola 13th May, in which he says Doctor West who left the Island yesterday (the 12th) will call upon me and inform me fully about him and that he has drawn upon me for 100£— what he is about I cannot conjecture for he makes no mention of having seen anyone to whom he had Letters of Introduction. He then concludes by saying he is very well but sadly bit by the musquitos—so it does not appear he would [have] thought about writing to me at all, if he had not recollected it was necessary I should be advised of his Draft. Perhaps you may have seen Doctor West and heard something about him.

William[157] took from hence half a dozen Books, and I shou'd have imagined must have sent one to Judge Robinson and another to Mrs. J Lettsom.[158]

When you send to Tortola I wish you would ~~sent~~ enclose the small paper parcel I send with this.

Every Book which has been enriched with the Head of my much valued friend is bound equally elegant and shall be choicely disposed of—but for fear you may be teazed I send you two Common Ones to send out occasionally, for when the Edition is gone it will never be reprinted. Those with your head have the New Impressions on very fine paper, of Newgate with additions as Engraving of it.

We are so near our Prison conclusion I would not have them appear oftener than every other month—Liverpool in the June mag.[159]—Maidstone August[160]—Oxford October,[161] and Portsmouth, Gosport, Southampton in December[162]—they will of course be published July, September, November, and January supplement.

---

[157] James Neild's eldest son.

[158] John Miers Lettsom's widow, Rachel Nanson, in the West Indies. It is tempting to read Robinson as Robertson and identify him as the same judge as in Neild [3] but it is almost certainly Robinson and a different person.

[159] 'Dr. Lettsom's fifty-ninth letter on prisons' appeared with 'Mr. Neild's Remarks on Liverpool Gaols', *Gentleman's Magazine*, 1809, **79** (i): 508–11.

[160] 'Dr. Lettsom's sixtieth letter on prisons' appeared with 'Mr. Neild's Remarks on Maidstone Gaol', *Gentleman's Magazine*, 1809, **79** (ii): 813–16.

[161] 'Dr. Lettsom's sixty-first letter on prisons' appeared with 'Mr. Neild's Remarks on Oxford Castle Gaol', *Gentleman's Magazine*, 1809, **79** (ii): 1017–19.

[162] Note that remarks on Portsmouth, Gosport and Southampton prisons did not appear in the December magazine, but rather a second account of another prison in Oxford: 'Dr. Lettsom's sixty-second letter on prisons' appeared with 'Mr. Neild's Remarks on Oxford City Gaol', *Gentleman's Magazine*, 1809, **79** (ii): 1099–101. In fact, Lettsom and Neild's remarks on these three prisons did not appear until October 1810: 'Dr. Lettsom's sixty-seventh letter on prisons', appeared with 'Mr. Neild's Remarks on Portsmouth and Gosport Gaols and on Southampton Gaol and Bridewell', *Gentleman's Magazine*, 1810, **80** (ii): 325–7.

I am, Dear Sir, yours truly,
James Neild

June 22^d

8. [E]

Endorsed: From James Neild Esq., July 9 1809, Chelsea

Doctor Lettsom

My dear Friend,
I set off tomorrow morning at five to Canterbury and as I must sleep at the Inn took my chance of meeting you in Basinghall Street to enjoy the pleasure of your Conversation for an hour. The Quarter Sessions begin on Tuesday and when they are over I shall visit the Gaols in Kent so that I probably shall not return before the Beginning of next Week. It will give you pleasure to hear that the last Edition of my Work has been beyond all calculation productive. I have not seen or heard of Doctor West so all that I know of my son is, that he arrived at Tortola in good health and what my neighbour the Revd. Mr. Butler informed me from a letter he had received from viz. that he had been engaged in one Cause for the Defendant and got a verdict.[163]
It shews the folly of a sending a letter by a <u>private</u> <u>hand</u> upon any interesting subject—for here you see a Father knows nothing about his son but what he hears from other people. If you should have a letter from Tortola which says anything about him, pray let me hear from you. Mr. Urban makes sad mistakes in numbering our Prison Letters. Leicester is 48 instead of 28.[164]
adieu and believe me yours truly
James Neild

Sunday Evening 8 Ju[ly] 1809

---

[163] This must refer to William Neild's activities in a legal capacity in the West Indies.
[164] John Nichols, editor of the *Gentleman's Magazine* (see note 135 above). It may, of course, have been a type-setting error, but it should have been picked up by Nichols' copy-editor.

9. [E]

Endorsed: Fr Js Neild Esq., July 21 1809, Chelsea

Dr. Lettsom

My Dear Friend,
I returned yesterday from visiting the Gaols in Kent, at Maidstone. I spent the Evening with Mr. Charles Coleman, surgeon,[165] and found he had received the Humane Society's Silver Medal for restoring to Life a Boy who had been under Water a longer time than I should have thought it possible for a spark to be retained.

He has never read any of the Society's reports, and this is not the only Case he has been successful in. I told him I would apply to you for One for him and send it in a parcel I should send to Maidstone.

I wish you to leave what is proper, directed for me at the Property Office. At the same time I recommend him to be appointed Medical Assistant at Maidstone. He is young and <u>very Active</u>, and that honour would I think be a stimulus. The Humane Society received the Knowledge of this very extraordinary recovery from a loose statement of it which appeared in the Kentish Papers.

I am very sorry to have neither seen Dr. West or receiv'd the letter which my son says he has sent by him fully explaining his situation late.

I found two letters from him on my return but they contain nothing of that Information a Parent expects to receive. He had many Letters of Introduction and recommendation, but except one from my friend Mr. Blackman to a Gent. at Barbadoes, no mention is made. He says Mrs. Lettsom's affairs are put into other hands and he has wrote for more Books, so I suppose he has not had any of the late Mr. P. Lettsom's,[166] and that is all that he says. I find he has recovered from two Fevers, but is terribly bit by the mosquitoes, otherwise he is in good health.

I am much concerned about him and fear he is in a Land of Strangers and uncomfortably of[f]—his natural Vivacity and temperate habits will do much for him, but I shall write and earnestly request his return—rather than suffer under those privations which Natural Humanity and Hospitality in most country's afford the unprotected stranger.

It is very wrong for any Person entrusted with a Letter from a Child to his Parent to protract the delivery—all that I learn about my son is from letters

---

[165] Charles Coleman was appointed surgeon to Maidstone Gaol in 1800. http://freepages.genealogy.rootsweb.com/~mrawson/sessions.html, 'West Kent Quarter Sessions Index', an electronic index of order papers for the Quarter Sessions for West Kent between 1788–1804, which were held at Maidstone each quarter.
[166] Pickering Lettsom, youngest son of John Coakley Lettsom, who had died on the island of Tortola in the previous year.

to his friends here—imagining that I have seen the Doctor. His letters convey nothing which is so essential to make me form any Conclusions, but leave me in a state of anxiety and suspense. If you should have receiv'd any letters with any mention of him, have the goodness to communicate it to
Dear Sir, your very sincere
James Neild

Fryday 21 July 1809

10. [E]

Endorsed: From James Neild Esq., July 25 1809, Chelsea. done

Doctor Lettsom
Sambrook Court
Basinghall Street

My dear Friend,
I was in hopes to have receiv'd the reports of the Humane Society to send to Mr. Coleman at Maidstone, but imagine you have not pass'd by the Property Office as I find they are not left there for me, and I will thank you to enclose in the Parcel Eight Impressions of your Head to put in some books which have it not. If you should hear any tidings of Doctor West, pray let me know. I am anxious to receive the letter he has for me. Everything I learn about my son is from other Persons. I propose setting out early in August on a very extended Tour, perhaps from 12 to 1500 miles. Believe me
Dear Sir, yours truly,
James Neild

Property Office
25 July 1809

11. [E]

Endorsed: From James Neild Esq., July 27 1809, Chelsea

Doctor Lettsom
Sambrook Court
Basinghall Street

My dear Friend,
I receiv'd your several Packets at the Property Office yesterday and should not so soon have troubled you with a letter, but in one of yours was a one

pound note and one shilling, without any mention from whence it comes or to what purpose it is to be applied. Maidstone I have just made some additions to, in consequence of the Alterations which have taken place there, and I believe it will appear in August mag. published in September.[167] I wish you would divide Oxford into two Essays—the Castle first, and at the conclusion, say, the City Gaol on our next. Mr. Urban may suit his own convenience about their appearing in his mag., but they must be in successive months. I have desired him to correct the proofs for Maidstone as I shall leave Town the 12th August and not return before the 29th October, to be present at Craven Street Committee,[168] therefore if Oxford appears sooner will beg that either you or him will correct my remarks. When I make my appearance in the different Countys the conversation generally runs upon Doctor Lettsom and Mr. Neild, your Essays are indeed so productive, and the Effect so very extensive, that I look to their End with regret, and if you are not tired, for your stores are inexhaustible, we will shorten description by only giving one Prison at time, and Mr. Urban tells me he shou'd prefer two short ones to one long one—what say to this, my dear Sir? We meet in Committee next Wensday, so you will let me know about the Guinea enclosed before that day. Adieu, my dear Sir and by a line to Chelsea.
Believe me, ever yours,
James Neild

Chelsea 27 July
1809

12. [E]

Endorsed: From James Neild, May 3 1810, Chelsea

[Doctor Lettso]m
[Sambrook] Court
[Basingha]ll Street

---

[167] As mentioned in note 160 above, Lettsom and Neild's account of Maidstone Gaol appeared in the September magazine: 'Dr. Lettsom's sixtieth letter on prisons' appeared with 'Mr. Neild's remarks on Maidstone Gaol', *Gentleman's Magazine*, 1809, **79** (ii): 813–16.
[168] The meetings of the committee of the Society for the Discharge and Relief of Persons Imprisoned for Small Debts were held in Craven Street.

My dear Friend,
   You will be pleased to hear that the Royal Burgh of Inverness and of Dumfries[169] have done me the honour to present me with their respective freedoms.[170]
I am, my dear Sir,
Your most obliged and grateful
James Neild

May 3^d
1810

13. [L]

Endorsed: From James Neild, Sept. 26 1810, Chelsea. answered.

Doctor Lettsom

My dear Friend,
   I returned to town last night, and found your favour of the 3^d. Instant. It unfortunately came to ~~Ch~~ Chelsea when my son was in Buckinghamshire, so that we were both absent. Of course it lay unopened till his return on the 17th.
   At Ipswich I found a Letter from him dated the 18th, in which he says he answered yours, as he is sure I should have done, and that was by complying with your request. I suppose the offer was too late as he tells me he received no answer. I am glad however that having it in his own power, he made no hesitation whatever in doing what he knew I would have done. I feel very much for the predicament it must have thrown you into, having experienced it myself. I have for some time ordered him to open all Letters addressed to me without they are wrote upon private, because my Prison Tours are so very extensive my Letters cannot follow me and some require immediate Answers.

---

[169] In Scotland, receipt of a Royal Charter makes a burgh into a city. In economic terms, a Royal Charter granted the merchants of a burgh a monopoly of trade in the town and its surrounding areas and entitled them to certain tax exemptions. Inverness received its Royal Charter in 1067 and Dumfries in 1186. Therefore, both were Royal Burghs of some antiquity.
[170] The freedom of a city or "the burgess ticket", was granted to distinguished individuals who were felt to be worthy of the honour. The freedom came from all the citizens of the city, but was granted through their elected representatives.

I shall stay at Chelsea a week at least before I set out again—perhaps a fortnight, for my son tells me he cannot return to Town sooner, and I do not like to leave my house to two women servants only.

Believe me, my dear friend,

yours sincerely,

James Neild

Sepr. 26 1810

Chelsea

PS/ When I came home last night it was my intention to have proceeded on Saturday to complete my intended Tour, but I am prevented—partly by a draft from Antigua—to provide "Ways and Means".[171] This I will put a stop to.

14. [E]

Endorsed: From James Neild Esq., Oct. 16 1810, Chelsea

My Dear Sir,

Your money concerns and mine differ extremely, so far from having <u>two</u> bankers, my account has not been worth the attention of <u>one</u> lately. My Extra funds are allmost totally absorbed, and I have been in a most extraordinary degree unfortunate with my tenants, so that it is with difficulty I can make things meet, and this embarrassment I am not likely soon to get over. Your draft is on Masterman,[172] and I had collected the money to pay a draft from Antigua. I shall take it tomorrow, and it will be sent, I suppose, for payment Thursday morning. I think the draft is not due till the day after.

I am in a good deal of anxiety about my son, William. In a letter from him dated 7th July by he appears to be in health and spirits at Antigua with fair prospects. Since this I have not heard from <u>him</u> but have received a letter from John Hall dated Antigua, 23d August in which he says "my intimate friend Mr. W. C. Neild was under the imperious necessity of leaving this Island by the advice of three of our most eminent physicians, for a change of climate, as the only possible means of preserving his Life. His extreme illness and dangerous disorder is the Chronic Thrush which had before he left this gone compleatly through him. He left this on the 10th Instant extremely regretted etc. in his Majesty's Brig Opossum, Capt Byam for Halifax".

---

[171] Neild's son, William, was drawing money in Antigua on his father.
[172] Messrs. Masterman and Co., bankers in London.

I have heard of Children having the <u>Thrush</u>. Will you be so good to explain this passage to me, and the transition from <u>Heat</u> to <u>Cold</u>, <u>Antigua</u> to <u>Halifax</u>.[173] How that cou'd be prescribed, I cannot reconcile, and why not come to England? I should have thought it a better climate. The medical Gentlemen are certainly more able to judge than myself—perhaps you can explain it?

I did intend, if opportunity presented itself, to have shewn you the enclosed letter which I found on my return from my Prison Tour. I rather think the writer is a relation of a very amiable lady you are acquainted with. I did not know there was a prison in the Isle of Man. It was unknown to Howard. Return the letter, I will answer it soon, and shall be glad if our Society can assist him, but we were obliged to adjourn our meeting from August to November for want of money, the Ballance in my hand being only Ten pounds and five pence.

I am, Dear Sir, yours truly

J. Neild

Tuesday 16th Oct. 1810

15. [E]

Endorsed: From James Neild, Nov. 10 1810, Chelsea. answered.

Doctor Lettsom

My dear Friend,

This very interesting letter written in Consequence of the one I sent you from Colonel Porter[174] will receive great additional weight if introduced by your enlightened Observations. I propose sending as [free?] number to Lords Beddesdale and Moira who mean to bring in a Bill this session, to the Marquis of Buckingham, Earl Romney and Mr. Wilberforce. I have written to the Colonel I hope a comfortable letter and I wish Mr. Urban to give it early insertion but not in the supplement. I have no Occasion to say I wish

---

[173] Halifax, Nova Scotia, Canada. The British navy had bases in Antigua and Halifax in order to consolidate its power in the North Atlantic. In the early 1800s, with the construction of the Royal Naval Dockyard in Bermuda, it further strengthened its position by adding a third base in the mid-Atlantic.

[174] Given the date and the rate at which Lettsom and Neild were producing their remarks on prisons, this probably refers to 'Dr. Lettsom's LXIXth letter on prisons' which appeared with 'Mr. Neild's remarks on Castle Rushen Gaol', *Gentleman's Magazine*, 1810, **80** (ii): 514–17.

you to be as animated as you can in your Preface, for upon that I think success in my Wishes will depend.

yours very sincerely

James Neild

Surrey is the only one before you and that may be postponed if you think better.

16. [E]

Endorsed: From James Neild, Nov. 27 1810, Chelsea

My dear Friend,

I had intended to have written to you before this, but have been in great domestic affliction occasioned by the death of my Eldest son at Falmouth the 19th ultimo.[175]

You express'd great satisfaction at my description of Castle Rushen[176] but receiving a letter from Colonel Porter in answer to several points I wish'd for information about, I was enabled to give a more prison-like description to the whole, and my friend Mr. Butler has given it a polish, and an addition of poetry, which will render it more interesting in the opinion of

Dear Sir yours truly

Jas Neild

27 Nov. 1810

17. [JCL][177]

Endorsed: to follow the memoir of Jas Neild

On James Nield [*sic*] Esq., By Miss Porter
Hence the true Christian, Lord of Appetite,

---

[175] William Neild died on board the ship that was bringing him back to England shortly after it docked at Falmouth.

[176] Castle Rushen, Isle of Man. The keep of Castle Rushen was the main civil prison in the Isle of Man. As early as 1765, there were three rooms for the confinement of debtors. Since debts incurred in England and Ireland could not be recovered in the Isle of Man, the island became home to some of the worst debtors. By 1791, only the smallest of these rooms remained and conditions had markedly deteriorated. The castle was remodelled in 1815, so that it functioned as a better prison for debtors and criminals.

[177] This poem is reproduced in Pettigrew, op. cit., note 87 above, vol. 2, p. 207.

The conqueror of low but fierce resentments,
Which in a painful fever keep the soul
Free from impediments, pursues with ardor
All that adorns and meliorates the man;
That polishes our life, or soothes its ills.
Where'er compassion with her glist'ning eye
Points to the squalid cottage of Affliction:
Jews, Moors and Infidels are all his Brethren.
Could he in some remote and barbarous land,
By powerful gold, or salutary arts,
Make pale Distress give way to blooming Joy,
He'd traverse wilds or swelling seas to court
The god-like office; his expanded heart
In every climate feels himself at home.

[JCL]

Endorsed: From Mr. Nesbitt, Aug. 21 1808, Lower Charlotte Street. done

Dear Sir,

I have to return you my best thanks for the Pacquet you was so obliging as send. In the Memoirs of your life[178] the only information I had to go upon was from the European Magazine.[179] I was glad to know there is another in the Public characters. In this number of the Spectator I shall take an opportunity of correcting what is wrong and in the next number I shall bring forward your observations on Vaccination and such other parts of your works as Dr. Lettsom has always a right to command from
Dear Sir
yours most sincerely,
Mr. Nesbitt

21 Lower Charlotte Street
Bedford Square
Augt 21 1808

---

[178] There is no specific memoir of Lettsom in the *European Magazine*. Nesbitt must therefore have been referring to the kind of incidental information that appeared in the magazine's notification of appointments, promotions and general social miscellanea.

[179] The *European Magazine* was published between 1782 and 1826 and was similar in type to the *Gentleman's Magazine*.

[JCL]

Endorsed: From Dr. Ontyd,[180] Jan. 31 1802, Hague. answered.

Dear Sir!
I have the honor to transmit to you the third and last part of the first volume of the Dutch Medical Journal[181] for the London Medical Society. If you would be so kind as to send me some cowpox matter you should very much oblige me as the Dutch practitioners at present are forced to leave of[f] inoculating with the vaccine virus for want of matter.
I am,
Sir,
Wholly yours
C. G. Ontyd

Hague 31 of January
1802

[JCL][182]

Endorsed: From E. Rack,[183] April 16 1779, Bath. answered (46)

Dr. Lettsom
I flatter myself that my Ingenious Friend Dr. Letsom's regard to every thing curious will induce him to excuse the liberty I take in sending him an animal of a species which I do not find either a drawing or description of in any author who has written on natural history. I call it an animal because it was alive, and vigorous more than a week after I found it. It was fix'd on the

---

[180] Coenraad Gerhard Ontyd (1776–1844), doctor in the Hague, who studied at Leiden where he gained his M.D. in 1797. He then came to London where he studied under Astley Cooper and met Lettsom.

[181] *Nederlands Tijdschrift voor Geneeskunde.*

[182] This letter is, as far as "It is however possible..." reproduced in Pettigrew, op. cit., note 87 above, vol. 2, pp. 308–10. We have found no one to make a confident identification of the beast described within it.

[183] Edmund Rack was the founder of the Bath and West Society in 1777. The son of a weaver, he was born in Norfolk in 1735 and his mother was a Quaker. Although he had a rather basic education, he became a writer and went to live in Bath in 1775, where he attended writers' groups set up by Lady Miller and Catherine Macaulay. In the late eighteenth and early nineteenth centuries, the Bath and West Society was a model for other agricultural societies set up round the country. Rack also formed the first Philosophical Society in Bath along with Thomas Curtis. The Philosophical Society was discontinued on his death in 1787.

side of a wooden pipe which convey'd a small stream of water into a Ditch. As it hung, its motion excited my attention while I was picking some liverwort which grew on the spout. I seperated it from its lodgment with the point of my knife, supposing it to be an aquatic plant and that its motion was occasion'd by the water which ran over it. On coming home, I put it in a tea saucer of water to spread, when, greatly to my surprize, the extremities of its branches or tentacula began to move. The motion gradually increas'd till at length the whole animal shifted its place and frequently extended its arms to the top of the water, curling them in fine spiral forms like a Corkscrew. I examined it with a lens of moderate power, and the brown spots seemed to be lamelae of a stony kind. Hence I concluded it to be one of the Crustaceous Polype. I then plac'd it on a thin plate of Glass, and examin'd it by the 4ᵗʰ magnifier in Cuff's double Microscope,[184] when, to my great surprize, I found the whole animal to be a congeries of innumerable fibres branching out ~~from~~ into infinitely fine ramifications, and ending in points. An undulatory motion was visible in all the principal arms, or branches, and in many of the smaller ramifications. The brownish spots at each joint, which I had suppos'd were Crustaceous Lamellae, I found to be tufts of fibres, which had other branches shooting from them so extremely fine, that even under the 1ˢᵗ magnifier they appeared no larger than a silk worm's thread to the naked eye. These tufts of fibres are transparent in the smaller branches of the animal and grow regularly between the joints in each limb, or branch. They appear'd to be hollow; and in some of the larger ones I could perceive a motion, which I took to be ~~a~~ the Circulation of some fluid. The smallest touch in moving the animal, I found displac'd or broke off some of the finer fibres. I could not find any appearance of a mouth, or distension of the Gelatinous parts, as is usual in other species of the polype, nor any Fibrillae at the extremities. In every thing, it had the appearance of a vegetable, except its frequent and vigorous motion. I gave it fresh water frequently; but going one day from Home I found the water had been spill'd and the animal was hanging dry to the edge of the saucer. After this accident it never discover'd any signs of life, although I immediately put it in water. I have shewn it to several ingenious Gentlemen in this city; they all agree in thinking it a species hithertoo undiscover'd. It is however possible we may be mistaken; but I thought thou wouldst be pleas'd with an opportunity of examining so singular a production, and accordingly send it for inspection. If thou hast never seen any of this species and think it worthy the attention of the Royal Society, thou art at

---

[184] John Cuff (1708–72) designed his "new constructed double microscope" at the suggestion of Henry Baker, author of *The microscope made easy* (1742). It is regarded as the first solid and stable microscope to be produced and was easy to use. It magnified specimens up to 320 times. It was extremely popular and imitated by other microscope builders. Cuff went bankrupt.

liberty to Communicate this letter with it to that learned body. I wish however to be favour'd with thy thoughts respecting it, and am, very respectfully thine etc.

Edmund Rack

Bath April 16th 1779

[JCL]

Endorsed: From Dr. Ramsey,[185] Dec. 19 1808, Carolina. answered.

Charleston December 19th 1808

Dear Sir,

I have drawn on you in favour of David Longworth, printer in New York[186] (who is to print my History of South Carolina) for the sum of six hundred Dollars.[187] I have seen a London paper of October 1807 advertising my Life of Washington by Caddell and Davis[188] which has induced me to believe that by this time sales have been made to authorise your calling on them for the above sum. I shall ever retain a grateful sense of you politeness in negotiating this business for me and am,

Your obliged Friend,

David Ramsay [*sic*]

Dr. Lettsom

---

[185] David Ramsey (1749–1815) (or Ramsay as he more often appears) was an M.D. of Charleston in South Carolina and a member of the Royal Physical Society of Edinburgh. He was also active in politics as a member of congress between 1782 and 1785 and was the author of a history of the American revolution—David Ramsay, *The history of the American revolution*, Dublin, printed for W. Jones, 1793. For a sample of his political writing, see David Ramsay, 'An address to the freemen of South-Carolina on the subject of the Federal Constitution: proposed by the convention, which met in Philadelphia, May 1787', Charleston, printed by Bowen and Co. [1788]). Also see David Ramsay, *Selections from his writings. Edited with introduction and notes by Robert L. Brunhouse*, Philadelphia, American Philosophical Society, 1965.
[186] David Longworth (born *c.* 1767) was a New York publisher who published many of the early directories of New York.
[187] David Ramsay, *The history of South Carolina, from its first settlement in 1670, to the year 1808*, Charleston, D. Longworth, 1809.
[188] David Ramsay, *The life of George Washington*, London, printed by L. Hanfard and Sons, for T. Cadell and W. Davies, in the Strand, and Longman, Hurst, Rees, and Orme, Paternoster-Row, 1807.

1. [JCL][189]

Endorsed: From Dr. Rush,[190] Febr. 7 1798, Philadelphia. answered.

Dr. John Coakley Lettsom
Physician in London.

My dear friend,
Accept of my thanks for your volume of <u>Hints</u>.[191] May you live to see all the ingenious and benevolent ideas contained in them realised in their utmost extent!
Herewith you will receive a volume of Essays upon moral, literary and philosophical subjects which [have][192] me as their author.[193] Should you think them worthy of being republished in L[on]don,[194] please to request the Editor to correct the <u>spelling</u> in <u>some,</u> and the <u>punctuation</u> in <u>many</u> parts of the [Work].[195] It was printed by a young hand, and during the [di]stracting months of the last Autumn in [soci]ety.[196]

---

[189] This letter is extensively blotted and the paper holed and torn.
[190] The Philadelphian Benjamin Rush (1746–1813) was a renowned physician and teacher who played a significant role in his country's affairs. He served a medical apprenticeship with Dr. John Redmond in Philadelphia for nearly six years and also attended the earliest lectures of Dr. John Morgan and Dr. William Shippen junior at the College of Philadelphia. In the autumn of 1766 he went to Edinburgh where he studied for two years and took his M.D. After graduating, he spent a year in London and in Paris before returning home to a chair of chemistry in the medical department of the College of Philadelphia (the first chemistry chair in America) at the age of twenty-three. He also developed a sizeable private practice. He was a great supporter of blood-letting. He opposed slavery and capital punishment and supported American independence. He helped to set up the Pennsylvania Society for Promoting the Abolition of Slavery and the Relief of Free Negroes Unlawfully held in Bondage, the first anti-slavery society in America. For Rush on himself, see Benjamin Rush, *The autobiography of Benjamin Rush; his 'Travels through life' together with his Commonplace book for 1789–1813*, edited with introduction and notes by George W. Corner, [Princeton], published for the American Philosophical Society by Princeton University Press, 1948. Lettsom published a quarto volume entitled *Recollections of Dr. Rush*, London, printed by J Nichols, Son and Bentley, 1815.
[191] As noted in 'Letters from Lettsom', note 55, his *Hints* were small tracts on various subjects that Lettsom published now and again and which he gave to his friends and enquirers. These tracts were on diverse topics, some of which brought Lettsom into controversy with the anonymous writers in the *Monthly Review* and the *Critical Review*, for which see John Coakley Lettsom, *An apology, for differing in opinion from the authors of the Monthly and Critical Reviews*...London, Nichols, 1803.
[192] Hole in manuscript. Word missing.
[193] Benjamin Rush, *Essays, literary, moral and philosophical*, Philadelphia, Thomas and Samuel F. Bradford, 1798. See also the modern edition with a scholarly introduction: Benjamin Rush, *Essays: literary, moral, and philosophical*, edited, with an introductory essay by Michael Meranze, Schenectady, NY, Union College Press, c.1988.
[194] There is no sign of the *Essays* having been reprinted in London.
[195] This word is heavily blotted, but appears to be "Work".
[196] This sentence is particularly heavily blotted and holed. The transcription of the last word is not completely certain.

I am now preparing for the ~~of an~~ press a 5th volume of medical inquiries and observations.[197] It will contain, among other things, an account of our late Epidemic.[198] Under the pressure of indisposition, great fatigue and the most unremitted newspaper scandal, I found leisure to take notes of nearly every case that came under my ~~review~~ care. The principles and practice contained in my former volumes,[199] will, I hope, be fully established by many facts to be communicated in the history of the fever of 1797. Its generation in our city will be proved by many documents.

Adieu. From my Dear Sir

Your sincere friend

Benjamin Rush

Philadelphia Feb: 7th 1798.

PS: If you conclude to republish the volume of Essays, you are at liberty if you please to introduce the words "to Dr. John C: Lettsom of London" instead of "a friend in Great Britain" in p. 189.[200] I suppressed your name only from a fear, that ~~it w~~ by mentioning it I might expose you to persecution ~~in~~ among ~~the~~ your fellow citizens.

2. [JCL]

Endorsed: From Dr. Rush, May 8 1811, Philadelphia.

Philadelphia May 8th 1810

My dear Old friend,

The bearer, Mr. James West, a member of the Society of friends, has heard and read so much of you, that he cannot return from London without

---

[197] The fifth volume came out later in the year. Benjamin Rush, *Medical inquiries and observations*, 5 vols, Philadelphia, Thomas Dobson, 1794–8.

[198] Volume five contained 'An account of the yellow fever, as it appeared in Philadelphia in 1797'.

[199] Yellow fever hit a number of towns and cities on the east coast of America in the 1790s, including Philadelphia where there were epidemics in 1793 and 1797. Rush published extensively on yellow fever. Volume three (1794) of his *Medical inquiries and observations* (Philadelphia, T. Dobson, 1793–4) included 'An account of the bilious remitting yellow fever, as it appeared in the city of Philadelphia, in the year 1793'. An edition of the 235-page text of this account was also published in Edinburgh by James Symington in 1796. Volume four (1796) was almost entirely devoted to yellow fever: *Medical inquiries and observations: containing an account of the bilious remitting and intermitting yellow fever, as it appeared in Philadelphia in the year 1794*. Some of the letters that Rush received on the subject of yellow fever are held in Bethesda, MD, USA, National Library of Medicine, MS B 76; Thomas Drysdale, Benjamin Rush and John Redman Coxe, *Account of the yellow fever of 1794 as it appeared in Baltimore… in a series of letters to Dr. Benjamin Rush*, Thomas Drysdale, 1794.

[200] Rush, op. cit., note 193 above, 'Information to Europeans who are disposed to migrate to the United States of America. In a letter to a friend in Great Britain'. Dated 'Philadelphia

knowing you. I have therefore taken the liberty of giving him a letter of introduction to you. He is the son of a wealthy and respectable merchant of this city, and visits Europe to acquire not property, but knowledge of men and things. He will give you all the information you may wish for respecting the state of Science, Commerce, and Government in our Country.

Health, Respect, and friendship!

from yours
sincerely
Benjamin Rush

Dr. Lettsom

[JCL]

Martis 10°. die Feby. 1801

At the Committee appointed to consider of the present high Price of Provisions.
The Right Honorable Dudley Ryder in the chair
Ordered,
That Dr. Lettsom do attend this Committee Tomorrow at one o'clock
D Ryder

1. [L]

Endorsed: From Lord Shelburne,[201] Aug. 13 1782, London. answered.

To
D^r. Lettsom
Basinghall Street

Lord Shelburne presents his Compliments to Dr. Lettsom and will be glad to see him next Friday between Ten and Eleven in the morning.

April 16 1790.' Presumably, not long after the War of Independence and in the midst of the French Revolution, Rush thought it prudent not to name a friend of an American.

[201] Sir William Petty FitzMaurice (1737–1805), second Earl Shelburne (from 1761), British statesman. Although he was one of the most liberal politicians of his time, he was also highly unpopular. He is usually credited with authorship of the anonymous Junius letters, which appeared in the London *Public Advertiser* between January 1769 and January 1772, attacking George III and his cabinet. He was a patient of Lettsom and possibly previously of John Fothergill. Lettsom and Shelbourne also seemed to have a rather informal relationship as well as their medical one. See Abraham, op. cit., note 29 above, pp. 270–1.

Shelburne House
Tuesday 13 Aug^t.

2. [L]

Endorsed: From Lord Shelburne, May 20 1783, High Wycombe.[202] done.

Lord Shelburne presents his Compliments to D^r. Lettsom and returns him many thanks for the Life of Dr. Fothergill. It could not fail to interest him on account of the Writer as well as the Excellent Man who is written of. He has since read it with great satisfaction and pleasure.

High Wycombe
20th. May 1783

3. [L]

Endorsed: From Lord Shelburne, June 5 1783, London. answered.

Lord Shelburne presents his Compliments to Dr. Lettsom, and if it's quite convenient proposes paying his respects to him about 12 o'clock to morrow in the Country. If any hour from 9 to 3 is more convenient to Dr. Let[t]som, Lord Shelburne can make it equally so to himself.

Lady Shelburne[203] propos'd herself the pleasure of waiting on Mrs. Lettsom till this Instant, but finds it impossible on account of different engagements in Town previous to her going next day to Wycombe.

Shelburne House
5th June 1783

4. [L]

Endorsed: From Lord Shelburne, July 13 1783, Aix La Chapelle.[204] answered.

To D^r. Lettsom

Aix la Chapelle
13th. July 1783

---

[202] High Wycombe, Wyckham or Chipping Wycombe in the county of Buckinghamshire was a large market town twenty-nine miles from London and on the road to Oxford. Lord Shelburne's seat was the manor house of Loakes, which he considerably improved.

[203] After the death of his first wife Sophia Cateret in 1771, Lord Shelburne married Louisa FitzPatrick (1755–89) on 19 July 1779. They had one child, Henry Petty-FitzMaurice (1780–1863) who, in 1809, became the third Marquis of Lansdowne.

[204] Called Aquisgranum by the Romans who founded a military outpost near hot springs, it was later the favourite residence of Emperor Charlemagne (742–814), whose palace was

Sir,

I was oblig'd to set out some days sooner than I intended, on account of some circumstances regarding Lady Shelburne's Health, which I cannot put on paper. This prevented my having the pleasure of seeing you as I intended, and makes me trouble you with this, both to make my excuse, and to acquaint you of what the attention you were so good to give to my complaints may make it agreeable to you to know, that I have found surprizing benefit from these Waters.[205] I stopp'd here as a preparatif for Spa,[206] but finding that the Waters, disagreeable as they are, instead of relaxing my stomach, gave me a better appetite than the Borrh did with constant exercise and strong Wine. Without either of these additions, I have prolong'd my stay. In truth I am satisfied that every complaint I have had has arisen from obstructed Bile, having voided a great deal both ways since I have been here. I propose continuing another Week and then going to Spa.

I am with great Regard Sir,

Your Faithfull and most obedient Servant

Shelburne

5. [L]

[Notes to Lettsom from Lord Lansdown][207]

[Note 1] Endorsed: From Lord Lansdown, May 30 1791, Lansdown house.

---

situated by the springs. The city was occupied by Napoleon in 1794 and annexed to France in the year 1801. It is now Aachen in Westphalia in Germany, near the borders of Holland and Belgium. By the eighteenth century, it had been a popular spa for centuries and its thermal waters were as celebrated as those of Bath.

[205] There are a number of eighteenth-century publications concerning these waters. See, for example, C. L. Von Pöllnitz, *Amusements des eaux d'Aix-la-Chapelle*, Amsterdam, Chez Pierre Mortier, 1736; Charles Lucas, *Essai sur les eaux minerales et thermales d'Aix-la-Chapelle et de Borset* Aix, s.n., 1786; M. D[e] B[arjole], *Lettres sur la ville et les eaux d'Aix-La-Chapelle*, The Hague, Gosse, 1784; Charles Perry, M.D., *An enquiry into the nature and principles of the Spaw waters ... To which is subjoined a cursory enquiry into the nature and properties of the hot fountains at Aix la Chapelle*, London, printed for James, and Paul Knapton, 1734; John Elliot, M.D., *An account of the nature and medicinal virtues of the principal mineral waters of Great Britain and Ireland, and those most of repute on the Continent ... And a method of impregnating water with hepatic air, so as to imitate the Aix-la-Chapelle and other sulphureous waters*, London, J. Johnson, 1789, 2nd edn.

[206] Spa, a town in Belgium, famous for its mineral springs discovered in 1326.

[207] Lord Shelburne was created Marquis of Lansdowne in 1784 as a reward for political service.

Dr. Lettsom

Lord Lansdown presents his Compliments to Dr. Lettsom, is sorry that all his Tickets had been previously engaged up to Monday inclusively, but the first sitting after that day he will be sure to have some, and due notice given.

Lansdown House Saturday morning. 5.

[Note 2] Endorsed: From Lord Lansdown, May 31 1791, Lansdown house. answered.

Dr. Lettsom
_____Court
Basinghall Street

Lord Lansdown presents his compliments to Dr. Lettsom; he will tomorrow receive three Tickets for Thursday to Mr. Hasting's trial.

Lansdown House Tuesday morning

[Note 3] Endorsed: From Lord Lansdown, June 1 1791, London.

Lord Lansdown presents his Compliments to Dr. Lettsom and sends him Two Tickets;[208] he is excessively mortified that he finds it impossible to send Three as he had hoped to do, but will make it up next time.

Lansdown House Wednesday Evening

[Note 4] Endorsed: From Lord Lansdown, May 16 1792, Lansdown house. answered.

Lord Lansdown presents his compliments to Dr. Lettsom, and sends him the inclosed letters. He would have sent them to him long since but was disap-

---

[208] Tickets for the trial of Warren Hastings (1732–1818), former governor-general of Bengal, who was impeached at the instigation of Edmund Burke. The trial before the House of Lords began in February 1788 and continued until 1795 when he was acquitted. See also Letter 2 in the 'Letters from Lettsom' section.

pointed by Count Zenobia, to whom he applied in the first instance; but Count Zenobia says he did not receive Lord Lansdown's letter: He abounds in excuses, which Lord Lansdown not accepting very readily, the Count intends to call on Dr. Lettsom, as he has great fear of offending the body of Quakers, or its being attributed to other motives which Lord Lansdown stated to him as the consequence. Dr. Lettsom however is no loser excepting in point of time, as the inclosed, Lord Lansdown hopes are more to be depended upon.

Lansdown-House
Saturday May 19th.

6. [E]²⁰⁹

Endorsed: to Marquis of Lansdowne, Sept. 10 1794, Lansdowne House

… of effecting this Herculean labour, the Crown may again call upon the Marquis, to rescue us from the ~~precipice~~ danger to which ~~weakness~~ ignorance has ~~brought~~ reduced us but ~~cannot~~ from which its ~~cannot~~ imbecillity cannot restore us.

My sentiments are unbiased by any other consideration than national good, and my acquaintance generally coincide with me— ~~May health~~ and I sincerely believe my sentiments are now the majority of the people—with these sentiments I beg leave to subscribe with the most
[My regard?] [and] esteem
J. C. Lettsom

1. [JCL]

Endorsed: From Dr. Stokes,²¹⁰ June 8 1812, Chesterfield.²¹¹ answered. about Pearce's Letters.

Chesterfield 8 June 12

---

²⁰⁹ A draft of part of a letter with much erasure and substitution.

²¹⁰ Jonathan Stokes (1755–1831) was a practising physician. He was one of the original fellows of the Linnean Society of London, the oldest natural history society in the country. In the late 1780s, he was a member of the Lunar Society of Birmingham. In the year that he wrote this letter, he published *A botanical materia medica, consisting of the generic and specific characters of the plants used in medicine and diet, with synonyms, and references to medical authors*, London, J. Johnson, 1812.

²¹¹ Chesterfield is an old market town in Derbyshire.

Dear Sir,

The treasure you have trusted into my hands arrived safe this morning, though it bore the very dangerous inscription of carriage paid. I have read nothing today but Dr. Pearce's letters.[212] I hope you will find time to give them to the world, with a sketch of the author's life. There is something quackish about him, especially when he talks about the remedy for cancer, and in his never telling us any instance of want of success. In his first letters he tells us that he used nitre with the lemon juice instead of Gunpowder, and at a future period he gives gunpowder without assigning any reason for the change. But if I indulge myself on animadversions on these interesting letters I shall disobey your injunction of acknowledging the receipt of the valuable manuscript. My son who is with me on his way to Buxton desires to unite in best compliments with,

Dear Sir,

Your much obliged and obedient servant

Jonathan Stokes

[JCL]

Buxton[213] 6th July 1812

My dear Sir.

I cannot let this letter of my father's to you,[214] (and which he sent me by a private hand in case I had anything to write to you about) leave this place without saying how much pleasure the short vi[sit] I paid you in Sambrooke Court gave m[e], and how truly I regret having managed so ill when in London, as to see no more of you than I did. I have attended this place[215] during the summer months, every year since I saw you in London.

Hoping you are well, I am

---

[212] Stokes' letter of 1 July 1812 makes it clear that these were not published, but manuscript letters.

[213] Buxton in Derbyshire is a small spa town in the Derbyshire Peak District famous for its thermal mineral waters. People had begun to flock there in the seventeenth century to sample the spring water which flowed from St Anne's Well. However, it was during the eighteenth century that the town began seriously to develop when the fifth Duke of Devonshire built the Crescent and the Great Stables. For more, see Mike Langham, *Buxton waters: a history of Buxton the Spa*, The Derbyshire heritage series, Derby, Hall, 1986.

[214] This letter is from Jonathan Stokes' son, J. R. Stokes, and is written on a half folio of the letter from his father dated 8 June 1812.

[215] Stokes senior was living only twenty-four miles from Buxton. His son was probably one of the attending physicians at the spa during its busy season.

Dear Sir.
your very obedient servant
J. R. Stokes

2. [JCL]

Endorsed: From Dr. Stokes, July 1 1812, Chesterfield. answered.

Chesterfield I July 12

Dear Sir,
It was not without considerable ~~difficulty~~ labour that I go through Mr. Pearce's letters, from the difficulty of making out a handwriting which became less easy to decypher as he advanced in years. How grateful did I feel to the discoverers of the art of printing who have so happily smoothed the way to science not only by multiplying the copies of a book at comparatively so small an expence, but in lessening the labour of reading. I cannot help repeating my hope that you will communicate your friend's discoveries to the medical world through the channel of the press. Should you do so, I shall save myself the labour of reperusing the letters and making extracts from them. On this account I again address you before I return you your manuscript. But possibly the greater part of the observations contained in these letters may be already before the public, in the 10 pieces he speaks of as having published in America. I am anxious to know if you have seen them, for he does not speak of having sent you a copy of his work, or whether I can procure it in the London sale catalogues or by means of my friends in the United States. If you are not able to give me a sight of them, I shall be much obliged to you for the title and place of publication, and year in which they appeared. I have sought in vain for the author's name in the medical journals of the day. Perhaps it may be found in Ploucquet.[216] If not, perhaps you may

---

[216] Wilhelm Gottfried Ploucquet (1744–1814) qualified in medicine at Tübingen in 1766 and was appointed professor of medicine at the university there in 1782, holding the chair until his death. He compiled a subject index to medical literature. He began to publish his elaborate subject classification in 1793 and published four *Repertoria* of current medical literature. In 1808, he published his best known work, a classified digest in four volumes, which took the current literature of medicine up to the year of the digest's publication: *Literatura medica digesta sive repertorium medicinae practicae, chirurgiae atque rei obstetriciae*, 4 vols, Tübingen, J. G. Cotta, 1808–9.

be acquainted with some medical bibliographist who may afford the desired information.
I remain,
Dear Sir,
Your very obedient servant
Jonathan Stokes

I have seen impressions of ferns in ironstone found some 20 or 30 years ago at Eastwood and West Hallam between Alfreton and Nottingham, in a cabinet at Eastwood, but none are found there now. I have heard of such at Mingerworth, but have never yet got a sight of any, but I shall make further enquiry after them.

3. [JCL]

Endorsed: From Dr. Stokes, Dec. 12 1812, Chesterfield. answered.

Chesterfield Dec. 12

Dear Sir,
I shall be much obliged to you to inform me whether you have had an opportunity of making the inquiries respecting your friend Dr. Pearce's medical pieces which he speaks of in his letters as having been published at Philadelphia. I mentioned Ploucquet as a likely book in which we might hope to meet with some account of the work. If you have it in your own library, or if it be in the library of the Medical Society, I shall be obliged to you at least to consult the index. Dr. Cope of Sommers town I think has the book. It perhaps may be found in Haller's Bibliographia Medica.[217] The extracts from the letters ought to be prefaced by some account of their author and of his works, if such have been communicated to the public through the channel of the press. I feel reluctant to begin the extracts til I know what is already before the public. I have read over Hoyes and Baynard[218] and wish much to see the 10th volume of Actae Naturae Curiosorum.[219] If you will lend it me,

---

[217] *Bibliotheca medicinae practicae*, 2 vols, Bern, E. Haller; Basle, J. Schweighauser, 1776–88.
[218] Hoyes not identified; Baynard may be Edward Baynard, author of *Health, a poem*, 2nd ed., London, J. Bettenham, 1719.
[219] Presumably he is referring to the transactions of the German Academy of Natural Sciences Leopoldina.

I will get some friend to call for it and return it with your volume of manuscript letters.

I remain,

Dear Sir,

your very obedient servant

Jonathan Stokes

1. [JCL]

Görlitz in der Oberlausitz

Den 24 Juni 1797

Für die mir gefälligst übersendeten Schriften vage ergebensten Dank. Das grosmüthige Geschenk der Königlichen Gesellschaft der Humanität hat mich bewogen dieser Gesellschaft mein Buch: Versuch über die Kunst Scheintodte zu beleben, Essay on the Resuscitativ Art.)[*sic*] zu widmen. Ich bin der Hoffnung die Societat werde dieses gut aufnehmen. zugleich habe meine Gründe in einem lateinisch Brief an die Gesellschaft erklert. Sie werden in diese Buche, so auch in den mitgesandten Miscellaneen Ph I pg. 119, einiges von dem Biß toller Hunde lesen. Ich verweise Sie hierauf, um Ihnen meine Gedanken über dieses Object mitzuteilen. Ich glaube die auseren Mittel, gleich nach dem Biß angewendet seyen die sichersten. Es ist in meiner Gegend nicht ungewöhnlich daß Menschen von wuthenden Hunden gebissen werden, auch sind vor ein paar Jahren zwei Menschen an der [Hyretdrophobia?][220] umgekommen. Ich arbeite an einer eigenen Schrift über dieses Object in lateinischer Sprache, welche Ich ihnen zueignen werde.

Ich bitte Sie, mir nicht nur den II Vol: Transactions of the human Society zukom[m]en zu lassen, sondern wen es seyn kann, um ein paar der neuesten Buecher medicinischen Inhaltes aus England, damit ich solche in die deutsche Sprache übersetzen kann, um meinen Landsleute Grosbrittaniens litterarische Schätze mitzutheilen. Ich werde Ihnen hingegen deutsche Werke senden, aber um neue Werke bitten damit die nicht schon übersetzt sind.Ich sende Ihnen noch mein Handbuch von den Kindlen Krankheiten / Essay on the Diseases of Children. Wollen Sie mir eine Adresse geben Damit die Briefe an Sie destogewisser Bestellt werden

Ihr

C. A. Struve[221]

---

[220] In spite of all attempts to read this as hydrophobia we could not do so.

[221] Christian August Struve (1767–1807) was an apothecary's son who became an M.D. at Leipzig in 1790.

2(a) [JCL] [A rough translation of this letter follows]

Dr. Lettsom in London

Görlitz in der Oberlausitz
den 22 April 1802

Das gefühl der unaussprechlichen Bangigkeit, welche man empfindet Wen ein freund den wir hochsagen, innig lieben uns verlassen hat und ein Jahr lang nicht wissen wie es ihm geht ist das meinige Seit zwei Jahren habe ich keinen brief von Ihnen gesehen ich schrub indeß einige mal an Ihnen und diese brief sind wahrscheinlich nicht in Ihr Land gekomen. Vor einig Wochen erhielt ich Lettsom's observations on the Cowpox [----] aber <u>keinen brief.</u> warscheinlich habe ich beider bucher, Ihnen zu danken der brief ist verlohren gegangen. Ich sand Ihnen 2 meiner Schriften In der Wissenschaft des Lebens habe ich meinen individuellen Carakter auszudrücken gesucht. Wan dz 2te Buch herauskommen wird, kann ich noch nicht bestimmen. Mit Dankbarkeit und einigem Stoltz habe ich gefunden, daß in London die meisten meiner schriften ubersetzt worden sind darf ich desmals von diesem oben hoffen. Sie geben Ihre Hint's vermehrt heraus—wie glücklich wurde ich mich schetzen Wen ich sie ganz besitze ich würde Sie für ein heiliges document der Freundschaft eines Lettsom's aufheben! Ich nehme underschiedlichen, den vaccination Buche so habe ich wuchentlich [----] ich menschen geimpft—und ich find ein sichers Schutzmittel gegen die Menschenpocken und als eine leichte Krankheit. Aber [----] mußen angelegenlich ihr [----] werden—sonst werden Sie noch von den Menschen vergessen. [----]—Wie angenehm wird mir Durch die Nachricht über die großen fortschritte im [----] Vaccin in England und in amerika [----]

Wieleicht habe Sie auch die Güte, mir eine der nächsten Ihrer Schriften uber diesen oder einen anderen Gegenstand zusenden. [----] Ich wüßte über folgende Punkte Aufschluß.

Lassen die wahren d[er] Pocken sich einem Subjekte mitführen welchs bereits die Menschenpocken gehabt hat? Beobachten Sie dan[n] ihren herkömmlichen Gang mit allen ihren Symptomen?—

Meine Erfahrungen hierüber sind noch zu unbestimmt das Neu ist noch nicht aufs Reine gebracht—daher [----] das [----] und neue Vaccin [----] den Menschen geben schon überstanden Subjecten sich zeigen kann, So [----] ein richtigen Unterschied gesehen und [----] dz Vaccin und den Menschengeben— Ich wollte lieber eine allgemeinen Pockenber[----] annehmen vor Der Menschengeben [----] sind—ich möchte Ihre und andere Englische Bedenken heruber wissen Von der Royal Society hab ich lange nichts gehört auch die Reports von 1800 und 1801 noch nicht herhallten! —[----]

die [----] bald etwas zu übersenden—Die Medical Society die die [----]
aufzunehmen habe ich im vorige Jahre [----] einen brief über den Zustand des
Vaccins in Deutschland übersendet—Weiß nicht ob in London angekommen
sind. Laßen Sie mich [----] bald etwas von Ihnen hören—Schreiben sie mir
recht bald.[222]
[C. A. Struve]

2(b). [JCL][223]

Endorsed: (59) From Dr. Struve, ~~Aug~~ June 1802, Gorlitz ~~(78)~~. answered
Oct. 15 1802.
Letter 88. from the same

Gorlitz in ~~der ober~~ upper lausitz.
June 1802

~~The sensation of an~~ The painful sensation from inexpressible anxiety which
one feels at the departure of an esteem'd and bel[o]ved friend, ~~and~~ not knowing what ~~is~~ may have become of him ~~for years such is mine~~ is what I suffer
at the present moment. ~~Since~~ It is now 2 years since I have I received a
Letters of from you, although I have written several times, ~~but never received
and an answer~~, but perhaps my Letters never ~~came to Hand~~, reached you. A
few weeks ago I received Dr: Lettsom's Observations on the Cow Pox ~~Bl.
Essays~~ but no Letter, most likely I have I to thank you for ~~both Books~~ the
Book, and perhaps the Letter ~~perhaps~~ is lost. I send you 2 of my works in the
"Knowledge of Life" I have endeavour'd to express my individual Character.
When the 2d volume will appear I ~~can~~ am not ~~determ yet~~ able to say. With
Gratitude and some Pride I understand most of my works have been trans-
lated in London; may I dare hope the same of the above? You give your Hints
out improv'd how fortunate should I think myselfe, if I posses'd the whole, I
should keep them in sacred remembrance of the friendship of a Lettsom.

I take the greatest interest in the Vaccine Pack and ~~have~~ inoculated weekly,
~~and shall do more~~, and I have found ~~them~~ it a sure easey and ~~safe~~ perfect
security against the Human Pock, which ought to bequite suppress'd or else
the savage angel of Natural Pock will again soon appear amongst us ~~again~~.
~~but~~ How happy should I be to have intelligence conserning the progress it has

---

[222] This was a very difficult hand and a number of words were indecipherable. It seems from
the translation that the final lines of this letter are missing.
[223] A draft translation from the German of Struve's letter dated 22 April 1802.

made in England and America, perhaps you'll have the goodness to favor me with a Work of on this or any other subject. I should wish to have the following points clear'd up. Will any subject who has had the small pox take the Vaccine? And if so, do you observe the regular progress of irritation and all its symptoms? ~~this now is not clear'd up, therefore when that tak's place and true vaccine take on = the Humain Pock on subjects all ready gone through it, apear, then there is a great difference between inoculation of vaccine an dsmall Pox. I would rather adopt a general disease of Pox's of the animal organismus, as small pox Cow pox sheep pox etc. etc. modifications, I should wish to know your or any Englishman's opinion.~~

From the Royal Humane Society I have heard nothing ~~this~~ for a long time nor have reciv'd the reports of 1800 and 1801. I hope to send somthing soon to the Medical Society who have had the goodness to elect me an honorary member ~~thereof~~. I have written a Letter on the subject of Vaccina in Germany. I don't know wether the~~y have~~ Society have received it ~~or not~~! Favor me with a Letter. The enclosed I beg you to forward to Dr: Fothergill also to him also I have written ~~some time ago~~, but have not received ~~the Letter~~ an answer. Please to send my Letter to Dr. Jenner, I know through you he will get it to a certainty. Fare well and favor me in future with your friendship. I enclose you my silhouette ~~and favor~~ me with yours. I am with esteem yours

C. A. Struve

[JCL]

Letter 89. Dr. Lettsom's reply.

London Octr 15 1802

Dear Doctor

I received thy kind expressions of friendship with a sincere and lively intrest in thy kind ~~of~~ sentiments ~~of a~~ on a distant correspondent who acknowledges himself to have been much improved by thy valuable communications. I have reminded my friends or Hawes, Dr. Fothergill and Dr. Jenner of the debt of literary correspondence they owe thee, and I hope to have some of their letters enclosed ~~with~~ in my packet now transmitted.

I have sent Dr. Pearson's new performance on the cow-pox, though not quite friendly to Dr. Jenner. We know very well that the cow pox prevents the smallpox; and the small pox in like manner prevents the calling the cow pox—That is, one is a certain preservative against the other; but with respect, it should only produce one pimple or pustule where the lancet touches and no where else. This pustule affords no danger, and requires no application in general. If there ever be a febrile action, it is a little, as scarcely to be perceptible, but the progress of this solitary pustule is very similar to the small pox, but the eruption is more like a vesicle of fluid matter, than a pustule of matter like the small pox. Dr. Pearson's book is particular as to this subject, as well as others.

At thy request, I enclose the 3 volumes of my "Hints", which I hope will be acceptable and meet with thy approbation. I send like wise some other little things which may amuse if not instructive and at the time evince the respectful esteem with which I am
thy friend
J. C. Lettsom

1. [JCL]²²⁴

Endorsed: from Dr. Vaughan July 26th 1783 Leicester. Ansd. To be examd.

… happens, removed these troublesome symptoms. The Patient returned to the use of it again, repeating it less frequently, and by this, and this alone, obtained a perfect cure, recovering but by very slow degrees his mental faculties long after his Corporal ones were restored. It was observable in this Patient that a total obliteration of whatever he had learnted years before took place, insomuch that he was obliged to learn his alphabet again. Since the above Case I have given it to a variety of patients, and often I think with very great advantage, but in that Paralysis which sometimes attacks the neck of the Bladder and where much might be expected from it, I have been disappointed in every case, though I had a Boy who could take without the least inconvenience in 24 hours nine grains of Cantharides in divided doses. The length of my Letter calls for an apology. Have the goodness to excuse it, and add to the obligations you have conferred already upon
your very obliged servant
J. Vaughan

Leicester
July 27 1783

---

²²⁴ The first part of this letter is missing.

2. [JCL]

Endorsed: From Dr. Vaughan, Mar. 2 1791, Leicester. answered.

Leicester March 2ᵈ 1791

Dear Doctor,

I thank you very heartily for your communication on the subject of Hydrophobia, as well as for your kind present, which Mr. Dilly neglected to convey to me until within these two days.

Of the good effect of Oil in hydrophobia I confess I have my doubts; nor can I believe you would have the least dependance upon it, were you to be called to a Patient under that terrible disease. What your Correspondent says of his Patient being insensible of the state he had been in is so opposite to what occurred in every one of those I have seen as to lead me to believe that the disease was totally mistaken; and I am confirmed in this opinion, by the success which is reported to have followed, the method by medendi. It is not every man who affects to make observation that he is capable of doing it; and I am sure it too often happens that the reporter loves fame better than health.

I am aware how strongly <u>perfect ablution</u> has been recommended as a powerfull Prophylactic where a wound has been inflicted by a Rabid Animal. I shall always prefer the Cautery, taking care to destroy the parts about the wound, and keeping the Ulcer open for some time. I have practised this method, in many cases, where there was no doubt of the Animal's being mad when the wound was given, and it has never failed me. But I believe the chance is as thirty to one against the Hydrophobia occurring where no means are employed to prevent it.

When the Virus begins to act, its power is rapid, and especially upon the Nervous System which it debilitates in a wonderfull manner. Was another case to occur, I should expect more from a high cordial tonic treatment, than from the most celebrated Antispasmodic remedies. The difficulty in swallowing, as it is called, arises from a sensibility in the [Tonces?], which brings on immediately a spasm of the diaphragm. When solids or fluids have once passed the back part of the [Tonces], the transit into the stomach, is ready [enou?]gh.[225] I believe it will be found that under the most violent affections of the nervous system, such as Tetanus etc., that they are always accompanied, with great debility in this part of the Frame and that this affords a very different indication to what is generally adopted. Does not the American treatment of the Locked Jaw coincide with the Ideas I am endeavouring to impress you with? I could carry this much further had I time and opportunity.

---

[225] There is a hole in the manuscript.

My Eldest Son, whose intention it is to settle in London, will be in Town in a few days and will do himself the honour of calling upon you. You will find him much better informed as to the treatment of diseases than young men generally are.

I remain, Dear Doctor, your very obliged and obedient humble servant

J. Vaughan

[JCL]

Endorsed: From Dr. Walker,[226] July 30 1781, Hull. answered

Doctor Lettsom
London

Hull July 30th 1781

Dear Doctor,

Though there is a great Chasm in our Correspondence yet knowing that our Friendship is not of yesterday, I take the Liberty to recommend to thy Acquaintance & friendly Notice a young Gentleman from Hull, who will deliver this Letter. He is at present attending St. Thomas's under the direction of Mr. Waring.[227] His name is Bolton, and I have no doubt thou wilt recollect his Father who called upon thee with a Letter from me about two years ago. Young Mr. Bolton has been one Winter at Edinburgh, and will give thee good Information respecting the medical Business transacted there last year, and the beginning of this. He has shewn great Attention and Assiduity hitherto, and I hope will prove an Ornament to his Profession and a blessing to his Friends here, who spare no Pains to give him every Opportunity of qualifying himself for the Profession he has chosen. As he is almost a stranger in London it would, I know, be of great use to him to have a few friends whom he might occasionally consult in any unforeseen difficulty; and as I am not acquainted with a person better qualified, or with better Inclinations than thyself, I could wish him to be acquainted with thee, though he is already under the Patronage of Mr. Waring, a Man, I am informed, of good abilities and who, I doubt not, will pay due attention to him.

---

[226] James Walker (1719–88) was an M.D. of St Andrews. He practised in Manchester, Jamaica and Hull. See Wallis op. cit., note 6 above, p. 621.

[227] John Waring was appointed surgeon to St. Thomas's on 31 March 1780, succeeding Joseph Else, deceased. By 24 January 1783 he was himself dead, for the governors again met on that day to appoint a successor to him. F. G. Parsons, *The history of St. Thomas's Hospital from the earliest times until A.D. 1600*, 3 vols, London, Methuen, 1932, vol. 3, pp. 239, 243.

A sight of thy Museum would be very grateful to Mr. Bolton, at some convenient Hour.

When are we to be favour'd with the 2^d Volume of the History of Medicine? I am much pleas'd to find thou hast undertaken to publish an Edition of Dr. Fothergill's works. I propose to order them when I hear they are to be had from the Booksellers. Pray, who is Dr. Elliott whose Advertisements and Extracts appear in the Papers? By his Extracts he does not appear to have been well inform'd respecting the first Period of Dr. Fothergill's Life.

I should be glad to hear from thee very soon. Is Beezley in the Land of the living? Or has he thrown himself into some Monastery abroad? I do not mean to offend him by asking this Question, but as I have heard nothing of him for some years, I have my Doubts as to his Existence. I suspect, however, he is writing some Philosophical Aphorisms as an Antidote to Matrimony, which may some Day surprize the world as the Posthumous work of the Author.

I remain with every good wish for thee and thine
Thy sincere and truely affectionate Friend
J. Walker

[JCL]

Endorsed: From Dr. Wall, May 18, 1789, Oxford. answered.

To be read in the Society May 25

Oxford 18 May 1789

Dear Doctor,

I seized this first opportunity of answering your kind letter and of thanking you for this new Instance of your friendly attention. With respect to the money, to which you allude, it was 7 Guineas, two of which were intended for the Howardian Fund and 5 for the Humane Society. Of the latter, I particularly hoped no other notice, than barely by the Initials of my name, might be taken in the public papers. If the money for the Howardian Fund has not been applied you will do me a kindness by presenting that also to the Humane Society.

You give me much satisfaction by informing me that your third Volume of Medical Memoirs is advancing. The two first have done great Credit to the Society, and your Papers in particular have conferr'd much Information.

I have found the Infusion of Quassia an extremely useful stomachic, especially in some Cases of [tophus?] affecting that organ from a gouty and hydropic disposition. Your remarks on the effects and operation of the Digitalis correspond so exactly with my own Observations that I could almost persuade myself that I had written the Paper. I am confident that very many Practitioners have seen the same and yet no one, unless we except Mr. Gickell, had Resolution before you to give the public an Account of their unfavourable trials of the medicine[228]—and, indeed, as most of the more valuable Papers were presented to the Society through the medium of your name, we may consider ourselves also as indebted to you for them. I should be extremely happy if it was in my power to promise you a mite for so valuable a Treasury.[229] But in truth my whole time is so totally occupied and has been for some years past, in very extensive country Business that it is very uncommon for me to be able to find an opportunity to write the whole of even such a letter as this at one time. My mind is therefore drawn aside from every regular pursuit. Even the little Reading in which I can indulge is irregular and desultory, serving more pour passer le Tem[p]s at an Inn or in a Carriage, than for any useful purpose. From such a life, what can be expected? We have much to envy in the situation of Physicians in Town. And yet I ought not to envy, because I have everything I ought in reason to wish for and I know at the same time that a town lif[e] be injurious to my Constitution. But [be][230] assured, Sir, and I request you to assure the Society, that their Interest will always be an important Object in my pursuits, and I shall be singularly happy at all times to promote them. If the College of Physicians should continue their periodical work they have, you know, a prior Claim upon me. There is, however, I find, an opening presented in your last preface, by which I may be enabled to show my gratitude to the Society and promote their useful Designs. I shall be extremely obliged to you if you will take the trouble of selecting from Murray's[231] or any other Medical Catalogue, any Books which may be not yet in the Library of the Society and order them (to the value of ten pounds) to be sent to the President in my name and with my proper acknowledgements. I will either transmit my Draught for

---

[228] A square bracket has been inserted here in the manuscript with the instruction: "go to next page" in the same pen as inscribed "to be read in the Society May 25". There is another square bracket on the opposite side after "be injurious to my Constitution", which clearly marks sections of the letter for reading.

[229] There are square brackets around this sentence, probably indicating that it was to be omitted from the reading to the Society.

[230] The manuscript is torn here, but this must be the sense.

[231] John Murray (1745–93), originally McMurray, was a Scottish bookseller and publisher, based at 32 Fleet Street. From the late 1770s Murray specialised in the publication of medical texts, averaging about ten a year. Murray's catalogue, was first published in 1778: *Murray's catalogue of books in medicine, surgery, anatomy, natural history for the use of the faculty, and*

the sum to you or to the Bookseller as you please. I rather prefer this method of giving Books to that which some of your [bene]factors have adopted of giving a sum of money, but at this distance I cannot know what you want and might therefore send you duplicates of what you have.

I am extremely obliged by your intended Present of the seeds but they are not arrived.

I remain

Your much obliged servant

H. Wall

Your Moral and Physical Thermometic[232] is ingenious if well applied

1. [JCL]

Endorsed: From Dr. Warren,[233] Aug. 10 1810, Boston

Boston N.A. August 10 1810

Sir,

Sometime since I had the honour of directing to you a small pamphlet on "Organic Diseases of the Heart",[234] which I hope you received. The occasion

---

practitioners in general, London, J. Murray, 1778. In 1785, he published his fifth medical catalogue. He also issued a more specialized one in 1787 designed for naval surgeons: *Catalogue of medical books, chiefly those upon the diseases of seamen, as well as those incident to hot climates and in long voyages*, London, J. Murray, 1787. See William Zachs, *The first John Murray: and the late eighteenth-century London books trade, with a checklist of his publications*, Oxford University Press, 1998.

[232] This refers to Lettsom's *History of some of the effects of hard drinking*, London, printed by Henry Fry, No. 5, Worship-street, Moorfields; and sold by C. Dilly, in the Poultry, 1789. At the end of this was '"A moral and physical thermometer:" or a scale of the progress of temperance and intemperance'. It went to six editions.

[233] John Collins Warren (1778–1856) was regarded as one of the best American surgeons of the early nineteenth century. He was born in Boston, Massachusetts, the son of John Warren (1753–1815), a surgeon, who became professor of anatomy and surgery at the small medical school which was set up at Harvard College in September 1782. Warren junior graduated from Harvard College in 1797, after which he became apprentice to his father. He went to Europe in 1800 in order to further his medical education in London, Edinburgh, Leiden and Paris. In London, he studied at Guy's Hospital, attending Astley Cooper's lectures and working as assistant to William Cooper. In Edinburgh, he took the classes of Charles and John Bell, Alexander Monro *tertius* and John Gregory. In Paris, he attended the lectures of Guillaume Dupuytren and Raphael Sabatier, as well as Jean Nicholas Corvisart's clinic at La Charité. He became adjunct professor of anatomy and surgery at Harvard in 1809 and when his father died, he became Hersey Professor of Anatomy and Surgery. He helped to found the quarterly *New England Journal of Medicine and Surgery* (Boston, 1812–28) in 1812. He also helped found the Massachusetts General Hospital, which opened to patients in 1821. See E. Warren, *The Life of John Collins Warren M.D.*, Boston, Ticknor and Fields, 1860.

[234] John C. Warren, *Cases of organic diseases of the heart. With dissections and some remarks intended to point out the distinctive symptoms of these diseases*, Boston, printed by Thomas B. Wait, 1809.

of my troubling you at this moment is to send you a publication lately made here on the "Petechial Fever",[235] which has within 3 or 4 years appeared in this country. Should your leisure permit, it would be gratifying to have your remarks on one or both of these pamphlets. I find myself represented in the Medical & Physical Journal,[236] as having communi[cated][237] a case of organic disease of the heart to that work. The truth was, that I sent to them the same printed pamphlet I enclosed to you.

The medical school lately existing at Cambridge is now removed to this place. Its plan is much enlarged and a clinical professorship[238] and the use of a hospital added to it.[239]

I have the honour to be, Sir,

With great respect your servant

John C. Warren

Dr. Lettsom.

2. [JCL]

Endorsed: From Dr. Warren, June 4 1815, Boston

Boston, June 4th, 1815

Dear Sir,

The unfortunate war which has lately existed between your country and ours[240] has broken off the intercourse I formerly enjoyed with you. I embrace

---

[235] The spotted or petechial fever. This refers to a report published in the *Medical Communications of the Massachusett's Medical Society* by Elisha North, 1810, **2** (pt. 2): 111–234. In the following year, it was published separately as a treatise: Elisha North, *A treatise on a malignant epidemic, commonly called spotted fever*, New York, Printed and sold by T. and J. Swords, 1811.

[236] *The Medical and Physical Journal* was published in London between 1799 and 1814, see W. R. Lefanu, *British periodicals of medicine: a chronological list, 1640–1899*, revised edn, Oxford, Wellcome Unit for the History of Medicine, 1984, p. 8.

[237] The word is unfinished at the bottom of the page and therefore, hyphenated: "communi-", but Warren either failed to complete the word on the reverse or it was completed at the bottom of the first page and cut off in the opening.

[238] The first clinical professor was James Jackson, who was unanimously elected professor of clinical medicine at Harvard College on 25 July 1810. He was formally inducted into office on 27 November 1810. Thomas Francis Harrington, *The Harvard Medical School: a history, narrative and documentary*, 3 vols, New York and Chicago, Lewis Publishing Co., 1905, vol. 1, p. 299.

[239] The medical school of Harvard College moved from Cambridge to Boston in 1810 in order to have improved access to clinical facilities. This was mainly at the instigation of John Warren senior. The school became known as the Massachusetts Medical College of Harvard University.

[240] The Anglo-American war of 1812–15, also referred to as the Second War of Independence.

the present opportunity of renewing it, through the bearer, who has charge of a packet to be delivered to you for the London Medical Society—and take the liberty at the same time to request the favour of your assisting with your advice this young gentleman, Mr. Codman, who has been a pupil of mine, and whose modesty and diffidence render him peculiarly desir[ous][241] to of instruction and advice. Any attention you may think proper to render him will be esteemed a great favour by you friend and servant, with great respect, John C. Warren

Dr. Lettsom.

I beg leave to request your acceptance of a few publications which we have made here, among which is a copy of a eulogy on your former correspondent and friend, my late father.[242]
Very respectfully, yours
J.C.W.

1. [JCL][243]

Endorsed: From Dr. Waterhouse, [244] May 8 1810, Cambridge.

Cambridge 8th of May 1810

Dear Doctor,
    What a tedious length of time has elapsed since I had a line from you, or indeed any of my old friends and correspondents in England! Our

---

[241] The last three letters of this word are overwritten, but this seems to be the sense.

[242] James Jackson, *An eulogy on the character of John Warren, M.D. ... Delivered at the request of the counsellors of the Massachusetts Medical Society*, Boston, C. Stebbins, 1815. Other publications relating to the death of Warren include Josiah Bartlett, Thaddeus Mason Harris and Susanna Haswell Rowson, *An oration occasioned by the death of John Warren, M.D. Past grand master*, Boston, printed by C. Stebbins, for Russell, Cutler and Co., 1815, as well as Joseph McKean, *A sermon, preached at the church in Brattle Square, Boston, on the Lord's Day after the decease of John Warren, M.D. ... who died IV. April, MDCCCXV. aged LXII*, Boston, John Eliot, 1815.

[243] This letter is reproduced in Pettigrew, op. cit., note 87 above, vol. 2, pp. 484–91.

[244] Benjamin Waterhouse (1754–1846) was born into a Rhode Island Quaker family. He travelled to London in 1775, where he became an apprentice in medicine to his second cousin, John Fothergill and to Lettsom. See Abraham, op. cit., note 29 above, p. 360. He afterwards went to Edinburgh and then to Leiden. He started up in medical practice when he returned to Rhode Island in 1782 and also taught botany at Rhode Island College (later Brown University). A few years afterwards, he went to Massachusetts and joined the Harvard Faculty, where he

non-intercourse has operated as cruelly on friendship as on trade. The commerce of both has~~ve~~ suffered by it, but I hope both will again revive with an encreased vigor, so as to make up in energy what has been lost by time. Where is Jenner?[245] and where is Ring?[246] There is, I hope, no embargo on their friendship. They, I hope, as well as yourself have not passed any non-intercourse resolutions with their transatlantic friend. Be assured yourself, and tell them, that I must still be allowed to send you my "raw materials" to be worked up by you all into those fine fabricks, which bear so high a price in every market of the civilised world. Are you aware that I have scarcely seen a sample from you these two years? For the honor of my country I am ashamed to tell Dr. Jenner how I have been treated by our legislature respecting remuneration. I have received nothing but abuse. I have been intrigued out of my place as physician to the United States Marine Hospital, worth £500 sterling a year,[247] and given me by Mr. Jefferson, as a reward for my labours in vaccination,[248] and this merely in consequence of his going out of office, and others coming in; so that at 50 years of age, I have now to contrive

---

co-founded its medical school along with Aaron Dexter and John Warren, becoming professor of the theory and practice of physic. He wrote on the dangers of smoking and drinking too much whisky. Waterhouse's diary was published in 1816: Benjamin Waterhouse, *A journal, of a young man of Massachusetts, late a surgeon on board an American privateer, who was captured at sea by the British ... to which is added, a correct engraving of Dartmoor prison, representing the massacre of American prisoners*, ed. Amos G. Babcock, Boston, printed by Rowe and Hooper, 1816.

[245] Edward Jenner (1749–1823), Gloucestershire surgeon, credited with discovering that vaccination with cowpox was a better defence against smallpox than inoculation with a mild strain of the human disease.

[246] John Ring (1752–1821), M.R.C.S., surgeon and vaccinator at New Street, Hanover Square, London.

[247] Waterhouse was physician at the Boston Marine Hospital at the Navy Yard in Charlestown for two years, between 1807 and 1809. He was dismissed on a charge of theft and dishonesty. In 1812, he was also forced to resign from the Faculty at Harvard. See Richard H Thurm, 'Dr. Benjamin Waterhouse and the Boston Marine Hospital', *Annals of Internal Medicine*, 1972, **76**: 801–13. Between 1813 and 1820, he was medical superintendent of the military stations in New England, in which post he continued to lecture and publish.

[248] Waterhouse heard of Jenner's cowpox vaccine through Lettsom. It is probably Lettsom who is referred to in the newspaper article published in Leominster, Massachusetts: Physician of the first eminence in London and Benjamin Waterhouse, 'Cow pox. Extract of a letter from a physician of the first eminence in London, to Dr. Waterhouse in Cambridge in July', *Political focus*, 31 October 1799, p. 2. Waterhouse was the first American physician to use the new smallpox vaccine which he did on his son. For more, see John Ballard Blake, *Benjamin Waterhouse and the introduction of vaccination, a reappraisal*, Philadelphia, University of Pennsylvania Press, 1957. Waterhouse published a number of his observations on smallpox, for instance, Benjamin Waterhouse, 'A prospect of exterminating the small-pox, or kine-pox, commonly called the cow-pox', [Cambridge, Mass.], printed for the author, at the Cambridge Press, by William Hilliard, 1800. For Thomas Jefferson's involvement with Waterhouse, see Robert Hurtin Halsey, 'How the President, Thomas Jefferson, and Doctor Benjamin Waterhouse established vaccination as a public health procedure', New York Academy of Medicine. Library, History of medicine ser., no. 5, New York, the author, 1936.

and execute some new plan to supply the deficiency. I propose to quit my quiet retreat in Cambridge and move into Boston, there to give my lectures on Natural History for medicine;[249] for here the <u>Botanist</u> I formerly spoke of has been forced into my place.[250] Were I a single man, and without children, I would go to England; if not to live there, at least to die there. You do not knock a man on the head in Britain because he exerts himself more than his neighbours do. The history of your mineral cabinet would make you weep.[251] If I have my health, and can hold a pen, you and the public shall know the whole of it. Sometimes one man influences, and impels the sentiments and conduct of the public. I am not calculated by nature or habit to combat intrigue.

The two parties in Massachusetts, the one called Fæderalists, or the English party and the other Republicans, have been most curiously ballanced. The latter party now predominates, and the partisans of England are daily loosing ground. The English party have been too confident, and too violent. They have pulled the string so hard as to break it. <u>John</u> <u>Bull</u> is a strong but violent animal. Bonaparte must make an Ox of him before he can tame him to his hand.

To compensate for embargoes and non-intercourse with England, a spirit of manufactoring has come to our existence. Almost every ship from Spain, or Portugal brings us the <u>marino</u> sheep.[252] Forty four arrived in one vessel, at Boston, a few days since, some of which have been sold for <u>one thousand</u>

---

[249] He went on to do this. See Benjamin Waterhouse, *The botanist. Being the botanical part of a course of lectures on natural history, delivered in the university at Cambridge*, Boston, J. T. Buckingham, 1811.

[250] It is not clear what he is referring to here. Waterhouse did not "quit" Harvard until he was forced out in 1812 but this letter is dated 1810. Jacob Bigelow (1786–1879) began lecturing in botany at the Harvard medical school in 1812 with W. D. Peck.

[251] Between 1794 and 1796, Lettsom gifted a collection of 700 mineral specimens from all over Europe to Harvard, in two consignments, to be used by the students there. The second consignment included between twenty and thirty stuffed birds and small quadrupeds. The mineral collection was placed in a mahogany cabinet. At that time, the United States apparently had no classified collection of minerals and rocks. The gift particularly pleased Waterhouse, who was more inclined towards natural history than medicine. He described the collection of minerals that Lettsom had donated, for which, see Pettigrew, op. cit. note 87 above, vol. 2, pp. 466–70, and Abraham, op. cit., note 29 above, pp. 361–3.

[252] William Jarvis (1770–1859), a native of Boston, Massachusetts, was a merchant and trader who sailed to Europe in 1797. In 1802, he settled in Lisbon and established a trading house there and was appointed United States *chargé d'affaires* and consul to Portugal, in which post he remained until he returned to America in 1811. In 1809 he took possession of a large flock of merino sheep (which were highly prized for their wool) for export to America. At that time, there were few merino sheep in the States. He sold some, but kept the majority for himself, buying a farm in Weathersfield, Vermont, where he bred and sold merino sheep throughout America. For more on Jarvis, see Mary Pepperell Sparhawk Jarvis Cutts [his daughter], *The life and times of Hon. William Jarvis, of Weathersfield, Vermont*, New York, Hurd and Houghton, 1869. The William Jarvis Papers, 1793–1845, are held in the Vermont Historical Society library.

dollars a head! If we go on as we have begun, we shall, in a year or two, be able to export <u>Hispanico</u> = <u>American</u> wool to England. While one party is vociferating that we cannot live without England, the other are trying to <u>demonstrate</u> that we can. While one depreciates our resources, the other extols them to the skies. Wisdom fi fixes her approbating eye on the line between both these extremes of party. France commonly magnifies our power, while the English delight to minify it.

We have something in the physical line somewhat alarming. The <u>spotted fever</u>, so called, has appeared here and there in Connecticut, and in Massachusetts. Several have died of it, in <u>less than 24 hours</u>. Two perished as speedily as that within a mile of my dwelling. It has appeared in high and dry situations, as well as low and damp ones. Is not this the plague? Those who have died in this neighbourhood appear to have perished as if by some subterraneous effluvia, rather than from a malignant state of the common air. Near upon, and after death, the sufferer appears spotted. Men, women, and <u>children</u> especially have been cut off in a few hours by this strange distemper. What author has treated of <u>such a</u> disorder? It differs widely from the yellow fever. It seems to merit the name of a <u>poison</u> rather than a fever.

I suspect that my manuscript, sent to you, has been stolen by some <u>governmental</u> emissary. Is it not a fact that the British government are disposed to suppress every book that contains such an account of America as would induce their mechanics and farmers to emigrate hither? I have heard some curious anecdotes to that purpose, which tend to strengthen my suspicion.

Should an opportunity occur do not fail to write to your affectionate friend Benjamin Waterhouse

Dr. Lettsome

2. [JCL]

Endorsed: From Dr. Waterhouse, July 16 1810, Boston. answered

Dear Sir,

I here send the last number in sheets of the Memoires of the American Academy of Arts and Sciences[253] and have only to apologize for snatching it

---

[253] The *Memoirs* were the proceedings of the American Academy of Arts and Sciences, a society founded at the time of the American Revolution in 1780 by John Adams "to cultivate every art and science which may tend to advance the interest, honor, dignity and happiness of a free, independent and virtuous people". Adams went on to become the second President of the United States in 1797. The *Memoirs* were first published in 1783 and ran to 1821, then there were another two series between 1826 and 1957 (including a temporary suspension between 1947 and 1956).

up just as my friend Harris was setting off, and when I had not time to get from the Bookseller's a better looking copy.
B. Waterhouse

Boston 16th July 1810

3. [JCL]

Endorsed: From Dr. Waterhouse, Mar. 29 1815, Cambridge. Received May 20 1815. Answered.

Cambridge 29th March 1815

My Dear Friend,

America and England having concluded to bury the hatchet, (and may it not be dug up again in our day) allows me an opportunity of once more addressing my old friend; and of enquiring after his health and wellfare.

I write this by Mr. Dana, a young gentleman in the medical line,[254] who lives very near me in Cambridge, and knows all about me, and my family. He is a well informed, smart young man, and is commissioned to purchase chemical apparatus for the University. After the curtain has been so long droped between the two countries, you will probably be gratified by conversing with a young American so intelligent as Mr. Dana really is.

Both nations have equal reason for rejoicing at the termination of the war, which had already begun to assume a terrible aspect. The bloody battles of

---

[254] James Freeman Dana (1793–1827) was born in Amherst, New Hampshire, and was a chemist. He graduated from Harvard in 1813, before taking a degree from the medical department in 1817. He was considered so talented that he was chosen by the college to fit out the chemical laboratory with new apparatus. He went to London in order to do so, working there in the laboratory of the chemist Friedrich Accum in Old Compton Street, Soho. On his return, he was appointed to the chair of chemistry in Cambridge, Massachusetts. In 1817, he was invited to give lectures on chemistry at Dartmouth College, New Hampshire, and, in 1820, became the first professor of chemistry and mineralogy there. He was responsible for the best known system of mineral classification and, with his brother, Samuel Luther Dana (1795–1868), also a chemist, published *Outlines of mineralogy and geology of Boston and its vicinity*, Boston, Cummings and Hilliard [at the] University Press [of] Hilliard and Metcalf, 1818.

Chippewa,[255] and Bridgewater,[256] and of Erie;[257] but above all that of New Orleans gave terrific indications of its destructive character.[258] Such an uninterrupted series of victories, without a single reverse, has rarely been allowed to any nation before. We deem ourselves a nation favoured of Heaven, who has helped us to come out of the war in a blaze of victory; and with so little loss on our side, that we have scarcely recovered from the astonishment it created. All our officers agree that the British exhibited great bravery, steady discipline, and good conduct; but what could they do before men inspired? I believe in the Scripture history from conviction, and Jackson's[259] extraordinary victory strengthens me in my belief. I am satisfied that the events on the banks of the Mississippi must be ~~owing~~ attributed more to the hand of Providence, than to the contingent powers of men. Our three great Generals are <u>Brown</u>,[260] <u>Scott</u>[261] and <u>Jackson</u>. The first was born and bred up a Quaker: his father and brethren all belong to the Society. Scott was a young Lawyer of Virginia; but Jackson towers above them all, and deservedly ranks among great men. He, too, was bred to the law and not to arms and yet he has proved himself one of the first generals of the age. The British general officers speak of him with admiration.

---

[255] The battle of Chippewa took place on 5 July 1814 near Fort Erie in Upper Canada, where a British force of about 1700 troops under General Sir Phineas Riall was guarding the Chippewa river. An American army of 1300 regular infantry under the command of General Winfield Scott defeated the British forces. The battle marked a turning point for the Americans after two years of defeats.

[256] The battle of Bridgewater was fought on 25 July 1814 before the Falls of Niagara. It is as well known as the battle of Lundy's Lane, a mile west of Niagara, and was the bloodiest exchange of the war. American troops succeeded in capturing the British artillery position, but were driven off by a strong counter-attack.

[257] Following through from the encounter at Bridgewater, General Drummond, the British commander, subsequently attacked Fort Erie, then held by the Americans. The engagement was again fierce, but the British attack was repulsed. However, its ferocity led General Izzard, the American commander, to retire, blowing up the fort before he and his troops returned to Buffalo.

[258] There were, in effect, a series of battles in Louisiana for New Orleans, from December 1814 through to January 1815. But what is remembered as *the* battle of New Orleans took place on 8 January 1815, when a diverse force including soldiers, sailors and militia, white, African and Native Americans defeated British troops from Europe and the West Indies on the plains of Chalmette below the city.

[259] Major-General Andrew Jackson (1767–1845), Commander of the Seventh Military District, who shared command with Commander Daniel T. Patterson, who was in charge of the United States Navy in the Gulf region. The 1812 war made Jackson a hero. He went on to become seventh President of the United States, winning two terms in office in 1828 and in 1832.

[260] Major-General Jacob Brown (1775–1828).

[261] Major-General Winfield Scott (1786–1866).

The consequences of this great victory surpasses that of Wolf's,[262] or that over Burgoine,[263] and over Cornwallis.[264] The difference between any other nation possessing <u>Louisiana</u> and that of the United States is immense; is incalculable. It secures an outlet to the ocean of a new world; and will make New Orleans the greatest emporium on the globe. It, more over, secures and consolidates the union of the States and fixes the <u>matchless</u> Madison[265] firm in the hearts of the people.

The war has not demoralized us. I cannot but think it has help our morals. I am Physician to the First Military District of the United States, comprehending the two states of New Hampshire and Massachusetts, and have acquired a considerable knowledge of the character of our troops, and cannot discover any traits of demoralization. They are citizen soldiers, and soldierly citizens, and most of them sons of farmers, and young mechanics, sober and industrious.

Where is our friend Jenner? My own family is yet entire. My second son, John Fothergill,[266] is making his way to good reputation and fortune in Philadelphia as a Physician, where he has considerable reputation as a Lecturer with Dr. Mease.[267]

Generally speaking, our country is contented and happy. The Republican Party is fast rising above the factious Federalists, who are an ambitious and unprincipled set of men, more attached to the good things of England than to the virtues of patriotism. Let me hear from you by the return of the Galen. Yours steadily,
Benjn Waterhouse

Dr. Lettsom

---

[262] General James Wolf's victory in 1759 over the French Marquis de Montcalm on the Plains of Abraham near Quebec. Both generals died in the battle.

[263] General Horatio Gates' defeat of the British under Lieutenant-General Sir John Burgoine (or Burgoyne) at Saratoga, New York, in 1777. The battle of Saratoga is regarded as the turning point of the American Revolution.

[264] The British Major-General Lord Charles Cornwallis (1738–1805) achieved a famous victory over General Horatio Gates at Camden in South Carolina in 1780.

[265] James Madison (1751–1836), fourth President of the United States (1809–1817). There was a surge of nationalism after America won the war.

[266] John Fothergill Waterhouse graduated from Harvard Medical School in 1813.

[267] James Mease was a graduate of the University of Pennsylvania Medical School and a surgeon during the 1812 war. He was also an officer of the Philadelphia Society for Promoting Agriculture and delivered the first lectures in Veterinary Medicine in 1814. The University of Pennsylvania School of Veterinary Medicine was established in part due to the influence of Mease and the Society.

[JCL]

Endorsed: From Dr. White,[268] Oct. 3 1784, Manchester. done

Dr. Lettsom
Basinghall Street
London

Mr. White presents his most respectful Compliments to Dr. Lettsom, and begs leave to return him his best thanks for his Edition of the late Dr. Fothergill's works.

Mr. W. takes this opportunity of introducing his son to Dr. Lettsom.[269] He has been spending his summer on the Continent and is now returned to London to perfect himself in Anatomy under the direction of Mr. Cruikshank.[270]

Manchester
Oct.[ber] 3 1784

[JCL]

Endorsed: From B. Wilmer, July 25 1796, Coventry. Answered. July 31 1796

Coventry 25 July 1796

---

[268] Charles White (1728–1813), surgeon and obstetrician in the north of England, studied medicine in London with William Hunter and in Edinburgh. After graduating he went into partnership with his father, Thomas White (1696–1776), a local physician. In 1752, he founded the Manchester Royal Infirmary with Joseph Bancroft, where he worked for thirty-eight years as a surgeon. In 1762, he was made a fellow of the Royal Society and a member of the Corporation of Surgeons. He was involved in the founding of a college of science, literature and art, in 1783, where he and his son, Thomas, lectured in anatomy. Later, in 1790, with his son and Edward and Richard Hall, he also helped to found Manchester's first "lying-in" hospital, close to the Old Bailey Prison in Salford, where he was surgeon for twenty-one years. He had an immense reputation as a man-midwife obstetrician and published his experiences in *The management of pregnant and lying-in women*, London, printed for Edward and Charles Dilly, 1773. His *An account of the regular gradation in man, and in different animals and vegetables*, London, C. Dilly, 1799, is regarded as an important work in the history of anthropology.

[269] White had three sons with his wife, Ann Bradshaw: Thomas White, Charles White and John Bradshaw White. Both Thomas (1763–93) and John Bradshaw (1771–99) followed their father into medicine. Thomas, like his father, studied in London and at Edinburgh, where he gained an M.D. and also practised as a man-midwife. He worked in the Manchester infirmary and the Lying-in hospital. John Bradshaw became medical officer at the Manchester Lying-in Hospital. Given the date of this letter and their respective ages, he must be referring to Thomas.

[270] William Cumberland Cruikshank (1745–1800) was William Hunter's anatomical assistant in his dissecting rooms in Great Windmill Street, London. In 1770, he became Hunter's partner, succeeding William Hewson. He published extensively on anatomical topics.

Sir,

I return you my sincere thanks for the ingenious pamphlets you were so good to send me some time since. I find myself much obliged also for the wish you express for a continuance of our Correspondence. There is now so large a collection of medical and surgical cases published, that it is difficult to select from private practice any that are either new or instructive. A surgeon of this Town did lately after a variety of sufferings which were attributed to water in the chest or Pericardiasm. But upon dissection no water was found in his chest. In the right auricle of the Heart was found a fleshy substance, which probably was the cause of death. This case resembled that published by Dr. Cheston; it also proves that the late Dr. Hunter was mistaken when he asserted that these concretions were the effect, <u>not</u> the cause of death.

A very worthy member of your society, John Cash, is at present under my care for a difficulty of deglutition. I ~~mentioned to~~ informed him yesterday that I was going to write to you, and that I should mention his case, at which he expressed much satisfaction. If you will be so good to send us your opinion and advice, both he and I shall be much obliged to you. He is about 50 years of age, and has enjoyed good health till the beginning of the present year. Four months ago he perceived that his food lodged above his stomach. This difficulty increased, and after some time he found it necessary to make efforts to bring it up. In this struggle, part of the food comes up, and he has a sensation as if part of it passed by the obstruction into the stomach. One day, being very sick, the contents of the stomach were forced through the obstructed part, but much difficulty occurred during this operation. Upon the whole, though he can swallow fluids, he is evidently getting worse, and has lost of his weight 24 Pounds. Seven or eight cases nearly similar have fallen within my observation, and they have all proved fatal. During the last month I have put him upon a mercurial course and have kept up during the greatest part of the time a gentle spitting by giving a grain of Calomel twice, thrice or four times a day. At the commencement of the spitting the disease appeared to give way, but this amendment has not been lasting.

Should you think the polypus case worthy your attention, I will endeavour to collect the particulars and am, with much esteem,
Your obliged humble servant
B: Wilmar [*sic*]

2. [JCL]

Endorsed: From B. Wilmer, Nov. 24 1796, Coventry. answered.

Coventry Nov 24th 1796

Dear Sir,

The directions you gave me relative to the case I some time since consulted you about, were observed as long as they could be with propriety. The symptoms went on, progressively increasing 'till about a month after I wrote to you, when a suppuration took place.

A considerable quantity of pus mixt with membranous filaments were discharged. This alteration produced not the least amendment, nor was he ever sensible that any thing taken into the Oesophagus found its way into the stomach. Nutritive Glysters appeared to keep up his strength till within this last fortnight when he died literally starved.

The day before his death he was much convulsed. I had no opportunity of examing the state of the parts, but the suppuration clearly shows the propriety of your opinion that the disease was occasion by some Tumor shutting up the [-]ake[?] of the Oesaphagus.

Mrs. Cash wishes you to accept the enclosed Fee with her thanks.

I am, dear Sir, your very obedient obliged servant

B. Wilmer

[JCL]

Endorsed: From Edward Withers, Sept. 7 1782, Newbury. answered.

To
Dr. Lettsom

Newbury Sepr. 7th

Sir,

I have thought it proper to transmit to you some account of your Patient, Mr. Clerk; this indeed happen'd, which may probably incline you to vary the method last prescribed. He bore his Journey Home pretty well, and early in the morning a Bleeding at the nose came on which continued for about two hours, however he seemed not at all the worse for it that following Day, and he continued as well as when he left Town until four or five Days since, the method you recommended agreeing very well with him. Wednesday night last he passed very indifferently getting very little sleep, and suffering great Pain in his Head, making also a large Chamber pot full of water, indeed that secretion has been upon the whole more copious since he left Town. On this account he has omitted the Millepede's Wine since Wednesday. Too great Exertion in Business, too much Company and too long Exposure in the Sun through the Day I believe contributed towards his Bad night.

He had last night a return of Vomiting and purging owing I presume to the Quantity, as well as Quality of what he had ate in the Day, and this morning he had a Return of the nasal Hamorhage to a considerable Degree. However, it was soon stop'd by a topical application, otherwise I had taken a few Ounces of blood from the arm. His Bowels being uneasy betwixt whiles I have directed him a saline Dr. with Rhubarb to be taken to night, and on account of the hamorhage, and the Heat of the Weether have for the present suspended the use of his Chalybeete Medicine.

Sunday Morn

The Rhubarb Draught has operated thrice and left his Bowels much easier, but he was alarmed this morning on passing off from the Urethra some fibrous Blood on straining for a stool. And just now another clot passed off on making water. He has slept tolerably but complains of being weak. His tongue is somewhat white, has a little thint, Pulse about 88. I have directed him a saline Dr. with $3 \times$ Decoct. Cost.

4

Letters from Lettsom

The letters transcribed and printed here owe their coherence only to the fact that they are all from Lettsom and are in the Medical Society of London. They come from separate collections and cover a range of matters, largely philanthropic and medical. Many are in draft. They show scarcely any overlap with the correspondence printed in our 'Letters to Lettsom' section, hence our decision to publish them separately. Within this section, however, the letters to John Nichols and his son form an identifiable group. John Nichols (1745–1826) was a printer, Fellow of the Society of Antiquaries of London, Edinburgh and Perth, and owner and editor of the *Gentleman's Magazine*. Nichols and his son, John Bowyer Nichols, traded under the imprint "John Nichols and Son" between 1800 and 1811 and as "Nichols, Son and Bentley" between 1812 and 1819. Lettsom published a great deal in the *Gentleman's Magazine* and had occasion to be involved in the publication of other authors there. Nichols also published other material of Lettsom's as books and pamphlets. The letters to Nichols mainly cluster around two subjects. First, prison reform, with which Lettsom was actively involved. In this work he was closely associated with the prison reformer, James Neild. Lettsom published a series of seventy-seven letters on prisons in the *Gentleman's Magazine*. Although there are sixteen letters from Neild to Lettsom in our 'Letters to Lettsom' section and some of them do deal with prisons, we have no letters from Lettsom to Neild. All Lettsom's references to Neild in what follows are in letters to Nichols. It seemed more sensible then to keep all letters from Lettsom separate rather than intersperse them with letters from Neild. Matters concerning prison reform are elucidated in detail in our footnotes at the appropriate points. The second matter to which much of the correspondence with Nichols was devoted was the affairs of the Royal Humane Society, an organization with which Lettsom was actively involved. The magazine was an important vehicle for bringing the Society's business to public attention. The Society's activities are detailed in our footnotes. We have arranged the letters from Lettsom chronologically.

1. [CF]

[No addressee]
~~Vol 5, Folio 91~~

Jan. 22 1788

The opposition to the slave business extends rapidly, and we shall make an excellent stand in the house of Commons. The object will not yet be carried, but it may prepare the way for the melioration of the chains, and gradually work total emancipation from them, and an abolition of future traffick in living blood. When I came of age the only property I possessed was a little land and some slaves; to the latter I gave freedom, when I had not 50£ besides in the world. I never repeated this sacrifice; indeed heaven has cancelled it long ago, by refunding innumerable unmeritted blessings, and what I estimate still more gratefully, a heart to diffuse them. Though I practiced but five months in Tortola, I acquired nearly £2000,[1] one half I gave to my mother; the other brought me to London, where I knew no individual. I had no address, no person or figure to show off, no relation whatever.[2] In short, I might have tumbled out of a balloon from the clouds and met with as many friends. I have not the presumption to suppose that such an object as I feel myself, when contemplating infinite perfection and goodness, could merit my present blessings; but I hope it is not presumption to thank him that blesses me, for rewarding my humble imitation of his beneficence. I did not liberate my slaves from any advices of our society. I do not say it was from religious motives, merely as such, I had early read much. I had considered the tenets of different religions and professions, and I thought there was only one true Religion consisting in doing unto others, as we wished that others should do unto us. A demure face and all the sanctimonious exteriors of individuals I appreciated as nothing, where beneficence was wanting. I hope to die in this

---

[1] Lettsom returned to Tortola to practise in 1767, which he did for only six months. £2,000 was an incredible amount for a relatively inexperienced practitioner to earn in so short a period. On Lettsom in Tortola, see James Johnston Abraham, *Lettsom: his life, times, friends and descendants*, London, William Heinemann, 1933, pp. 49–64. For an account of the family in Tortola, see Alan Waller Woodruff, 'Lettsom and his family in Tortola', *Proceedings of the Royal Society of Medicine*, Section of the History of Medicine, 1973, **66**: 7–12.

[2] While he certainly had no blood relations in London, the rest of this assertion is quite inaccurate. Lettsom was able to begin practising in London because of the friendship and patronage of Samuel Fothergill who befriended him during his schooling in Lancaster and who sent him to London with a letter of introduction to John Fothergill. See Lettsom's own 'Recollections or reminiscences' published here.

religion, not having yet found a better. These sentiments overcame worldly interest, and I was a voluntary beggar at 21.

Pardon these Egotisms and believe me to be affectionately thine.

J. C. Lettsom

2. [E]

Dr. L May 14 1791

Dr. Sutcliffe[3]
Sheffield

My Dear Friend,

I begin this letter, under the pressure of much business, and the want of time to ensure today's post; on account of an application made to me by Mrs. Nowell's attorney, a friend also of mine in Basinghall Street to pay her bond off, for £50. I request to know of thee what to do, The bond is due to Friend Squire; it is in my custody.

I am much to my shame, and to my loss, three letters in debt to thee. The first of Jan. 23. mentions Thomas Camm, as likely to make a good servant. I imagine he was engaged by W. Lawson. I generally keep 8 or 10 men at my Villa at Grove Hill[4] and might as a labourer employ any recommendation of thine, as I am sometimes putting up, and at others pulling down, so that I am

---

[3] Lettsom's former master. On Sutcliff, see the 'Recollections or reminiscences' published here, and Abraham, op. cit., note 1 above, pp. 20–1, 24–5.

[4] Lettsom purchased $2\frac{1}{4}$ acres of land on the east side of "The Grove" in Camberwell and built a country villa there in 1779. The house was almost at the top of Grove Hill and was approached by a tree-lined avenue known as Camberwell Grove. The library and museum were open to medical practitioners on Saturdays and he frequently used to hold social gatherings for professionals, for which see 'A rural retreat ... given by Dr. Lettsom, at Grove-hill, Camberwell', *Gentleman's Magazine*, 1804, **74** (i): 473–4. When John Fothergill died in 1780, Lettsom purchased some of his greenhouses and a large number of his tropical plants, for which see John Coakley Lettsom, *Hortus Uptonensis; or, a catalogue of stove and green-house plants, in Dr. Fothergill's garden at Upton*, [London, s.n., 1783?]. By 1792, when his property was surveyed, Lettsom had increased his landholdings to ten acres. A pleasure garden of about an acre was placed immediately behind the house, facing south. Adjacent to it was the kitchen garden, including fruit trees, and hot houses. Adjoining this was the *arbustum* or plantation which contained over 400 European plants along its path, arranged in the Linnaean system and over 100 more fruit trees. On another side of the house was a bowling green. Lettsom also produced a large quarto volume entitled *Grove-Hill: a rural and horticultural sketch*, London, printed by Stephen Couchman, 1804. It includes a catalogue of the fruit trees in the garden and a catalogue of plants. A copy of this is bound into the volume of letters 'Dr. John Coakley Lettsom 1744–1815', bequeathed to the Medical Society of London by Sir Thomas Colyer-Fergusson.

enabled to employ many poor people. Thou would not now know Grove-hill. I have purchased the land to Camberwell; made a canal on the hill, and a bason of water and fountain, between my house and the town of Camberwell. The alterations of last year cost me about £8000, but I can, however, gratify thee, with the money mentioned in thy letter, and when the amount shall be £500, thou may keep it, under a bond, at thy own interest, for it has always been and continues to be the greatest pleasure of my life to evince my readiness to serve thee and thy family in every point of view. I have ever felt a pride in owning thee as my Master, and by thy principles I have felt how much I have been indebted to thee. William Hargraves still resides with me, and is much valued. I had proposed to have his sister with me at his request, but I concluded upon the whole that she would be happier where she is, and at all events probably safer. Give me sometime thy opinion on this matter.

With respect to Burke, and the political state and government of this country, I believe we have only one mind. I think we differ about Hastings, but I dare say we shall not long do so.[5] My dear and intimate friend Dr. Sims,[6] was a violent opponent to Hastings. In vain I told him there was not one ~~sit~~ single charge proved, though much declamation and abuse substituted—that India not only was saved by Hastings, but that the country said to be ruined, is the most flourishing in India—that the people injured by him, have universally acknowledged their gratitude for his patronage and protection—that his political measures are adopted by Lord Cornwallis, who by the bye has not half his abilities—that his seizure of the Begum's treasury, kept our army from a mutiny, and saved Bengal—that the contract for bullocks was wise, and that the defeat of Colonel Lloyd now shews it. All these irrefragable proofs, had not effect on the doctor, till he read Burke's book and mad[e] speeches on the French Revolution the most glorious in history—and now he is convinced that Burke is no more to be depended upon, as his wild imagination can conjure up facts where none existed, and substitute crimes for virtues.[7] It would give me pleasure to find thee a convert to Hastings, who

---

[5] Warren Hastings (1732–1818), governor-general of Bengal 1772–84, see note 208 in the 'Letters to Lettsom' section.

[6] James Sims (1741–1820) joined the Medical Society of London on 13 July 1773. By 5 October of the same year, he had been appointed the third member of the Committee (along with Lettsom, and John Millar, the first president) responsible for codifying the laws of the institution. See James Sims, *A discourse on the best method of prosecuting medical enquiries; delivered before the medical society of London, at their annual meeting, on Tuesday, January 18, 1774*, London, printed by H. Hart, 1774. Sims was appointed the third physician to the Aldersgate Dispensary (or the General Dispensary) in 1774. He was also associated with the Inoculation Dispensary.

[7] Edmund Burke (1729–97), philosopher and independent Whig MP, author of *Reflections on the Revolution in France: and on the proceedings in certain societies in London relative to that event* (1790).

will sometime appear, one of the first characters of modern times. Mr. Pitt, who is an arch prerogative man,[8] must have sufferred this impeachment to employ and amuse the opposition, and to keep Hastings from the board of control for India, when no man in this kingdom is so fit for that office as this great character, thus excluded by impeachment, equally cruel, and in matter, unfounded. Thy letter of the 29th of January, introduced a syphilitick patient, who I hope was satisfied with my attention.

Thy last letter of May 28 mentioned thy resolution not to part with thy navigation shares, which I am glad of, and I mean to keep mine also.

I have known some go to America under views similar to those of thy son, and they have returned with disappointment.[9] I conceive America an excellent place for a farmer or labourer with 50 or £100, to buy land, and improve it for his posterity, but as to getting into a mercantile or counting house, I fear there are more clouds than sunshine. I have my fears that it will not succeed, but recommendations, were they necessary, I can give, and procure.

I expect to hear from my nephew by the present G. India ship, as I suppose he wrote by her. I wish our correspondence may not be diminished. I usually am 100 letters behind hand, but I am working hard to overtake time—alas however in vain. It will overtake me, but till then let us commune together.

I have got over one troublesome affair—the question of the Medical Society "What diseases are most prevalent in great towns, and the best means of obviating them". I answered, and gained the Fothergillian Medal.[10] My work is 600 folio pages—when did I write it? In my carriage chiefly—from business I leave no relaxation—I must die in the shafts or thills.[11] Remember me to Mistress and the whole family. We are all well at Grove-hill, and am affectionately,

J. C. Lettsom

London
May 14 1791

---

[8] William Pitt, the younger (1759–1806).

[9] Abraham Sutcliff and his wife, Sarah Barnes of Langford, had five sons, Samuel (1754), Robert (1757), William (1759), John (1762) and Richard (1764), at least one of whom did not survive. The middle son, William, took over his father's practice at Settle, after he retired to Sheffield. It was, presumably, therefore, one of Sutcliff's other surviving three sons who went to America. See Abraham, op. cit., note 1 above, p. 27.

[10] See the Introduction to this volume, p. 3.

[11] The thin strata of fire-clay underlying coal seams.

3. [JCL][12]

Endorsed: To Dr. Zimmerman,[13] July 21 1794, Hanover. P.

Dear and Respected Friend,

Thy letter, for which thou makes an apology on account of its length, ~~and~~ I have repeatedly perused, and as often lamented that I had not more to read. I felt indeed a proud pleasure in experiencing so much ~~affection~~ notice from a ~~philosophers whose celebrity~~ person whose literary productions have ~~been~~ arrested the attention of potentates and philosophers [whose celebrity?] must have entailed upon him a ~~great~~ more extensive correspondence, than a man whose moments are so precious to the world at large, could sacrifice to the importunities of individuals. It brought to my recollection a saying of Ned Hyde, as he was called before he ~~became~~ was created Lord Clarendon,[14] that he never thought so highly of himself as when he was the least in the company, and so I feel from the honour done me by such correspondents as a Zimmerman.[15]

I have to request thy acceptance of a few pamphlets, which our friend de Luc[16] has the goodness to take the care of. I have not yet had leisure to enlarge upon the yellow fever of Philadelphia, but I am collecting all the facts I can upon the subject. ~~If however~~ The Gentleman's Magazine for April, herewith sent, contains a little essay of mine on Human dissections under the signature of one of the Faculty.[17] It is merely a jeu d'esprit, without any other merit.

---

[12] A draft letter with alterations and substitutions. This letter is reproduced in Thomas Joseph Pettigrew, *Memoirs of the life and writings of the late John Coakley Lettsom, with a selection from his correspondence*, 3 vols, London, printed by Nichols, Son, and Bentley, for Longman, Hurst, Rees, Orme and Brown, 1817, vol. 2, pp. 484–91.

[13] The Swiss physician, Johann Georg von Zimmerman (1728–1795) studied at Gottingen where he took the degree of doctor of medicine. After travelling in Holland and France he set up practice in his home town of Brugg in the canton of Argau. His books *Uber die Einsamkeit* (1756) and *Vom Nationalstolz* (1758) were extremely well received in Germany and translated widely into most European languages. In 1768, he became physician to George III in the court at Hanover. In 1788, he attended Augustus (1773–1843), the fifteen-year-old son of George III, when he fell ill. He attended Frederick the Great of Prussia in his last illness and wrote a number of books about him.

[14] Edward Hyde, first Earl of Clarendon (1609–1674), English historian and statesman.

[15] The "s" of correspondents and the final "a" before Zimmerman are crossed out with pencil (probably by T. J. Pettigrew) so that it reads: "by such correspondent as Zimmerman".

[16] Jean André de Luc (1727–1817), Swiss geologist and meteorologist. He came to live in England in 1773, leaving behind business problems and devoting himself entirely to scientific pursuits. He was appointed a fellow of the Royal Society in the year that he arrived and also became reader to Queen Charlotte, an honour which came with an income.

[17] 'Reflexions on human dissections', *Gentleman's Magazine*, 1794, **64** (i): 134.

There are only two parts of the 4th volume of Medical Memoirs yet published, which I have enclosed.[18] The third part is in the press, and will include a ~~paper~~ memoir of mine on the prison of our Newgate with the plan of a hed for their use.[19]

With respect to the German language, I never was acquainted with it, and painfully experiencing this inconvenience, I sent my eldest son two years to a German University, and who speaks it fluently. I requested him to return by Hanover purposely to see thee, but submitting his rout to the inclination of his companions, the opportunity was lost, and I fear will never again offer.

Some days ago, I gave a seat in my coach to a patient of mine who is a German. He pulled out of his pocket as his companion to read in travelling Zimmerman on the pride of nations. I immediately applied to him to make a translation, which I think he will do, not as a bookseller's labourer, but as a Classical gentleman above pecuniary emolument.[20] He and Dilly[21] dined yesterday with me at my Tusculum.[22]

I ought to have observed that with my packet is the life of my late patron, Dr. Fothergill.[23] We were born and educated Quakers (~~Les Amis~~ Friends) ~~but~~ I trust I ~~tr~~ entertain no narrow selfish notions of Religion, as I believe all are ~~all~~ equally children of one supreme beneficent creator—equally regarded by their common parent in proportion to their intellectual improvement. Indeed,

---

[18] Lettsom is referring to the *Memoirs of the Medical Society of London: instituted in the year 1773*. Six volumes of the *Memoirs* were published in London between 1787 and 1805 by Charles Dilly. Volume four was published in 1794.

[19] The memoir was also published separately: J. C. Lettsom, *Hints respecting the prison of Newgate*, London, printed by Darton and Harvey, 1794.

[20] Zimmerman's *Strictures on national pride* had been published in England some two decades earlier in 1771 and the first American edition in Philadelphia in 1778. The book was a study of national pride that advocated cosmopolitanism and a tolerant attitude. However, the reference here is probably to Johann Georg Zimmerman, *Essay on national pride; to which are added memoirs of the author's life and writings, translated from the original German of the late celebrated Dr. J. G. Zimmerman, by Samuel Hull Wilcocke*, London, printed for C. Dilly, 1797. Thanks to Sibylle Naglis for assistance with this reference.

[21] Charles Dilly and his elder brother Edward were booksellers with a shop in the Poultry in London, who published on medical topics. Edward was interested in politics and spent a lot of his time talking, while Charles was a modest man. He loved to entertain both authors and friends, and when away on business that pleasure was sometimes deputized to his friend James Boswell. He was a frequent visitor to Lettsom's villa in Camberwell. Charles published material for the Royal Humane Society, for example, Charles Kite, *An essay on the recovery of the apparently dead, being the essay to which the Humane Society's Medal was adjudged. To which is prefixed, Dr. Lettsom's address on the delivery of the Medal*, London, C. Dilly, 1788. When Charles Dilly died in 1807, he left Lettsom £500 in his will. See Abraham, op. cit., note 1 above, pp. 94–5, 310.

[22] Tusculum was the name of the villa of Marcus Tullius Cicero (*c.*106–43 B.C.), Roman statesman, orator and philosopher.

[23] John Coakley Lettsom, *The works of John Fothergill*, 3 vols, London, printed for Charles Dilly, 1783–84, vol. 3.

I have often thought that if any thing we could do could possibly add to the pleasure of ~~the~~ our Author, it would be to see the ~~individua~~ individual 3000 different religions (for so many there are supposed to exist) adoring him ~~with~~ in different modes, for the sacred mount of ~~suprem~~ divin~~de~~ mercy is accessible every way to the humble traveller. I even think there are not two natural objects in the whole universe exactly similar. There are not two bodies, nor do I believe there are two minds. Hence we should hear and forbear with each other, and ~~detes~~ avoid every species of persecution for opinion, as well as for difference of bodily construction, or difference of age.

I believe that our Society, though respected in England and America, is almost unknown to you. In France we were <u>once</u> respected, and I remember, when I visited Macquer—Daubuctou—Le Roie and Derbourgh in my youth with letters from Franklin, Dubourgh said to me "I thought Franklin had been a Quaker and I did not like him better when he told me he was not["].[24] The short sketch of thy life gave me singular pleasure, ~~I thought I could perceive~~ because, although I could perceive a bodily constitution much broken down, there remained a natural vigour that triumphed ~~th~~ over the material system[25] and reminded me of an observation applied to Dr. Humbert[26] by thy late royal patient, Frederick the Great—while he entered the other world he continued to teach the members of this. Happy indeed is it for the community that thou hast thus cheated away the tædia vitae, by raising monuments to laudable fame, by thy instruction and philosophic works, and realized the beautiful theory of our Bolingbrok on retirement.[27]

I should but sympathize with thee on the murders thou hast suffered by Translators, but do not regard a cloud in the atmosphere, which shades for a time even the meridian sun. The refulgent power will ~~resist~~ resist and dissipate the haze. ~~I cry t~~ Time is the arbiter of things, and truth will prevail when we can no longer defend ourselves. Linnaeus waded as he was, when he first ~~made a~~ waterd his vegetable creation, wisely observed.[28]

---

[24] Benjamin Franklin (1706–1790), printer and natural philosopher.

[25] Zimmerman died in 1795.

[26] Claude Humbert Piarron de Chamousset (1717–73), reformer and philanthropist, spent his entire fortune of 500,000 livres in philanthropic activities, especially in providing hospital expenses for the poor. His complete works were collected by the Abbé Cotton des Houssayes, librarian at the Sorbonne. See Claude Humbert Piarron de Chamousset, *Vues d'un citoyen*, Paris, Lambert, 1757.

[27] Henry St. John, first Viscount Bolingbroke (1678–1751), *The true use of retirement* (1738). Most surviving copies are of the 1752 French edition: *Lettre de mylord Bolingbroke à mylord Bathurst, sur le veritable usage de la retraite & de l'étude. Traduite de l'anglois* [by J. Barbeu Dubourg], Berlin, Etienne de Bourdeaux, 1752.

[28] This sentence is crossed through in pencil and does not appear in Pettigrew's version of this letter.

I ~~had~~ was about to close this letter, when I received one from Dr. Seybert[29] whose ~~observation~~ relation of thy kind reception binds me under renewed obligation, as thou will suppose from the following extract of his letter.

4. [JCL][30]

Endorsed: Abuse of Mr. Pitt N.P.

To Dr. Thornton,[31] Aug. 10 1794, Philadelphia

About the time thy letters came to my hand, I imagine ~~might~~ mine would arrive at Philadelphia, so that in the only sense in which distant friends can converse, we should at this time be conversing together. Under what equitorial degree they met in their different routes I cannot ascertain, but I should imagine from their unaffected cordiality, it would under the sign of Gemini and on a calm unruffled sea. Thy last indeed dated Feb. 21 which was warm if not violent in politics, must have occasioned a little turbulence in the ocean, ~~as they and raised a white spray~~ with bocaps and sprays as they passed each other, and even had thy letter contained no politics, the ocean will be turbulent and will have calms, and so it in kingdoms and so it was, and so it will, for although prophets ~~and~~ have said that swords shall be made into plowshares, ~~and~~ but till the nature of man is changed, the effects will continue.[32]

I think as meanly of Pitt as thou doest, and his whole political career has ~~been~~ born the aspect of a noisy orator, with a superficial head, that is great in cunning and little in great national concerns. Had he possessed a capacious

---

[29] Adam Seybert, M.D. (1773–1825), a physician and chemist who had a pharmacy in Philadelphia. Seybert was in Europe at some time before 1797, where he continued his education. His commonplace book for 1810 is held in the American Philosophical Society Library in Philadelphia, Pennsylvania, B Se95.

[30] A draft letter.

[31] The West Indian-born physician Dr. William Thornton (1759–1828) was a graduate of Edinburgh University. Like Lettsom, he was born in the Quaker settlement of Jost van Dyke. Thornton's classically inspired and domed design was chosen by the President, George Washington, for the Capitol building in Washington. He was awarded $500. Thornton also designed Library Hall (1789–90), home of the Library Company in Philadelphia. See Elinor Stearns and David N. Yerkes, *William Thornton: a Renaissance man in the federal city*, Washington, DC, American Institute of Architects Foundation [c.1976], and C. M. Harris, *Papers of William Thornton*, Charlottesville, VA, University Press Virginia, 1995.

[32] "And they shall beat their swords into ploughshares and their spears into pruning hooks. Nation shall not lift up sword against nation, neither shall they learn war any more". Isaiah 2: 2–4.

mind, with integrity, he would not have suited our Cabinet. ~~He~~ With little sense, he might have foresen that the present French Crusade was impolitic and impracticable. It was incongruously organized like Nabuchadnezzar's image, and must tremble to pieces.[33] He raised himself by opposing the American Crusades, and prating for a reform in Parliament when in power. ~~As soon as he secured~~ In power he has plunged the nation into another frantic crusade, out of which he cannot extricate it without humiliating sacrifices. He spent 4 millions sterling for an acre of land at Nootka Sound, and was laughed at by Spain.[34] He spent one million to frighten the empress from Oozahow, while she ridiculed him for his folly of presuring t[w]o men of war into the narrow and inhospitable Baltick.[35] He has already lavished 35 millions to shut the Scheldt when it would have been worth 5 millions to have it opened, as a ~~port~~ mart for our manufactures.[36] He has suspended the Habeas

---

[33] Daniel 2: 31–34 refers to the dream of Nebuchadnezzar, king of Babylon, who built an empire in the ancient Middle East. In the dream was revealed a great image with a head of gold, arms of silver, belly and thighs of brass, legs of iron and feet partly of iron and partly of clay. The image was smashed into tiny pieces by a stone, which then grew into a mountain and filled the earth. The dream was interpreted by Daniel, who said that the king's own powerful kingdom represented the head of gold, but that, afterwards, other inferior kingdoms would arise, the last of which, like iron and clay, would be partly strong and partly broken.

[34] Between 1789 and 1794, a diplomatic dispute occurred between Britain and Spain for control of the northwest coast of Canada. Spain asserted its claim to the whole west coast of America and, in 1774, an expedition anchored off Nootka Sound. Britain's claim was based on a visit made by James Cook to the coast of British Columbia that stopped at Nootka in 1778. In 1789, a Spanish expedition under Estéban José Martínez built a fort at Nootka Sound, seized British fur trading vessels and imprisoned their crews in Mexico. The Spanish proclaimed their possession of the entire area. John Meares, a retired naval lieutenant who sponsored the traders, stirred up political and public opinion in England, trying to encourage the government to extract compensation. The Cabinet resolved to demand satisfaction. Taking advantage of the fact that France, Spain's traditional ally in Europe, was not in a position to assist due to the French Revolution, Pitt threatened war on the principle of freedom of the seas and the right of Britons to trade where there were no established foreign settlements. However, on 28 October 1790, war was averted when Spain signed the Nootka Sound Convention, agreeing to restore British property and to grant the British access to the northwest coast. Matters were not eventually resolved until the signing of the Convention for the Mutual Abandonment of Nootka on 11 January 1794, which again confirmed British access to the coast for trading purposes. The Spanish fort was dismantled in the following year. See Christon I. Archer, 'Retreat from the north: Spain's withdrawal from Nootka Sound, 1793–1795', *BC Studies*, 1978, **37**: 19–36.

[35] One of Peter the Great's (1682–1725) main aims was to expand Russia's Baltic shores, a policy continued by Catherine the Great (1762–96). She also fought a short war against Sweden, in 1790, in which Sweden hoped to regain territory that it had previously lost at the Finnish border. The Swedes were unsuccessful and relinquished their attempt by the Treaty of Värälä, signed on 3 August 1790. Catherine commented: "One paw we have pulled out of the mud". At the same time, perturbed by the growing power of Russia, Pitt put forward the idea of a united federation of all northern European countries, but had to abandon his policy as problems loomed with revolutionary France. See John T. Alexander, *Catherine the Great: life and legend*, Oxford University Press, 1989, pp. 279–82.

[36] In 1792, the French allowed free navigation on the Scheldt estuary within Dutch territory and opened the port of Antwerp to international shipping. In doing so, the French Republic was

Corpus Act, and affirmed that the king can bring in foreign troops without consent of parliament; and in short I consider him as a worse minister that [*recte* than] Lord North[37] was. Granting all this, I do not go the length of thy letter. If all men were Thorntons, the world would be happy; but the great mistake in politics is that virtuous men seem to suppose that virtue may become general in a nation. In all governments, a wise legislator will take men as they are, Solon said.[38] He did not make Laws which he though the best, but they were the best the people could bear. We have read of free states, but where is Sparta, Athens or Rome? Every state has within the seeds of depravity, like as every man, said a wise prince, has a wild beast within him that requires chaining. All men have passions, ~~h~~and Fenelon, in the gloom of mysticism remarked ~~Les passions~~ "La vertu en dirige[a]nt nos passions n'éteint pas le sentiment."[39] The great art of government is to direct these passions to noble actions. However impolitic the conduct of our Ministry may be, were the original constitution maintained, I think ours one of the best suited to the frailty and folly—to the virtue and dignity of human nature. I thought much of governments, and in a state like ours, where talents may rise to accept or refuse titles and emoluments, a stimulus is given to the energy of the mind, which perhaps otherwise would sink into depravity and littleness. The greatest politician in Europe, Lord Shelburn,[40] said when we lost America—"The sun of England was set forever". To compare America with any populous country is not candid. In the latter, labour is ~~chea~~ Cheap and provisions dear. In a new Country with few Inhabitants and spare lands, labor is dear and provisions cheap. Here America has a specious superiority, but in a small extent like England's many inhabitants, there is increased energy, and velocity augments in a geometrical ratio. A million of men in a small extent of territory will often defeat 2 millions in a great extent, as history proves. Besides, England possesses within itself sources of inexhaustible wealth independent of her wool, corn, lead ~~and~~ tin and Iron. She has two articles

---

rescinding a long-established right of the Dutch. Britain entered the war against revolutionary France in opposition to this opening, as an ally of the Dutch, since French control of Holland would lead to France being Britain's main maritime rival. John Holland Rose, *William Pitt and the great war*, London, G. Bell and Sons, 1911, pp. 71–2, 79.

[37] Frederick North (1732–92), eighth Baron North, fourth Earl of Guildford, Whig politician and Prime Minister (1770–82).

[38] Solon (638–539 B.C.) Athenian politician and lawmaker.

[39] François de Salignac de la Mothe Fénelon (1651–1715), archbishop of Cambrai (1695), a celebrated theologian and author. In 1689, he became tutor to the Duke of Burgundy, grandson of Louis XIV and future king of France, and wrote his *Fables, dialogues des morts and Télémaque*, in which he taught the prince the qualities and attributes necessary for his position. They were not published at the time. Lettsom was possibly quoting from Fénelon's, *Dialogues des morts anciens et modernes: avec quelques fables, composez pour l'education d'un prince*, Paris, Chez Florentin Delaulne, 1721.

[40] See Shelburne's correspondence in the 'Letters to Lettsom' section.

overlooked by politicians, which will always render her the first power in the world of the same extent—these are coals and salt. The last is the most prolific article to vegetation—the other is the source of every manufactory that requires as Iron etc. It was a saying of Kobli Khan,[41] that whoever can use Iron will ever command Gold; and it will hold good in a commercial view better than in a military one.

There are two other things will preserve the ~~freedom~~ liberty and prosperity of England—I mean the freedom of America, and our national debt. The latter, if our war continues a few years longer, will be 400 millions—the interest of which must be paid or a revolution must ensue. To raise a revenue to pay it, trade must be encouraged, but trade cannot thrive without freedom ergo, the government will promote freedom and trade to prevent a revolution. Again, America opens her bosom to Emigrants—no law, if freedom of trade be maintained can prevent emigration. What then? Government will sooner or later endeavour to obviate this, by meliorating the condition of the people.

In short, my dear friend, view mankind not as we wish them to be, but as it pleased the Almighty to make them, and as they have been since the world began, and considering that even titles may excite mental energy and velocity, I submit, with chearfulness, to our present condition, which though not quite in health, has the seeds of renovation in its constitution. Moral evils, like ~~natural~~ diseases, have often natural cures. I repeat, we must take men as they ~~eare~~ are in different situations. A mercantile nation ~~with~~ surrounded with water—a hilly country or a cold one, will ever be free—a warm valley with a luxuriant soil will tend to slavery and despotism. Voltaire well said "Events govern us; we do not govern them."[42]

5. [S]

Endorsed: To Deputy Nichols[43] in England.

Dear Brother Traveller,

I am now at our comrade's, Charles Dilly's, talking over a new addition of my Tea-plant,[44] and having our pre-dilection fixed for your press, we propose

---

[41] Kublai Khan (1214–94), the youngest son of Genghis Khan by his favourite wife, Tolui, was elected khan over the Mongols in 1260.

[42] François-Marie Arouet (dit Voltaire) (1694–1778). We have been unable to trace this quotation.

[43] John Nichols is discussed in the introduction to this section. He was known as "Deputy Nichols" because he was deputy to John Wilkes in the London Ward of Farringdon Without.

[44] J. C. Lettsom, *The natural history of the tea-tree, with observations on the medical qualities of tea, and effects of tea drinking*, London, printed for E. and C. Dilly, 1772. As soon as it

to have it immediately under its pressure; ~~but~~ and as your son is coming into business,[45] it is with us a stronger inducement to send to you; but as he is beginning business he must begin with a new type, for as all authors expect the whole world will read their performances, I can entertain no doubt of my child's admission everywhere,[46] and particularly among the Ladies, and hence I am more anxious of his appearing well drest.

I am your friend

J. C. Lettsom

Sept. 7 1799

6. [S]

~~Dear Mr. Deputy~~

In my publication, I mean to introduce the profiles of those respectable characters, who have been founders of, or particularly active in, the Institutions to be described. The revd. D. Williams was the founder of the Society for a Literary Fund,[47] and I should be very happy to have the favour of prefixing his Silhouette to the history of this interesting Society, but not having the honour of his acquaintance I am induced to trouble you to request that he would permit Mr. Myers in the Strand, to take a shade for me.[48] You

---

appeared, the book was pirated in Dublin. The edition Lettsom is discussing was indeed produced in 1799 by Charles Dilly.

[45] See the introduction to this section.

[46] "Child" is used as a metaphor for the book, but it has added poignancy in that Lettsom's first child, Mary Ann, was born on 20 June 1771, the year in which he was preparing his manuscript on the tea-tree for publication. Her birth certificate survives in the Medical Society of London, in the bound volume, 'Lettsom Relics, 1768–1810', presented by John Hugh Armstrong Elliot. There is a note on the back of the birth certificate saying that she "exhibited peculiar marks of a sweet disposition, passing some months of her infancy in a calm unruffled temper, ever upon the smile and ready to rush into the arms of those she had the least knowledge of" and recording her death on 16 March 1774.

[47] We have not found a Society for a Literary Fund but it is surely what became the Corporation of the Royal Literary Fund in 1790. Lettsom seems to have taken an interest in the project, because he published 'Hints for establishing a society for promoting useful literature', *Gentleman's Magazine*, 1780, **50** (i): 183.

[48] John Miers or Myers (1756–1821) was the most renowned English painter of miniature silhouettes during the golden age of silhouette taking (1770–1820). He had a shop at No. 62, the Strand in 1788. The trade label on his silhouette portraits read "Miers, Profile Painter and Jeweller, Exeter Change, Strand, London". See Leonard Morgan May, *A master of silhouette, John Miers: portrait artist, 1757–1821*, London, M. Secker, 1938.

know he will be in very good company—such as a Blizard[49]—a Neild[50]—a Colquhoun—and similar characters; and this permission would not only oblige me, but I trust can serve the Society by diffusing a knowledge of it.

Every head is now completed for the work, except this I now request, and I have much hope in your application, ~~to~~ as our cause is good.

I am sincerely etc.

J. C. Lettsom

~~Sambrook Court~~

Mar. 25 1801

7. [L]

To Dr. Roots
Kingston

Dear Doctor,

After having tried powerful diuretics without effect, I think it would be adviseable to avoid everything that tends to nauseate the stomach, and to endeavour to support the strength; and at the same time to interpose anodines[51] as the case may require.

---

[49] Sir William Blizard, the surgeon who founded the London Hospital Medical School. He was elected to the Medical Society of London on 13 July 1773.

[50] James Neild (1744–1814), the prison reformer who published with Lettsom on the subject in the *Gentleman's Magazine*. Neild was a jeweller by trade, having been apprenticed in 1760 to Mr. Hemming, the king's goldsmith, in London, where he developed a flair for designing ornaments. He had a business in St. James's Street by 1770, but was fascinated by prisons. Lettsom and Neild first met through a mutual interest in the Wood Street Compter, a prison for debtors. Neild had been deeply interested in such prisoners from 1762 when his elder apprentice was thrown into the King's Bench for debt. Lettsom became responsible for the medical care at the Wood Street Compter when appointed Physician to the General Dispensary in 1773. See Abraham, op. cit., note 1 above, pp. 242–65. It was mainly through Lettsom's influence with the editor of the *Gentleman's Magazine*, that Neild's accounts of the prisons he visited became widely known. Neild himself wrote that "to his [Lettsom's] suggestions alone the publishing of my prison remarks owe their origin.... If Howard owed anything to Fothergill, I am in a ten-fold degree indebted to Doctor John Coakley Lettsom". Pettigrew, op. cit., note 12 above, vol. 2, pp. 204–5. Between 1804 and 1812, Neild visited many jails in order to ameliorate and amend the prison system and create so-called "model prisons". By 1804, he was High Sheriff of Buckinghamshire and J.P. for the counties of Middlesex and Buckinghamshire, and the City and Liberty of Westminster. He was a magistrate of Aylesbury and closely connected with its jail. See C. Norton, *English laws for women in the nineteenth century*, London, printed for private circulation, 1854.

[51] Anodynes or pain-relieving drugs.

I fear tapping[52] would do no good, as th[e] whole frame is diseased; but to relieve the anararia. I see no objection to scarify the legs, if the breathing become more intolerable
I am sincerely
J. C. Lettsom

Sambrook Court
Jan. 7 1802

8. [S]

March 26, 1803

Dear Mr. Nichols,

I enclose the paper respecting Mrs. Church, which I wish you to print on the cover of the Gentleman's Magazine, the expence of which I will discharge when I meet you.

I imagine some person must have borrowed my Gentleman's Magazine, but if you could easily refer to it, I should be obliged to you, merely for the references to the volumes and pages wherein you review
"Hints designed to promote beneficence".[53]
"Apology for differing from the Reviewers".[54]
J. C. Lettsom

Mar 26. 1803.

---

[52] The drawing or tapping of accumulated watery fluid from the body, as in dropsy.

[53] Lettsom published small tracts on various subjects now and then, which he designated "Hints". He disposed of them to friends and enquirers, but finding that there was a steady demand for certain of them, he had the more popular ones reprinted and collected in three volumes in 1802 (though the imprint states 1801) under the title, *Hints, designed to promote beneficence, temperance, and medical science*, London, J. Nichols for J. Mawman, 3 vols, 1801. These tracts, on subjects as diverse as infectious fevers and the treatment of female servants, brought Lettsom into controversy with the anonymous writers in the *Monthly Review* and the *Critical Review*. See Abraham, op. cit., note 1 above, p. 384.

[54] John Coakley Lettsom, *An apology, for differing in opinion from the authors of the Monthly and Critical Reviews; on 1. Literary communications. 2. Variolous and vaccine inoculation. 3. Dr. Jenner's discovery of vaccine inoculation. 4. The means of preventing febrile contagion. 5. The establishment of charitable institutions*, London, Nichols, 1803. Later in the same year, Lettsom refuted criticisms of his 'Apology' in John Coakley Lettsom, *An appeal addressed to the calm reflection of the authors of the Critical Review: on 1. abusive language, 2. ambiguity and embarrassment, 3. espionnage and detraction, 4. the Jennerian discovery; with letters to the authors of the Monthly Review and British Critic*, London, printed by J. Nichols and Son, Red-lion Passage for J. Mawman, 1803.

9. [S]

Note: Should the quotations from Reviews and Magazines be of a smaller type?

May 7, 1803

Dear Mr. Nichols,

I enclose you another controversial MS. and I hope it will be the last I shall have to publish. It is to be printed in the manner of my "Apology", one of which I send, that the type etc., may be similar.

As I know your friendship, I should be obliged to you ~~to~~ should you cast your eye over the press to suppress what you disapprove. It has only been subjected to Dr. Jenner's[55] perusal who did not offer any single alteration, but approved it generally.

I am respectfully etc.

J. C. Lettsom

May 7 1803

10. [S]

Jan. 12 1804

Dear Mr. Deputy,

I hope you will be able to place Mr. Neild's paper in a prominent part of your next number. Both his name and the importance of the subject, merit I think, this distinction, and it certainly gratifies our mutual friend. When you print it, I must again trouble you for a dozen copies. Some I shall send to him on the next month. I trust I shall send you a paper still more interesting on prisons, and rather longer than the present one.

The paper I now return signed Philanthropos is incorrect. I shall be at home all this evening, and were you to send me a Revise, your boy might have it at 7 or 8 tomorrow mor[n]ing: But you will judge if this be requisite.

---

[55] Edward Jenner (1749–1823), see note 245 'Letters to Lettsom' section.

Besides my next letter on prisons, I shall trouble you with some observations on the Cow-pock as connected with the last year's bills of mortality. These you may have by the first of February.[56]
Respectfully etc.
J. C. Lettsom

Sambrook Court
Jan. 12 1804

11. [S]

Endorsed: July 1 1804

To
Mr. Nichols
Red Lion Passage[57]
Fleet Street.

Dear Mr. Deputy,
Mr. Maurice[58] is desirous of having the enclosed in the Gentleman's Magazine. You may act agreeably to your own pleasure.
The 8th letter on prisons is under the inspection of Mr. Neild, and I hope tomorrow, or the day after, to receive it, when it will [be] further transmitted for its intended destination[59] to your friend
J. C. Lettsom

July 1 1804

---

[56] No observations on the cow-pock by Lettsom appear in the *Gentleman's Magazine* for 1804. However, the following appear in 1808: John Coakley Lettsom, 'Letter I. Small-pox and cow-pock', *Gentleman's Magazine*, 1808, **78** (i): 191–3; 'Letter II. Small-pox and cow-pock', ibid., 1808, **78** (i): 308–9; 'Letter III. Small-pox and cow-pock', ibid., 1808, **78** (i): 507–9.

[57] The Nichols' business premises was at 48 Red Lion Passage, Fleet Street.

[58] The Rev. T. Maurice, 'Epithalamium on the marriage of Col. Elliot and Miss Lettsom', *Gentleman's Magazine*, 1804, **74** (ii); 664; *idem*, 'Epitaph on Mrs. De Medina, wife of Solomon De Medina, Esq. of Stoke Newington', ibid., p. 954. This is the same Rev. Thomas Maurice who wrote poems about Grove House, Lettsom's Camberwell residence. See, Abraham, op. cit., note 1 above, pp. 301, 304.

[59] This refers to Lettsom's 'Eighth letter on prisons', which appeared with James Neild's 'Remarks on prisons, lunaticks, &.', *Gentleman's Magazine*, 1804, **74** (ii): 607–1.

The 7th letter excepting my department does your Magazine credit.[60] The prison department has produced considerable sensation among numerous readers.[61] Should you print the Epithalamium I should thank you for a few copies, but do not print it on my account. I wish you to do nothing that can in the least atom discredit the high character of your Magazine.

12. [CF]

Endorsed: Mr. Mudford, 12 Church row, Pancras

Mr. Mudford,

I regret much that you directed your letter to Grovehill, instead of my residence, as I could then have conveniently paid you a visit on Monday (yesterday) but your letter arrived in Sambrook Court only at noon today, and I am particularly engaged both on this day, and on Wednesday, but will endeavour to see Mrs. Mudford on Thursday, when she shall be welcome to the advice of

J. C. Lettsom

Sambrook Court
Basinghall street
July 17 1804

---

[60] Lettsom's 'Seventh letter on prisons' appeared with Mr. Dale's, 'Management of the Lanark cotton mills', *Gentleman's Magazine*, 1804, **74** (i): 491–5.

[61] Lettsom is presumably referring to how the 'Letters on prisons', collectively, were received. Letters published in the magazine, in the following year, demonstrate that the public's reaction was not uniformly positive. See [Rev. Weeden Butler (Sr. or Jr.)], 'On the lucubrations of Dr. Lettsom and Mr. Neild', *Gentleman's Magazine*, 1805, **75** (i): 319; [Zachariah Cozens], 'Mr. Neild's researches into prisons encouraged', ibid., 319–21. Authorship identified from James Marquis Kuist, *The Nichols file of the* Gentleman's Magazine: *attributions of authorship and other documentation in editorial papers at the Folger Library*, Madison and London, University of Wisconsin Press, 1982, pp. 41, 53. In his letter, Butler expressed the opinion that Neild was a man of sufficient stature in himself not to require the commendatory introductions of his friend, Lettsom: "His goodness needs not, his modesty desires not, the incessant panegyricks of any individual, or of any set of men". Cozens, on the other hand, wrote in reply to Clericus Londinensis, who had said, in a letter in the *Gentleman's Magazine* (Supplement, 1804, **74** (ii): 1182–3) that he was tired of the praiseworthy and Christian-like exertions of the venerable physician and the indefatigable magistrate on behalf of unfortunate prisoners. "But", said Cozens, "I verily believe Mr. Neild might have perused his enquiries, and have made public his observations with impunity, nay, even to have brought on the *filthy* subject of the privies, which so mightily offered the olefactory nerves of the polite Clericus, had he not dared to practice the neglect of the Clergy or Magistrates, in not providing or not enforcing a due attention to the moral improvements and spiritual concerns of the prisoners."

13. [S]

Mr. Nichols
Red Lion passage
Fleet Street.

Sep. 8 1804

Dear Deputy,

I hope you have been so good as to strike off for Mr. Neild and myself, a few copies of the last letter on prisons.[62] I send you a few disputation letters between Mr. Knight[63] and myself; if you find it inconvenient to introduce them this month, perhaps you may not think them improper for the next month. The publication of them appears to me a tribute due to our deceased friend Forsyth. In a day or two I will send the conclusion, or extract of our signature to the certificate or testimonial in the last edition of his valuable work.[64]

---

[62] Lettsom's 'Tenth letter on prisons' appeared with Neild's 'Remarks on prisons in Bury, &c.', *Gentleman's Magazine*, 1804, **74** (ii): 799–801.

[63] Thomas Andrew Knight was the author of a *Treatise on the culture of the apple and pear, and the manufacture of cider and perry* (1797). In 1804, he was in contention with William Forsyth, F.S.A., His Majesty's gardener at Kensington, and author of a *Treatise on the culture and management of fruit trees* (1802). Forsyth was an authority on forestry and claimed to have invented a secret plaster that mended both holes in trees and hollow trees, bringing them "in a few years to such a state of soundness that no one could distinguish the new wood from the old". This had huge implications for the navy, and Forsyth had been paid £1,500 for his process in 1791 with the promise of another grant once its success had been verified. Knight, however, cast doubts on his process in the *Gentleman's Magazine* in 1804 and no further grant was paid. See 'Correspondence between Thomas Andrew Knight, Esq. and Dr. Lettsom, on the late Mr. Forsyth's composition for the restoration of decayed trees', *Gentleman's Magazine*, 1804, **74** (ii): 823–6; B. S. to Mr. Urban on the same subject, ibid., p. 1006; Thomas Andrew Knight, to Mr. Urban with a proposal for settling the controversy, ibid., pp. 1095–6. The magazine also drew attention to Knight's 'Experiments and observations on the motion of the sap in trees', *Philosophical Transactions of the Royal Society of London*, 1804, **i**, that he used to confirm his conjecture that the vessels of the bark were better arranged to carry fluid towards the roots than in the opposite direction, *Gentleman's Magazine*, Supplement 1804, **74** (ii): 1220. Forsyth arranged a demonstration for his friends, who included Lettsom, Nichols, William Woodville, physician to the Smallpox and Inoculation Hospital, and Astley Cooper, surgeon to Guy's Hospital. They were convinced and issued a statement in his support, which Lettsom was first to sign. Knight rose to the bait, offering a bet of 200 guineas (to be lodged with the President of the Royal Society) that Lettsom could not show him a single foot of wood thus restored after injury. As a Quaker, Lettsom wrote denouncing the wager. Not knowing that he was a Quaker, Knight apologized. Although Forsyth died on 25 August 1804, the dispute continued. The *Gentleman's Magazine* (1805, **75** (i): 513) published a picture of a cross-section of restored timber submitted by Lettsom. Commenting on the section, Knight, an experienced horticulturalist, pointed out Lettsom's errors, although acquitting him of any intention to deceive. The *Gentleman's Magazine* dropped the subject.

[64] Letter No. 4 is addressed to William Forsyth, Esq., Royal Gardens, Kensington, and fully supported the efficacy of his process for the restoration of decayed trees. He is described as

My next paper on Prisons will not exceed half the pages of the last.[65] I have not yet begun it, but I hope to have it completed by this day week at the farthest.

I am respectfully

J. C. Lettsom

Sept. 8 1804

14. [S]

To
John Nichols Esq.
Red Lion passage
Fleet Street.

Oct. 10 1804

Dear Mr. Nichols,

I address now for your candid opinion. James Neild and I could go on with our prison letters for 12 months longer, but I have long been afraid lest you and the public, should think we may say too much, or too long. It is true that we receive very flattering compliments for what we have already done, but friends you know will be partial to us, and we to ourselves. But if you think it would please the public to suspend our essay for 5 or 6 months, we shall do it. Mr. Neild and I have corresponded over this subject and wish to know your opinion, which we know will be unbiased.

At the commencement I little thought to exceed 2 or 3 papers, but the importance of Mr. Neild's communications have encouraged me to proceed beyond what I originally designed. The letters have certainly made a great impression on the public mind. Money has flowed into the Society for relieving small

---

having "had the goodness lately to give us an opportunity of examining several trees in Kensington Gardens, in the various stages of renovation, or filling up with new wood", *Gentleman's Magazine*, 1804, **74** (ii): 826. It was signed by: "John Coakley Lettsom, M.D. F.R.S. &., William Woodville, M.D., Physician to the Smallpox and Inoculating Hospitals, James Sims, M.D., President of the Medical Society of London, William Norris, Surgeon to the Charter House, &c., Joseph Hart Myers, M.D., Physician to the General Dispensary, Aldersgate Street, Astley Cooper, Surgeon of Guy's Hospital, Edward Coleman, Professor of the Veterinary College, and H. N. Willis, F.R.S."

[65] Lettsom's 'Eleventh letter on prisons' appeared with Neild's 'Remarks on prisons in Cambridge', *Gentleman's Magazine*, 1804, **74** (ii): 895–8.

debtors[66]—many of the nuisances have been removed—and many prisoners restored to liberty—many more to the amelioration of their situation.

A bookseller applied to me last week to be allowed to print them in a pamphlet which I refused; nor do I mean to take them out of the Gentleman's Magazine.

I confess that recently we had a view of describing every prison in England, Scotland and Wales, which would constitute the most minute prison history in these kingdoms. Waving, however, every other view, mine is to please the Readers of the Gentleman's Magazine without fatiguing or disgusting them, and I implicitly depend upon your judgement for the dose and the application of it to the public gratification.

The next Essay destined for your pages, is on <u>outcasts</u>, which completes the 12th.[67] I have ~~alr~~ another ready on the Lincolnshire prisons, to await your fiat or veto. As I repeat that I have no other objects than public good and private pleasure to gratify you will g[ive] you[r] veto in due time to your friend. J. C. Lettsom

Sambrook Court
Oct. 16 1804

15. [S]

To
John Nichols Esq.
or Mr. Bowyer[68]
Red Lion Court
Fleet Street.

~~Dear Mr. Nichols~~

The attack on our friend Neild ~~calls~~ in your last magazine, demands an early reply; and if it be not too late I wish the letter I now send, might appear,

---

[66] Stimulated by the sermons of the Rev. Dr. William Dodd, founder of Charlotte Chapel, Pimlico, advocating the reform of prison laws, James Neild was one of several people who formed a committee to found the Society for the Discharge and Relief of Persons Imprisoned for Small Debts in May 1773. See James Neild, *An account of the rise, progress, and present state, of the Society for the Discharge and Relief of Persons Imprisoned for Small Debts throughout England and Wales*, London, printed by Nichols and Son, 1802. Neild was elected Treasurer of the Society in 1774 and remained so until his death in 1814. It was in this capacity that he compiled his great survey of the prisons of England, that was published in the *Gentleman's Magazine* from 1801 onwards. See Abraham op. cit., note 1 above, pp. 256–7.

[67] It actually appeared in the thirteenth letter. Lettsom's 'Thirteenth letter on prisons' appeared with Neild's 'Remarks on labour in prisons', *Gentleman's Magazine*, 1804, **74** (ii): 1087–9. Lettsom's letter discussed founding an asylum for the employment and restoration of outcasts.

[68] John Bowyer was the name of John Nichols' son. When John Nichols died in 1826, the *Gentleman's Magazine* was continued by John Bowyer Nichols.

instead of that I sent you, which may come in on the subsequent month. ~~They are of nearly the same length.~~

~~You may have a running title of~~

~~Dr. Lettsoms 25th letter on prisons,~~

~~Mr. Neild's notes (or notices) on the prisons of Norwich.~~

I know our worthy friend at Chelsea feels very much from the letter of his Brother Magistrate, Mr. Firth.[69] Neild has seen my MS. and is satisfied with it, and it would add to his satisfaction were this answer to appear immediately. If you should take the trouble of reading it, I think you will deem it moderate manly, and decisive. I have avoided all severe language and introduced dispassionate argument. If I judge right, as an old man[70] (I hope not partial to his worst productions) it is the best letter, yet written by

yours sincerely,

J. C. Lettsom

Dec. 24 1805

~~Neild is very poorly indeed, confined to his chamber. He has to have a copy to correct, and I hope the post will allow it to pass and repass in time. Of this letter I must beg 50 copies.~~

16. [S]

To
J. Nichols Esq.
Red Lion passage
Fleet St.

~~Dear Mr. Nichols~~

When I had a family of children, I was anxious to collect various subjects of Natural history etc., both for instruction and amusement at home; but they are all settled from me, and I should now be willing to dispose of a portion

---

[69] William Firth, 'Norwich Magistrates, &c. vindicated', *Gentleman's Magazine*, 1805, **75** (ii): 1019–21. Lettsom's 'Twenty-sixth letter on prisons' (ibid., pp. 1185–90) was a refutation of the charges levelled against Neild by Firth.

[70] At this time, Lettsom was sixty-one years of age.

of my collection to the Surrey Institution, with the greater pleasure, as I could still have access to them.[71]

Of Minerals there is a pretty complete collection.

Of Mechanical and philosophical instruments, those from which Ferguson formerly lectured.

Of Books too big for my private collection, Boydell's Shakespeare,[72] the 10th subscription Bowyer's History of England.[73]

My view is, that if the Managers should think those objects worthy of their attention they might be seen by any competent person, and after the valuation to deduct 5 L per cent in favour of the Institution.

J. C. Lettsom

~~Sambrook Court~~

May 21 1808

---

[71] The Surrey Institution was in Blackfriars Road, Southwark, London. It was housed in the Surrey Rotunda, built around 1788 by James Burton for the land agent James Parkinson, so that he could exhibit the collection of Sir Ashton Lever (the Leverian Museum), which had been won in a lottery. The Surrey Institution promoted science, literature and the arts, and took over the building in 1806, at which point Parkinson reconstructed the interior. The Wellcome Trust Library holds a collection of printed ephemera, drawings and water-colours relating to the building: *Surrey Rotunda (Sir Ashton Lever's Museum &c.) 1784–1858*, London, s.n., 1784–1878. It had a lecture hall in which popular chemical lectures were given for audiences of gentlemen and ladies. See, for instance, Sir Goldsworthy Gurney, *A course of lectures on chemical science, as delivered at the Surrey Institution*, London, G. and W. B. Whittaker, 1823.

[72] John Boydell (1719–1804), an alderman for the City of London, made his money publishing books, illustrations and engravings. In 1786, he and his business associates planned an edition of Shakespeare's plays with illustrations by the best artists in England. The paintings were exhibited in the Shakespeare Gallery in Pall Mall in 1789. The catalogue for the exhibition, John Boydell, *A catalogue of the pictures in the Shakespeare Gallery, Pall-Mall*, London, s.n., 1789, contained passages from Shakespeare that the paintings illustrated. The first set of engravings from the paintings was produced in 1791. A nine-volume folio edition was published in 1802. In 1803, the two-volume elephant folios of the complete engravings were published. It may be this last to which Lettsom was referring, given that the book was too big for his private collection. See, *A collection of prints, from pictures painted for the purpose of illustrating the works of Shakespeare by the artists of Great-Britain*, London, published by John and Josiah Boydell, 1803.

[73] In 1792, Robert Bowyer, the miniature painter, announced his intention to commission sixty painters to illustrate David Hume's *The history of England* (1754–62) in *Prospectus of the general design and conditions for a complete history of England, superbly embellished*, London, 1792. Bowyer took his idea for his Historic Gallery from Boydell's Shakespeare Gallery. The paintings were exhibited in the Historic Gallery, Pall Mall, in the following year: Robert Bowyer, *Exhibition of pictures, painted for Bowyer's magnificent edition of the History of England*, London, 1793. See also, Robert Bowyer, 'Elucidation of Mr. Bowyer's plan for a magnificent edition of Hume's History of England, with a continuation by G. Gregory', London, R. Bowyer, 1795. Bowyer's illustrated edition of Hume's *History* was never completed.

17. [S]

Mr. Nichols
Red Lion passage
Fleet Street.

~~Dear Mr. Nichols~~

I do not imagine that my presence is necessary or even proper. I thought that if the Institution[74] wished to avail itself of an elegant apartment at a moderate expence, it would be an opportunity that might not again offer. Indeed half the collection would be ample as affording models for lecturing etc.
I am respectfully
J. C. Lettsom

May 24 1808

18. [S]

Dear Mr. Nichols
As I know you feel an interest in my happiness, I have the pleasure to inform you that on the 22^d of last month my youngest Son Pickering married Mrs. Georges, Mother-in-Law of Mr. Combe.[75] She has at her own disposal about £20,000 per annum, but I do not know the conditions of the Union.
Dr. Hawes continues dangerously ill ~~with a disease of the neck of the bladder~~. The event is to be greatly feared.
I am sincerely
J. C. Lettsom

Nov. 18 1808

---

[74] The Surrey Institution, mentioned in Lettsom's letter of 21 May 1808, see note 71 above.

[75] Pickering Lettsom (1782–1808), Lettsom's fourth and youngest son, was a barrister. He visited Tortola in a judicial capacity in 1808. Shortly after his arrival he met Ruth, the widow of William Payne Georges. She was the wealthiest planter in Tortola and had more than a thousand slaves on her estates. Abraham states that they were married on 22 September 1808 (op. cit., note 1 above, p. 454). But, in this letter, Lettsom says that they were married on 22 October. Abraham must be in error, for Lettsom states later in his letter of 10 December 1808 to Nichols that his son had been married little more than a month when he died. Ruth was sixteen years older than her new husband and, at the age of forty-two, old enough to have a daughter married to Charles Combe junior, son of one of Lettsom's oldest friends. Shortly after the marriage, Pickering contracted the island fever. He died on 28 October 1808. His father did not yet know of his death when he wrote this letter. Abraham, op. cit., note 1 above, pp. 263, 407, 453–5.

19. [S]

To
John Nichols Esq.
Red Lion passage
Fleet street.

~~Dear Mr. Nichols~~

No. 24—How chequered are sublunary prospects! After I last wrote to you of the marriage of my Son, I determined to call on my old friend Dr. Combe, to congratulate him, and felicitate myself on the union of families on the basis of long friendships.[76] On my way I called on my Son's agent and learnt that emigraverit ad sedes aethereas, unde negat redire quemqua[77] I do not know that I ever before felt so many contending sensations, where pleasure was rendered more pensive by affliction and friendship more tendered by sympathy. I left my card with my new relation, but I had no spirits to see him, nor he to receive me, nor has my mind been since tranquillized. As we advance in life, how the branches of our enjoyment fall off in the autumn of our friendships, and leave a trunk with some root indeed but no sap to invigorate it ~~remaining branches~~. Thus I pensively muse in the removal of one associate after another, quae demum conficiens ad celestem aulum properaverit.[78]

Today indeed our excellent friend Dr. Hawes is somewhat better, but I fear his disease will be too violent for the efforts of constitution to overcome. I intimated to him, the concern you experienced on his account. He is alive to the attention and sympathy of his friends; and he appears more amiable on the bed of languishing than in those convivial moments, when so often we have mingled humanity of heart with rationality of intellect. Should heaven demand him, we may conclude brevi denique luctu opus fuit, et migravit ad superos.[79] You will overlook the sombre of this letter,[80] but I have lost a Son which I never shall overcome, and I sympathize with Dr. Combe, with whom I have maintained without intermission, a friendship of little short of forty years.

It remains for us, my friend, as we lose one associate, to cling with closer attraction to survivors, to concentrate esteem, and the ardour of affection to encrease with the loss of extension.

---

[76] Charles Combe senior was one of Lettsom's oldest friends. When Lettsom was made a Fellow of the Society of Antiquaries in 1771, Combe was one of his proposers. Combe was also one of the founding members of the Medical Society of London. Abraham, op. cit., note 1 above, pp. 110n, 125, 337n, 454.
[77] "Finally, putting an end to this, he has hastened to the celestial hall".
[78] "He has passed to a heavenly seat whence it is said no one returns."
[79] "He has passed to the heavens but needs little grieving."
[80] Should be read with the sense "sombre [nature]".

This is felt by,
your sincere friend
J. C. Lettsom

~~Sambrook~~ Court
~~Nov. 24~~ 1808

20. [S]

~~Dear Mr. Nichols~~

Dec. 10 Awful are the reverses, which it pleases ~~provi~~ divine wisdom to dispense. The little sunshine in Tortola was soon overspread by a dark sky. My dear son had been married little more than a month, when sublunary objects terminated. He died on the 28th of October. The affectionate attention of his wife was worthy of the sensibility and goodness of her heart. He was buried near his namesake, the late Major Pickering.[81]
I am sincerely
J. C. Lettsom

Sambrook Court
Dec. 10 1808

21. [S][82]

~~Dear Mr. Nichols~~

I had heard of the bequest of your old friend Mr. Gough to the Royal Humane Society,[83] and with still more pleasure of ~~his~~ recollection of his personal esteem to you.

---

[81] John Pickering (1707–1768) was lieutenant-governor of Tortola and was Lettsom's friend. He had over 500 slaves. Abraham, op. cit., note 1 above, pp. 6, 52.

[82] The following letters deal largely with the affairs of the Royal Humane Society, mainly with the printing of its annual reports. Lettsom assisted Thomas Cogan and William Hawes in founding the Royal Humane Society in 1774, although Hawes was its prime mover in the early years. The Society was devoted to the resuscitation of those apparently drowned. Thomas Cogan was the son of a Northamptonshire surgeon. It was through reading Cogan's translation of the memoirs of the Dutch Society that Hawes became interested in resuscitation. Cogan took his M.D. in Leiden and practised in Amsterdam, Leiden and Rotterdam before he settled in London in 1772. Cogan apparently made all the money he required by 1780, after which he retired to Holland, living comfortably on his wife's inheritance from her banker father. He returned to England in 1795 when the French invaded Holland. He kept busy by writing on theological and philosophical topics, as well as writing for the Royal Humane Society. Abraham, op. cit., note 1 above, p. 141.

[83] Richard Gough, Esq., Enfield, was a governor for life of the Royal Humane Society. *Royal Humane Society annual report*, 1808, p. 82. Gough also collaborated with John Bowyer Nichols in finishing John Hutchins' account of Sherborne: *The history and antiquities of*

I warmly approve of the whole inscription etc. on our deceased friend Dr. Hawes. Perhaps you may favour me with a few copies, to accompany the tribute you previously sent me.[84]

~~In a few days I hope to find an opportunity of collecting for the annual report of the Royal Humane Society. The introduction is ready. How soon will you want it for the press?~~[85] ~~I regret that there is scarcely a novel or interesting case to introduce. Indeed, I think we may compress the whole, and omit the picture and the poetry. I do not think that even the emperor of Russia merits renewed notice.~~[86]

~~Should any thing occur to you worthy of insertion you will favour by communicating it to your friend~~

J. C. Lettsom

Sambrook Court
Mar. 24 1809

22. [S]

~~Super Strata viarum~~
~~March 25 1809~~

~~Dear Mr. Nichols~~

I wish much to have a moment's conversation with you respecting the report of the present anniversary of the Royal Humane Society. Can you command any time this evening from 6 to 12 tonight?

Sherbourne, in the county of Dorset; By John Hutchins ... augmented ... by Richard Gough, Esq. and John-Bowyer Nichols, London, printed by and for Nichols, Son and Bentley, 1815.

[84] William Hawes, M.D., died on 5 December 1808. The Royal Humane Society erected a memorial tablet to him in Islington Church in honour of his philanthropy (Hawes was born in Islington in 1736.) Abraham, op. cit., note 1 above, p. 411.

[85] After Hawes died, Lettsom became the mainstay of the society and had responsibility for compiling its annual reports.

[86] When Alexander I became Tzar of Russia in 1805, a romantic story had been disseminated of how he risked his life to save a Polish peasant from drowning. It was an ideal means of self-promotion for the Royal Humane Society that, in 1806, awarded the Emperor its gold medal in recognition of the deed. However, the peace of Tilsit, signed on 7 July 1807, made Alexander into an enemy of Britain and it was not politic to draw attention to the case at this particular juncture of the Napoleonic Wars. Once Napoleon fell, the Tzar came back into favour and, indeed, visited England in June 1814. Abraham, op. cit., note 1 above, pp. 426–7. The case was published separately by the Society in 1814, clearly in order to mark the Tzar's visit: Royal Humane Society, 'Case of resuscitation by His Imperial Majesty, the Emperor of Russia, published for the anniversary festival', London, Nichols, Son and Bentley, 1814.

I have been harrassed with professional avocations, beyond the courses and of time, but I will command tonight if requisite.

I am sincerely

J. C. Lettsom

Super Strata viarum[87] ~~Mar 25~~

23. [S]

~~received late March~~

~~March 28 1809~~

~~Dear Mr. Nichols~~

March 28 1809 I received today your friendly letter; at the same moment a foreign one dated January last, informing me of the decease of my Daughter-in-Law Mrs. Pickering Lettsom on the 24th of that month! My friend says she died of a broken heart.[88]

My path seems to be over the ashes of my children. May heaven be more propitious to the advancing years of my esteemed friend is the prayer of

J. C. Lettsom

Sambrook Court

Mar. 28 1809

24. [S]

March 31/1809

Dear Mr. Nichols,[89]

I enclose you the whole of Section 3. You have Section 4th [90] to which I think it would be proper to add some remarks on the dissection of persons who have died by drowning.

---

[87] Above the Strand (that is beyond the Strand i.e. Fleet Street).

[88] After the death of her husband, Pickering Lettsom (see note 75 above), his widow, Ruth, became ill and survived only two months, dying on 24 January 1809. This was an event of some financial consequence to Lettsom because instead of leaving her estate to her children or other relatives it was left to Lettsom and, after him, to his grandson, William Nanson Lettsom. Given the brevity of the marriage, the will was disputed and was only finally decided in Lettsom's favour on 2 March 1813. Lettsom died just two years after that, on 1 November 1815, before he could either enjoy the estate or decide what should be done with it.

[89] John Nichols was a governor for life and a member of the Committee of the Royal Humane Society. *Annual report of the Royal Humane Society*, 1809, pp. 75, 94.

[90] Section III was entitled 'Directions for the recovery of drowned persons, and prevention of premature death', *Annual report of the Royal Humane Society*, 1809, pp. 14–27. Section IV was

Mr. Beaumont[91] has engaged to take tea in Sambrook Court at 7 on Saturday. Could you favour us with your Company? I have some questions to ask and have explained respecting the Section vi. All the subsequent sections you can complete.

Section v. I shall prepare in advance as I have abridged about 150 letters on resuscitations. I had no idea of the labour I have undertaken, till the documents were sent to me, which I ought to have had a month ago.

I am respectfully

J. C. Lettsom

Mar. 31 1809

25. [S]

Endorsed: Lettsom

April 2 1809

Dear Mr. Nichols,

You will see by Mr. Addington's letter enclosed, that he wishes to see a Revise[92] and to have 2 or 3 copies stuck off.[93]

Have you got the enclosed print of a place, which is to form as usual the Title page?[94] It should be prefixed and with a title like this

> Royal <u>Humane</u> Society
> Annual Report,
> <u>1809</u>

and the plate under.

'Suggestions respecting the mode of narrating cases', ibid., pp. 28–9. On page 29 was an account of the appearances of the brain, the bronchia, the lungs, the heart and the arteries on dissection of drowned bodies.

[91] John Beaumont was, in 1791, treasurer of the Royal Humane Society and a founder member of the General Sea-Bathing Hospital, Margate. He went on to become registrar and secretary of the Royal Humane Society, a position that he held until 1813. Abraham, op. cit., note 1 above, pp. 282, 419.

[92] Revise = a revision.

[93] John Addington, of Spital Square, was a steward of the Royal Humane Society in 1809. He communicated and made remarks upon 'Case 15165th—the 3213th recovery; being the 106th restoration out of 164 claimants for 1808. Case of recovery from the effects of suspension by the cord', *Annual report of the Royal Humane Society*, 1809, pp. 31–48.

[94] The title page of every annual report carried two figures—a little boy "represented blowing an extinguished torch, with the hope, as the Legend imports, that a little spark may still remain"—this was the Society's motto: Lateat Scintillula Forsan—and "a civic wreath, which was the Roman reward for saving the life of a citizen" with the motto: *Hoc Pretium Cive Servato Tulit*. "The inscription around the wreath expresses the merit which obtained the honour conferred by the Royal Humane Society". These emblems also appeared on the honorary medals that the society awarded. See, *Royal Humane Society annual report*, 1808, p. 74.

at least I would avoid names, titles, poetry and Latin quotation. With Daniel's life preserver[95]

Frame for conveying the apparently dead.[96]
Dr. Cogan's drag,[97] and
The Society's apparatus[98]

We shall have four plates, and as the two pictures are much worn, I think we had better omit them this year, for I find we are very much in debt and every saving may be adviseable.

The gentleman[99] last night proposed to have 600 copies of the Reports. Of the last year's reports there are above 300 copies remaining.

On any of these matters if you think differently, inform your friend

J. C. Lettsom

Apr. 2 1809

---

[95] 'Some account of Mr. Daniel's life-preserver', *Annual report of the Royal Humane Society*, 1809, p. 67, with plate which reads "patronized by His Royal Highness the Duke of Sussex; the Society for the Encouragement of Arts, Manufactures, and Commerce; and the Royal Humane Society". The life-preserver was made of pliable water-proof leather, large enough to encircle the body of the wearer, and was attached by straps at the shoulders and around the thighs of the wearer. Once fixed, it was then inflated with air by the wearer through a cock fitted with a stop-cock. It would keep up to four people afloat.

[96] There is no plate of this description in the annual report for 1809, though it may refer to 'Explanation of the engraving of the portable bed invented by the Rev. Mr. Davies of Leicester, 1805', *Annual report of the Royal Humane Society*, 1809, p. 65. This was a six-foot long enclosed bed, with a belly of steel in which the body was warmed.

[97] Plate I, *Annual report of the Royal Humane Society*, 1809, p. 57. This was an iron instrument with three arms, each with two hooks at the end, for dragging drowned people from the water. Originally designed in Holland for the aid of those who fell into the water with their clothes on, the hooks pierced the drowning person's clothing. Ibid., p. 61. On Cogan see note 82 above.

[98] Plates I and II, *Annual report of the Royal Humane Society*, 1809, p. 17. Plate I is a view of a pair of bellows for inflating the lungs and for injecting stimulating vapour of rosemary, lavender, valerian and asafoetida, a brass nozzle by which to inject the stimulating vapours and a long flexible tube. Plate II is a view of short and long flexible tubes to fit to the bellows, a brass box to contain the stimulating substance, a curved silver pipe to be passed down the throat to inflate the lungs, a cannula for bronchotomy, nostril pipes, clyster pipes of various sizes and a syringe with a flexible tube for injecting cordials into the stomach.

[99] Presumably Mr. Addington on behalf of the committee of the Royal Humane Society.

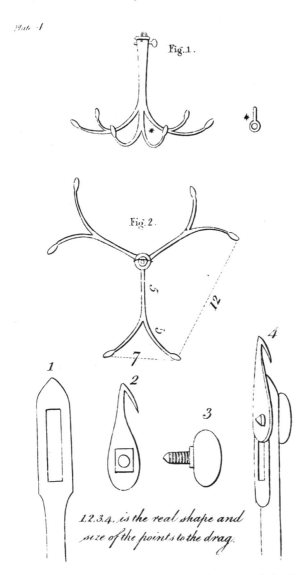

Figure 2: Dr. Cogan's drag. From *Annual report of the Royal Humane Society for the recovery of persons apparently drowned*, London, Royal Humane Society, 1812, Plate 4 opposite p. 72. (Wellcome Library, London).

26. [S]

Apr. 3 1809

Dear Mr. Nichols,

I enclose you a Section ө for the Report.[100] I have not been able to collect the other cases to which medals have been awarded,[101] but have wrote to Mr. Beaumont to enquire.

I send the 4 plates for the reports that you may know which to order of Mr. Norris, Engraver, but as I have no history of the Drag, perhaps striking off the plate may be postponed till I hear from Dr. Cogan, to whom I have written on the subject.[102]

You have, I find, mentioned the Medical Society in the last magazine fully and politely.[103]

The only section I now have to complete is on the apparatus, which will be finished on the receipt of Dr. Cogan's references, hence the press will not wait for

Yours respectfully
J. C. Lettsom

Apr. 3 1809

27. [S]

April 10 1809

Dear Mr. Nichols,

I think the vice presidents of the Royal Humane Society have not for some years past attended the festival of the Society[104] so fully as heretofore. To recall their attention it occurred to me that if the Report could be finished in

---

[100] This presumably refers to Dr. Cogan's section, whose drag was awarded a gold medal by the Society.

[101] No notification appears in the report for 1809 of medals awarded, but a list of Honorary Medals granted in 1807 was printed, for instance, in *Royal Humane Society annual report*, 1808, p. 74. In that year eleven medals were awarded.

[102] Dr. Cogan was clearly able to supply a history of the drag, which is given in the *Annual report of the Royal Humane Society*, 1809, pp. 56–61. See note 99 above.

[103] The Anniversary Meeting of the Medical Society was flagged up in the Literary Intelligence section, *Gentleman's Magazine*, 1809, **79** (i): 251. Lettsom was elected President at the meeting of 8 March.

[104] The Royal Humane Society held an anniversary festival, for which see *Account of the anniversary festival of the Royal Humane Society, 1810*, London, J. Nichols, 1810.

time, and as many neatly, but not extravagantly bound, as there are vice presidents, and a copy presented to each V. P.,[105] it would rally their feelings and their suffrages, on the present melancholy event in the loss of Dr. Hawes.

I think it would be a compliment to them not merited, and a respect to the deceased Founder; for the present report containing so many memoirs of him,[106] should not be received as waste paper, but preserved in the libraries of the Friends of humanity.

I have not surmized these ideas to any, but should you approve them; and we can realize them so far as to have the report ready before the anniversary, I would myself wait upon every V.P. in town, and write to every absentee.

If you approve, I will communicate the same to the Committee of Managers, and am sincerely
J. C. Lettsom

Apr. 10 1809

28. [S]

April 14 1809

Mr. Nichols,

I know that Capt. Manby's letter was inserted in the last report,[107] but there was not any explanation, I think, of the mode recommended by him. I say I think because I have not the Report, as the only one in my possession I sent you which perhaps you can return.

---

[105] V.P. stands for "Vice President". This was an office held by a large number of people and designed to attract support to the society. In 1809 there were no fewer than eighteen.

[106] The 1809 report contained an account of the 'Rise and progress of the Royal Humane Society, with a tribute to the deceased founder', *Annual report of the Royal Humane Society*, 1809, pp. 1–12, as well as a list of 'Subsequent institutions of other humane societies', ibid., p. 13.

[107] The 1809 report contained a brief account by Captain G. W. Manby, B. M. Yarmouth. It stated that in the previous February, H.M.S. *Snipe* had been stranded near the Haven's Mouth at Yarmouth only fifty yards from the shore. However, because of the violence of the sea and the strength of the storm, no communication could be established between the vessel and the shore and "upwards of sixty persons perished in the presence of their sympathizing countrymen". Manby recommended a method of avoiding this in the future: "I was led to infer (although repeatedly told it was impracticable), that, if a rope could be thrown from the shore, security would at once be given, and every soul saved". Manby started to experiment in this regard, submitting his reports to the Society. See 'Varieties of apparatus for the preservation of life, communicated to the Society', *Annual report of the Royal Humane Society*, 1809, p. 54.

The Resolution of the Managers I confess is not well drawn up, and perhaps the following would be clearer:

The Managers are unanimously of opinion that W. Whiteworth Esq. having been the primariry means of saving the life of Mr. Lill, merits the Society's honourary medal. They regret that they cannot grant a second medal, but they earnestly hope that Mr. Smith may in future be equally successful, and it will afford them abundant satisfaction to offer him a similar reward. ~~verte~~

After reconsideration, I think it would be best to omit the paragraph of censure p. 49,[108] as useless—also the whole resolution of the Managers as well as Mr. Neild's opinion p. 50. Also the first sentence of Mr. Teasdale's letter introducing the hope of a medal.[109] If you think otherwise I acquiescence [*recte* acquiesce].

I approve the idea of doing up the annual report in neat boards, uncut. I have proposed that each Vice President and the President have one neatly bound and lettered with the name of each. I think it would induce them to open their purses and to visit us also. Certainly they should be uncut in general. It gives the appearance of amplitude and elegance, and with your <u>neat type</u> I think the Report will suit a library or study. It will at least contain useful information
I am etc.

J. C. Lettsom

Apr. 14 1809

29. [S]

Endorsed: ~~Mr.~~ Dr. Lettsom

April 15 1809

Dear Mr. Nichols,

I am truly glad to see the progress you have made. The audit will be ready on Monday and I shall urge Mr. Beaumont to forward it to you as soon after 12 o' clock as possible, that being the hour of meetings.

---

[108] 'Case 15166th—the 3214th recovery; being the 109th restoration in the year 1808. Case of recovery from drowning. (By W. Whitworth, Esq. and Mr. T. P. Smith, jun.)' was an account of Mr. Lill, of Church street, Bethnal Green, aged 65, who was taken out of the New River on 27 May 1808. Neither Whitworth's account of the case nor the account of Thomas Smith junior, surgeon, which follows it, include a paragraph of censure. *Annual report of the Royal Humane Society*, 1809, pp. 48–50.

[109] 'Case 15167th—the 3218th recovery; being the 110th restoration in the year 1808. Case of recovery from drowning. (Communicated by Mr. Teasdale)', *Annual report of the Royal Humane Society*, 1809, pp. 50–2. The sentence was not published.

Twenty minutes before I received your copy I met Alderman Ansley[110] in the street, who assured me he would attend our Anniversary. You may depend upon it, the presentation of a copy to the President and Vice Presidents will prove beneficial to the Society, whilst it is but a due respect to them.

I must beg to have 24 copies to send to Humane Societies here and abroad.[111] I shall make good use of them. I just now met at a patient's Mr. Owen, surgeon, Chancery Lane,[112] who wishes to become a governor and will attend our anniversary. I wish you therefore to insert his name among the present governors.[113]

I am respectfully

J. C. Lettsom

Sambrook Court

Apr. 15 1809

30. [S]

Note: Perhaps if the table of contents is not printed off, the last section and audit may be omitted altogether.

Mr. Nichols

Red Lion passage

Fleet Street

April 17 1809

Mr. Nichols,

We cannot I think wait for the audit, if we conclude to wait upon the President and Vice presidents in time to induce them to attend the anniversary.

---

[110] John Ansley, Esq. Ald. V.P., Bread Street, was an ordinary member of the society in 1809. *Annual report of the Royal Humane Society*, 1809, p. 81.

[111] There were Humane Societies in a number of other European and American towns and cities by this time, for example, the Dublin General Dispensary and Humane Society, the Bath Humane Society, the Paisley Humane Society, and the Humane Society of the Commonwealth of Massachusetts.

[112] Titus Owen (fl. 1765–1826), MRCS, surgeon, Chancery Lane, London.

[113] "Mr. Owen, Surgeon, Chancery-lane" was put into the 1809 report as a governor. *Annual report of the Royal Humane Society*, 1809, p. 94.

Might not the audit be printed against the anniversary, on a separate half sheet or sheet, to be added afterwards by a little paste by the governors themselves if they chuse to complete the Report? I think we should not allow a trifle to delay the report for the reason above mentioned.

J. C. Lettsom

Apr. 17 1809

Against the 26th I should like to know the annual expenditure.

31. [S]

Mr. Nichols,

If you have not printed the table of contents—I repeat that the audit may be wholly omitted. If it be printed off, then I conceive the Report may be finished without it, and the audit may be ready to deliver on Wednesday, loose or separate.

J. C. Lettsom

Apr. 17 [1809?]

32. [S]

Endorsed: Lettsom

Note: I think with their names gilt, thus

To Lord Macdonald
From the Royal Humane Society
Report of 1809   so to the others

Please to return the enclosed.

To
Mr. Nichols
Red Lion passage
Fleet Street.

Apr. 17 1809

Mr. Nichols,

If you think the enclosed request of Mr. Benjamin Hawes should be complied with, you will order the Reports to be bound according and transmitted to me.

Persons are sending to me for Reports. I wish you would order a dozen to be sent to me—I just now parted with one to Mr. Park who sent me ten guineas.[114]

I am sincerely

J. C. Lettsom

Sambrook Court
Apr. 17 1809

33. [S]

Mr. Nichols
Red Lion Passage
Fleet Street

~~Mr. Nichols~~

As Capt Godall (Christophe's Admiral) is a steward of the Humane Society,[115] should you approve a report for Christophe who gives £20 per annum, it might be delivered at the Anniversary after the Report of his Donation. Should a Report be presented to the Lord Mayor, I think it would be well and decently applied, as we cannot get too many friends in the Court of aldermen; but this I submit to you. My wish is that as we shall need the animation of our departed Founder, we must exert ourselves in the best manner, to join propriety and dignity in our proceedings.

I think we shall have a respectable anniversary, with more of the vice presidents than we have recently been favoured with.

I am etc.

J. C. Lettsom

~~Sambrook Court~~
Apr. 20 1809

~~Should Christophe leave the epithet or title of His Excellency precede his name?~~[116]

---

[114] Park does not appear in the list of members of the society for 1809. He was therefore presumably a member of the public who sent in a donation. However, a James Allan Park, Esq., of Lincoln's Inn Fields, appears in the list of members for 1812. *Annual report of the Royal Humane Society*, 1812, p. 139.

[115] See *Annual report of the Royal Humane Society*, 1809, p. 75, for a list of stewards in 1809, of whom there were twenty.

[116] This refers to Baron de Robeck. The title was left in the published report.

~~Pray print me off some cards early — My house and time are occupied in answering applications about the rewards of the Humane Society. It is unfortunate that I have hourly to send as far as Villiers Street the numerous Claimants.~~[117]

Apr. 21 1809

34. [S]

Endorsed: D[r.] Lettsom, Feb. [*sic*] 1810.

Jan. 23 1810

Dear Mr. Nichols,
    Although I would ~~avoid~~ practise oeconomy with the affairs of the Royal Humane Society, I would parsimony;[118] and I think last year we printed 100 too small an edition of the Reports, as that performance was called for and read. Suppose then, we have 700 instead of 600 last year, which I imagine will suffice.
Respectfully
J. C. Lettsom

Jan. 23 1810

35. [S]

Mr. N[ichols]
Red [Lion Square]
F[leet Street][119]

~~Dear Nichols~~

I enclose you some lines which I thought, from what you intimated to me, might be introduced respecting Dr. Mitchill ± which, if you judge anyhow

---

[117] John Beaumont, register and secretary, at No. 9, Villiers Street, the Strand, received subscriptions for the Royal Humane Society. *Annual report of the Royal Humane Society*, 1809, p. 102. Beaumont was responsible for maintaining the list of members of the society.
[118] This obviously has the sense of "I would [advocate] parsimony".
[119] Most of the address has been cut off in opening the letter.

admissible, alter and use them as you please.[120] I hope the paper I enclose by Dr. Mitchell might suitably appear in your magazine.

I am respectfully

J. C. Lettsom

Sambrook Court
Jan. 24 1810

± An eminent Physician at New York; of whom I have a Portrait with Manners, ~~in Gentleman's Magazine LXXX, pp. 33~~, advert? what were begun ---- page.[121]

36. [S]

April 14, 1810

Mr. Nichols,

As Mr. Curwen[122] is now proceeding in the House of Commons to procure a reward to Captain Manby of £2000, might it not be adviseable to send Mr. Curwen the present sheets of the Report?

---

[120] Samuel Mitchill, 'City trash and offal convertible into excellent manure, and rendered safe to handle, and good for farming, by the alkalies with which it abounds. In a communication from Dr. Mitchill to John C. Lettsom, LL. and M.D. &c. dated New York, Sept. 21, 1803', *Gentleman's Magazine*, 1810, **80** (i): 33–5. The paper was prefaced by the following introductory paragraph presumably written by Lettsom: "We were sometime since favoured with a Likeness of Dr. Samuel Mitchill of New York, accompanied by some Memoirs of this highly distinguished Physician, which unfortunately perished in the Fire of 1808; and we should hence be much obliged to our unknown Correspondent, could he favour us with a copy of his former Communication.... with permission to publish it; ... Dr. Mitchill, we also learn, is the Author of many Literary Essays, and, with Dr. Edward Miller of New York, conducts *The Medical Repository*, a work which has been extended to upwards of ten volumes, and has justly acquired considerable celebrity in Europe as well as America, Samuel Harvey of New York later wrote on 19 May 1810 to 'Mr. Urban' stating that 'you have given a very inaccurate portrait of Dr. Mitchell of this city'". Harvey stated that Mitchill was born in New York in 1751, that he went to Princeton University aged only fourteen in order to get a good education before returning to New York, where he took a B.M. in 1773 and, shortly afterwards, his M.D. He had a career in the army, ending his service in 1783 with the rank of brigadier-general and afterwards settled in New York, employing his leisure hours in philosophy and belles lettres. He was elected to the Senate of the United States in 1798 and continued in office until 1807. *Gentleman's Magazine*, 1810 (Supplement), **80** (i): 614.

[121] This addition is in a different hand, possibly Pettigrew's.

[122] John Christian Curwen (1756–1828) was elected Whig M.P. for Carlisle in 1786, after a House of Commons' inquiry reversed a decision in favour of Lord Lonsdale achieved on the addition of fictitious freemen to the electoral roll.

On the anniversary festival, I mean to make a very short speech, but as if to introduce slightly the case of the young woman page 45 (first paragraph only) and then propose that someone should read to the Meeting Mr. Pridden's excellent letter, ~~which~~ p. 47,[123] which I think would produce a happy effect for in it every thing is interesting and appropriate, and it will be entirely novel to the meeting. On Monday I shall hope for your opinion.

~~Of these two sheets G&H,~~[124] ~~please to send me one (of each) that I may prepare to make use of them. I think also the person who reads Mr. Pridden's excellent letter should do it from a loose sheet and not from the book.~~

I am sincerely

J. C. Lettsom

Apr. 14 1810

37. [S]

Dec. 16 1810

Dear Mr. Nichols,

Accept my thanks for your valuable present∓ which I shall ever estimate in a particular manner, from the esteem I have for the donor, and from the kind manner of his conveying it.

~~This week my MSS. etc. will be ready for the press.~~[125] ~~Mr. Mawman will receive them today, and he told me last night, that he would transmit them to you.~~

I am affectionately

J. C. Lettsom

Dec. 16 1810

~~∓ A very uncommon Edition of Horace.~~

---

[123] The Rev. John Pridden was a founding member of the General Sea-Bathing Hospital and was appointed secretary at its first meeting. The land on which the Infirmary was built was bought in 1793 in the name of Dr. Lettsom, the Rev. John Pridden and John Nichols. Pridden was Nichols' son-in-law. Abraham, op. cit., note 1 above, pp. 282, 285. Pridden was also one of the Royal Humane Society's chaplains. In 1806, he was their anniversary preacher, responsible for delivering the anniversary sermon of the Society. *Annual report of the Royal Humane Society*, 1809, pp. 75–6. Mr. Pridden's letter, here referred to, does not appear in either the 1809 or 1810 annual report.

[124] Presumably the numbered sheets of a proof for the next *Royal Humane Society annual report*.

[125] Lettsom was responsible for compiling the annual reports of the society between 1808 and 1813.

38. [S]

Endorsed: Lettsom 16

~~Mr. Nicols~~

I hope you [are] proceeding with the engraving of Dr. Hawes' tablet and I wish particularly to receive from you, as early as you can favour me with, the account of the tablet, that I may add, if requisite, and prepare by the first of March, to go to press with the Report, that matters may not be hurried just before the festival[126] ~~as I have the Report now ready for you to print. Can you tell me Count Zenobio's address?~~

I am respectfully etc.

J. C. Lettsom

Sambrook Court
Febr. 23 1811

39. [S]

Endorsed: Dr. Lettsom.

Mr. Nichols
Red lion passage
Fleet Street

Oct. 5 1811

Dear Mr. Nichols,

The revd. Mr. Nightingale is writing the County history of Staffordshire,[127] on which account he applied to me, and to request [if][128] in your power to permit him to see Shaw's Staffordshire.[129] As he pursues an object of literary information, I thought you would be disposed to aid his exertions, and I know him too well to doubt his making a proper use of your kindness.

I am sincerely

J. C. Lettsom

Sambrook Court
Oct. 5 1811.

---

[126] The Society's anniversary festival.

[127] J. Nightingale, *The beauties of England and Wales: Staffordshire*, 18 vols, London, J Harris, 1813, vol. 13, pt. 2.

[128] The manuscript is holed, but the flourish of the "f" remains.

[129] The Rev. Stebbing Shaw, *The history and antiquities of Staffordshire*, 2 vols, London, J. Nichols, 1798–1801.

[a pencil reply from Nichols is appended]

Dear Doctor

I am sorry I have not a second Copy of Shaw's Staffordshire, which would be much at Mr. Nightingale's service. But the only ~~Copy~~ one I have being a fine Large Paper Copy, handsomely bound, with loose Additions I am unwilling to let out of my Library; if, however, Mr. N. can make <u>use of it</u> for Consultation at N°· 4 Canonbury Lane ~~it~~ he will be very welcome, if he wants it for the purpose of comp[aring?].[130] There is a Copy, however, in the Library of the <u>London Institution</u> which perhaps ~~he~~ Mr. N. could consult with greater Ease to himself.

40. [S]

Endorsed: Lettsom

Bowyer Nichols Esq.[131]
Red Lion passage
Fleet Street
For himself.

Nov. 18 1811

Dear Mr. ~~Nichols~~ Bowyer,

In consequence of the letter of the Committee of the Royal Humane Society, on the affair of the Medal, an illusion is made to some improvement in consequence of the useful experiments of Captain Manby.

~~I have desired Mr. Beaumont to summons the Committee for Friday evening, the[132] of December and I have applied to Mr. Page[133] to furnish us with the dye.~~

As a man of taste, you know, from Roman and Grecian models, that simplicity and unity of design constitute the beautiful and elegant; and every person whom I have consulted has expressed their approbation of our medal,

---

[130] The manuscript is holed where the seal has been removed, but the flourish of a "g" remains.

[131] John Bowyer Nichols was a steward, one of the annual directors and a member of the Sub-Committee of the Royal Humane Society. *Annual report of the Royal Humane Society*, 1809, pp. 75, 94.

[132] The manuscript is holed where the seal has been removed.

[133] Perhaps a medal maker. He was not on the committee of the Society.

which is scarcely rivalled by antiquity, and in my humble opinion it is so perfect in the leading attributes of medallic expression, as to preclude any addition without injury. The whole design, with the most elegant simplicity, in a single figure, ~~is a~~ comprizes a narrative of the Humane Society, in the act of restoring suspended life. It is a volume in epitome and I should be grieved to see this noble [monument?] of taste and [adornm]ent[134] frittered away, on subjects of dubiety, and any abstraction of the leading object introduced.

Do weigh this matter against the time when I hope you will meet your friend.

J. C. Lettsom

Sambrook Court
Nov. 18 1811

41. [S]

Endorsed: Dr. Lettsom, 8 Feb. 1812.

To
J. B. Nicholls Esq.
Red Lion passage
Fleet Street.

Feb. 7 1812

Dear Mr. Bowyer,

I now send you the copy of the Report of the Royal Humane Society.[135] I regret that I have acted for so many Governors, without aid, lest my endeavours may not have answered their expectations; and hence during the printing, I shall hope for such hints and improvements as may occur to you. I have so far improved the third section as to enable any person without the aid of an apparatus to act with probable success.[136] Experience has long convinced me of the danger of tobacco, to the use of which my predecessor was very

---

[134] The manuscript is torn and has been repaired here. Most of the word is missing.

[135] The master copy of the *Royal Humane Society annual report*, 1812, sent to the printers.

[136] Section III of each annual report comprised 'Directions for the recovery of drowned persons, and prevention of premature death'. This section was expanded to four and a half pages (twice its previous length) in the report for 1812. *Royal Humane Society annual report*, 1812.

partial; but the Remarks of John Hunter,[137] and of every man of science, and now the experiments of Dr. Brodie,[138] all confirm my own experience as to the deleterious effects of this vegetable.

I am sincerely etc.

J. C. Lettsom

~~Sambrook Court~~
~~Febr. 7 1812~~

~~12 copies of the last prison letter~~

42. [S]

Endorsed: <u>Lettsom</u>

Mr. Nichols
Red Lion passage
Fleet Street

March 4 1812

Dear Mr. Nichols

I have communicated to Mr. Neild your resolution or admission respecting the prison letters, which I think would be beneficial to the public and I hope not disreputable to your scientific and useful miscellany. I would not wish to appear oftener than every 3 months.

At the Surrey Institution last night, I met with Capt. Manby, who promises something to one of the Humane Society's meeting[s], prior to the festival which he purposes to attend.

J. C. Lettsom

Mar. 4 1812.

---

[137] John Hunter (1728–93), surgeon, condemned the use of tobacco clysters in resuscitating unconscious subjects. Abraham, op. cit., note 1 above, p. 411.

[138] The surgeon, Sir Benjamin Collins Brodie (1783–1862), was against tobacco in all its forms. Some of Brodie's work was published in the *Lancet* in the early nineteenth century. His anti-smoking stance was later taken up with some enthusiasm by both the British Anti-Tobacco Society and the Anti-Narcotic League in Manchester, who republished some of his work.

43. [S]

Endorsed: Dr. Lettsom, Mar. 1812

March 4, 1812

Dear Mr. Nichols
On full consideration of my friend William Knight's poetry,[139] I do conclude that it would be aviseable to cancel and reprint it whatever the expence may be, which may be settled between him and the society.
I am respectfully
J. C. Lettsom

Sambrook Court
Mar. 4 1812

44. [S]

Endorsed: Dr. Lettsom

c/o
Bowyer Nichols Esq.

Mar 6 1812

Dear Bowyer
I mentioned the cancelling the incorrect poetry of my friend Knight, and reprinting it fair, which indeed must be done. You must, I think, charge the society, not the author, with the expence.
Sincerelyle [*recte* Sincerely]
J. C. Lettsom

Mar. 6 1812

Turn over

---

[139] Mr. Knight of Gainsford Street is listed as an ordinary member of the society in 1809. *Annual report of the Royal Humane Society*, 1809, p. 91. Possibly William Knight, F.S.A., who died in 1847. See *Catalogue of the exceedingly choice…library of the late William Knight… which…will be sold by auction by Messrs. S. Leigh Sotheby and Co.….on…August 2d, 1847, and five following days*, London, Compton and Ritchie, 1847.

It was, I think, resolved that Mr. Martin's speech with Dr. Fothergill's poetry should be reprinted in a seperate pamphlet.

Do you think that this should be done preparatory to the anniversary, and then distributed?

It was resolved to print Mr. White's sermon.

Have you received the MS.?

Should it not be printed to be distribut'd at the festival?

Perhaps these distributed, would open the pocket and purse of the company present.

Your opinion should decide the judgment of

J. C. Lettsom

Mar. 6.

45. [S]

Endorsed: Dr. Lettsom, April 9 [*sic*] /1812.

Note: White, and Print from p. 1. to 18. of Annual Report 1810.

Mr. Bowyer Nichols
Red Lion passage
Fleet Street.

March 26, 1812

Dear Mr. Bowyer,

About three days ago, I saw the Rev^d. Mr. White, who told me then that his sermon was ready, and that he would send it, but I will write to him and urge the matter.

I have not any thing to add to Mr. Martin's elegant performance. It was directed, I think, to print Dr. Fothergill's Triumph with it, and if I recollect right the doctor has mentioned in a letter to me some trivial correction which I will find in time, when I shall have with your permission a sight of ~~the~~ it when subjected to the press.

Sincerely etc.

J. C. Lettsom

Mar. 26 1812

46. [S]

Endorsed: Lettsom D^r

April 3, 1812

Dear Mr. Nichols,

I hope you will have been able already to have sent to the Binder, a sufficient number of Reports, for him to prepare to present to the vice presidents on or before the 15th of this month. By such attention, I think that our Anniversary has been more productive.

You know that Dr. Fothergill's Triumph is to [be] added to Martin's oration. The Doctor observes "In page 5 line 3 from the bottom, I remarked the printer put over for o'er, which destroys the harmony of the verse".

I hope you have received Mr. White's MS. which should be printed to appear on the 20th after dinner.

Do not forget to press the Binding of as many Reports as shall correspond with the number of President and Vice presidents—one to Mrs. Hawes and on[e] Dr. Hawes' Brother (Benjamin I think his name).
I am sincerely
J. C. Lettsom

Sambrook Court
Apr. 3 1812

47. [S]

Endorsed: Dr. Lettsom, Apr. 9 1812

PS I wish the vice Presidents would have the Report soon sent to them, as it might engage their attendance, or open their purses.

April 9, 1812
$\frac{1}{2}$ past 1 A.M.

Dear Mr. Bowyer

I think with you that an appendix to Mr. ~~White's~~[140] sermon would be not only superfluous, but even lessen the importance of his pious work. The

---

[140] This word is struck through in the manuscript, but he may have intended to underline it.

Report will anticipate any extracts from Captn. Manby or any other performance. It will stand more dignified alone, and I hope I can persuade our Revd. Friend to acquiesce in the same.

You and I have had no little trouble in this publication, and with other things pressing upon my time and years, I long for quiet and retreat.
sincerely ~~sinly~~ yours
J. C. Lettsom

~~Sambrook Court~~
~~Apr. 9.~~ $\frac{1}{2}$ ~~past one AM~~

48. [S]

Endorsed: Dr. Lettsom, Feb. 23

Feb. 18 1813

Mr. Nichols,

All that depends upon me is completed of the Report of the Royal Humane Society. I request of you individually draw up something respecting the long services and usefulness of Mr. Beaumont to accompany his head.

And of you and Mr. Beaumont, to draw up some account of Mr. Brookes' Ropes for drawing drowning persons out of the Water, of the nature and mode of using these Ropes I am ignorant. I wait for Dr. Cogan's Boat hook for the Engraver,[141] and some explanation of it for the Printer. I suffer imbarrassment and inconvenience from the tardiness of those I depend upon, and thus my labours in the Humane Society are increased, and perplexed. If you should see Dr. Cogan, do urge him to complete his department, that the Engraver may be in readiness, as well as
yours respectfully
J. C. Lettsom

Sambrook Court
Febr. 18th 1813.

---

[141] This is Dr. Cogan's drag, see note 97 above.

49. [S]

Endorsed: Lettsom 18.

Feb. 26 1813

Mr. B^r: Nichols
Red lion passage
Fleet street

Dear Mr. Nichols
    I have read and approve of the Eloge designed for Mr. Beaumont, as far as it has proceeded. When you want Copy, I have some ready for the Report. Is there any account of the spear to ~~me~~ be directed by the hand of Dr. Cogan?
J. C. Lettsom

Febr. 26 1813.

50. [S]

Endorsed: Dr. Lettsom.

~~PS. I will prepare tonight, and send tomorrow (probably) the whole remaining Report.~~

Mr. N[ichols]
Red [Lion Passage]
[Fleet Street]

Mar. 4 1814[142]

~~Dear Mr. Nichols,~~
    ~~I approve the advertisement as it respects Mr. Beaumont,~~ but as I am mentioned in so very polite a manner, and as I am known to draw up the Reports, would it be improper to say by whom the advertisement was prepared; ~~or at least to say by a Friend to the Humane Society, or by any other medium~~ to exonerate from self-complacency or egotism?
Your friend
J. C. Lettsom

Mar. 4 1813

---

[142] Although this date is not consistent with that following the signature, the content places it in March 1813.

51. [S]

June 3 1813

Dear Mr. Nichols,
The death of Dr. Anthony Fothergill[143] has appeared in many of the Newspapers, but I do not know by whom introduced.
I wait for the decision of Doctors' Commons[144] to send you the will, and then some document may be inserted with fuller explanation in the Gentleman's Magazine.
I wish to have a few copies of the last prison history.[145]
I am sincerely
J. C. Lettsom

Sambrook Court
June 3 1813

52. [S]

Endorsed: Lettsom

Mr. Nichols
Red lion passage
Fleet street

Dear Mr. Nichols,
I have been applied to by Mr. Nightingale, an author as you will see by the enclosed printed paper, who requests some gratuity from the Literary fund[146]

---

[143] Anthony Fothergill died on 11 May 1813. See the Introduction to this volume, pp. 2, 5. Lettsom compiled a memoir of Anthony Fothergill for publication in Nichol's, *Literary anecdotes of the eighteenth century*, 9 vols, London, printed for the author, vol. 9, pp. 211–14.

[144] The court of the Bishop of London sat in Doctors' Commons near St Paul's Cathedral as well as the registries of various other church courts, such as the Bishop of Winchester, the Archdeacon of Surrey, the Archdeacons of London and Middlesex, the Deans and Chapters of St. Paul's and Westminster.

[145] Lettsom's 'LXXVIth letter on prisons' appeared with Neild's 'Account of Ludgate Prison' in *Gentleman's Magazine*, 1813, **83** (i): 431–2.

[146] The Corporation of the Royal Literary Fund was established in 1790. It aimed to provide relief to distressed authors of genius, learning and literary merit, and to help them when enfeebled and in declining life. See Royal Literary Fund, *An account of the institution of the Society for the establishment of a literary fund: constitutions of the Society, list of subscribers*, London, printed by John Nichols, 1799.

as a distressed author, now in the rules of a prison. His friend, who desired me to address you, speaks of him as a fair character.

I am ignorant, though a subscriber, of the plan adopted on such application, but it would oblige me to give me an answer as to the propriety of this application and the rules to be adopted to claim relief. Your reply as to the mode of conduct to be pursued, and the time as well as prospect of having relief.

I am respectfully

J. C. Lettsom

Sambrook Court
Feb. 27 1814

53. [S]

Endorsed: Lettsom, March 4.

March 1, 1814

Dear Mr. Nichols,

I believe no life was ever published of Mr. Neild.[147] I will write to his son to get if possible some materials: From what he has occasionally said to me, I did expect some interesting papers, but I fear that we shall be disappointed: He has not even left a will.

If, however, no part of his biography remain with his son, I think I could patch up something and certainly it should be at your service, though I have had some other applications on the subject.

I am sincerely etc.

J. C. Lettsom

~~Sambrook Court~~
~~Mar. 1 1814~~

---

[147] James Neild died at his Chelsea home on 16 February 1814. Neild's 600-page *State of the prisons in England, Scotland, and Wales, extending to various places therein assigned, not for the debtor only, but for felons also, and other less criminal offenders*, London, printed by John Nichols and Son, 1812, appeared two years before he died. Lettsom attempted to get a statue raised to him, as he had done with Howard, but failed due to Neild's treatment of his eldest son, which was "so notorious as to thwart my endeavours", wrote Lettsom in 1814. Cited in Abraham, op. cit., note 1 above, p. 261.

54. [S]

Endorsed: Lettsom

March 14 1814

Mr. Nichols,

~~I thank you for your indulgence. I have dated the note the 14th, for I think the dividends at the Bank are often delayed till the 14.~~

Mr. Neild has wrote to me, saying he possesses extensive memoirs of his father which he hopes in a few weeks to transmit to your friend.
J. C. Lettsom

~~Sambrook Court~~
~~Mar. 14 1814~~

~~When we meet I will give you the discount. The stamp would not do for anything above £100.~~

55. [S]

Endorsed: Dr. Lettsom. Mr. J. B. Nichols.

Mr. Bowyer Nichols
Red Lion passage
Fleet Street

April 26, 1814

Dear Mr. Nichols
I have not since heard from Mr. Neild (surviving only son)[148] but shall renew my application.

---

[148] Neild had two sons (and one daughter). He had a very poor relationship with his eldest son, William, to whom Lettsom thought he was unkind and abusive. Lettsom helped the boy to get a legal post in Barbados in the West Indies, where he contracted the disease that ended his life. Letters received by his father in May and June 1809 said that he had recovered from two fevers and was badly bitten by mosquitoes. James Neild's correspondence to Lettsom, at this time, none the less shows some concern for the boy about whom he professed himself "in a good deal of anxiety". He also stated, on 16 October 1810, that his son had "the *Thrush*". Abraham has taken this to be syphilis. The previous correspondence makes malaria seem just as likely. William died on 19 November 1810 when his ship docked at Falmouth at the end of his return journey to England. James Neild's younger son was John Camden Neild, who was educated at Eton and Trinity College, Cambridge, and called to the bar in 1808. Abraham, op. cit., note 1 above pp. 262–5. See also the various letters from Neild in the 'Letters to Lettsom' section.

I do not well know what you mean by the portraits of Cuming and Fothergill.[149] If you mean the copper plate engraving of the first, and the painting of the latter, they are at your service. I have also the half length of Cuming by Bentley, also at your command.

You may let me know perhaps by tomorrow morning what is meant, and which you may command from

yours sincerely

J. C. Lettsom

Apr. 16 1814

[Bowyer Nichols' original note to Lettsom is appended]

Dear Doctor,

Both my Father and myself are greatly obliged by your kind letter. What he wished was to have the use of <u>the two Copper Plates</u> ~~Dr.~~ <u>Dr. Cuming</u>, and that of the first Dr. <u>Fothergill</u>, in your very excellent Life of him.

yours etc.

56. [S]

Endorsed: Dr. Lettsom

May 31, 1814

Dear Mr. Nichols

I have twice searched for the plates of Grove Hill[150] without success, but will make another diligent one, by opening all my plates lest they may be placed with others.

I have no ~~engraving~~ plate of William Curtis, but I possess an engraving given to me by himself—my own head I enclose.

I thank you for the heads of our worthy friend Dr. Cogan, and am respectfully

J. C. Lettsom

Sambrook Court
May 31 1814

---

[149] See 'Letters to Lettsom' section, Letter 1 from Dr. Cleghorn.

[150] When Lettsom built his country mansion at Grove Hill, Camberwell, in about 1779, Camberwell was then a rural village. His wife loved the country and all Lettsom's children were raised there. Engravings were made of his property in 1795, by which time he had over ten acres of garden. Abraham, op. cit., note 1 above, pp. 105, 296, 298; a map of Grove Hill and its grounds in Lettsom's time is reproduced on p. 303.

The ~~plates~~ engravings herewith sent are at your service. Curtis, horticulturist at Walworth, married his cousin Miss Curtis, only daughter of William Curtis. He, I think, has a plate of his Father-in-Law.[151]

57. [S]

Endorsed: Lettsom 20

~~Dear Mr. Nichols~~

You have condensed an excellent epitome of the Memoirs of our deceased friend and meets my approbation.

I want much to prepare some account of James Neild, the visitor of Prisons, but, alas <u>tempus fallit, et forsan semper fallebit,</u>[152] <u>to the exertions</u> of yours sincerely
J. C. Lettsom

~~Sambrook Court~~
Nov. 11 1814

58. [S]

Endorsed: Lettsom Feb. 14 1815

Dear Mr. Nichols
I have read the enclosed with satisfaction, thinking that it cannot be mended. The copy is preparing for the subsequent portion of the Report.
I am sincerely etc.
J. C. Lettsom

Sambrook Court
Febr. 4 1815

---

[151] An authority on botany, the apothecary William Curtis (1746–99) was the translator of Linnaeus and the author of *Flora Londinensis*. He had a botanic garden in Higler's Lane, Lambeth Marsh, close to Blackfriars Bridge. He met Lettsom when they were both students and was another of Lettsom's life-long friends. Indeed, it was mainly owing to Lettsom's financial assistance that he was able to publish his *magnum opus*, the *Flora*. The second volume is dedicated to Lettsom. Abraham, op. cit., note 1 above, p. 82, 266. A deed of covenant, dated 25 November 1786, between Curtis and Lettsom, relating to the copyright of the *Flora Londinensis*, survives in the Society's volume 'Collection of letters, to and from John Coakley Lettsom'.

[152] "Time deceives and will always deceive".

59. [L]

Endorsed: Dr. Lettsom's Prescriptions, July 1815

[Recipient and address unknown]

Dear Colonel,
   I received your kind letter, and thank you for the note enclosed.
   I hope the prescription will answer more effectually with Eliza. It is the consequence of most laxative medicines to render the body more costive after their operation. It is usually otherwise with salts; and perhaps they might agree with Eliza.
   To dissolve an ounce, in a pint of water, of Epsom salt and take a fourth part every second or third morning, if prefer'd nearly lukewarm. In effect this is similar to Cheltenham water, and is agreed in its salutary qualities.
   However, I hope the pills will suffice.
   I do not know when you leave town; but as I purpose to call soon, it will be prior to your departure.
I am affectionately
J. C. Lettsom

Sambrook Court
July 1 1815

60. [S]

Endorsed: Lettsom

Mr. B. Nichols
   I think I shall call upon you, if I can, between 12 and one—but do not be at home on my account, as the subject is unimportant—merely something about Dr. Fothergill's MSS.
J. C. Lettsom

July 25 [1815?].

[Mr. Bowyer Nichols' original note to Lettsom is appended]

Dr. Lettsom for the purpose of asking your Advice about Dr. Fothergill's works. He wishes to know if you have glanced at the volumes he left with you. He will call again soon.

61. [S]

[no addressee or date]

Endorsed: <u>Lettsom</u> P[153]

Dear Sir

Mrs. Smith[154] has requested me to inform you that a Copy of her verses with various alterations appeared in yesterday's Observer,[155] without her being previously informed of such alterations; I am therefore persuaded she will feel herself much hurt should you transpose a single word and you will perhaps have the goodness to print them exactly as they stand in the original.
very respectfully
your obedient servant
P Lettsom

Sambrook Court
Basinghall Street
Monday morning

---

[153] This letter is probably from Pickering Lettsom and possibly dates from *c*.1804.

[154] Possibly the romantic poet, novelist and political radical Charlotte Turner Smith (1749–1806). Smith wrote the first edition of her *Elegiac Sonnets* (1783) when she was in a debtor's prison with her family. Her husband went to France to escape his creditors, until he was able to return, largely due to Smith. However, she left him in 1787, supporting her twelve children through her writing. For her poetry, see Stuart Curran (ed.), *The poems of Charlotte Smith*, Oxford University Press, 1993.

[155] The *Observer* newspaper reference has not been found.

5

Family Business

In his will Lettsom decreed, "I leave to my son John Miers Lettsom all my manuscripts, he to destroy all that may tend to hurt the tenderest mind".[1] John Miers Lettsom predeceased his father and the executor was Lettsom's son-in-law Philip Elliot. If he had carefully scrutinized all Lettsom's manuscripts, he might have found material in the letters we publish in this section "to hurt the tenderest mind". There are fifty-four letters here, all dealing with family matters. All were loose when first seen by us. As with the letters in the 'Benevolent Favours' section, their provenance is uncertain but, given the Elliot connection, it is most likely they were lent by Mrs. Jill Martin (see Introduction, p. 10). We do not know if Abraham saw them. He quotes from none of them.

Forty-nine of the letters are to Lettsom from his nephew William James Archer or his wife J. Elizabeth Archer (Betsy). William was the son of Lettsom's wife's sister Mary Miers (see genealogical chart). Elizabeth was of Dutch descent, the daughter of Le Chevalier Horngacher de Dardagni. The Archers lived in Switzerland. The correspondence begins with an extremely ill-tempered letter (in French) from Elizabeth's father to Lettsom (whom he seemed to hold in high regard) complaining of the conduct of William with regard to Elizabeth. The basis of the complaint is difficult to fathom. They had seemingly recently married (in Switzerland, almost certainly) and Archer was incensed by the marriage contract. The details are perhaps unimportant. What is significant is that William and Elizabeth's daughter, Maria, was born in that year suggesting she was conceived out of wedlock.[2] One letter from Elizabeth hints at estrangement from her father (Letter 6). Elizabeth never left Switzerland in the period covered by this correspondence and never met Lettsom, yet her letters to him are full of expressions of love, gratitude and esteem suggesting Lettsom intervened on her behalf in this business. Indeed

---

[1] 'Abstract of the will of John Coakley Lettsom', cited in James Johnston Abraham, *Lettsom: his life, times, friends and descendants*, London, William Heinemann, 1933, p. 485.

[2] Even more interesting is that at a later date William refers to his "eldest" child, John, prompting the inference that the latter was illegitimate (Letter 24). But in Letter 5 Elizabeth implies Maria was the eldest. This seems more likely to be correct.

at one point she talks of the "protestations of ~~the~~ affection I allways bore you from the moment you shewed so much interested in my favor." (Elizabeth's English was not always up to scratch). Perhaps Lettsom prevailed on William to do the honourable thing and marry her.

Elizabeth's first letter is dated 1 November 1793 but clearly she had written earlier. Most of the correspondence until 1802 is from her (there is only one short letter from William before this) (Letter 12). William spent the bulk of this period in England and his absence was the source of much lamenting and indiscretion on Elizabeth's part. Lettsom might well have wanted these letters to have been destroyed after his death. Given Lettsom's fondness for women, it is likely he encouraged Elizabeth's outpourings, but we do not have his share of the correspondence. She complained to Lettsom that William's long absence made her a "widow" (Letter 3). She remarked on his "coolness" and how he was "childish". Money, she said was his "sole consideration" (Letter 4). By 1799 when he went to England again she was blessing the day he left (Letter 9). There might have been some truth in her accusations. William's first letter to Lettsom that we have was written from Ramsgate en route to Switzerland and was about income tax (Letter 12). After 1802 William settled back in Switzerland and does not seem to have returned to England by the time the correspondence we have finishes in 1811. In fact after his last return in 1802 domestic matters seem to have got distinctly better. The Archers had a farm and a vineyard and were clearly as prosperous as was possible in a war-torn country. Money matters dominate William's letters to Lettsom but he reports with pride on the growth of the children, including Maria's marriage in 1810 (Letters 47 and 48). Elizabeth's letters cease to contain any criticism of her husband. Aside from the domestic tribulations these letters betray, they tell a story of a family in a country riven by war. In one way or another nearly every letter makes reference to the effect of occupation or the local reverberations of events further afield. The difficulties of ensuring that letters arrived in either direction were not the least of these. William, many of whose financial affairs were managed in London, was particularly concerned by this. What is striking too is that Lettsom, whose workload was clearly massive, was also undertaking financial errands for William. As noted, the correspondence we have ends in 1811 but with a perfectly ordinary letter from William and it is hard to imagine there were not many more (Letter 50). There follows a brief note from Lettsom to one of his grandchildren that we have not included in the other Lettsom correspondence because it deals with family matters. The next three letters do not concern Lettsom at all and were written after his death. They are from John Elliot, Lettsom's grandson, to his father and sister. We have included them for the sake of completeness. They were among the loose letters we first saw.

SWISS ARCHERS

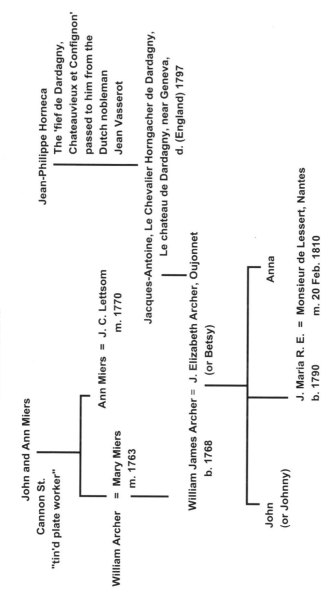

John and Ann Miers
Cannon St.
"tin'd plate worker"

William Archer = Mary Miers
                 m. 1763

Ann Miers = J. C. Lettsom
            m. 1770

Jean-Philippe Horneca
The 'fief de Dardagny,
Chateauvieux et Confignon'
passed to him from the
Dutch nobleman
Jean Vasserot

Jacques-Antoine, Le Chevalier Horngacher de Dardagny,
Le chateau de Dardagny, near Geneva,
d. (England) 1797

William James Archer = J. Elizabeth Archer, Oujonnet
b. 1768   (or Betsy)

John
(or Johnny)

Anna

J. Maria R. E. = Monsieur de Lessert, Nantes
b. 1790   m. 20 Feb. 1810

1. [L]

Endorsed: Mr Horngacher, Nov. 19, 1790, Dardagny.

à Monsieur
Monsieur le Docteur, J. C. Lettsom
Bazinghall Street, Sambroock house
à Londres.

Mon cher Parent,

A mon retour de Flandres ou j'avois eté voir mon fils en garnison à Valenciennes, j'ai trouvé icy il y a quelques jours la lettre que vous m'avès fait l'honneur de m'écrire le 4 9.bre. seul, privé de ma fille, je ne puis faire traduire votre lettre, et le peu de connaissance que j'ai de la langue Anglaise fait que ne comprenant pas d'une manière bien certaine le contenu de votre lettre, je n'ose de hazarder d'y répondre, je suis forcé de renvoyer jusques à ce que je puisse la faire traduire, et je ne scais pas trop encore par qui: etant assès délicat de communiquer ces lettres, cependant je m'en occuperai le plus tot possible.

Je crois toutes fois Monsieur avoir compris que vous répétés huitante neuf livres Sterlings pour divers frais occasionés par l'affront indigne que M^r: votre neveu n'a pas craint de faire à ma signature. Il n'a pas craint non plus de me donner à entendre dans une de ses lettres qu'il regardoit comme infidèle le contract de mariage passé entre lui et ma fille, ce qui ne va rien moins qu'a m'accuser du crime de faux ainsi que les avocats, et notaires qui ont dressés le contract. Malgré mes sollicitations préssantes et soutenues durant plusieurs mois M^r: W: J: Archer n'a pas jugé a propos de me donner aucune espèce de satisfaction a cet égard, je ne scais pas comment cette nouvelle vilaine affaire se terminera.

Je reviens à ce que je crois avoir compris que dans la fin de votre lettre vous répétés 89 Livres Sterlings de divers frais. J'ignore qui sera obligé de payer cette somme ce que je n'ignore pas <u>c'est que très certainement ce n'est point vous qui devés supporter les susdits frais, et que tot ou tard ou M^r: votre neveu ou moi devons les rembourser;</u> cette question se decidera, vous pouvés y compter et vous serés satisfait.

La conduite de M^r: W: J: Archer à l'égard de ma fille est mauvaise et répréhensible, les détails facheux m'en sont connus. Je doute que ma fille puisse supporter longtemps de pareils procèdés malgré la resignation et toutes ses bonnes intentions.

Je suis affligé de n'avoir jamais à vous entretenir que de choses tristes. Recevés je vous prie Monsieur tous mes voeux pour votre santé, votre conservation et le bonheur de toute votre famille et soyés bien

convaincu de tous les sentiments d'est[]³ et d'amitié avec lesquels. J'ai l'honneur d'être
Mon cher Parent Votre trés humble et trés obeissant serviteur

Le Chevalier Horngacher de Dardagni⁴

Château de Dardagny 28 9.ᵇʳᵉ 1790
pré Genève.

2. [L]

Endorsed: From Betsey Archer, Nov. 1 1793, Oujonnet. answered.

Dr. J. C. Lettsom, Sambrook House, Basing-hall Street, London, England.
Via Allemagne

I am so much ashamed my dear Uncle of my long silence that I hardly dare begin my apology. I hope though you'll accept of it and will excuse me, particularly if William has mentionned to you the high esteem, regard and love I bear you. You cannot imagine, my dear Sir, how sincerely I regret to have lost this last opportunity of seeing you for I fear it will be a very long while before Mr Archer goes again to England and consequently before I'll be able to go my self, for notwithstanding the pleasure it would give me to be acquainted with Mr. Archer's relations, I cannot think of leaving my dear little ones behind and that would have been the case lately. I must hope for a more favourable opportunity and beg of you to continue me your affection.

I hope all your family is well, Wife and Children. My health is much better. Nothing agrees so well with me and does me so much good as riding on horseback. It strengthens me amazingly, and gives me a strong appetite, and luckily I have had all this last month very fine to ride.

My little ones are very healthy thank God and very good. My little Maria is the most engaging child I ever saw. I hope John will be the same when older, though he is a riotty little fellow now.

---

³ The rest of the word is covered by the back of the seal.
⁴ Betsy's father always used this spelling for his name. The first "seigneur de Dardagny", Aymon, knight and vassal of the Comte de Genève (in whose will he received 30 livres) is mentioned in 1280. At the Reformation, the "fief de Dardagny, Chateauvieux et Confignon" became a vassal of the République de Genève. Having been in the hands of the Lullin family, the fiefdom was acquired, in 1721, by the Dutch nobleman, Jean Vasserot. In 1775, it passed to Jean-Philippe Horneca, whose son, Jacques-Antoine (father of Betsy Archer), changed his patronym to Horngacher. André Locher, *Les châteaux suisses*, 'Le château de Dardagny', http://www.swisscastles.ch/Geneve/dardagny.html (10 May 1997).

We have no political news now, though yesterday I was told by a Bernois that the king of Prussia wanted the little republic of Neufchatel to decide on his side,[5] which would be likely to bring war in this country. He only left them 36 hours to decide about it; it is thought that the republic of Neufchatel would require the assistance of the Helvetic Body which by the treaties is obliged to give them help, yet no body seems anxious about it. I wish my dear Uncle you will be so good as to remember me kindly to all your family and believe me most sincerely your affectionnate devoted servant
J[e.] Elizabeth Archer

1[rs.] of November

You may expect to hear from me by Mr. Macnamara who purpose seing you on his arrival in London. He left Lausanne Wednesday last, they have been very civil to me.

3. [L]

Endorsed: From Elizabeth Archer, Apr. 28 1794, Oujonnet.

Dr. J. C. Lettsom
Sambrook House
Basing-hall Street
London
England

Oujonnet April the 28th 1794

My dear Uncle
Our Correspondence has from so long a time droped that nothing less than a letter of congratulation could be I fear acceptable. Believe me, my most beloved Sir, I never have forgot you nor never possibly could. I wrote you

---

[5] A canton of Switzerland, bordered by the canton of Bern, the Pays de Vaud, the lake of Neufchâtel and the French border. It had extensive cotton, linen and woollen manufactures. Neufchâtel and the district of Valengin formerly constituted a small state with considerable freedom. In 1707, when the Duchess of Nemours died, the state acknowledged the King of Prussia's claims to its sovereignty. A century later, in 1807, Prussia ceded Neufchatel to France, upon which Napoleon Bonaparte gave it to Louis Alexandre Berthier (1753–1815), prince of Neufchâtel and Wagram, then French minister of war. In 1814, it was acknowledged as a Swiss canton by the Congress of Vienna, though Prussia's nominal sovereignty was preserved.

(I dare not say when) in the month of October but never received an answer and to my shame never ventured an other letter, but you are so very Good and so indulgent that all my hopes lays in your forgiveness. Was you to know how sincerely I love you I am confident you would not refuse it me. What I am sorry for is that I [have] never yet been in the way to make you sensible of the truth of the protestations of ~~the~~ affection I allways bore you from the moment you shewed so much interested in my favor. How much you would wrong me was you ever to think me ungrateful. If William has told you how often I talk'd about you, how much I wished it to be in my power to show you my everlasting gratitude you cannot doubt the sincerity of what here I say. I must wish you joy on the happy marriage of your Daughter which is attended with my best wishes for her future welfare.[6] May Heaven Bless her in this new state. May she for ever be a stranger to the bitters of it never to experience, but the sweets. Tell her many kind things for me, though I have not the advantage of been known to her. I hope she will receive them. Where is your son I saw here two years ago? I wish he was to pass through here in his way back to England. He seemed then a very accomplished young man, now he must still be improved by his travels and still more pleasant.[7]

My little Children are perfectly well. I think them charming but you know a mother is allways a little partial and they are both so remarquably fond of me so that every day more and more it endears them to me. It is such a comfort to be loved that we cannot help returning love for love: it is very natural. You would laugh to hear and see them. When I leave them behind they are in agonies, but it's soon over and when I return they are as happy as can be. They rejoice much to see their future brother or sister. They are very fond one of an other and very entertaining. When I shall be able to make them acquainted with their family, God knows. I hope though they~~'ll~~ shall never be strangers to you. I hope Mrs. Lettsom is in good health. The last letter

---

[6] On 16 June 1794, Mary Ann Lettsom married Philip Elliot (1767–1847), M.D., son of Welsh surgeon, George Elliot, at St. George's Church, Hanover Square, London. They had four children: Mary Ann, George Lettsom, Henry Capel and Margaret Eliza. Lettsom was initially perturbed that Elliot was not a Quaker and had little by way of fortune. In moving from Swansea to London, Elliot hoped to increase his practice substantially. Dr. and Mrs Elliot settled in Barnet, where he practised until 1801. After John Miers Lettsom died, in 1800, the Elliots moved in, for a time, to Sambrook Court, while Dr. Elliot acted as his father-in-law's assistant. Elliot afterwards succeeded John Miers as physician to the General Dispensary in Aldersgate Street. However, London practice seems not to have suited him and he soon left. See Abraham, op. cit., note 1 above, pp. 293, 460.

[7] John Miers Lettsom went on the Grand Tour between May 1792 and October 1793, accompanied by Dr. James Sims, Lettsom's friend and President of the Medical Society of London. They visited Flanders, France, Switzerland, Italy, Germany and Prussia, where Lettsom junior spent most of his time studying medicine under his father's friend, Johann Friedrich Blumenbach (1752–1840), professor of medicine at Gottingen, who did his main work in comparative anatomy. Ibid., pp. 289, 292.

I had from Mr. Archer which was of the eighth of this month you were, as he wrote me, all well, and he mentionned his intention of leaving England soon to return here. I have been a widow so long that I don't know how I'll bring it about to be a wife again or he to be a husband. It's to be hoped we'll manage it if not better at least as well as we [did].[8] We have no particular n[ews] about politics. Them French goes on a great deal too well. If this Campaigning is not ~~now~~ attended with more success than the last I fear then we must give them over, which would be horrid. The Wildest brutes never was so cruel as they are. They brought the Guillotine last week at a little place nigh here called Pontarliers[9] where they begin now to execute the poor unfortunate wretches who are either too good or too rich for their new principles. Farewell my dear Uncle. Lett me hear from you and believe me most affectionnately your humble servant
Je. Elizabeth Archer

4. [L]

Endorsed: From E. Archer, May 6 1794, Oujonnet.

Dr. John Coakley Lettsom
Sambrook House
Basing-hall St
London
England

Oujonnet, May the 6th

It is impossible for me, my most dear and beloved Uncle, to acknowledge my gratitude for the very kind letter you have favored me with. What I feel I is too much above what I can express even to try it. To find such a friend such as you, when entirely left to myself, when allmost alone in this wide world is the Greatest, the only, comfort I felt from a longful while.

At the same time I received your letter, one from William came to hand announcing me his leaving England on the 1st of this month. Though not living perfectly happy with him, I am glad of his return. His long stay from me

---

[8] The top layer of the paper has been taken off by removal of the seal, but there is a trace outline of two "d"s.

[9] This is in the east of France, now in the département of Doubs, in the region of Franche-Comté, bordering Switzerland.

and my Children may easily make you perceive that his love to either me or them is not very strong. I own, notwithstanding my endeavours to make up my mind to his coolness, I cannot often help regretting the happy days that a more loving husband and father would have made me pass. He has a good heart and many good qualities but unfortunately he has none of those delicate affectionnate feelings that in a private life can only make one happy. He is fond of teasing those he lives with, but I hope that nine months will have made him more settled and less childish. I fear by his never saying a word about his father that they are not on good terms. I hope to God it is not the case for is there any thing so wrong as for a father and son to be continually at variance together? My dear Sir, if you did but know how I hate quarrels and if you consider that ever since I married there has been a continuance of them either with one or t'other, you would pity me. It wears my health out entirely. You would hardly know me for having been without disputing these eight months. I am as well as ever I was in my life, yet have I had many painful moments, few friends, many people jealous of the liberty I enjoyed. In this little paltry contry scandal is never at an end, and a young woman without her husband is too good a theme to escape it. To that I never would have been exposed had Mr Archer been like any other man and taken me with him. It was so natural for him to make me acquainted with his own family, but money is for ever his sole consideration and the fear of being annoyed with a Wife and Children was too much for him. I am sadly affraid, my dear Uncle, that still for a great ~~wh~~ while I must be doomed only to know you by correspondence, though nothing in the world I wish more than to see you to enjoy the blessing of your company. I am confident that I must be happy with you. You shew me so much tenderness to be otherwise. You are a second father to me. Oh, I beg, I beseech of you to be one to me. Mine is so wretched, so unhappy, that his own sufferings are already too much for him to bear. How then could I be so hardhearted as to make him a confident of mine? You see that when I tell you that your letter is the greatest comfort I experienced for a long while, it is not too much said, for what can be more wretched than not to have a friend to unbosom oneself. Though I have particular and, I hope, sincere friends, yet there's many things that cannot be said. To you I can lay my hea[rt] open without fear. I beg you will keep this letter to yourself, my dear Sir, as Mr Archer sees all ~~my~~ the letters that came for me. You'll oblige me to be particular in your answer, if you only ~~have~~ wish it to be seen by me.

I am happy to hear about your son.[10] You run a fair chance of increasing your family, but there is never too much of a good thing, and I have no doubt

---

[10] This presumably refers to the engagement of John Miers Lettsom, who married Rachel Nanson, daughter of William Nanson of New Bridge Street, on 9 April of the following year, 1795. See Abraham, op. cit., note 1 above, p. 293.

but the choice of your Children must be an agreable one to you and Mrs. Lettsom,[11] whom I beg to be particularly remembered to. I hope you received the letter I wrote you last week. I am so unwell today that I must end this scrawl. I am so big and so heavy, I am sure I shall be delivered soon, what I wish with all my heart, the last days being so unpleasant, for I am a great coward and the expectation is to me near as painful as the pain itself. Farewell, my dear Uncle, loove me and my sweet little babes. Think of us sometimes, and believe me most sincerely, your affectionnate and grateful niece,
J. Elizabeth Archer

Oujonnet May the 9th.

5. [L]

Endorsed: From Mrs. Archer, May 29 1798, Oujonnet.

Dr. J. C. Lettsom, Sambrook House, Basinghall Street, London.

May the 29th 97[12]

It has been a great pleasure to me, my dear Sir, to receive the very kind letter you have been so good as to write me. The far distant hopes you give me of passing once over our mountains to see me fills my heart with gratitude and joy. I cannot tell you how happy I would be to see you. I am sadly affraid the dismal state of this poor ruined Country will prevent your putting this charming plan to execution for a long time to come, at least before Peace is made, and sorry I am to say but I don't think it will be yet.[13]

I have the pleasure to hear often from you, my dear Uncle, by William's letters who repeats often how good and kind you behave to him which is indeed a great comfort to me, for I am certain he must be sometimes much

---

[11] Unlike his sister, Mary Ann, who married only two months after him, John Miers chose a Quaker for his wife. Lettsom had to announce Mary Ann's secession and was criticized for allowing the marriage. Abraham, ibid., p. 293.

[12] The date at the head of the letter clearly says 97, while Lettsom's endorsement reads 1798. That it was written in 1797 is further proved by the fact that Elizabeth Archer's father was still alive when the letter was written. He was dead by November 1797.

[13] France overthrew the Swiss Confederation in 1798 and proclaimed the Helvetic Republic on 19 March 1798.

uneasy on our account, particularly as there's no possibility for his return till the affairs takes another turn.[14] I hope he will profit of his stay in London and of your good advices to manage his fortune, and his Childrens' fortune to their greatest advantage and with prudence. We all tremble for the credit of old England. What horid expense does it sustain. It is really impossible not to dread the end of all this, when I consider how near I have been to be sent out of this here place, consiquently near loosing it for ever, and that perhaps I am not yet safe. I own I wish much William had courage enough to make perhaps a loss in selling some of his English funds and to place it somewhere sure, if there's such thing to be found. He is on the spot and directed by you. I hope he will prevent the blow. Excuse my anxiety, my dear Uncle, but think what would become of us if unfortunately poor old England was to fall like every other Country. I think it is prudent to have a little money every where. I you don't think like me, do not even mention my fears to my poor William. It is unnecessary then to make him uneasy. You will do me a great pleasure and render me a great service if you can with any certainty quiet my mind about the Placements of his money. It is very fortunate he is absent for he would not be safe here. When they will put the taxes on the fortunes, they would put it w[ith?][15] his whole and detain him untill h[e] had paid his Contribution. I am resol[ved] to deffend my propriety as much as I can and not to leave the place untill it becomes absolutely necessary for my safety and for my dear beloved little ones. I am much affray'd, my dear Uncle, it will be out of your power to read and understand this scrawl. I have entirely lost the habit of writing English and my hand shakes so much that I can scarce hold my pen, yet I hope you will excuse all my blunders and believe me with a true filial affection, yours
J[e.] Elizabeth Archer

My father is with me and desires to be kindly remembered to you: he means to [re]turn to Italy in a short time. Will you be so good to say many things to all your family. If you favour me with a letter you will render me very happy. I will write you again in a short time, if it does not bore you too much.

---

[14] With the French occupation of Switzerland, William Archer seems to have left the country to safeguard his investments. As a British national, he would not have been safe in Switzerland.
[15] Word covered by seal.

6. [L]

Endorsed: From Mrs. Archer, Nov. 10 1797, Oujonnet. answered.

Oujonnet 10th November 1797

My dear Uncle

We received your afflicting letter of the 19th October the day before yesterday. I need not tell you how severely we have felt the loss we have just sustained, so unexpectedly: it's out of William's power to write to-day but he intends to do it in a Post or two. We have the consolation ~~to~~ of being assured our dear Father has received all medical assistance and attention it was possible for you to bestow on him, for which my dear Uncle we return you ~~our~~ most sincere thanks. We are happy to be informed you and your family enjoy good health and wish with all my heart you may continue long the same. It's a cruel trial to part with those we love.

My dear little ones are well thank God. Maria is much afflicted of the loss of her Grand father whom she remembers perfectly well and whom she loved tenderly. John was too young to recollect him and Anna was unknown to him. I Beg my dear Uncle you will excuse the badness of the stile not being used to write in English and being much agitated at present. William joins me in affectionnate love to you and your family. Believe me your afflicted niece J^{e.} Elizabeth Archer

I'll be very happy my dear Uncle if you do me the favour to write me, for several times I have had the pleasure to write to you as well as to my poor father but never receiv'd any answers since above three years. I feel it much at present that my father never answered me. If you knew how much I love and respect you my dear Uncle you would not forgett me.

7. [L]

Endorsed: From Betsey Archer, May 12 1798,¹⁶ Oujonnet

Dr. J. C. Lettsom
Sambrook House
Basing-Hall Street
London

---

¹⁶ The considerable delay between the date of sending from Switzerland and the month of receipt in England may be due to the Napoleonic Wars or delivery of the letter by hand.

12 Feb.ʳ 1798

Though I wrote you several times my dear Uncle without ever receiving any answer from you, once more I take the liberty to address myself to you to ask you to be so good to remit the inclosed to William. I hope he is safely arrived amongst you. You will render me a great [ser]vice my dear Sir to let me know if [he ha]s[17] arrived or not. You cannot think how anxious I am about him. I thought he did not look well when he went away. The Length of the journey and the news we have here of the French taking possession of Hanover puts me in a great anxiety about him. If you favor me with an answer be so good not to tell me of any news and particularly nothing about mo... matters;[18] tell him so if he is with you, it's of the greatest importance. I only wish to know how you all do. Thank God I am better than I expected; my children are very well. Will you remember me to Mrs. Lettsom, to your family, particularly to your son John I had the pleasure to see. I wish I was with you my dear Uncle for I love you allways with all my heart and beg of you not to forget me.

8. [L]

Endorsed: From Elizabeth Archer, July 21 1798, Geneva.

<u>To England Via Hamburgh</u>
Dr. J. C. Lettsom
Sambrook Court
Basing-Hall-Street
London
England

Genèva July the 21ˢᵗ·

I had the pleasure to write you, my Dear Sir, about a couple of months ago. I hope my letter has reached you by this time and found you in good health as well as your family. I have often the pleasure to hear of you by William's letters, who knows very well how much I interest my self on your welfare particularly at this moment of War. The Papers in general gives such dreadful accounts respecting England and particularly Ireland, that it frightens the friends of those contrys to Death. The French are become so daring that

---

[17] The manuscript is holed here, but this seems the most likely wording.
[18] Money matters presumably.

I begin to think that no earthly power can resist them. Yet the fact is that no nation but England has as yet employed the proper means to do it. I must make an apology, my dear Sir, for the liberty I am going to take, and beg of you to excuse me. A friend of mine[19] is particularly interested to know the direction of the Gentelmen under-named, and would be exceedingly obliged to you if you had the kindness to enquire where they lives and where their letters may be directed. One is Mr. Silvester Douglas[20] whose House is N⁰· 32 or 33 in Bedford Square. He married Lady Marguerite North. The second is Sir James or John Burgess, who was under Secretary of State in the year 1792 and lived at that time in a House near Downing Street. The third is General R. Abercrombie, who was C[om]mander-in-Chief of the British forces in the East Indies.[21] If it is not too troublesome, my Dear Sir, for you to make these enquiries and send me the directions, you'll render a very important service to my friend. I know you are so obliging that it has induced me to be so indiscreet.

I hope William do not think of leaving you; Germany cannot be an agreable stay for a foreigner as there's every appearance of beginning again a continental War. It is a dreadful prospect for the inhabitants of poor wreched Switzerland to become the theatre of War.[22] Their existence then will be truely horrid to the last degree. But lett us end such a dismal subject. Tell me How you all do? It appears that your family increased much. I felicit you, for nothing is so agreable as a pretty heap of sweet little babys. Mine are charming. They have very good tempers and good faces. My boy has the sweetest disposition of the three. Maria is very sensible and witty.[23] Anna is as pretti a little girl a[s] can be, always merry and full of humour, [so] excessif giddy she

---

[19] Possibly Mrs. Hatley, whom she mentions in the next letter.

[20] Sylvester Douglas (1743–1823), Baron Glenbervie, Tory politician and diarist. When this letter was written, he was Lord of the Treasury, a post that he held until 1800, when he was appointed governor of the Cape of Good Hope and was created Baron Glenbervie of Kincardine in the Irish peerage. He was a supporter of the Scottish manager, Lord Melville and, therefore, of Pitt the younger. His correspondence, family papers and diaries are held in the National Library of Scotland. *Dictionary of National Biography* (1917), vol. 5, pp. 1253–4.

[21] Sir Ralph Abercrombie or Abercromby (1734–1801) was the general credited, alongside Sir John Moore, with improving the military reputation of the British soldier. In 1795–7, he was Commander-in-Chief of British Forces in the West Indies (rather than the East Indies), sent to reduce the French sugar islands. He took St. Lucia and Demerara and relieved St. Vincent. He also examined the state of health of the soldiers in the West Indies, adapted their uniforms for a hot climate and set up mountain stations and sanatoria. When this letter was written, he had just resigned his command of the troops in Ireland. *Dictionary of National Biography* (1917), vol. 1, pp. 43–6.

[22] This letter was written just after the establishment of the Helvetic Republic. For the rest of the Napoleonic wars, Switzerland had a French army of occupation and was technically under French rule.

[23] The manuscript reads "vitty". Both Betsy and William Archer often interchange "v" and "w".

amuses me from morn till night with all her tricks. She is too young yet to be troubled with leçons, and has nothing to do but to play, yet she knows all the letters and will soon be able to read. How happy I should be, my dear Sir, were they known to you and was you affectionnate to them. I hope once to be more particularly known to you than by letters, and then to experience the friendship of which you have so often given me proofs. En attendance, believe me most affectionately yours.

9. [L]

Endorsed: From Elizabeth Archer, Nov. 29 1799, Oujonnet. answered.

Dr. John Coakley Lettsom
Sambrook House
Basing-Hall Street
London

Oujonnet 29ᵗʰ of November

My Dear Sir,

Permit me to take the opportunity of my friend Mrs. Hatley going to London to write you a few lines. I desired her to call on you on her arrival. I know so well your Goodness and your friendship for me that I am sure you'll hear with interest of our Welfare. She'll tell you how happy I would be to be acquainted with you to present you my Children. They are brought up to love and respect you, my Dear Uncle and I hope if ever Mr. Archer will permit me to take them to England that you'll be pleased with 'em. They are very good natured and of agréable disposition.

I received the other day a letter from William, wherein he says that you had had the goodness to write me above ten weeks before the dâte of his letter. I never received it, which I regret much. It'll come to hands perhaps within these twelve months. At any time it will be a very wellcome Epistle. We have had a most wretched year to pass. Thank God we are at the End of it and it's to be hoped the next will be better though there's kind of miserys that can never be recalled. When you see so many unhappy, it is impossible to enjoy any thing.

I am going in a few days to town where I mean to pass my Winter. Here I have no possibility of giving any lessons to my children, and to put them to scool and be left alone I owne I have no courage. My dear Boy John wants masters. He is a charming little fellow, for the figure the picture of poor John and his temper is possible too soft for a boy. It would be a great pity not to take the greatest care of his education, as he has lived continually in the Contry and at liberty. It is a hard task to curb him to dipendance. Maria my Eldest girl wishes very much to be acquainted with all her English Cousins. She has been very ill this Summer but is quite recovered now. My little Anna is very pretty and has really the temper of an Angel. Reading all these praises of my offsprings, won't you think me a little out of my senses, my good Sir, but you know what is a mother's Eye, then pardon me. I am happy to hear of the increasse of your family.[24] If they are like you, there never will be too many. If my cousin, John, remembers me, pray say many kind things to him. I hope Mrs. Lettsom is well. When Peace is made you must bring her to breathe a little of our sharp Winds. I'll receive you both as well as in my powers. William is very happy to be with you all. Oh, how I Bless the day he went off. I hope he amuses himself. He writes me often in a very kind manner, but yet he never said he wished we were with him in his own Contry, at which I am a little Angry, for out of civility he might very well have paid me such a compliment, but likely he feared I should go and thank him my self. What do you say, my dear Uncle, to this long tiresome letter? You must think me a terrible Chatterer, but ask Mrs. Hatley. It is only when you are the subject that I fall into such fits. I'd never end was I to assure you of all I feel for you. Believe me, most respectfully yours. J.E. Archer

10. [L]

Endorsed: From Elizabeth Archer, June 23 1800, Oujonnet. answered.

Dr. John Coackley Lettsom
Sambrook-House
Basing-hall Street
London
England

Oujonnet 23[d] of June 1800

My dear Sir,
    Though I have not been so happy as to receive any answer to my two last letters to you, I will not deprive myself of the pleasure of corresponding with

---

[24] This refers to the birth of Lettsom's various grandchildren. John Miers Lettsom and his wife, Rachel, had three children in quick succession, after their marriage in 1795. Mary Ann, who became Mrs. Philip Elliot in 1794, had two children by the time this letter was written. See Abraham, op. cit., note 1 above, pp. 293, 460.

you, my dear Uncle, and assure you that my respectful love for you, notwithstanding your long silence, is for ever the same. Give me leave to return you my best thanks for the affectionnate manner in which you talked about me with my poor unfortunate friend Mrs. Hatley. She wrote me she had had the pleasure of a long Conversation with you, the result of which increased if possible my wish of being personally acquainted with you. I allways flattered myself William would have proposed me to take a Trip to England during this War which would have been very easy for me in passing through France, and I think he could well afford to let me pass two month with his relations. I ask for no more, but I believe he is too much affraid of the Money it would Cost him to Grant me such a favor (he says when Peace is made). Don't you think, my Dear Sir, that is to say as much as <u>never</u>. I am very angry with him to love his money better than either his Wife or Children, et[25] to deprive me of the pleasure of seing you. I believe I'll finish by givin you a Rendezvous at Dover or some Where about without asking his permission. I'll pass six Weeks in old Dear England whilst he'll be bathing ~~in~~ at Buxton.[26] I'll not even pay him a visit to punish him, and when I'm returned to my Wineyards, he'll have nothing to do but to pay the Journey. Now, Dear Uncle, what do you think of my Plan? Don't you think he deserves it? Now without joking do what you Can to persuade him to lett me Come. If he will not this Summer, I'll wait till next April. If I have but the certainty of going, I'll be happy. Really, you have no idea how much I wish to be acquainted with you. Mrs. Hatley, who knows what a regard I have for you, says it would be still increased was I to see you.

You know by the Papers all I could tell you about this wretched Contry. I suppose you all pity us. If you ~~don~~ do, you do right, for it is impossible to be worst than we are and no hopes of being better. There's no more money, scarce any food, and what little is left is to the order of the first troops that's pass. Yet we must think ourselves very happy that the Austrians have been so kind not to resist the French Army. Had the French been beat, the Theâtre of War must, of Course, be in this Contry, then all was over. But we have no such fears at present. We have never been better guarded—I hear the Cannon this moment. It announces the Compleat defeat of the Austrians and a suspension of Arms between the armies.[27] Really, this Emperor and his Ministers are [a] sad pack of scoundrels. I dare say he will make up such a Patched-up Peace as he has already done, which will last 6 month. Yet they say that all the French Army who went to Italy is coming ~~again~~ back to Cross

---

[25] A momentary lapse into French.
[26] Buxton in Derbyshire.
[27] On 14 June, Napoleon won the battle of Marengo against Austria. The battle took place during a French offensive in Italy and by it France regained northern Italy.

this Contry to Go to the Rhine, ~~to se~~ to do there again the Emperor's business.[28]

I hope, my dear Uncle, that all your family is in good health. I just receiv'd a letter from William who says Mrs. Lettsom is much better and that you are so kind as to enquire often about me. I have been very indifferent the whole Winter, with a bad Cold, which lasted so long that I have been ordered to drink asse's milk. I hope it'll do me good. I find by William's letters he seems quite bored. Good God, was he in this Contry [how][29] would it be? I wish you would give him some good Remedys against this disease, the ~~greatest~~ Worst of all on Earth. You will do me a very great Pleasure to write me, my dear Sir. A letter from you will make me quite happy. I beg of you to remember me kindly to all those who think about me. I must end this too long scrawl by assuring you of my most sincere Wishes for your Welfare and happyness. My Children who wishes as much as their mother to be acquainted with you joins with me to assure you of our respectful affection.

J. E. Archer

11. [L]

Endorsed: From Mrs. Archer, Oct. 1 1800, near Geneva. answered.

Dr. John Coakley Lettsom
Sambrook Court
Basing-Hall Street
London

Plongeon near Geneva 1st of 7[ber]. 1800

My dear Uncle,

I cannot express you the pleasure your very affectionate letter afforded me. It was so long since I have been deprived of hearing from you: but yet this dear letter of yours was damped with my tears. Yet I find my self happy you gave me an occasion of lamenting with you the loss of my amiable Cousin John. My dear Uncle, be assured if I did not mention this most lamentable event it was for fear of openning a fresh, a cruel wound in your respectable

---

[28] Marengo dashed all hopes of an Austrian invasion of Provence. The French General Moreau crossed the Rhine and broke allied opposition at Hohenlinden on 3 December 1800.

[29] Hole in paper caused by seal.

bosom,[30] a loss I felt my self so deeply, I thought would not be a subject I even dared to mention. But your fortitude is equal to all your Christian virtues, and you show your self above human kind. The little I saw of your beloved deceased John increased much my affliction of his untimely death. It was impossible to see him and not to feel a strong affection for him. His amiable behaviour, his sweetness of Temper painted on all his lovely features gained him every heart, but alas he is no more and nothing can return him to our wishes. He is happy, much happier, than the friends he left below to regret him. I hope his poor little babes, particularly his little boy, will be a consolation to you, a comfort to his unfortunate widow. Good God, I can write no more. I am struck with Grief and fear. Indeed, I too was not long ago near to be separated from my John. He was very ill and I feel I could never have supported to part with him. Unhappy Mrs. Lettsom. You, my dear Uncle, how I do pity you.

I accept with gratitude the Challenge of a letter every month. It is a favor, a kindness I little expected, and for which I return you my most sincere thanks. You'll judge by my exactness to write of ~~the~~ my pleasure to correspond with you. I am very glad your daughter Mrs. Elliot is with you. Her little family must be a great comfort to you. How happy I would think my self to be transported amongst you all, to be acquainted with you, my respected, my beloved Parent, you who ever since I entered your family have proved my best friend.

You tell me you look sometimes at our Pictures. I own I am very sorry you know us by such ugly likenesses. If I remember well, they all squint in a terrible manner and I do assure you, without flatery, we have all of us a pair of pretty Eyes Enough and not at all squintish. My boy is so pretty that they run after him in the street to look at him and he is just as good as he is handsome. Maria is so much like me that I can say nothing of her. Anna is extremely pretty, and what is still better than their faces is the goodness of their little hearts. You may easily suppose how happy they make me, and how much I doat on them.

We have a great number of Troops now in the Contry. The Second Army de Reserve which they rise to 30 thousand men, is Crossing Switzerland to Go to Germany.[31] We are very quiet here and we know no more news than if

---

[30] John Miers Lettsom died on 29 January 1800 from a "putrid fever" caught at the Aldersgate Dispensary, where he was physician. He bled himself while distracted and his father declared that he might as well have shot himself. He soon became delirious and died within a day. He was only twenty-nine years old. His father had invested so many hopes in his eldest son that he was said never entirely to have recovered from his death. See Abraham, op. cit., note 1 above, p. 293.

[31] The Army of the Reserve was organized and commanded by Louis Alexandre Berthier, chief of staff and the most senior of Napoleon's Marshals. It was this army that had crossed the Alps in 1800 and won the battle of Marengo.

we were in Africa. They say Buonaparte is again expected here. Yesterday they talked of Peace, to day of War. No body knows nothing. For example, what we know perfectly well in Switzerland is that we are ruined and eat up to our last, never to recover. You never can form a just idea of the misery of the Contry, of the wretchedness of the inhabitants. I am sure when William will return it'll break his heart to see to what is reduced a Contry formerly so happy.

The heat of the Summer has been so unwholesome that there's a terrible mortality, particularly amongst young People and Children. The SmallPox is of such a malignant kind as never was k[nown].[32] All those who have it dies. They even pretend[ed the] other day that it was something of the Plague.

I'm very happy you seem to like my poor friend Mrs. Hatley. She is very miserable and you are so good that I hope you'll pity her and help her. I love her much and am sorry that she is at such a distance of me that I can be of no service to her. In what ever you oblige her, you'll oblige me likewise. I must end this long scrawl for fear of teazing you so that you would not keep our agreement. I remain, Dear Sir, yours most sincerely,

J. E. Archer

12. [L]

Endorsed: From William Archer, Nov. 5 1800, Ramsgate. done.

D^r: J: C: Lettsom
Basinghall Street
London

Ramgate 5 Nov. 1800

Dear Uncle,

I received your favour of yesterday this morning. As I gave in my income last year at Bath, I did not know it was necessary to give in my income every year, but I thought I was to continue to pay it yearly at Bath. The person who I pay'd ᵐ the income tax last year never sent me a Notice to give in a fresh statement of my income this year. If the Commissioners in London wish me to give in my income there instead of sending it to Bath, I will do it directly and pay the different installments that are due and for which I have never

---

[32] The mark of the seal covers this word.

been call'd for. I thank you kindly for your goodness towards M^rs: Hatley. I heard the other day from M^rs: Archer she and the Children were verry well. May I request of you to communicate as soon as possible to the Commissioners what I have written relative to my income, that I may know where in future to send an yearly statement of my income, and where to pay it. I suppose as I paid it for one year at Bath am to continue to pay it there.

In expecting your answer,

I am your affectionate Nephew,

William James Archer

PS. I hope to be in London about the middle of next Month. Please to direct to me at M^rs: Hooper's Boarding House, Ramsgate.

13. [L]

Endorsed: From Mrs. Archer, Dec. 5 1800, Oujonnet. answered.

Dr. J. C. Lettsom

Sambrook Court Basing-hall

Street

London

My dear Sir,

I was extremely happy in the receipt of your very kind letter of the 14th October, and I return you my best thanks for it, as I do for the affectionate things you are so good as to tell me. Believe me, my dear respected Parent, your friendship, your love, is what I wish most to deserve. Permit me to express you my gratitude for your kindness to my poor friend Hatley. I received a letter from her t'other day where in she says you are the best of men and that if it hadn't been for you she would not have been able to send her Niece to Scotland. I'm the more obliged to you as I look upon it that you had in view to oblige me in what you did for her. Really, her situation is so shocking that I think she can do no better than to return in this Contry. She has two Ladys, her proven friends, besides me, who wrote to her to endeavour to come. They will receive her by turns at their Houses and provide for her expenses. She'll not be near so badly off as she is now. She is so much beloved by all those who knows her that it will be a comfort to her wretchedness to be amongst such true friends.

I always thought that a widow and a Child was looked upon as first creditors and I can't think but that if M^rs: Hatley had been well advised she would be gott an alimentary allowance from the other creditors. I wish much she had asked you for your advice, as she understands nothing about these kind of affairs. She has perhaps been afraid of disturbing you. As I know, you are all goodness, and allways ready to oblige the unfortunates. I believe you would render her a great service to talk with her about all this, as Mr. Hatley had settled so much upon her at his death; she might possibly get something. Pardon me, my dear Uncle, for the liberty I take of intruding this upon your well-employed moments, but I know you will not taxe me with indiscretion for applying to you.

I am still at Oujonnet, but am going soon to Genèva for the Winter. I have no resource here whatsoever for my Children, and they are of an age to have lessons. In town they have all kind of masters. The little time they have had them it is astonishing how much they improved. I am not pleased with my poor boy's health. The tumour he had last year in his breast is beginning again. He spits continuously something very thick and nasty, and is very short breathed. The Cold weather does not agree with him at all. He is very thin, but strong and very gay. He sleeps well, but eats very little. He was so ill last spring that I am perhaps more affraid than I ought. M^{rs}. Batini, under whose care he was, called his disorder a <u>Vomique</u> and made him drink for upwards of 3 month over the herbe called in French, Marhube des Sommités de sapins et du miel blanc. I wish, my Dear Uncle, you would tell me what you think of this disorder. The Child does not coughs much but his breast is allways full. It makes me more unhappy than I can tell you, for he is such [a] good sweet-tempered Child that it puts me out of my mind to think something might happen to him. Do not mention this to William for it would make him uneasy, and I hope John will be better. What I would wish to know is if my brother John had not something of the same kind, for the phisicians asked me much if I knew if any of the family had been in a Consumption. I told him I did not think it, but you would render me a great service to write me what you know about it without letting William know I made you such a question. It is my anxiety for my Child that urges me [to] flatter my self you will not take it amiss, but answer me according to what you know, for if John does not inherit this Weakness from any of the family it may be nothing, but if the contrary they must look upon it more seriously. Maria and Anna are very well. In your letter you say you inclose a Piece of Poetry of your friend the Reverend M^r. Maurice,[33] but you forgot to send it me. I should be happy to have it and beg of you the favour to inclose it in your first letter. I hope all your family is in good health. I wish to be kindly remembered to M^{rs}. Lettsom and Children. I wish them and you, my Dear Uncle, a happy New Year that you may enjoy all the quiets and blessing you so much deserve.

---

[33] See Introduction to this volume, p. 6, and 'Letters from Lettsom' section, July 1 1804.

I beg the continuation of your valuable affection for me and mine and remain
with respect and affection,
yours
J. E. A.

Oujonnet. 5th of December 1800

14. [L]

Endorsed: From Elizabeth Archer, Mar. 20 1802, Geneva. answered

Dr. John Coackley Lettsom
Sambrook House
Basing-hall Street
London
Via Calais.

March the 20th 1802

My dear Uncle,
     Being just informed by a letter from William of the marriage of your son
with Miss Garrow,[34] permit me to write you on the subject and express you
my pleasure of an event that appears to be so agreable to both families and
which I have no doubt will no doubt turn out to their mutual satisfaction. The
young people's respective choices having so much obtained their Parents'
approbation, I wish with all my heart, my dear, respected Uncle, you may
long, very long, enjoy the happyness at seeing your family all well settled. I
was in hopes you would have done me the favor of a letter, but I suppose you
have been too busy to think of answering me. But I do not renounce my claim
and beg that you will do me the pleasure to write to me as soon as <u>you can</u>.
I have been expecting William every day since near four months, which I do
assure you is not a state of life in the least agreable, for expectations ever
followed by disappointment becomes very tiresome. Yet I think he does
perfectly right not to return untill Peace is decidedly signed. For my own
quietness, I like it much better, Switzerland being till then quite in a waver-
ing situation, nobody knowing what will be made of the Contry. One day we
are to become French, another Austrians and so on, everybody talking

---

[34] The marriage of Lettsom's second son, Samuel Fothergill Lettsom, to Eliza Sophia Garrow,
only daughter of Sir William Garrow, took place on 6 April 1802. Like his sister, Mary Ann, Samuel
also married outside of the Society of Friends. See Abraham, op. cit., note 1 above, pp. 288, 451.

according how they wish the things to turn.[35] En attendance, I pass my time as well as I can and to tell you the truth I succeed very much to my satisfaction. We have particulars, Concerts, Comedys and Balls where I amuse my self remarquably well. My Children have likewise their little Balls and I am proud when I see them so much admired. You have no ideas how well they turn out, both for their understanding and their figures. They take many lessons and their masters are pleased with 'em. For their healthes, Maria and Anna are perfectly well. Unfortunately, John is very delicate. The Cold and damp weather disagree so much with him that he is indifferently ~~the~~ most part of the winter. I spoke t'other day to Mr. Dijean who arrived last week from London. He had seen Mr. Archer and I was excessif sorry to hear he found him grown so very thin that he did not know him. I fear he is not well. I hope he profits of the happiness of being under your Eyes, to ask your advices and follow them. When you do me the favor to write me, you'll oblige me much to lett me know if he has been ill, as he never wrote me about it, and how he does at present. I hope Mrs. Lettsom is well. I beg her to accept my best compliments and Congratulations on the acquisition of a Daughter of her Choice. I hope when Peace is made you'll [put into][36] execution the long made plan to paying us a visit which will be more agreable to me than I can tell you. I allways wished to be acquainted with you and as it does not appear that William has a mind to lett me pass even three months though he promised it at Peace, I have no chance of seeing you unless you comes. I own to you I find his behaviour in this respect far from being as it ought to be. I must end this scrawl, my dear beloved Parent, in assuring you of my most tender and respectfull affection.
J. E. Archer

15. [L]

Endorsed: From W. Js. Archer, May 5 1802, Paris. answered.

Dr: J: C: Lettsom
Basinghall Street
London
Via Calais

Paris 5 May 1802

Dear Uncle,

As you desir'd me to write to you from time to time when I should be on the continent, I address you these few lines from Paris where I have been

---

[35] Another revolt occurred in Switzerland in 1802, which resulted in Napoleon restoring the old Swiss Confederation in February 1803, with a federal diet subservient to France.

[36] There is a hole in the manuscript. The missing words should read something along these lines.

allmost a fortnight, being detain'd here longer than I expected relative to Passports, but having got them I intend to sett off for Geneva, Saturday or Sunday next; I had a verry pleasant jorney from Calais. Contrary to what I had hear'd, I found the country in a high state of cultivation for more than 200 miles, hardly a piece of waste land to be seen, but verry little timber and hardly an enclosure, the horses of the peasants as good as ours in England, their tackling bad. Paris has far exceeded my expectations. I have not seen a tenth part of what is worth seeing. Strangers are admitted 9 days out of ten to the most noble collection of statues and Pictures in the world. Amongst the former is the famous Apollo of Belvidere, the Antinoüs Larcoon,[37] Hercules etc. etc. The Venus of Medicis is not here.[38] The collection of Pictures is ~~bea~~ grand byond idea, containing the master pieces of Raphael, Titian, Van Dyke, Rubens etc. etc. I have found the people of France as civil as before the revolution and verry glad to see the English; I am sorry I did not bring a few letters of introduction. Though unknown here, I have mett with much politeness. On the whole Paris is, I think, the first place ~~in~~ for a person out of business to reside ~~h~~ in, especially if one is fond of the fine arts and sciences; there are vast numbers of Theatres open every night; the Grand Opera in point of musique and singing detestable, but the dancing far superior to ours, as they are in genteel and low comedy. Everrything is excessive dear here, especially lodgings and fireing. The dress of the French women is elegant, like the genteel women in England. They are not loaded with much cloathing, in generall are not as handsome as the English but are better made, having remarkable good legs and feet, and in conversation lively and entertaining. Religion or morals are little attended too [*recte* to] by any ranks of society in this country.

I hope this will find you and your familly in good health. Since I have left England I ~~am~~ have been pretty well. I cannot finish this without returning you many thanks for your ~~d~~ goodness towards me during my stay in England, and believe me

Your affectionate Nephew

William James Archer

---

[37] Napoleon brought back a number of European art treasures to Paris, particularly from Italy, Austria and Germany, which were shown in the Louvre. The statue of Apollo and the Laocoon were the main attractions. For a near contemporary excursion mentioning the statue, see Ircastrensis, *A short excursion in France, 1814: embellished with plates of the Venus di Medici and the Apollo di Belvidere*, London, printed for J. J. Stockdale, 1814.

[38] The statue of the Venus de Medici or Venus Pontia. In 1680, it was removed by Cosmo III from the Medici Palace in Rome to the Imperial Gallery in Florence. Tobias Smollett gives his impression of seeing it in Florence in Letter xxviii of his *Travels through France and Italy*, Edinburgh, J. Mundell and Co., 1796.

P:S: When you favour me with a letter, please to direct at Rolle, Canton du Leman en Suisse.[39]

16. [L]

Endorsed: From W. Js. Archer, Jun. 18 1802, Oujonnet. answered.

D^r: J: C: Lettsom
Sambrook Court
Basinghall Street
London
par Pontarlier et Calais

Oujonnet 18 June 1802

Dear Uncle,
    I receiv'd your favour of the 28 May this morning. I thank you for having paid M^{rs}: Archer's bill on me for 70£. You mention'd you had paid another bill for me for 100£. I cannot conceive what bill it is, as since I left England I have not drawn on you, nor before my departure did I leave any order on you, having paid all my accounts. You will oblige me to inform me as quick as you conveniently can what the above-mention'd bill for 100£ was for. Be so good to direct to me at Messrs: Calandrini et Cie, Banquiers à Genève, Department du Leman, Republique Française (via Calais) as letters come much quicker than through Switzerland.[40] Betsy and my little ones desire to be kindly remember'd to you and your familly. I assure you it would make us all verry happy to see you here. We are well, thank God. Since I have been here and at Geneva my health is much improv'd and my friends say I begin to gett a little more flesh. The Climate of England never agreed with me. We are come for a little time here and shall return for the remainder of the summer in the neighbourhood of Geneva. Betsy's aunt[41] has lent us an excellent house about a mile from the town, which is verry convenient for the education of the Children. For my own part, I should prefer living the whole year

---

[39] A district of Switzerland bordering France. On 16 May 1803, Archer asked for money to be directed to him "à Rolle, Canton du Vaud, République Helvetique". Rolle commune is still in the Vaud Canton of Switzerland.

[40] Messrs. Calandrini et Cie, bankers, Geneva, Department du Leman, République Française, according to Archer's letter of 6 January 1803.

[41] Possibly Madame de Tourne (the only aunt mentioned by name in the letters) who died in the following year.

at Oujonnet and take to my old amusement of farming. I had the pleasure of finding every thing in good condition at Oujonnet, thanks to the care of my dear Betsy. The house and furniture considering the number of soldiers we have lodg'd has not suffer'd the least. The plantations are so much improv'd that I shall be oblig'd to cut some trees. They begin to spoill the Wines [*recte* Vines]. We have but a poor crop of hay. The wheat and oats look pretty well. The last severe frosts in the month of May have hurt the Vines, but should the season continue favourable, I hope to make more wine than last year; in about Geneva allmost all the Vines are frozen. Things are by no means quiet in this once happy part of the Globe. We expect daily more French soldiers as the peasants are verry riotous relative to the feudall Rights, which they were made to believe would all be abolish'd.[42] As Oujonnet has no feudal rights, we are ~~quiet~~ verry quiet and easy here.

I remain,

Your affectionate Nephew,

William James Archer

17. [L]

Endorsed: From William Archer, July 19 1802, Oujonnett. answered.

D^r: J: C: Lettsom

Sambrook Court

Basinghall Street

London

par Calais

Geneva July 19 1802

Dear Uncle,

I receiv'd some time ago your favour of the 30 June, for which I return you many thanks. I am going tomorrow to Oujonnet and shall draw on you from there for £178 à 3 jours de vue, payable a Mes^{rs}. Calandrini et Cie or their order. You will please to pay the said draft and put it to my account.

---

[42] On the proclamation of the Helvetic Republic in 1798, cantonal sovereignty and feudal rights had been abolished in favour of one, indivisible republic. When the Swiss Confederation was restored in 1803 with a diet subservient to France, cantonal sovereignty was also largely restored.

You mention'd you have 114£ 18s, 10d remaining of what Masterman and Co.[43] transfer'd of mine to you. The beginning of this Month there is a dividend of 4100£ bonus annual £61, 10 and of £265 Navy 5 per Cent 6£ 12s, 6d due, to which said sums of 61£ 10 and £6, −12, 6, and 114£ 18, 10, forms the sum of 183£ 1, 4. I would be oblig'd to you to send Jane Hewson, at M[r]: Francis's near the Plow, Clapham,[44] five pounds for me. Therefore there remains £178, −1, 4, which paid £178 I shall draw in a few days. It is not worth drawing for the remainning 1 shilling and 4 pence. The Exchange on London is rather unfavorable, but I can allways make some interest of my money here till I want it. Should the exchange get more favourable, I hope you will not take it amiss if I should draw on you for 200 or 300£, but should I draw, the bills will not be made payable before the 20th of next October, consequently after the dividends at the Bank are payable, should some commerciall arrangement take place between England and France, the exchange on London will most likely get better. Some years ago we got 10 per Cent clear by drawing on London[45] and at present I believe we loose from 3 to 4. Geneva is full of English goods, which are as cheap as in the retail shops in London. If you could gett me the best treatise on the cultivation of hops, I should me be much oblig'd to you. A person who is going soon to London would bring me the book. Beer is become more common here and is recommended by the first Medical Gentlemen here. Vi[ne]s in a good year are verry profitable but subject to many accidents. I intend to try to grow hops at Oujonnet. Pray remember us kindly to all your familly, and believe me, your affectionate Nephew
William James Archer

P.S. We went the other day to Dardagny.[46] The frosts and a most dreadfull haill storm has done a great deall of mischief. The whole village will not make 2 pipes of wines and verry little corn. Switzerland is much quieter and I hope will continue so. I think of staying about 10 or 12 days at Oujonnet, during the harvest.

---

[43] Messrs. Masterman, Peters, Walker and Co., 2 White Hart Court, Lombard Street, London. See *Leigh's new picture of London*, London, printed for Samuel Leigh, 1819.

[44] The Plough, Clapham.

[45] Presumably this refers to a more favourable exchange rate to be had in London.

[46] Betsy Archer's father was Chevalier de Dardagny, see Letter 1 above.

18. [L]

Endorsed: From William James Archer, Aug. 30 1802, Geneva. answered.

D^r: J. C: Lettsom
Sambrook Court
Basinghall Street
London
Via Calais

Geneva 30 Aug: 1802

Dear Uncle,

I did myself the pleasure to write to you about the middle of last July. I hope you receiv'd my letter. As the exchange on London is getting worse and worse every day, I shall take the liberty of drawing on you from Oujonnet the 1st of September for 200£ Sterling payable the 20th of October next, consequently after the dividends are payable at the Bank. About a month ago it was the general opinion that a commercial treaty would be form'd between England and France, and the exchange on London was getting better, but as there is no appearance of any commercial treaty being concluded, and as the French have laid a heavy tax on Sugars, Coffee etc. which comes from England, the exchange on London is fallen and in all probability will be lower. Things are by no means quiet in the little cantons of Switzerland. It appears they are determin'd to form a separate republick. About Oujonnet all is ~~peaceable~~ tranquil at present. The harvest has turn out but very poor, and for these last two months we have hardly had a drop of rain. The vintage promises to be plentifull especially between Lausanne and Vevay. I hope that you and all your familly are well. We all of us here enjoy pretty good health. Johny is getting much stronger; riding on horseback does him a great deal of good. We shall be verry happy to hear from you, ~~wh~~ when you can find time to write to us. An American who pass'd a few days here told us he had call'd often at your house, but you was so much engag'd that he could not see you. The great affair concerning the indemnitys in Germany seems likely to be soon terminated, though not to the satisfaction of all Partys.
I remain,
Your affectionate Nephew,
William James Archer

19. [L]

Endorsed: From W. J. Archer, Oct. 27 1802, Oujonnet. answered.

D^r: J: C: Lettsom
Sambrook Court
Basinghall Street
London
par Pontarlier et Calais

Oujonnet 27 Oct. 1802

Dear Uncle,

It is some time since we have had the pleasure of hearing from you. We hope you and all your familly are well. We all of us here enjoy pretty good health, notwithstanding the cruell situation of this once happy country. As the publick News papers have undoubtedly inform'd you of the different events that have taken place in Switzerland, I shall not repeat them, but only mention that all is quiet in our part of the country. I assure you we pass'd some disagreable moments, the theatre of ~~the~~ war being but a few milles ~~of~~ from our house. I have taken the liberty of sending you from Strasburg, ~~30~~ 36 dwaf apple trees as these trees take up but a verry little place, and produce most excellent fruit and, as I believe you have none in your Garden, I hope they will be acceptable. Last year 50 dwaf trees were planted here, which have all succeeded and some have produced fruit allready. Our vintage, owing to the severe frosts last May has~~ve~~ not been very productive. The wine is good and I hope will fetch a good price. We have most delightful weather, but are in great want of rain, as we have hardly had any for these 4 months. I desir'd a Carrier by the name of Lacombe to call at your house. I would be oblig'd to you if you could give him some seeds of the <u>Sea Cole</u> for me,[47] if any of your acquaintances are coming to this part of the world, Lacombe would be verry glad to bring them. If you could send me some seeds of the ~~Zeela~~ New Zealand flax,[48] or of any other plants, I should take it ~~as~~ a particular favour. As the exchange on London is a little more favourable, though still below par, I intend drawing on you for 100£ in a short time. We shall return to

---

[47] Possibly a reference to the vegetable sea kale (*Crambe maritima*).

[48] New Zealand flax (*Phormium spp.*) are large strap-leafed evergreen perennials that used to be placed in the Agave family (Agavaceae), but recent taxonomy places them in the family Phormiceae. The Maori used the roots as a medicine and the pollen to make face powder. Harvey Wickes Felter in John Uri Lloyd, *King's American Dispensatory* (1898) states that the roots and leaf-bases in a concentrated decoction, with carbolic acid added, were used later in the nineteenth century as a surgical dressing for amputations and fresh wounds.

Geneva in about a month for the education of ~~our~~ the children, who are well advanced for their age. Betsy desires to be kindly remember'd to you, and believe me,

Your affectionate Nephew

William James Archer

20. [L]

Endorsed: From Elizabeth Archer, Nov. 2 1802, Oujonnet. answered.[49]

Dr. J. C. Lettsom

Basing-hall Street

Sambrook Court

London

England

Par Pontarlier and Calais

Oujonnet the 2nd of November 1802

Dear Uncle,

William had the pleasure of writing to you last week. A day or two ago, he received your favor of the 4th of October informing us of the melancholy death of Mrs. Elliot.[50] It is impossible to express you how much we are affected, and how we sympathise in your pain at the loss of so amiable a daughter. I hope that your health and that of the rest of your family is good notwithstanding the troubles of your minds and I beg you to be kindly remembered to Mrs. Lettsom and your Children. William likewise desires to be kindly remembered to you and your family and begs of you when you do him the pleasure of writing to him, you will direct your letter for him at Messrs. Calandrini and Companie à Genève R. F.[51] by way of Calais, as your last letter has been above three weeks a coming. We are still at Oujonnet where notwithstanding the disturbances of the Contry we have been perfectly quiet. The French troops re-entered the Contry last Friday. They say they will not make a long stay. It is to be hoped so, for this poor unhappy Switzerland is very poor and wants no strangers to eat her up, but if they reconcile all the parties we shall think ourselves very happy to have had their visit.

---

[49] Black lines have been drawn round the letter in indication of mourning.

[50] Mary Ann, Mrs. Philip Elliot, died of consumption in 1802. See Abraham, op. cit., note 1 above p. 461.

[51] République Française.

My Children are very well. They play with their Papa the whole day and they are very fond of him. Farewell, my dear Uncle, believe me most respectfully your affectionnate niece
Je. Elizabeth Archer

P.S. I hope you have received a sett of small prints of views of Switzerland and a cup and saucer of the China manufacture of this contry which an American Gentelman took charge of about 3 months ago. He wrote lately to William from Paris where he stays that he has given it to one of his friends who was going to London to remit it you.

21. [L]

Endorsed: From Elizabeth Archer, Dec. 24 1802, Geneva. answered.

Dr. J. Coackley Lettsom
Sambrook House
Basing-Hall Street
London.
Calais

Genèva 24th of December 1802

My Dear and Respected Parent,
I take the liberty to put under your cover the enclosed for William in case he should be sett off for this contry, begging of you the favor, if he is still in London, to give it him, or if he is gone to tear it. I not knowing the name of his Bankers, I directed to him at your House a Draught of 100 Pounds to be Paid the 20th of February. If William should be gone, you will oblige me much my Dear Uncle, to give proper orders for the Draught to be paid. I hope you will excuse my boldness in presuming so much of your Goodness, yet the Weather has been so continually bad that I hardly suppose William would have undertaken his journey. Then my precaution will be quite unnecessary.
I saw the other day a Lady (Mrs. Cazenove) who is a great admirer of yours. What she told me increased, if possible, my wish to know you more particularly than by letters, but I fear if you dare take a trip to this Contry my wish may never be exhausted. Though William had given me his word of honor when Peace should be made to lett me come go to England and pass 2 or 3 months, I own to you I think it is very odd he remembers so little his promises. But you must come, pass a few months with us and then I'll return

to pay your visit before I'm quite old, blind, or lame. Really, you cannot imagine how much I wish to see you, how happy I would be if my Children were known to you. I am sure you would love them. They turn out very well. They are very good-hearted and have a good understanding. Their figure is genteel and agreable. My little John's health is better but he is still very delicate. I hope all your family is well. You must have a good many little Grand Sons and daughters. I am sure you and Mrs. Lettsom are very happy among this little People. I hope her health is good. I beg you will remember me kindly to her. I cannot express you, my dear Uncle, how much pleasure you would give me to write me. My direction is J. E. Archer, au Bâtiment neuf de la Treille à Genève, Départment du Liman R. F.

Farewell my dear Uncle, believe me most sincerely your affectionnate and respectful niece.

Je Elizabeth Archer

Excuse this bad scrawl but I think I qui[te] forget writing English

22. [L]

Endorsed: From W. Js. Archer, Jan. 6 1803, Geneva. Rec'd Jan. 18 1803. answered.

Dr. J. C. Lettsom
Sambrook Court
Basinghall St
London
par Calais

Geneva 6 Jan 1803

Dear Uncle,

I received yesterday the different kinds of seeds you was so kind to send me, for which I return you many thanks, allso your favour of the 2 December 1802, which is the only letter I have receiv'd from you since yours of the 4 Oct. Before I left England, I left a power of attorney ~~with~~ (which I sign'd and was witness'd by Demattos and his Clerk)[52] to enable you to receive

---

[52] De Matos and Podmore, brokers, were based at the appropriately-named 12, Change Alley, Cornhill, London. Henry Kent, *Kent's Directory. For the year* 1794, London, R. and H. Causton, 1794.

my dividends of what I have in the New 5 per Cent stock, amounting to £2435. As you mention in your letter of the 2 December that I must send you a power to receive my dividends. I am afraid the power of attorney I left you (the 15th of Aprill 1802) is lost. I have written to England and desir'd that a propper power of attorney may be made out at the Bank, which I must sign and return you, that you may receive my dividends. Would you be so kind to inform me if you ~~have~~ have lost the power of attorney I left with you, or if it was not well made out, which would be rather surprising, as Demattos the Broker, who I allways employ got it for me. I am sorry to give you so much trouble. I am much concern'd of hearing of different persons of poor M^{rs}: Hatley continuing in distress. Would you be so kind as to send her five pounds for me; she is at 49 Warren Street Fitzroy Square. And if you would be so good as to send M^{rs}: Hewson at M^{r}: Francis near the Plough, Clapham, allso five pounds for me, I would take it as a particular favour. As letters now and then miscarry, I would be oblig'd to you to desire Demattos to gett a propper power of attorney made out at the Bank to enable you to receive my dividend of the New 5 per Cent and be so good to send it me here, directed chez Messrs: Calandrini et Cie, Genève, Department du Leman, République Française, par Calais. ~~w~~ I must sign the said power here or in Switzerland, before, I believe, two witnesses, and I will return it you directly.

I hope you and your familly continue well. The winter is mild, very wett, and people rather sickly. We have nothing new in our part of the world, believe me

Your affectionate Nephew

William James Archer

P:S: Betsy received your favour by Lacombe yesterday and in a short time will have the pleasure of writing to you. She and the Children are well. ~~I know of no person~~ I know nobody in Switzerland [----]^{53} can make out a propper power of attorney. In Geneva, every power must be made in French, which I suppose the Bank would object to. I must have one from the Bank, which I must sign before witnesses and send it to you.

---

[53] Hole in manuscript where the seal has been removed. What remains of the tail of the first letter does not appear to be a "w", which might have suggested "who".

23. [L]

Endorsed: From William James Archer, Mar. 19 1803, Oujonnet. answered.

D^r: J: C: Lettsom
Sambrook Court
Basinghall Street
London
par Pontarlier et Calais

Oujonnet 17 March 1803

Dear Uncle,

It is some time ago I have had the pleasure of hearing from you. I hope that you and all your familly enjoy good health. I left Betsy and my children all well at Geneva, about a fortnight ago, as I came here to look a little after the work in the wineyards, and other work going on my domaine. The last letter I receiv'd from you was brought me ♭ by Lacombe the 4th December 1802. T: H: Masterman wrote to me the 19th January 1803 and mention'd you had inform'd him you had found the power of attorney I left with you to receive the dividends of what I have in the New 5 per Cent stock and that you had written to me on that subject. Your favour must have been lost as I never receiv'd it. I have given M^r: Jacques Dejean a draft on you for twenty pounds, if you have any seeds or any thing else to send me he will take charge of it. I would be much oblig'd to you to send me a Copy of the power of attorney I left with you relative to what I have in the new 5 per Cents, as if by any accident the one I left with should be lost or mislaid, I could get a new one made out in Switzerland and send it you. The exchange on London is pretty steady yet below par. I intend returning to Geneva in a few days, and shall draw soon on you from Oujonnet for one hundred pounds. I hope London has not been as sickly as Paris and Geneva. In the latter place some time ago no less than 5000 people were ill at once, and mostly of a complaint called La Gripe[54] which fortunately was not dangerous. M^{rs}: Archer has lost her old aunt Madame de Tourne aged 77 years. You are inform'd by the public papers of the new Helvetique constitution, which in general seems to give satisfaction. Poor Switzerland is in great want of tranquility. When you are so kind to write to ⅄ us please to direct chez Mes^{rs}: Calandrini et Cie, banquiers, Genève, République Française. I have received at Geneva a letter from London in 8 days. We have fine cold weather at present. I am going to form

---

[54] Influenza.

a small plantation of hops. Pray remember me kindly to all your family and believe me
your affectionate nephew
William James Archer

24. [L]

Endorsed: From W. J. Archer, May 16 1803, Geneva. answered.

D^r: J: C: Lettsom
Sambrook Court
Basinghall Street
London
par Calais

Geneva 16 May 1803

Dear Uncle,

It is more than 4 months we have had the pleasure of hearing from you. I hope that you and your familly continue to enjoy good health. People are much afraid here, that a fresh war is on the point of breaking out between England and France. ~~Su~~ Should such an ~~event~~ event take place, I have no thoughts of leaving Switzerland, where thank God I enjoy much better health than in England. If unfortunately there is a war and any acts of Parliament are passed relative to bills of exchange drawn from any parts of the continent on England, you will be so good to obtain a Licence to pay what I may draw on you for yearly, namely ~~what~~ the interest of what my Brother left, and of what I have in the new 5 per Cents. Please to direct to me should a war take place, à Rolle, Canton du Vaud, République Helvetique. If peace continues, be so good to send your letters to me chez Messrs: Calandrini et Cie, Banquiers, à Genève, Department du Leman, République Française. In a few days I shall draw on you for 100£ à 2 mois de date, which you will please to accept and put to my account. Should the exchange be low I shall only draw for 50£ Sterling. In generall, people in Switzerland seem well pleased with the new constitution.[55] It is impossible to please all partys. The French troops I hear are on the point of leaving the country; I hope the poor Swiss will continue long to enjoy peace and tranquillity. Pray remember me kindly to

---

[55] February 1803 had seen the re-establishment of the Swiss Confederation. See note 41 above.

D^r: Elliott;[56] when he was here last December he promis'd to write. I have never received a letter from him. My daughters sent you some time ago, some artificiall flowers of their own making. They as well as Betsy desire kindly to be remember'd to you. It would make us verry happy to have the pleasure of seeing you in this delightfull but <u>at present</u> cold country. We have a return of winter; I am afraid the wineyards will suffer, which will be a great pity, as there is a verry fine show of grapes.

My children continue to improve in their education. The eldest in particular, John, is got quite strong. He rides and dances verry well. They find the English language rather difficult. In hoping to hear from you, believe me,
Your affectionate Nephew,
William James Archer

25. [L]

Endorsed: From Elizabeth Archer, May 26 1803, Geneva. done

Dr. J. C. Lettsom
Sambrook Court
Basing-hall Street
London
England

Genèva 26th May 1803

My dear Uncle,
I received you kind favor of the 10th May about a week ago for which I return you many thanks. The breaking out of a new War between England and France has caused great uneasiness in Genèva as it is impossible to foretell when we shall enjoy again the blessings of peace.[57] William wrote to you the 17th of this month. I am affraid you will not receive his letter as we hear the Port of Calais is shut up. He mentioned as he enjoyed better health here than in England. He had no thoughts of quitting Switzerland at present. He requested of you, my dear Uncle, if there should be any new Acts of Parliament passed relatives to Bills of Exchange drawn from any part of the Continent on England, you would be so good to obtain a Licence to pay the different bills my husband may draw on you from Switzerland. When you write, please to direct to us a Rolle, Canton de Vaud, République Helvetique. In your favor of the 10th you said you would write to William in a week's

---

[56] Dr. Philip Elliot, who married Lettsom's daughter, Mary Ann in 1794.
[57] Peace had been declared between England and France by the Treaty of Amiens on 25 March 1802. War broke out again in May 1803.

time. I fear he will not receive your letter as we hear Dover is shutt up. This unfortunate War will make all communication with England very difficult as all letters must pass by Hamburgh.

I need not tell you, my dear Uncle, how pleased I was at the short ~~wis~~ visit of Dr. Elliot, and with what pleasure I heard all the particulars relating to your family. He had promised to write me on his arrival in London but he has not and I am very angry with him. My daughters were very happy to send their little work to their dear Cousin Eliza. I hope for their sakes she'll wear with pleasure the artificial flowers which are likewise their own work. As the Winter was so bad and the Spring came all of a sudden, ~~the~~ I suppose the Gardner ~~from~~ at Strasburg thought impossible to send the apple trees in any good condition to England. Those we received begun to bud on the road. The Wineyards in the neighbourhood of Geneva have much suffered by the late frost. Fortunately in Switzerland no mischief has been done. Corn in general looks remarquably well, the Grass but indifferent, fruit trees promiss a good crop. As society at Geneva is on a pleasing and easy footing, we passed our Winter pleasantly. We were last night at Madame de Staël, daughter of the famous Necker,[58] whom we saw, and where we mett several English who were very dejected at the news of this war. Mrs. de Staël is a most agreable and witty woman, her lively conversation is very interesting and amusing. She is very partial to the English and receives them exceedingly well. In hoping that you, my dear Uncle, ~~enj~~ and your family enjoy as good health as we do, believe me, your affectionnate niece J[n] Elizabeth Archer

26. [L]

Endorsed: From William Archer, Aug. 12 1803, Oujonnet. answered.

D[r]: J: C: Lettsom
Sambrook Court
Basinghall Street
London.

Oujonnet 12 Aug. 18[03?]

Dear Uncle,

I receiv'd your kind favour of the 8 July some time ago, for which I return you many thanks. It afforded Betsy and me particular satisfaction of being

---

[58] Anne-Louise Germaine Necker, Baroness de Staël-Holstein (1766–1817), French woman of letters, daughter of the French politician, Jacques Necker, minister of Louis XVI, and Suzanne Curchod.

inform'd that you and your worthy familly enjoy good health. I am glad that my friend Sam's child has had the cow pock. Vaccination is become pretty generall at Geneva, and, as I have been inform'd, allways attended with great success.[59] In Switzerland it is not quite as common, many people, and some who should know better, having sett their faces against it. As severall of the Children of my vignerons have not had the small pock, they wish them to be vaccinated. The matter can be a easily procur'd from Geneva. The crop of hay in this quiet part of the world has been but little, the same of oats, barley etc., but that of wheat and Rye verry good. The vines promises a plentifull vintage. Consequently w wine will be cheap for near 3 Months. We have not had a drop of rain; all our meadows are burnt up, and if we have not a great deall of rain in a few days there will be no after crop of hay, on which we chiefly depend for feeding the cows in winter. The taxes we shall have to pay here next year are verry moderate indeed, the land and house tax not quite 6 £ Sterling a year; those on servants, carriages and horses verry little. I see by the news papers that there is a new income tax in England.[60] I would be oblig'd to you to pay M^{rs}: Jane Hewson five pounds for me; she is at M^r: Francis's near the Plow, Clapham. For these last two months the weather has been allmost insupportable on account of the heat; at present it is much pleasanter. Your friend D^r: Odier[61] some time ago was thrown from a carriage and much hurt; and so but was soon cured. When you see M^r and M^{rs}: Nanson pray remember me to them, as likewise to all your

---

[59] Samuel Fothergill Lettsom had a son, William Garrow, born on 23 January 1803. He died on 20 July of the same year, perhaps as a result of vaccination. Geneva adopted Jenner's cowpock vaccination relatively quickly, mainly because some physicians such as Louis Odier studied in Edinburgh and then spent time in London hospitals (see note 61 below). For more on this topic, see Louis Odier, 'Mémoire sur l'Inoculation de la vaccine à Genève', *Bibliothèque Britannique*, t. XV, pp. 71–89. Léon Gautier, *La médecine à Genève jusqua'à la fin du dix-huitième siècle. Mémoires et documents publiés par la société d'Histoire et d'Archéologie de Genève*, Geneva, J. Julien and Georg, 1906, pp. 407–16. Thanks to Philip Rieder for his help with this reference.

[60] Income tax was first introduced by Prime Minister William Pitt in 1799. When a peace treaty was signed with France in 1802, Henry Addington, the next Prime Minister, hurriedly repealed the new tax only to be forced to bring in a new Income Tax Act in the following year.

[61] Louis Odier (1748–1817) was the first of a group of his Geneva contemporaries to study medicine in Edinburgh. He also visited London. When he returned to Geneva in 1773, he worked mainly as a journalist on medical and natural history topics. He co-authored, with Daniel Delaroche and Charles William Dunant, the *Pharmacopoea Genevensis* (1780). He also founded the largely ineffective Société de Médecine de Genève, which, during the period of French occupation (1798–1815), acted as a substitute for the abolished Faculté de Médecine. He was made honorary professor of medicine in 1799. He was one of the founders of the *Bibliothèque Britannique* in which, in 1798, he published notes on a translation of Edward Jenner's *Inquiry*. Through that and subsequent reports, he became an authority on vaccination on the Continent which he helped to introduce into Switzerland and France.

amiable familly. Betsy and my little ones desire to be remember'd to you, and
believe me,
Your affectionate Nephew,
William James Archer

27. [L]

Endorsed: From Elizabeth Archer, Jan. 26 1804, Oujonnet. answered.

Dr. John Coakley Lettsom
Sambrook House Basinghall
Street
London

26ᵗʰ of January 1804

Dear Uncle,
    It is such a long while since we haven't had the pleasure of hearing from
you that I must write to you to beg of you the favor to lett us know how you
and your family do. The last letter William ever received from you was in the
latter end of July. He answered it directly and has wrote several times since.
We sincerely hope your silen[ce is] owing only to the difficulty of forwarding letters. At present the Post comes regular from England and a communication is open between England and Holland. This letter is going through the
latter place and I hope, dear Sir, you'll receive it time enough to accept of the
compliments of the season. Wishing you and yours many happy new years.
We are all in good health and spirits and our Children continue to improve in
their education. Maria is as tall as me and grows a fine figure. She is a very
clever girl at anything she undertakes. John's health is, thank God, much
better. He is a remarquably good-natured. My little Anna is the best-hearted
child I ever knew. She dances extremely well. I would be very happy were
they acquainted with you. ~~you~~ They are taught to love and respect you.
    The Wintage was abundant and good but unfortunately money is so scarce
that there's no selling the Wine at any reasonable prices. Switzerland enjoys
quietness. There are few French troops in the contry. The taxes are moderate,
and many of the Co[ntry?]⁶² are pleased with their Constitution. The Winter
is uncommonly mild. We have had but very little frost and snow the first days

---

⁶² The paper is torn from the removal of the seal.

of December. Ever since we have had an April wheather which we fear will bring things to[o] forward and prove fatal to the Vines and Corn. As the Exchange in London is very favourable, and as it may fall from one day to another, William intends drawing on you for one or two ~~hun~~ hundred pounds. Poor Richard broke his leg in the beginning of October and unfortunately it has not been very well sett, so he continues lame and he suffers much. I hope Miss Eliza enjoys her winter and that she attends Balls, as there's but one time of life for dancing. I regret heartily mine is over, and own I am very sorry of growing old. I ~~g~~ beg you will be so kind to give my best compliments to Mr. Elliot whom I was very sorry to know for so short a time. I [know?] all his little family ~~are~~ wer[e well?][63] When you do us the pleasure of wri[ting] to us, please to write by way of Holl[and], should the communication continue open and direct your letter at Oujonnet, près de Rolle, Canton de Vaud, république Helvetique. If not, write by the way of Germany. William desires to be kindly remembered to you and Mrs. Lettsom, and never will forget the marks of friendship he received from you. I remain, dear Uncle, your

most affectionate niece,

J$^{e.}$ Eth Archer

28. [L]

Endorsed: From Elizabeth Archer, Apr. 12 1804, Oujonnet. received May 4. answered.

Dr. J. C. Lettsom ~~Esqr~~
Sambrook Court Basing-hall
Street
London

Oujonnet 12th of April 1804

My dear Uncle,

We received your favors of the 7th and 24th of February but a few days ago. They were a long time a coming. We were several weeks without any intelligence from England. I assure you it gives us great pleasure to be informed that your amiable daughter is so well married according to your desire and

---

[63] The paper is torn and the final word missing. "Well" is only a suggestion.

wishes.[64] We sincerely hope that she may enjoy many years of health, comfort and happyness. I wish with all my heart when peace is made that you would accompany her and take a trip to our contry. If not, I'll be very happy to obtain of my husband leave to pay you a visit and make acquaintance with you, dear Sir, and my pretty young Cousin.

William will do himself the pleasure of writing to you in a short time. His health is very much improved and his old enemy, the Rhumatism, has not been very troublesome this winter. The Children are all very well. The famous Mr. Necker is dead.[65] He was buried yesterday at his Estate at Copet by the side of his Wife. He is much regretted by his family, his friends, and the poor people. His private character was most amiable. His continuals endeavours was to make all those about him happy. As to his publick character, opinions are very different. His intentions were pure, no doubt, but unfortunately they did not succeed.

The season is still cold, but as it is better to feel it now than in the month of May, we make up with it. Till at present we have not felt the effects of the war in Switzerland, our taxes are moderate. The only articles that are getting dear is the Colonial produces. I hope Mrs. Lettsom and all your amiable family are well. I beg to be kindly remembered to them, and believe me, dear Sir, you affectionnate niece,

J[e.] Elizabeth Archer

29. [L]

Endorsed: From W. J. Archer, ~~May~~ Apr. 25 1804, Oujonnet.

D[r]: J: C: Lettsom
Sambrook Court
Basinghall Street
London
England

Oujonnet 25 April 1804

Dear Uncle

Betsy did herself the pleasure of writing to you about 3 weeks ago, in answer to your favour and wherein you inform'd us of the marriage of your

---

[64] Lettsom's youngest daughter, Eliza, married Colonel John Elliot of Pimlico Lodge on 27 February 1804, at St Margaret's church, Westminster.

[65] Jacques Necker (1732–1804), the Geneva-born Protestant banker and politician and father of the above-mentioned Madame de Staël, began as a clerk in a Swiss bank of Isaac Vernet. He became director-general of French finances on two occasions.

amiable daughter to M^r: John Eliott,[66] which gave us great pleasure as you so much approve of it. Please to give my compliments to the new married couple, wishing them all health and happiness. I receiv'd some little time ago, the power of attorney. When I wish to sell what I have in the five per cent annuities 1797, I can send it to you. Last year I saw in an English Newspaper an article relative to the Income tax, but which I did not clearly understand, if no deductions are allow'd for children; I think you must have paid about forty six pounds sterling for me, for one year. The exchange on London is favourable at present. In a few days I shall draw on you for one hundred and seventy six pounds sterling à 2 mois de date, which you will be pleased to accept and put to my account. The present is a busy time with the farmers; we have had a verry late spring. The appearance of grapes is favourable. We now only dread frosts and hail storms. There is a good show of grass and of fruit except apricots. The ~~eo~~ corn is fine. We continue to enjoy, thank God, peace and quietness in this part of the world. You certainly have seen by the publick papers that the disturbances which broke out in the Canton of Zurich are appeased. I hope my friend Sam's wife has been safely deliver'd and that she enjoys good health. We have most delightfull weather—rather warm. In hoping, my dear Uncle, that you and yours are en bonne santé,

believe me, your affectionate Nephew,

William James Archer

30. [L]

Endorsed: From W. J. Archer, Oct. 3 1804, received Oct. 25, Oujonnet.

D^r: J: C: Lettsom
Sambrook Court
Basinghall Street
London
Angleterre

Oujonnet 3 Oct. 1804

Dear Uncle,

It is a long time since I have had the pleasure of hearing from you. I hope that you and your worthy familly are all in good health. Betsy (who desires to be kindly remember'd to you) and my Children as well as myself are well.

---

[66] See note 64 above.

In a few days we begin the vintage, which in generall promises to be one of the most abundant ever remember'd in this country. I do not think the new wine will sell for 3£ Sterling the pipe,[67] hardly sufficient to pay the expences of cultivation. Our crops of corn have been much hurt by continuall rains; the hay in generall has been good and plentifull. We continue to enjoy peace and quietness in this part of the world. Should a war break out between France and Russia, it is not likely to be felt in Switzerland, especially as Austria seems ~~ded~~ determin'd to remain neutre. Pray what is the opinion in England concerning the invasion?[68] Some accounts say it causes universall alarm, others that people are verry easy about the matter. Stocks according ~~the~~ to the French papers continue high. They have often the news in 8 or 10 days from London by way of Rotterdam. In a few days I intend drawing on you for two hundred pounds Sterling à un mois de datte. The Exchange on London is not as favourable as some time ago, and it may gett worse. Does trade and commerce go on well in England? The fleets that are arriv'd lately must have brought an immense quantity of merchandise Coloniall produce is ~~verr~~ dear here Every thing as I have been inform'd is got to a great price in London, and taxes verry high. Ours in this country continue moderate. Pray give my kind respects to M^rs: Lettsom and your familly.

I remain your affectionate Nephew
William James Archer

31. [L]

Endorsed: From Elizabeth Archer, Jan. 22 1805, Oujonnet.

Dr. J. C. Lettsom
Sambrook Court Basing-
hall Street
London

Oujonnet 22^d· January 1805

Dear Uncle,

In the month of October last I receiv'd your kind favor for which I return you my best thanks. I should have answered it much sooner had not I been

---

[67] A pipe (from the Portuguese word for barrel, *"pipa"*) is a large, long barrel or cask with tapered ends used for ageing and shipping port, marsala and madeira.

[68] During the period from 1801 to 1805, Britain was hostile to any form of non-monarchical government in France and, throughout much of these four years, the Royal Navy maintained a commercial blockade of the Continent. Britain kept pressure on France and all countries trading

unwell and continued so November and December owing to a fever, which didn't last long but left such pains in my Eyes that it is only since a few days that I have been able to read or write for any length of time. Thank God at present I am well but still rather weak. The disagreable Winter we have, continual rain and snow and little frost makes it very uncomfortable and unwholesome. Notwithstanding it, William and my Children are very well. We continue to enjoy peace and quietness in this part of the world. The Wintages in général have been the most productives ever remembered, but the Wine does not sell. The Cellars are full and we may [be] said to be head and ears in Wine, which I believe is the Case all over France. We have no accounts lately from England, seven or eight mails being due owing to the Cold Weather settling in the North. I hope to be informed by your first letter of the safe delivery of your amiable daughters Mrs. Elliot[69] and Mrs. Sam: Lettsom.[70] I am allways happy to hear of the Wellfare of you and your worthy family. You certainly have seen in the Public News Papers an account of the Grand fêtes and rejoicings which have taken place lately at Paris during the time of the Coronation.

My Children continue to give us great satisfaction in the improvements they make in their different leçons. Maria is taller than I am, rather too tall for her age, but enjoys at present a very good state of health. John is an exceeding Good Boy but unfortunately continues to be rather weak and subject to bad Colds. Anna is all vivacity and liveliness, more fond of Play and dancing than of her leçons, yet she does them and succeeds in what she undertakes. As to news, we have none. How is the Spanish War liked in England? I suppose it must please the Navy, but by no means the merchants.[71] I am affraid it will affect this Contry as the greatest part of the Current species are ~~dollars~~ Spanish dollars.

We made a very agréable excursion this year with our Children in the Valey and Lake de Tours after having passed some days with Mr. J. ~~Mr~~ Dayrolles, an Englishman who maried a Swiss lady and settled in this Contry. The Children were much pleased with the magnificent prospect they enjoyed from the Dent de Voglion,[72] one of the highest mountain[s] of

---

with her. Napoleon thus planned an invasion of England. However, the French Navy was unable to lure away the English Navy to ensure safe passage of the force across the Channel. With the conclusion of the Third Coalition of Britain, Austria and Russia in April 1805, the invasion plans finally came to nothing when Austria and Russia declared war and invaded the south of Germany.

[69] Eliza, Mrs. John Elliot.

[70] Mrs. Eliza Sophia Lettsom gave birth to a son, William Garrow Lettsom, on 24 March 1805.

[71] Spain declared war on Britain on 12 December 1804.

[72] This is now spelt Dent de Vaulion.

the Jura, from which we discovered seven different lakes, Mount Blanc and the Glaciers of Savoy. We purpose going this year, if the weather is fine, to see the Glaciers of Switzerland and the little Cantouns. I wish, my dear Uncle, you might be of our party. Believe me most sincerely, your affectiônate nie[ce],

J^{e.} Eth Archer

32. [L]

Endorsed: From W. Js. Archer, Mar. 7 1805, Oujonnet.

D^r: J: C: Lettsom
Sambrook Court
Basinghall Street
London

Oujonnet 7 March 1805

Dear Uncle,

I received your kind favour of the 6 November and should have answered it much sooner, had not the communication with England been so often inter-rupted this winter, owing to the frost in the North. Even at present 7 English maills are daily expected. You inform'd me the Bank have given a Bonus of 5 per Cent on Bank Stock. Has it been paid in money, or in another stock in the same manner as some former Bonus? The French News papers mention that something has been done, relative to the Loyalty Loan or new 5 per Cent. Would you be so good to inform me if anything has taken place relative to the said stock? Has it been paid of[f], or only in part, or transfer'd to another Stock; or is it to be paid in a given time? If what I have in the new 5 per Cent Stock has been paid you for me, pray be so good to buy for me for the amount of that sum in the 3 per Cent consols[73] and send me the certificate or receipt of the Bank. What I have in the new 5 per Cent stands in my name, of the York Hotell, Blackfriars. I believe if you buy any stock for me it ought to be placed in like manner. If what I have in the new 5 per Cent has been transfer'd to the Navy 5 per Cent, be so good to send me the certificate or receipt of the said transfer, and I suppose I must send you a new power of Attorney to receive the dividends. Betsy wrote to you some time ago.

---

[73] "Consols" is a contraction of "consolidated annuities", that is, a bond issue which consolidated two or more outstanding issues, used in relation to British government stock.

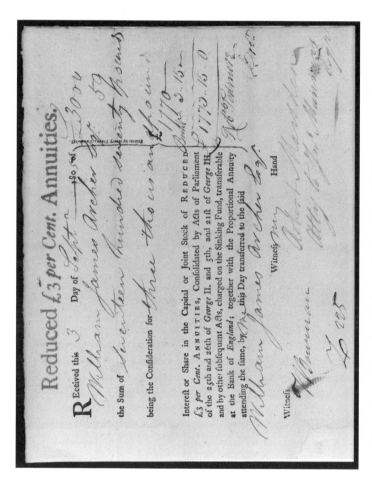

Figure 3: Three per cent Consols, purchased on 3 September by John Coakley Lettsom for his nephew, William James Archer, as instructed in Archer's letter of 7 March 1805. (Courtesy of the Medical Society of London.)

At present she is verry well, though subject now and then to pains in her eyes, a complaint that is common this damp, rainy, ~~sn~~ snowy winter. We have hardly had 8 days fine since the 1 November.

We have often news quick from London in the French papers. Yesterday I saw Mr: Pitt's ways and means for the service of the year, and his loan of 20,000,000£. It is the general opinion, at least in this part of the world, that a continentall war will not take place; it is hoped that a general peace is not far of[f]. The taxes in the Canton de Vaud are moderate and all is peaceble and quiet. May it long and long continue so. I hope that you and your excellent familly are well. Pray remember me kindly to them all, and believe me,

Your affectionate Nephew,

William James Archer

33. [L]

Endorsed: From William James Archer, July 16 1805, Oujonnet.

D^r: J: C: Lettsom
Sambrook Court
Basinghall Street
London

Oujonnet 16 July 1805

Dear Uncle,

I receiv'd your kind favour of the 21 June last Friday and answer[ed] it as soon as I could gett the enclos'd power of Attorney properly made out. You mention that you intend purchasing some freehold land adjoining to your premises between Camberwell and Peckham to the amount of about 2000£ Sterling and ask me if I wish to lay on any sum from 500 to 1000£ Sterling. The sum I should like to lend you mortgaged on the above mention'd purchase is seven hundred and fifty pounds sterling, for which sum you offer five per cent per annum. I will desire M^r: Geldard to see the deeds properly executed on my account; would you be so good to pay him five or six pounds. I believe I am in his debt, as likewise any expense he may be at on my account in seeing the deeds properly made out. When you have sold out the two thousand four hundred thirty five pounds, 5 per Cent annuities 1797 for me, after deducting 750£, please to buy for me (of the York Hotell Blackfriars, but now residing at Oujonnet near Rolle in Switzerland) in the 3 per Cent reduced annuities a sum equal to the remaining 1685£ Sterling and be so kind to send me the receipt or certificate of the Bank. Pray make the above-mention'd purchase for me in the 3 per Cent reduced annuities as soon as possible, that I may receive a dividend next October. You must send me a power of Attorney, that I must sign to enable you to receive the dividends for me. I think the bonus of 265 receiv'd on Bank Stock should be placed in our names in the 3 per Cent consols, or if there is no inconvenience to place it on your intended purchase of land between Camberwell and Peckham. Betsy and my daughters have been on a visit at a Madame d'Hautville near Vevay. They intend crossing the lake today to see part of the road which is cut through the Rocks of Mellerie.[74] The road over the St: Plom is a most astonishing and noble undertaking. Next year I hear carriages will be able to cross it without locking the wheels.[75] The communication with Italy over the Alps will be verry easy. Betsy and my Children are going next week with a Dutch familly to see the Glaciers of Savoie.[76] I was there some years ago. We have cold weather unfavourable for the grapes of which I have a great show. The hay has turn'd plentifull, oats and barley verry promising, the wheat and rye but poor. Pray remember me to all your familly, and believe me,

your affectionate nephew

William James Archer

34. [L]

Endorsed: From W. J. Archer, Oct. 8 1805, Oujonnet.

Franco Engen[77]
To
D^r: J: C: Lettsom
Sambrook Court
Basinghall Street
London

Oujonnet 8 Oct 1805

Dear Uncle,

I receiv'd your kind favour of the 5 September a few days ago and a power of attorney which I will gett properly made out a Lausanne to enable you to receive the dividends for me of the 3 per Cent reduced annuities, which you

---

[74] This was a common stop on the Grand Tour. Mary Wollstonecraft Shelley mentions it in her *History of a six weeks' tour through a part of France, Switzerland, Germany and Holland*, London, T. Hookham Jun. and J. Ollier, 1817.

[75] The wheels would have been locked to stop them spinning on ice.

[76] The English were the first, in the eighteenth century, to make the journey to see the glaciers of Savoie. These were the famous "*voyages aux glaciaires*". Chamonix in the upper Arve valley was a popular destination.

[77] "Franco" means carriage-free. The nature of "Engen" eludes us.

inform me you have bought in my name. Would you be so kind to send me the receipt or certificate of the Bank of what you have bought in my name in the 3 per Cent reduced Annuities. I believe it is necessary I should have the said receipt or certificate. You likewise mention there remains in your hands £694-14-7 of mine after the purchase you have made for me in the 3 per Cent reduced Annuities, which I desire to make up 750£ out of the 265£. I have drawn on you a few days ago for 200£ à 2 mois de datte. I am afraid this letter will be some time before it getts to England as the French and Austrian armys are in Germany.[78] Hostilities have not yet begun though their different outposts and patrouilles[79] often meet. Great hopes are entertain'd that Switzerland will be able to remain neuter, as the most positive assurances have been given by France and Austria to that purpose. Should the war break out, letters to and from England will be a long time on the road. I expect daily a letter from Mr: Geldard. Richard Paris is still with me. Betsy, who desires kindly to be remember'd to you, is returned from Geneva, where she had been to bathe in the icy waters of the Arve, on accounts of violent pains in her Eyes.[80] The Baths have done her much good. She intends in a short time to have the pleasure of writing to you. My Children are all well. Owing to the continentall war our wines have risen in price; this year's vintage will be bad in quality and quantity, but I hope will sell well. People must be much pleas'd in England that the French have broke up the camp at Boulogne.[81] The German papers mention the Russians are daily expected in Germany; they are said to be 100 or 150,000.[82] The exchange in London is getting worse and worse, owing, as is supposed, to the sending so much ~~redy~~ ready cash on the continent and the immense subsidies England has to pay. Pray remember me kindly to your worthy familly, and believe me,
Your affectionate Nephew
William James Archer

---

[78] After the signing of the Treaty of St Petersburg in April 1805 and further agreements signed by Austria in the July and August following, the Austro-Russian Third Coalition began planning a major campaign in Europe, to include four different offensives and half a million men. As one offensive, 85,000 Austrians under the command of General Mack were to conquer Bavaria, a staunch ally of France, there to be joined by 85,000 Russian reinforcements under General Kutusov. Mack invaded Bavaria on 10 September and occupied Ulm and waited for his Russian back-up. But the Grande Armée marched with dazzling speed, so that by the end of September Mack was in danger of being encircled. A series of clashes followed at Wertingen, Hasslach and Elchingen, but, on 20 October, Mack, almost entirely surrounded and with the Russians nowhere in sight, was forced to surrender his army of, by that time, 30,000 men.

[79] Patrols.

[80] The Arve descends from the glaciers of Mont Blanc to join the Rhône outside Geneva.

[81] The 200,000 men of Napoleon's Grande Armée, located in training camps along the Channel were based at Boulogne sur mer, where Napoleon was collecting his flotillas.

[82] Mack's surrender was still twelve days away and Russian reinforcements were still anticipated in Bavaria, at this stage.

35. [L]

Endorsed: From Elizabeth Archer, Nov. 12 1805, Oujonnet

Double lettre franco Engen
John Coakley Lettsom M.D.
Sambrook Court Basinghall
Street
London
England

Oujonnet 12th of November 1805

My dear Uncle,

I have been a long time in expectation of the pleasure of hearing from you. Owing to the events in Germany, the communication with England is long, and perhaps letters may be lost. However, several have been received from London. My husband sends you the enclosed Power of Attorney to enable you to receive this dividends for him of the 3 per Cent annuities. He desires to be kindly remembered to you and all your family. We hope you enjoy as well as all your family a good state of health.

We have just finished our Wintages, which have turned out but indifferent, the wine being of a very ~~bad~~ bad qualite owing to the dampness of the season. As for news, I can inform you of none, as it's likely you have been informed of the wonderful events in Germany which in all probability will oblige the House of Austria to a disgraceful Peace. Switzerland enjoys a perfect state of tranquillity. Her neutrality, till the present moment, has been respected by the different Powers.

I hope your daughter Mrs. Elliot has been safely delivered. I shall be happy to hear of her welfare. I wish we had a Peace that you, dear sir, and your daughter might take a trip to our beautiful Contry. I made an excursion this Summer with my Children to the Glaciers of Savoy and the adjacent vallies. I need not inform you how we were delighted with the beautiful views of the several Glaciers and Mount Blanc covered with eternal snows and yes, I wish I had strength to go up. The Children supported this fatiguing journey with a great deal of courage and good humour, and wishes as well as me to make next year an other excursion among the Swiss montaignes. It would be all pleasures, if the Savoy inns were not such horrid dirty places, but we were so happy that we made up with every little inconveniences. We took another turn round the pretty lake of Annecy,⁸³ where we had the pleasure to see

---

⁸³ Lac d'Annecy is fed only by springs and rainwater and is situated in the mountains (now in Haute Savoie) in eastern France, near the borders of Switzerland and Italy, 64 km or 40 miles

a newly-discovered coal mine which in quality and quantity is supposed to be one of the finest in the world, the whole mountain being allmost one solid bed of Coal. It's a pity it is so far from Genèva. Wood, the only fuel, is excessif scarce and dear and the Winters bitter Cold. We visited several Glass houses where the Children were very much amused in seing the different process[es] employed in blowing of Glass. We were much disappointed in not being allowed to see a newly erected manufactury ~~of~~ for spinning of Cotton on the English principle which is said to succeed very [much?].[84] My Children continue to improve and give me great pleasure. Maria is much taller than me. We are in great hopes in the part of the world that the King of Prussia jointly with the Emperor of Russia will be able to bring about a general Pacification.[85]

I shall be very happy if you favour me with an answer, being a great pleasure for me when I hear from you. I beg you will ~~remeber~~ remember me to Mrs. Lettsom and your family. I remain, dear Uncle,
your dutiful niece
J^e. Elizabeth Archer

I beg you will excuse this scrawl, but I have very bad pains in my Eyes, yet I do not suffer as I did since I bathed in the Icy waters of the Arve, a torrent which takes its rise amongst the Glaziers [*recte* Glaciers].

36. [L]

Endorsed: From Elizabeth Archer, Aug. 22 1806, near Geneva

fo Engen
Dr. J. C. Lettsom
Sambrook Court, Basing-Hall
Street
London

Plongeon near Geneva 22^d. of August 1806

My dear Uncle,

I had the pleasure of receiving your letter about a month ago and wished to answer it sooner, but my Eyes have been so bad that it had entirely

---

south of Geneva, a long distance over difficult terrain in the early nineteenth century. On the shores of the lake were the towns of Annecy, known as the "Venice of Savoie" because of its canals and cobbled streets, and Talloires.

[84] The manuscript is torn and only the first part of the first letter, which looks like an "m" survives. Cotton was still being produced in Annecy in the early twentieth century.

[85] In the event, Napoleon destroyed the Third Coalition by routing the Austro-Russian army at Austerlitz on 2 December 1805.

prevented me from writing. It is almost a general complaint in this Contry. William is likewise affected with it so we came here to take the Cold Bath in the Arve, which does us much good. I wish, Dear Sir, you would try ~~of~~ this remedy to cure yours, though I hope they continue better. I cannot help wishing for an occasion to bring you near us. I am very sorry to hear ~~good~~ Mr. Elliot is not well. I beg you will give him my best Compliments. You must come altogether to our fine airy Contry to Cure you. Mr Elliot will tell you, this House is large enough to receive you <u>en famille</u>. If ever you take this ~~Grand~~ Grand resolution, think what a happy day it will be for me, for I wish nothing more earnestly than to be more particularly acquainted with you.

The harvest had a very fine appearance, but unfortunately a great deal has been spoiled by the wet. We have had plenty of Hay. The Wineyards have not such a good appearance as these two late years it rains too much and if we have not some fine warm weather I am affraid the Grapes will not ripen well. I am quite happy to hear by your letter my Good friend Hatley is in a better situation, but what surprises me much is that I had given order to my Banker in London, Mr Duval, to enquire for her and to remit her a little token of my remembrance this last month of May; and he has answered me that he went to Mrs. Hatley's house but they answered him she was gone on the Continent and did not know her Direction. If she is still in London, pray be so good to desire her to write me for she may be assured my friendship for her is allways the same.

We had great hopes that Peace between England and France would have been announced this day week, the Festival of the Great Napoleon,[86] but it appears that the Negotiations have met with unforeseen difficulties. However, hopes of a Peace are not yet vanished. The French Papers mentioned that a terrible inondation had taken place in London and the environs the 24th of July. I hope your beautiful house on Camberwell Grove Hill has not suffered by the hurricane and the dreadful storm of thunder and lightening, which according to the French Papers, took place on the same day. William will have the pleasure of writing to you in a short time, as the Exchange in London is a little better. He intends drawing on you for "100" Pounds à deux mois de date. My Children continue to enjoy a good state of health and improve in their education. We return ~~bak~~ to Oujonnet in a month, and we beg of you to continue to direct your letters as usual. The Post comes now very regular from England in about three weeks time. Pray remember me kindly to Mrs. Lettsom and all your family, and believe me, your affectionnate niece.

J[e.] Elizabeth Archer

---

[86] Napoleon was born on 15 August 1769 at Ajaccio in Corsica.

37. [L]

Endorsed: From W. Archer, Nov. 12 1807, Oujonnet.[87] done.

To
D^r: J: C: Lettsom
Sambrook Court
Basinghall Street
London
England

Oujonnet 12 Nov: 1806

Dear Uncle,

I receiv'd your kind favour of the 26 September some time ago. It afforded ~~us~~ me great pleasure to be inform'd of your wellfare and that of your worthy familly. You certainly have by the publick papers as early information as we have here of the astonishing ~~ev~~ military events that have taken place in Prussia.[88] The seat of war being such a distance from Switzerland, was it not for the French Bulletins, it would hardly be perceiv'd. The taxes in this part of the world are moderate and hopes are given that they will be diminish'd next year. The taxes last year exceeded the expenditure. The surplus, I hear, is to be lent at a moderate interest to persons of small landed property (who owing to the vintage in many places having been so bad, and the great want of ready money) stand in need of momentary relief and may not be forced to sell their property. Land continues to be dear here. Trade, manufacturys and commerce all over Switzerland is much on the decline. A generall peace is wanted.

You mention that the Bank have ordered a bonus of 5 per Cent on their stock. The exchange on London is got a little better but it is supposed will not continue so. In a few days I intend drawing on you for 265£ à 2 mois de datte. For some time we have little or no news from England except by the French papers. Letters come but irregularly. Betsy received one from Mrs. Hatley that was nine weeks on the road. We have a most delightfull Autumn; the weather today is as fine and as warm as in May. Our vintage has been but indifferent but not as bad as in some parts of the country. The wine

---

[87] Lettsom has inaccurately endorsed this as 1807. The correct date is 1806, as given at the head of Archer's letter.

[88] Prussia became increasingly concerned at the spread of French influence in the smaller German states and decided to join Britain and Russia to form the Fourth Coalition against France in October 1806. Napoleon reacted swiftly, launching an attack on Prussia on 8 October. Prussia suffered a double defeat on 14 October at Jena and at Auerstadt, where the Prussian army was defeated. Frederick William III of Prussia fled to Russia.

is of a good quality, that of last year verry bad. We sold all ours of the last vintage at a pretty good price. There are but few purchasers of wine owing to the want of ready money or a representative of it.

Betsy desires kindly to be remember'd to you and yours. In a little time she will have the pleasure of writing to you. The accident which happened the 2 of September in the Canton of Switz destroyed one of the most fertile and beautifull valleys of Switzerland.[89] The number of persons who perished according to official returns is I think 474, and a vast number of cattle. Betsy met with in a society at Geneva, a German Gentleman who was an eye wittness of the calamity, and who with a few others miraculously escaped for the avalanche finish'd but at about forty yards from them; they saw the first avalanche and the mountain wave before the great fall.

I am your affectionate Nephew
William James Archer

38. [L]

Endorsed: From W. J. Archer, Dec. 18 1806, Oujonnet.[90]

Oujonnet 24 Dec: 1806

Mon cher Oncle,

J'ai eu le plaisir de vous ecrire il y a quelque tems. J'espère que vous avez reçu ma lettre; je crains d'être longtems sans reçevoir de vos nouvelles; car la correspondance va être bien difficille. Le change a été bien mauvais. Il y a quelque tems jusqu'a 8 a 9 per Cent de perte. Heureusement il c'est [*recte* il est] un peu bonifié. C'est pourquoi j'ai tiré sur vous pour deux cent cinquante £ivres Sterling (250£ Sterling) à trois mois de datte. C'est fort possible que la Change vient bien plus mauvais encore, ou presque impossible.

Betsy me charge de vous dire mille choses de sa part de même qu' à toute votre bonne et excellente famille. Nous sommes tous bien. Nous avons un hiver detestable après un bell Autumn. Il fait des brouillards et des pluies continuelles. Ce tems est bien mall Juin. Je vous prie de faire bien mes amities à toute votre famille, et croyez moi,

Votre affectioné Neveu
William James Archer

---

[89] On 2 September 1806, a part of Rossberg Peak broke off, falling into the Goldau valley, one of Switzerland's central valleys. It swept away four villages and almost 500 people.

[90] The date discrepancy is probably a mistake by Lettsom on his endorsement.

39. [L]

Endorsed: From W. Archer, Dec. 24 1806, Oujonnet.

Monsieur D^r. J. C. Lettsom
Sambrook Court
Basinghall Street
Londres.

Oujonnet 24 Dec: 1806

Au Dr. J. C. Lettsom

Mon cher Oncle,
   C'est avec plaisir que je vous informe, que ma famille et moi sont bien.
J'espère que vous et la vôtre sont de même, et tire sur vous pour deux cent
cinquante livres Sterling à trois mois de datte.
Je suis votre affectioné Neveu
William James Archer

40. [L]

Endorsed: From W. Js. Archer, Sept. 25 1807, Oujonnet. answered.[91]

To
D^r: J: C: Lettsom
Sambrook Court
Basinghall Street
London

Oujonnet 25 Sept: 1807

Dear Uncle,
   I receiv'd the day before yesterday your kind favour of the 14 July. I assure
you it gave me infinite pleasure to hear from you as it is allmost a year since
I received any letter. All communication with England is verry difficult and
I am afraid will be still more so. You mention that you have paid
T: H: Masterman £700 for me and that he purchas'd exchequer bills to that
amount on my account. As I am to place about £600 the beginning of next

---

[91] This letter is written on blue paper.

year, I wrote to T: H: Masterman to sell the Exchequer bills he bought for me and that I should draw on him for £600 in the following manner, about the middle of October next for £150 à trois mois de datte, the beginning of November for £150 à deux mois de datte, and in December for £300, à deux mois de datte, and that if agreable to him I would leave one hundred pounds sterling in his hands at 5 per Cent per annum. I would be much oblig'd to you to communicate this letter to him, that if the one I wrote is should be lost he might be inform'd of my intention of drawing on him, for the above-mention'd £600. Has not the Bank of England augmented their yearly dividend of 7 per Cent to 10 per Cent?

We are going soon to begin the vintage which is promising. The 14 of August there was a most dreadful haill storm, which did great dammage to the vines at Lausanne and between here and Copet.[92] Fortunately we have had but little harm here. Our harvest has been plentifull, and we have had a good deal of hay, but a poor after crop. We continue to enjoy most perfect peace and tranquility. Switzerland may look on herself as one of the happyest countrys in Europe. Taxes are moderate. If there was but a generall peace, trade and commerce would encrease. Betsy desires to be kindly remember'd to you and your worthy familly. I read in the News papers that Mr: Elliot had stood candidate for Westminster.[93] There was allso an account of Sir Burdett's parading and his speech.[94] I was verry sorry that the English Government refus'd passing the bill in favour of the Roman Catholics[95]—what a different conduct to that of Bonaparte. We have just receiv'd accounts of the surrender of Copenhague and the Danish fleet.[96] I am afraid there is little probability of a generall peace, though much to be desired as well by the Continent as by England. How does trade go on? We have various accounts by the French

---

[92] Copêt or Coppet is two kilometres over the Geneva-Vaud cantonal boundary, by the shores of Lake Geneva (French: Lac Leman). It was the home of Madame de Staël and the group of brilliant intellectuals that gathered round her.

[93] John Elliot was persuaded to stand against Richard Brinsley Sheridan (1751–1816), dramatist and politician, for the Westminster division, but after the poll had been running for a number of days, Elliot realized that he had no chance and gracefully retired. See Abraham, op. cit., note 1 above, pp. 465–6.

[94] Sir Francis Burdett (1770–1844) was elected MP for Westminster in 1807. He stood because the constituency had a large electoral roll and a reputation for electing radicals. Burdett polled more votes than the other three candidates put together and his election was hailed as the first reform victory. He had formerly been MP for Boroughbridge in Yorkshire and for Middlesex, and was married to Sophia Coutts, daughter of the wealthy banker, Thomas Coutts.

[95] In March 1807 the Grenville Ministry broached the question of allowing Catholic officers to serve in the army. The King demanded a pledge not to meddle in this question. On refusal of this pledge the Ministry was dismissed.

[96] One of the results of commercial warfare between England and France, at this time, was English bombardment of neutral Copenhagen in October 1807 and the seizure of the Danish fleet on 21 October 1807. Almost 2,000 Danish civilians died. The bombardment caused a shock

papers how their stocks have risen, two years ago they were at fifty and lately at 92. Pray remember me to Mrs. Lettsom and all your familly and believe me,
Your affectionate Nephew
William James Archer

41. [L]

Endorsed: From William James Archer, Apr. 28 1808, Oujonnet.

To Dʳ: J: C: Lettson
Sambrook Court
Basinghall Street
London.

Oujonnet 28 Aprill 1808

Dear Uncle,
I received your kind favour of November last some little time ago, which afforded us much pleasure to be inform'd that you and all your excellent familly were well. We have had a long and tedious winter. At present, it is allmost as cold as in February. The 2 of this Month we had a slight shock of an Earthquake. Nobody felt it here, but many people at Geneva, Lausanne and Berne. Considerable damage has been done in some of the vallies at Piedmont, where according to the last accounts, there has been upwards of 100 shocks. Many people have left ~~there~~ their houses, as severall ~~has~~ are down and many not safe to inhabit. All communication by letters with England is getting more difficult. The French papers that gave regular extracts from the English have of late no News from England. In a short time it will perhaps be impossible to negociate bills on London, which would be a most distressing circumstance. I have drawn on you today for 100£ Sterling à trois mois de datte. All Coloniall produce is getting verry dear, as likewise all articles of dress, except silks. Corn and Wine is cheap. The last article I suppose is dear in England. Betsy desires to be kindly remember'd to you. I remain,
Your affectionate Nephew,
William James Archer

---

wave throughout Europe; George III even declared it an immoral act and Thomas Jefferson in America spoke of the "extinction of national morality". A. D. Harvey, *Collision of empires: Britain in three world wars 1793–1945*, London, Phoenix, 1994, pp. 98–102.

42. [L]

Endorsed: From W. J. Archer, July 14 1808, Oujonnet.

D^r: J: C: Lettsom
Sambrook Court
Basinghall Street
London

Oujonnet 14 July 1808

Dear Uncle,

It is a long time since I have had the pleasure of hearing from you, which I attribute to the difficulty of receiving letters from England. I hope that you and your worthy familly are all well. We continue here to enjoy pretty good health. I have drawn on you today for 250£ Sterling payable the 30th of October next, consequently after the dividends are paid at the Bank. The exchange in London is verry bad, more than $6\frac{1}{2}$ per Cent loss, and it is a most difficult matter even to negociate bills. We have now and than [*recte* then] news from England in the French papers. It is surprising how verry high the stocks are. What can be the reason, as the trade and commerce of England is much diminis'd? Since some time, all coloniall produce has more than doubled in price here, Coffee allmost 5s. a pound, sugar 3s.6d., and cotton, hardly any to be had, which is likewise the case for all drugs for dying and for the apothicarys. Should the war continue between Russia and Turkey,[97] there will be a total want of Coffee,[98] Cotton and different drugs. We have just finish'd hay making, which has not been verry plentifull. The corn in generall ~~lo~~ looks well and is allmost fitt to cutt. The vineyards never had a more promising appearance. Corn and wine will in all probability be excessive cheap. Our taxes here continue to be moderate; I suppose they are verry high in England. Betsy desires to be kindly remember'd to you. The hot weather is just begun, I am afraid it will be as warm as last year. You certainly are inform'd of the great events that have taken place in Spain. Yesterday's papers contain the new Spanish Constitution.[99] Is there any talk of peace in

---

[97] Russia declared war on Turkey in 1807. The conflict was costly to both sides. Russia lost 120,000 of its infantry and 7,000 cavalry, though technically it was the winning side. Turkey lost 100,000 regular soldiers, its entire feudal cavalry and three corps of feudal infantry.

[98] Coffee arrived in Constantinople in the mid-sixteenth century as a result of Muslim expansion. By 1765, there were about 3,000 coffee houses in England.

[99] On 10 May 1808, Napoleon forced both Ferdinand VII and his father Charles IV to abdicate the Spanish throne, which he then gave to his brother Joseph. The Constitution of Bayonne, signed on 8 July 1808, contained Napoleon's reforms of the Spanish state. It was replaced by a new constitution in 1812.

England? I am afraid this war will continue for many years; thank God we are perfectly quiet in this part of the world. Agriculture is much improv'd but trade much on the decline. Some few manufactures go on well, but what can they do if there is a want of cotton, Indigo etc? If you see T: H: Masterman, would you be so kind to tell him I have written severall times to him and request he will ~~answer~~ write to me as soon as possible. I am afraid my or his letters have been lost. In hoping, dear Uncle, to hear from you soon which I assure you will give me great satisfaction,
I am
your affectionate Nephew
William James Archer

43. [L]

Endorsed: From W. J. Archer, Febr. 1 1809, Oujonnet.

D^r: J: C: Lettsom
Sambrook Court
Basinghall Street
London

Oujonnet 1 Feb: 1809

Dear Uncle,

   It is now more than a year since I have had the pleasure of hearing from you. I have often wrote to you, but I am afraid my letters are lost. I hope that you and all your worthy familly are well. We continue to enjoy pretty good health; my son who some years ago was rather of a weak constitution is grown tall and strong. The difficulty of communication with England is a distressing circumstance, ~~for~~ the continent I believe suffers more than England, especially the commercial interest, if we may judge by the vast number of bankruptcies which have lately taken place and many more are dreaded. Now and than [*recte* then] there is news from England in the French and German papers. The stocks continue high, and it appears that the British manufactures, especially the Irish linens, have more work than for many years past. The exchange on London is verry bad, from 12 to 15 per Cent loss; and it is a difficult matter to negotiate bills. ~~On~~ tomorrow I intend drawing on you for 200£ Sterling à 20 jours de vue (20 days after sight). Nobody would take bills ~~at~~ as formerly ~~at~~ à trois mois de datte. You would render me a particular service, when you see T: H: Masterman, to desire him to inform me if he has not receiv'd for me ~~the~~ a dividend arising from J: Masterman's Estate. I sent him an order to that effect a long time ago, that money would be of use to me now, as perhaps in a short time, it will be impossible to draw on London or perhaps at a loss of 20 or 30 per Cent.

We continue to enjoy perfect peace and quietness in Switzerland. If we look on other states of Europe we may consider ourselves as a fortunate nation. Betsy desires to be kindly remember'd to you. In hoping to hear from you soon, believe me my dear Uncle,
Your affectionate Nephew
William James Archer

44. [L]

Endorsed: From William James Archer, May 1 1809,[100] Oujonnet.

D^r: J: C: Lettsom
Sambrook Court
Basinghall Street
London

Oujonnet 11 May 1809

Dear Uncle,

I did myself the pleasure of writing to you some time ago. It is now more than a year since I have heard from you. I hope that you and all your family are well. We continue to enjoy good health. You are certainly inform'd in England of the new war that has broke out between Austria and France, and of the great success of the French.[101] There is everry reason to hope that the neutrality of Switzerland will be respected by the Belligerent powers.[102]

---

[100] The discrepancy in the dates is presumably a mistake on Lettsom's part.

[101] Following the peace of Tilsit on 7 July 1807, when Russia and Prussia submitted to French terms, the majority of the Grande Armée had been withdrawn behind the Rhine. The Austrians took advantage of this weakness. On 9 April 1809, the Austrian army marched and took Munich, the capital of Bavaria. On 13 April, Napoleon hastened towards the front and the Austrians were defeated at Wagram on 6 July.

[102] The Napoleonic Wars did much to strengthen Swiss neutrality (which had first been declared by the Cantons in 1674). Both the French and the various allies in league against them made the country into a war zone and much of Switzerland was annexed by France. However, Switzerland's "*neutralité perpetuelle*" was constitutionally recognized, after Napoleon's defeat, by the Treaty of Vienna on 20 November 1815.

Of late letters have come quicker and safe from London, but the exchange is verry bad, and I am afraid in a short time it will be allmost impossible to draw on London. I have drawn today on you for 200£ Sterling <u>à un mois de vue</u> (a month after sight) and I am afraid I cannot negotiate the Bills at less than 17 per Cent loss. During the last war, the exchange on London was never more than 8 per Cent loss, and at one time 12 per Cent in favour. All colonial produce continues excessive dear, as everry article of dress, especially cottons, Wine and corn are too cheap. A universall peace is much to be wish'd for. When you see T: H: Masterman woul'd you be so kind to tell him I have written severall times, and request he will answer me as soon as possible. The difficulty of having letters from England is a distressing circumstance for many people; if Sweden remains neuter, perhaps letters may go and come by that way.[103] Betsy desires to be kindly remember'd to you. She as well as myself wish much to hear from you.

I remain,

Your affectionate Nephew

William James Archer

45. [L]

Endorsed: From W. J. Archer, Oct. 3 1809, Oujonnet.

To

D^r: J: C: Lettsom

Sambrook Court

Basinghall Street

London

Oujonnet 3 Oct 1809

Dear Uncle,

It is a verry long time since I have had the pleasure of hearing from you, owing I suppose, to the difficulty of corresponding with England; however, many letters of late have arriv'd from London. I have drawn on you today for 250£ Sterling à trente jours de vue (thirty days after sight). The exchange on

---

[103] Napoleon had prompted Russia and Denmark to declare war on Sweden in 1808. Sweden lost the war, huge amounts of money, land and a king. By the time of this letter Sweden was obviously regarded as neutral again.

London is verry bad, more than 20 per cent loss, and I am afraid it will gett worse till a generall peace. If you see T: H: Masterman, will you be so good to desire him to write to me as soon as possible. Betsy and my familly, who are all well, desire to be kindly remember'd to you. She wishes much to hear from you. We have had a most miserable summer. Today is cold as in December; we shall make but little and very bad wine. The harvest has been indifferent, but a great deal of hay. You certainly are inform'd by the publick papers of the continentall news, how happy Switzerland has been during the late events in Germany. Coloniall produce continues verry dear. I see by the French papers, that sugar is so cheap in England, that cattle are fattened with it. Corn and wine continues cheap, though we have a bad seed time. All articles of dress except silk is high. A̶g̶r̶ Agriculture is improving. Many machines invented in England have been introduced. As to trade and commerce is allmost at a stand. A general peace is wish'd for, but I am afraid is far of[f]. Pray, dear Uncle, lett me hear from you as soon as possible, and believe me,
your affectionate nephew,
William James Archer

46. [L]

Endorsed: From W. Js. Archer, Dec. 18 1809, Oujonnet.

To
D^r: J: C: Lettsom
Sambrook Court
Basinghall Street
London

Oujonnet 18 Dec 1809

Dear Uncle,

It is now near two years since I have had the pleasure of hearing from you.[104] I have wrote verry often, and am afraid many of my letters have been lost. All communication with England by letter is getting more and more difficult, and the exchange worse and worse. I have drawn on you today for two

---

[104] Archer states six months earlier, in his letter of 11 May 1809 that "it is now more than a year since I heard from you".

hundred Pounds sterling à un mois de vue (a Month after sight). The ~~exchange~~ exchange on London is at a loss of 25 per Cent; perhaps in a short time it will be worse, or impossible to negotiate Bills on London. The exchange on Russia is at 50 per Cent loss, on Danemark 65; I assure you the war is severely fellt. When shall we have peace? How does trade and Manufactures go on in England? We have such various accounts in the French papers, that it is impossible to form a just idea.

The last vintage has been one of the worst and less productive for many years past; Money consequently scarce in Switzerland. Some cotton manufacturys are going on verry well. How happy poor Switzerland has been during the war with Austria, and especially since the most positive assurances have been given by the French Government of maintaining her independence. Pray dear Uncle lett us hear from you, it will give us great pleasure, believe me

your affectionate Nephew

William James Archer

47. [L]

Endorsed: From William Archer, Jan. 16 1810, Oujonnet.

Oujonnet 16 Jan: 1810

Dear Uncle,

I did myself the pleasure of writing to you some time ago; it is now near two years ~~ago~~ that I have heard from you. When you write to me, be so good to request Messrs. William Mellish and Co. merchants in the City[105] to forward your letter under cover to Messrs. Delaroche, Delessert et Cie à Nantes,[106] or if your letter is sent to Holland, to desire their correspondent to send it to me in Switzerland. The exchange on London is got a verry little better, but I am afraid will not continue so, therefore I intend drawing on you for 100£ Sterling à 30 jours de vue (30 days after sight). As you my dear Uncle have allways been good and kind to me, and in many instances a second father, I inform you that my eldest Daughter is soon to be married, to a Swiss Gentleman who is engaged in a commerciall house in one of the sea

---

[105] John and William Mellish, merchants, 112, Bishopgate, within. See Henry Kent, *Kent's Directory. For the year 1794*, London, R. and H. Causton, 1794.

[106] A French firm of forwarding agents. It may have been the company for which Archer's son-in-law worked, see Letter 49.

ports of France. He is near 30, of a good figure and of an excellent caracter, and nearly related to one of the first Merchants of Paris. My daughter is all-most 20. This marriage, as the French say, ne me rendra pas plus jeun.

Betsy desires to be kindly remember'd to you, and all your worthy familly. It is now near 8 years since I have had the pleasure of ~~hearing f~~ seeing you. believe me, my dear Uncle,
Your affectionate Nephew
William James Archer

48. [L]

Endorsed: From W. Js. Archer, Mar. 8 1810, Oujonnet.

D^r: J: C: Lettsom
Sambrook Court
Basinghall St
London.

Oujonnet 8 March 1810

Dear Uncle,

I did myself the pleasure of writing to you, in the month of January last. As you have allways been verry kind and affectionate to me, I thought it would give you pleasure to hear that my eldest daughter was going to be married, which event took place the 20th of last February. Mr Delessert is the name of my daughter's husband. He is engag'd in a commercial house at <u>Nantes</u>, which in time of peace and when the American flag was respected by France and England, did a great deal of business with America. Severall persons of my acquaintance in a short time have made large fortunes in that line.

As for news, you certainly are inform'd in England of the Emperor of France's marriage with the Daughter of the Emperor of Austria,[107] an event for the continent of Europe of great importance, and certainly in many respects for Switzerland, especially if a war should take place between France and Russia, as in that case, the seat of a war would be at a great dis-tance from her frontiers. All communication with England by letters is verry

---

[107] On 15 December 1809, Napoleon and Josephine were formally divorced. In March 1810, Napoleon married the Archduchess Marie Louise of Austria.

difficult. The exchange on London is a little ~~better~~ better, but is still at 20 per cent loss, some time ago as bad as 25. I intend drawing on you for 200£: Sterling à un mois de vue (a month after sight).

The middle of last month we had excessive cold weather, the thermometer as low as 14, the lake for 2 days was frozen near Geneva. At present the weather is fine and too warm. The 23 of February was a difference of 16 degrees between cold and heat in the 24 hours.

Betsy and my familly desire to be kindly remember'd to you and yours. In hoping, dear Uncle, to hear from you soon
I remain
your affectionate Nephew
William James Archer

49. [L]

Endorsed: From W. J. Archer, Apr. 6 1810, Oujonnet.

D^r: J: C: Lettsom
Sambrook Court
Basinghall St
London

Oujonnet 6 Aprill 1810

Dear Uncle,
During the course of the winter I did myself the pleasure of writing to you. I hope you have receiv'd my letters, and that I shall soon hear from you. I mention'd that my eldest daughter was married to a Mr: de Lessert, who is engaged in a commercial house at Nantes. Tommorrow I intend drawing on you for 100£: Sterling à trente jours de vue (30 days after sight) payable to my daughter J: M: R: E: de Lessert[108] or order. The exchange on London is got much better. It is impossible to say how long it will continue so. I hear that many licences have been given by the French Governtment to export certain articles. There is allso a great talk of peace, of which the continent as well as England I think is in great want, but which event I am afraid is far of[f].

You certainly are inform'd in England of the Emperor of France's marriage, and of the great rejoicings and illuminations that ~~ar~~ have been at Paris,

---

[108] Known by her second name, Maria was the Archers' eldest daughter.

and in many other cities in France. It appears that Holland will be allow'd to keep her independance but it is supposed she will be oblig'd to pay verry considerable sums of money.

Betsy desires to be kindly remember'd to you and all your worthy familly. Believe me my dear Uncle,
your affectionate Nephew
William James Archer

50. [L]

Endorsed: From William Archer, Feb. 8 1811, Oujonnet. answered.

D:ʳ J: C: Lettsom
Sambrook Court
Basinghall Street
London

Oujonnet 8 Feb: 1811

Dear Uncle,

I receiv'd the beginning of last November your kind favour of the month of June. I need not mention how sorry and distress'd I was to be inform'd of the death of your worthy son, and my good friend, Pickering.[109] I certainly should have wrote sooner, had an occasion offer'd of sending letters to England. Sometimes they come and go quick, at others are many months on the road, are often open'd and lost.

Our last vintage was good in quality, but by no means abundant. As for news, you certainly are ~~inford~~ inform'd in London by the French papers, what concerns the continent. In Switzerland, thank God, we enjoy perfect peace. Our taxes are moderate and all ~~we~~ we can reasonably wish for is a general peace. Trade and commerce is dull and money scarce. The cotton manufactorys, which were flourishing, are almost at a stand; and many hundred workmen want employment.[110]

---

[109] Pickering Lettsom (1782–1808), a barrister and Lettsom's youngest son, died on 28 October 1808 on the island of Tortola from island fever. He had just been married, a month earlier, to Ruth, widow of William Payne Georges, one of the wealthiest planters on the island. Pickering's wife died three months later, allegedly of a broken heart. Archer, it seems, did not have news of his friend, Pickering's death until two years after it occurred, in November 1810. See notes 75 and 88 in the 'Letters from Lettsom' section, and Abraham, op. cit., note 1 above, pp. 454–5.

[110] The cotton industry in Switzerland had grown rapidly in the eighteenth century to become a significant economic activity. It also was linked to the growth of fine white embroidery that was usually exported. By 1814, three years after this letter was written, there were around

The exchange on London was never ~~so~~ so bad and perhaps may gett worse. In a few days I intend drawing on you for 150£: Sterling à un mois de vue (a month after sight). The winter has been pretty severe, and a great deal of snow in the environs; past the Jura and the Alps verry little. Pray, dear Uncle, lett me hear from you soon, and

believe me, your affectionate Nephew

William James Archer

51. [L]

Miss Eliza Elliott
Pimlico Lodge

Dear Eliza!

I do not forget how good you were when you staid a few days at Grovehill; and to encourage you to continue to be kind, dutifull and affectionate, your Grandpapa sends you a box and threads. Your Grandmama joins in love with

J. C. Lettsom.

Sambrook Court,
November, XI 1811.

52. [L]

Endorsed: N°· 10, Marsala, 8 May

<u>Per Messina e Napoli</u>
John Elliot Esq., Pimlico Lodge, Westminster, London, Inghilterra
Single

No. X Marsala, Thursday May 8<u>th</u> 1823

My Dear Father,

We left Palermo on Monday morning, with four mules and two muleteers, and after a scorching ride of two hours arrived at the Village of Monreale: the only thing to be seen there is the ancient Cathedral: the great nave of which,

---

twenty-four spinning firms in the textile area in eastern Switzerland. Once the continental blockade, maintained by the Royal Navy during the Napoleonic Wars, was lifted the Continent was inundated with cheaper yarn of a better quality and the operatives were no longer able to survive.

is supported by corinthian pillars, taken, no doubt, from some ancient building at Palermo: we then proceeded through a wild mountainous country till we came in sight of the lovely bay of Castell à Mare, formerly the famous port for the commerce of Segesta:[111] to the east of this bay was the ancient town of Riccari, destroyed by Nicias, and of which nothing remains but the memory of the famous Lais, the daughter, according to Plutarch, of Alcibiades and his mistress Timandra—when Riccari was laid waste, Lais was but seven years old: she was taken by Nicias to Greece, and sold at Corinth where she remained some time, and received the appellation of "the Corinthian". Princes, Warriors, Philosophers, Apelles, Demosthenes, all flocked to Corinth and all were captivated with her beauty. Nay, even the callous heart of the Cynic felt the influence of her charms, and Diogenes himself became a candidate for her smiles. She sold her favors at so high a price that it gave rise to the well-known proverb

"Non cuivis homini contingit adire Corinthum".[112]

We arrived about eight in the evening at Alcamo, thirty miles distant from Palermo, having been on our mules twelve hours, which is tiresome work. The country around Alcamo is very picturesque, and abounds with the Indian fig, which makes, I think, a very pleasing addition to the beautiful scenery of this fertile country. Our host was a priest who, although a dirty-looking fellow himself, gave us very clean beds, a comfort we did not expect. The next morning, however, at starting, we found the <u>Holy Father</u> not only dirty, but a cheat; a happy illustration of that <u>wonderful</u> Trio which you may remember in the Latin grammar.

Fur, sus atque sacerdos![113]

We left Alcamo at five o'clock Tuesday morning, and after a ride of eight miles through a romantic country we arrived at the beautiful temple of Segesta, situated on the summit of a small round hill. The remains of the ancient city are but trifling: I was searching for them but could not find any traces of them: Wathaius, who was at the bottom of the hill drawing, told me this morning that he must have seen them: for he discovered several flat stones and part of an old Wall without being aware at the time that there were any remains of the ancient town. At the foot of this hill flows the River Crimisus, now called S. Bartolomeo. This River under the shape of a swan,

---

[111] Segesta, Sicily.

[112] "Not everyone is lucky enough to get to Corinth". Horace, Epistles I. xvii. 35. That is, it is not in every man's fortune to see great cities. In the first century B.C., Corinth was considered to be the centre of luxury and refinement.

[113] "Thief, pig and priest". This is part of a mnemonic poem used to memorise common nouns that can be male or female. We are grateful to Professor Vivian Nutton for this information.

enjoyed the embraces of a Trojan Girl who became the mother of Accotes or Egestus. When Aeneas, after the sacking of Troy, arrived in Sicily, Acestes founded, near the River Crimisus, the city of Egestas, in which Aeneas left all his followers who were unwilling or unable to go with him to Italy. Aene. V. 715.[114] This city, after continual quarrels with the inhabitants of Selinunte, became subject to the Carthaginians, who were called upon by the Egestans to help them against the Selinuntines, and who, after having subdued the latter, fell with their usual "Punica Fides"[115] upon their friends. Egestas remained under the power of the Carthaginians till the first Punic War: when she found means of throwing off the yoke, and espoused so warmly the Roman cause that she was declared by that power a free city. Agathacles inflicted terrible vengeance on this unhappy town—at the destruction of Carthage, Scipio generously restored to the Egestans the celebrated Bronze statue of Diana, which had been carried away amongst other treasures. When Sicily became a Roman Province, the Egestans were again robbed of this statue by that shark Verres. [Vide nota I][116] The Romans, not liking the inauspicious name of Egestas, prefixed to it an S: it is mentioned as existing as late as the third century: when it was destroyed is not known: probably during the invasion of the Saracens in the ninth century. The Portico of the temple which attracted our admiration at Segesta is perfect, whilst the Cell is entirely destroyed: so much so that we could not tell there had ever been one. It is of the Doric order, and infinitely more beautiful than the temples at Pastum.[117] [certainly not, Aug 1824][118] Its length is 174 feet and its breadth 70, exclusive of the basement: it is supported by 36 pillars: 14 at the sides and 6 in the front and back including the angular columns in each side. Each pillar is 20 feet in circumference and diminishes gradually in circumference from the Base to the Capital. Its superiority over the Pastum temples is owing to the length of the shafts which gives it a lightness and elegance so different from their squat, dumpy appearance. Immense blocks of stone about ~~14~~ 12 feet in length meet at the centre of each capital: the frieze is about $3\frac{1}{2}$ feet high and is ornamented with triglyphs: above this are the remains of the cornice. It is

---

[114] The passage referred to is: "Huic trade, amissis superant qui navibus et quos pertaesum magni incepti rerumque tuarum est; *longavosque sense ac fessas aequore matres* et quidquid tecum invalidum metuensque pericli est delige". "To him [Acestes] entrust those who, their ships thus lost, are left over, and those who have grown aweary of thy great emprise and of thy fortunes. Choose out *the old men full of years and sea-worn matrons*". Virgil, *Aeneid* V.715, italicized.

[115] "Carthaginian faith".

[116] This is superscripted in the text, in red ink, presumably by the recipient.

[117] A group of three temples built in the Greek version of Doric in Paestum, near Naples, in southern Italy, was rediscovered in the 1750s.

[118] This is superscripted in the text, in red ink.

unknown to whom this temple was erected. After having breakfasted inside this magnificent monument of Antiquity we proceeded on our journey. Since we left Alcamo we have felt no inconvenience from heat or dust: we have always enjoyed a sea-breeze, and, as there are no roads, our way lies over commons or through corn-fields. I have seen but one Letica (the carriage of the country) which to a person who comes from a <u>civilized</u> country has a most extra-ordinary appearance. It is a coach without wheels carried by two ~~horses~~ mules, one before and one behind, like a sedan chair. About five o'clock we arrived at Trapani, the modern Drepanum, so called because the coast[119] bends like a scythe. This spot is celebrated for the death and burial of Anchises. Aene. III, 707,[120] and as the ground where Aeneas celebrated his games in honor of his deceased Father. Aene. V, 65.[121] Virgil would not have selected a better place than this extensive plain—The "procul in pelago saxum" where

> – viridem Aeneas frondenti ex ilice metam
> Constituit, signum nautis pater, unde reverti Aene. V, 129
> Scirent, et longos ubi circumflectere cursus.[122]

stands exactly as the Poet describes. Near Trapani, Mount Eryx, (now Monte S. Giuliano) rises majestically out of the plain. Eryx, king of Sicily, was the son of Butes and the courtesan Lycasta, so famed for her beauty that she had a temple raised to her on Mount Eryx, and was worshipped there as Venus Erycina. [Aen. V, 760][123] [Vide note III][124] Thus the whole scene of the fifth book of the Aeniad is laid in this interesting spot. The modern town contains nearly 40,000 inhabitants, is strongly fortified, and is famous for its salt and coral. Edward the first landed here twice on his voyage to, and from, the Holy Land—you can imagine how we were devoured by the fleas at Trapani: I am now nothing but a <u>continued flea-bite</u>. We left Trapani about seven o'clock

---

[119] The word is in a fold of the letter and is discoloured and worn.

[120] The line referred to is: "Hine Drepani me portus et inlaetabilis ora"; "Next the harbour of Drepanum and its joyless shore". Virgil, *Aeneid* III.707.

[121] The passage referred to is: "Si nona diem mortalibus almum *Aurora extulerit radiisque retexerit orbem*, prima citae Teucris ponam certamina classis"; "Should for mortals the ninth *Dawn lift her kindly light and with her rays lay bare the world*, I will ordain contests for the Trojans". Virgil, *Aeneid* V.65, italicized.

[122] "Here as a mark father Aeneas set up a green goal of leafy ilex, for the sailors to know whence to return and where to double round the long course". Virgil, *Aeneid* V.129.

[123] This is superscripted. The passage referred to is: "Tum vicina astris Erycino in vertice sedes *fundatur Veneri Idaliae, tumuloque sacerdos* ac lucus late sacer additur Anchiseo"; "Then, on the crest of the Eryx, nigh to the stars, *a shrine is founded to Venus of Idalia*, and to Anchises: tomb is assigned a priest with breadth of hallowed grove". Virgil, *Aeneid* V.760, italicized.

[124] This is superscripted in red ink.

yesterday morning, and proceeding through a flat, fertile country arrived about two o'clock at Marsala, built on the site of the "splendidissima civitas Lilybaetera"[125] as Cicero calls it. There is nothing like an Inn in the town, and I do not know what travellers would do without the assistance of Mr Woodhouse, of whose hospitality we had heard before our arrival and to which we can bear ample testimony. Mr W is an elderly Bachelor, and is the exporter of all the famous marsal[a] [w]ine, by which means he has amassed an immense fortune. He lives about a mile from the town, and on our arrival we determined on paying him a visit. He was just going to dinner: two covers were immediately added to the table and he ordered our baggage to be taken off the mule <u>and carried upstairs</u>. He is a plain, hospitable, John Bull, character, and from his riches and goodness, is looked up to, as a king, and Father by the people in the neighbourhood. After dinner we rowed out to his Breakwater, which is at present his hobby-horse. About nine we had supper, and went to bed immediately afterwards. I never was more tired in my life, and never slept more soundly. G! the blessing of a <u>flea-less</u> bed. It was eleven before either of us was dressed this morning, and we found the old gentleman waiting for us to begin breakfast. We have seen to-day the small remains of the ancient port of Lilybaeum, now Capo Boco, so famous in the Punic Wars, and the Cathedral church, in which are sixteen handsome marble pillars, and of which, Thomas à Becket was the patron. The rest of the day has been devoted to writing—Tomorrow we go on towards Girgenti, which we expect to reach Sunday night. The cleanliness of Mr Woodhouse's beds has greatly refreshed us. I have often derived pleasure from a hospitable reception, but never till now did I feel its blessings. I have now surveyed the lane of eight books of the Aeniad: the fifth at Trapani, the sixth near Naples and the six last from the Alban Hill: for the other four I have nothing to do but take a trip to Carthage. How triumphant would she appear amidst her ruins to the eye that has contemplated the little All that remains of her successful Rival?

"O magna Carthago, probrosis
Altior Italiae ruinis".[126]

A fair wind would carry me thither in twelve hours: but "miserabile dictu"[127] there is a fortnight's Quarantine, which puts the matter quite out of the question. The same obstacle prevents my seeing Malta.

---

[125] Marsala was on the site of the Roman city of Lilybaeum. Cicero visited in 75 B.C. and described it as a "Splendid City".

[126] "O Great Carthage, greater still by the shameful fall of Italy". Horace, *Carmina (Odes)* III.5.

[127] "Sad to say".

With best love to all at home, believe me, my dear Father,
your most affectionate son,
John Lettsom Elliot

[L]

[A loose page—this is obviously the notes, superscripted in red, to John Lettsom Elliot's letter from Marsala, endorsed: N°· 10, Marsala, 8 May]

Note I/ Cicero with regard to this says Itaque aliquando multis malis magnoque metu victi Segestani Prætoris imperio parendum esse decreverunt. Magno cum luctu et gemitu totius civitatis, multis cum lacrimis et lamentationibus virorum mulierumque omnium simulacrum Dianae tollendum locatur.[128] In Verrem. lib. IV.

Note II/ After mentioning a variety of Duties to whom different authors have allotted this temple Biseari says "A quale di queste Divinità possa essere stato questo Tempio dedicato, lo giudichi il Viaggiatore: ma ponga mente, che potè Cerere essere quì venerata: perocchè i di lei Tempj solevano <u>fuorì la Città</u> innalzarsi, per le ragioni, che ne adduce Vitruvio". Viag. per le Antichità della Sicilia. This, however, was not always the case, for the temple of Ceres at Paestum is <u>within</u> the walls.

Note III/ Hic Veneri Idaliae—etc. Idalian = Cyprian, from a grove in that island consecrated to Venus: Virgil does not call Venus Idalia to distinguish her by that name, but to shew that the Venuses Idalian and Erycinica were the same.

Note IV/ The present town of Marsala was rebuilt by the Saracens. Marsala in Arabic signifies "Harbour of God". About 12 miles off Marsala are the islands of Levanso, Favignana, and Maretimo: anciently called Phorbantia, Aegusa, and Hiera: or Aegades Insulae. These are certainly not the νησοι μακαρων [islands of the blessed] as I was informed there were no less than twenty thousand persons confined in them, chiefly on account, of the late political disturbances.

---

[128] "And thus, in the end, crushed by their many sufferings and fears, the Segestans agreed that the governor's command should be obeyed. Amid the grief and lamentation of the whole community, with tears and cries of grief from every man and every woman in it, a contract was authorized for the removal of the image of Diana". Cicero, *Against Verres*, IV.34 76.

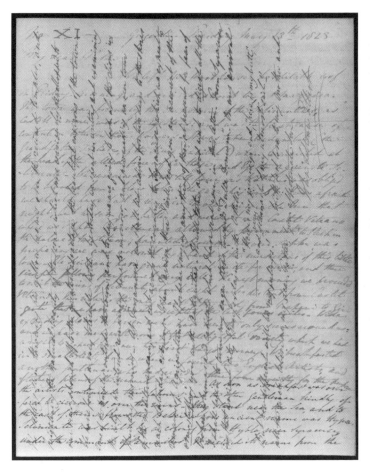

Figure 4: The first page of John Lettsom Elliot's letter from Girgenti, May 13 1823, to his father, John Elliott Esq., of Pimlico Lodge, Westminster. Letters were often cross-written during this period to save paper. (Courtesy of the Medical Society of London.)

53. [L]

Endorsed: N$^{o.}$ 11, Girgenti, 13 May[129]

Per Messina e Napoli
John Elliott Esq., Pimlico Lodge, Westminster, London, Inghilterra
Single

No. XI Girgenti Tuesday May 13th 1823

My dear Father,
    We left Mr Woodhouse's hospitable roof on Friday morning, and arrived about ten in Mazzara.[130] The town was formerly the Emporium of the Selinuntines,[131] as Castell à mare was of the Egastans: and was the first cause of the contention between those powers. It was taken by [H]Annibal (the grandfather, I believe, of the "dirus Annibal") when he succeeded at the head of the allied forces of Carthage and Egesta against Selinunte. We remained there till four, as Wathias[132] was obliged to be blooded from a blow which he gave his wrist. I was afraid we should have had to remain in our miserable inn that night, but he soon got better and we went on to Castel Vetrano where we slept. Travellers are allowed by government to sleep in the palace of Monteleone haunted of course. As our supper was preparing, we were welcomed by a band of the musicians of this little town. The Sicilians have great natural taste for music, and these simple fellows performed very well. The next morning we proceeded to visit the ruins of Selinunte about eight miles distant from Castel Vetrano. This ride is the only part of the road from Trapani to Sirgenti that we have admired excepting the last four miles. Wide extending plains or barren rocks have been the only scenes around us: and we have met with none of that delightful variety which we had a right to expect from our two first days' journey. We breakfasted in a small dirty house where we found two English Artists, and another gentleman who had resided these four months for the purpose of taking plans of the ancient temples. As soon as breakfast was over, the artists continued their labours, and the other gentleman kindly offered to Cicerone[133] us over the ruins. They stand near the sea, and to the east of them flows the Beliei, whose ancient name was Hypsa.

---

[129] The first page of this letter is cross-written to save paper and is difficult to read in parts.
[130] Mazara del Vallo, a seaport on the west coast of Sicily, at the mouth of the Mazaro river.
[131] In the early sixth century, the Selinuntines possessed the southern coast of Sicily as far as Sciacca (between Marsala and Agrigento).
[132] In Letter 52 this was spelt Wathaius.
[133] A verb made from Cicero.

Selinunte was built by a colony from Hybla near Syracuse, under the command of Paminibus. It received its name from the Greek word Σελινον [Selinon] as this country was famous for its parsley.[134] 242 years after its foundation Selinunte was taken by the first Annibal after obstinate resistance, and entirely destroyed. The women fled in vain to the temples, as places of refuge from the fury of the conquerors. Even these sacred edifices were razed to the ground, as Annibal declared that the Gods had deserted them the moment the city was reduced to slavery. Those who escaped out of the hands of the Carthaginians were received by the inhabitants of Agrigentum: and after some time succeeded in restoring Selinunte to a situation almost equal to that of former times. But 141 years after it was rebuilt it was again destroyed by the Carthaginians who led the inhabitants in captivity to Lilybaeum. It appears the city was built on the two hills which rise with a gentle slope from the sea. There are remains of six temples, all of the Doric order; three on each eminence. The largest was raised to Jupiter Forensis; of this, there is but one column standing, and that without its capital; the other pillars lie in ruins around. Its length is about 334 ft and its breadth 146. It had eight pillars in the front, and back; and seventeen at the sides; including the angular pillars in both directions: the two angular columns of the portico were fluted, which shows that they intended having the others so. It is singular enough that they were fluted after they had been erected. The diameter of the capitals is twelve feet and a half: of the columns, ten. Their height was five times their diameter. At Paestum it is not above four if I remember rightly: whilst the elegant Corinthian columns in the Roman form are nine or eleven times the length of their diameter. Some of the blocks of stone which formed the architrave were 27 ft long: the two other temples on the hill are considerably smaller than their gigantic neighbour. They are completely in ruins, and as no inscription has been found, it is unknown to whom they were dedicated. These remains, from their immense magnitude, are called by the country people "i pilieri dei giganti".[135] There is a peculiarity in these temples, as in the one at Segesta, which is to be met no where but in Sicily: namely, that at the bottom of the capital there is a deep groove, instead of the accustomed projections <u>beyond</u> the shaft. About eight miles distant is the quarry from which the stone was taken: it is a singular circumstance that the immense masses of stone which formed these columns were worked in the rock; as a proof of it, the grooves are still remaining. The dimensions of

---

[134] The Ancients identified two *selinon* plants, celery which they called *heleioselinon* or "marsh selinon" and parsley which they called *oreoselinon* "mountain selinon" or *petroselinum* or "rock selinon". The latter became corrupted into *Petrocilium*, which was anglicized into Petersylinge, Persele and eventually Parsley.

[135] "The pillars of the giants".

the three temples on the opposite hill are considerably smaller than either of the others, and are all in a state equally ruinous. One of them was most curiously proportioned; six columns in the fronts and seventeen at the sides. Some have supposed that the destruction of these temples was occasioned by an earthquake; but the columns have in many instances fallen so regularly, that I prefer laying the blame on the Carthaginians. The pillars of one whole side, in one of the smaller temples, lie extended outside of the temple, with their shafts and capitals in complete order. About fourteen years ago a Roman architect was employed in making excavations in this temple. Signore set to work inside the cell, and found nothing. He forgot that as the capitals were thrown out of the temple with the columns, the frieze and cornice could not have fallen in the <u>interior</u>: the two English Architects who are here at present (Messrs Angell and Harris) [– the latter died here six weeks after of the Malaria].[136]—made the trial <u>outside</u> the temple, and found some figures in alto relievo on the frieze, between the trigliphs. They are of an order hitherto unknown: between the Egyptian and Aegina. They have also made another interesting discovery—namely—that the foundations of the cell were not formed of one solid mass of stone: but that they were built like walls with hollow spaces between them which they afterwards filled up with rubbish: and the stones which formed the pavement of the cell, were laid across these interstices, from one wall to another. Thus, considerable expense was spared, without taking from the strength of the construction. The same kind of economy was used in the mole ~~in the mole~~ at Puteoli[137] which I believe, I mentioned to you in No. VIII. This same temple had, at some period, been turned into a Christian church, for we were shown a stone there, with a coffin and cross carved on it. Two skeletons were also found there. I can imagine nothing so interesting to professional men than these ruins, but, I must confess, that as I understand nothing about architecture, <u>I</u> prefer a temple that is <u>standing</u> to one that is <u>down</u>. Having taken some refreshment we mounted our mules

Teque datis linquo Ventis, palmosa Selinus Aeneid III, 705.[138]

Virgil calls it "palmosa" from the quantity of palms with which the environs still abound. We arrived a little after sunset at Sciacca and passed through the market-place—a busy scene every where—and here heightened by all the

---

[136] This is superscripted in the text, in red ink, above "Messrs. Angell and Harris".

[137] A maritime town on the northern shore of the Bay of Puteoli (part of the Bay of Naples) in Campania, Italy. Its modern name is Pozzuoli. The harbour was rendered safe by an artificial mole that consisted of piers connected by arches to masonry. It dates from around the second century B.C.

[138] "With a fair wind, I leave you, palmy Selinus, behind." Virgil, *Aeneid* III.705.

animation which a warm climate inspires, and to which Billingsgate[139] itself cannot offer a parallel. The ancient name of Sciacca was Thermae, so called on account of its hot springs which are on the summit of a neighbouring mountain. We did not think it worth while to remain here a morning to visit them, as we had seen them in their greatest perfection at Naples. Thermae was the birth-place of Agathodes, king of Syracuse. The inn was a dreadful hole: so dirty we could not make up our minds to undress, though very much fatigued: we filled our bags with straw; and lay down with our clothes on: but I got very little sleep, being perpetually annoyed by fleas and mosquitoes. At day-break we left our miserable quarters, and breakfasted on the sea shore "sub Dio". We rested during the heat of the day at Monte Aleaco, a village built near the site of the ancient city Eraclea. According to Diodorus, the Cretans who came with Minos into Sicily, after the death of their king, and after having their fleet burnt by the inhabitants which prevented their returning to their country, settled themselves in this city, which they called Minoa. Dorilus, a descendant of Hercules, then got possession of it, and it then received the name of Eraclea Minoa. It made such rapid strides to wealth and power, that it soon excited the envy, and even apprehension, of the Carthaginians, who, accordingly laid siege to it with a large army and entirely destroyed it. It rose again to distinction and was taken by Agathocles. Cicero mentions it as a considerable city, and in his time, its numbers were increased by a Roman Colony. Nothing now remains of it but the "campos ubi-fuit".[140] About seven in the evening we arrived at the port of Girgenti fortified with a strong mole: and in a few minutes came in sight of the modern Agrigentum, occupying a most commanding and beautiful situation about four miles from the Harbour. "Arduus inde Acragus ostentat maxima longe" Aen. III, 703.[141]

The setting sun throwing his yellow beams over the ruined temples, and heightening the natural beauty of the scenes which were variously devellopped to our view, showed off to the greatest advantage the beautiful environs of the town. We have found a very tolerable hotel. Yesterday we spent in visiting and examining some of the temples outside the town, and to-day we are going to look at the Lions in the city. We intend remaining here to-morrow and proceeding on our tour Thursday morning. At Terranova we shall bid adieu for two days to the shores of the Mediterranean, and cut across the country to Syracuse,[142] which we expect to reach Saturday

---

[139] Billingsgate fishmarket, London, was established by act of parliament in 1698. The market opened in the morning to the ringing of bells, closed at noon for two hours and then continued until five o'clock in the evening.

[140] "The fields where it was".

[141] "Then steep Acragas shows in the distance". Virgil, *Aeneid* III.703.

[142] Syracuse in the east of Sicily was founded in the eighth century B.C. by Greek settlers from Corinth.

evening. When I arrive there I will send you an account of the remains of Agrigentum: I forbear saying anything of them at present for fear of <u>over-stuffing</u> you with Antiquities. It will take a good week to <u>digest</u> all the broken columns and capitals which I have sent you in this letter. From Syracuse I shall begin to turn my eager steps towards "Dulce Domum".[143] On my arrival in that ancient city I may exclaim with Othello

> "Here is my journey's end; here is my butt;"
> and very sea-mark of my utmost sail".[144]

But how different will be <u>my</u> feelings! With best love to my mother and all the circle; believe me, my dear Father, your affectionate son,
John Lettsom Elliott

54. [L]

Endorsed: Nᵒ· 9, Vienna 21 May[145]

Miss Elliott
Pimlico Lodge
Westminster
London

No. IX. Vienna Friday May 21ˢᵗ 1824

My Dear Eliza,
I leave Vienna to-morrow with le Chevalier de Guttenberg who is going to Paris. I have had two pleasant bachelor dinner-parties at his house and he seems a very gentlemanlike man. The route I take as by Saltzburg, Munich, Stuttgard and Carlsrue. Here my companion will proceed to Strassbourg and Paris and I shall go on to Francfurt and Mayence where I expect to be by the first of next month. I shall then embark on the Rhine and probably go down nearly to the mouth of that river, then return by Antwerp to Brussels. I do not think I <u>can</u> be in England before the 17ᵗʰ and as I <u>must</u> be there by the 21ˢᵗ you know tolerably well about what time to expect me. Now for a few more of the curiosities of Vienna. The imperial and city arsenals are well worth visiting. The latter belongs to the town and contains arms for 16,000 men. There

---

[143] "Sweet home".
[144] William Shakespeare, *Othello*, V. ii. 264–71.
[145] The first page of this letter is cross-written to save paper and is difficult to read in parts.

are several suits of ancient armour [ve]ry[146] well arranged. A large musical clock excites attention also, as well as the head of Kara Mustapha, the grand vizier who commanded the Turkish army at the last siege of Vienna and who was strangled the following year at Belgrade.[147] The imperial arsenal is admirably arranged and contains arms for 150,000 men. There are many suits of armour which belonged to German Emperors, amongst them Charles V. They keep the leather jacket worn by Gustavus Adolphus, (the Lion of the North) at the fatal Battle of Lütgau. They even pretend to show the armour of Attila. The rooms are ornamented with several flags taken from the Turks, the Poles, and French. I could not help smiling at seeing inscribed on almost all the French flags, Wagram, Austerlitz, Marengo, etc., words little calculated to excite any feelings of triumph in the minds of the bons bourgeois de Vienne. In the vaults of the church of the Capuchins are the tombs of sixty seven members of the House of Austria. The mausoleum of Francis and Maria Theresa is magnificent. The imperial library is said to be one of the largest in Europe; it is comprised of more than 300,000 volumes and 12,000 manuscripts. The cabinet of antiques is particularly valuable. The apotheosis of Augustus is the largest cameo in the world and as admirable for the composition as for the size of the stone. There is also a very fine Etruscan vase, and a sarcophagus taken from the environs of Ephesus with some beautiful sculpture in basso relievo. Since I last wrote the weather has in general been unfavourable, and I have not been able to make as many excursions into the country as I would have wished. I wanted very much to visit Dürenstein, a small village on the north up of the Danube, about forty miles from Vienna. On the mountain which rises near it stands the ruins of the castle in which Richard, Coeur de Lion, was confined on his return from the Holy Land. It is certainly interesting, as connected with the most romantic story of the most romantic times the World ever knew. The dust is a great annoyance here. Even after heavy rains, there is generally dust the next day. This is one of the principal causes to which medical men attribute the frequency of declines here. It is now past midnight, and I must finish this letter tomorrow before I go. Somebody has been serenading me on the harp for t[he] last half hour. Now I have nothing to do but to fancy myself Richard, prisoner, and the harper, Blondin;[148] and there I have the whole story illustrated gratis.

---

[146] A hole in the manuscript has removed most of this word, but it seems likely to be "very".

[147] On 12 September 1683, a combined Austrian and Polish army defeated the Ottoman Turks at Kahlenberg and thus ended the siege of Vienna. 20,000 Turks, including the Grand Vizier, were slaughtered and another 10,000 drowned. Kara Mustapha's severed head was preserved in Austria as a souvenir of the siege of Vienna.

[148] The minstrel, Blondel de Nesle, enjoyed the patronage of Richard I (the Lion Heart) (1189–1199), king of England. On his return from a crusade in the Holy Land, King Richard was ship-wrecked in the Adriatic and captured in December 1192 by Leopold V of Austria, with

Saturday morning—I have spent three week very agreeably here, but I leave Vienna without regret, having seen every thing, and having no particular friends here. If I had had four months more, I should have gone to St Petersburg. The prince Barclay de Tolly who started three days ago offered me a seat in his carriage which I was obliged most reluctantly to refuse. Had I had enough of the one thing needful I think I should have accepted it, and put off the 21st June <u>for a short time</u>. I should have seen Norway and Sweden on my return at the finest time of year. There was such a hurricane here last Saturday that it rent and nearly destroyed my venerable hat which I had fondly hoped would have lasted me till messengers Lock and Lincoln supplied me with a new one. The dust was so great that I could not see five yards before me in the faubourg through which I was passing. My eyes and ears have not yet recovered from its effects. The next evening we had one of the most tremendous thunder-storms I ever heard. I just arrived before the heavy rain came on; there were more than four hundred carriages in the prater who got a glorious benefit.[149] It was a most ludicrous sight to see the poor folks in their Sunday best hurrying through the streets half desperate. I have made some few excursions in the environs with my friend the Baron de Boch. Schon Brüm, one of the Emperor's villas, about two miles from the town, is prettily situated. The pleasure grounds are well laid out in the continental style, and are open to the public. This was Napoleon's residence when he was here. Laxenburg is another imperial residence about eight miles to the south of Vienna. The palace itself offers nothing remarkable. The park is well laid out and contains many interesting buildings. The most striking is the castle, a building which represents an old baronial residence and is fitted up completely in the style of the middle ages. The antiquities which are collected there from all the monasteries and old castles render it extremely interesting. They shewed us a magnificent helmet of the Emperor Charles V. Some of the painted glass was marked 1036. Baden is an imperial town about 18 miles to the south of Vienna, and one of the most favourite places of resort during the summer for the Vienna fashionables.[150] It owes its celebrity principally to its baths which are taken for purifying the skin etc. The environs are delightful,

---

whom he had quarrelled on crusade. Leopold delivered Richard to the Holy Roman Emperor Henry VI, who imprisoned him. When news reached England, Blondel pledged not to rest until Richard had been found and wandered the banks of the Danube looking for him. Coming one day to the castle of Dornstein on the Rhine, he took his harp and sang one of the king's favourite songs. Richard replied from a window of the castle. Blondel returned to England, where ransom was raised to liberate the king, who was released in 1194.

[149] The Prater was 2,000 acres of park and woodland on the east side of Vienna between the Danube and the Danube canal, which attracted many visitors.

[150] The history of the spa town Baden bei Wien can be traced back to the Romans. It was at the height of its popularity during the early nineteenth century when the imperial court routinely spent its summers at the spa.

to which the new palace of the Archduke Charles makes a magnificent addition. Wednesday evening we paid a visit to Bruhl, a little village near Medling about eight miles to the south west of Vienna. It rained when we arrived; but being provided with umbrellas, we ascended a neighbouring hill, on the summit of which is situated a temple to Minerva, erected by Prince Lichtenstein, the proprietor of this lovely spot. By the time we reached the top, the rain had ceased; and I have seldom seen any thing more romantic than the view which presented itself. To the north on a height seperated from us by a small and fertile valley we beheld the venerable remains of the ancient castle of the Lichtenstein family, whose mouldering walls half gray and half green have stood the test of six centuries. Beyond this lay Vienna and many villages scattered here and there over a spacious plain, intersected by the rapid Danube, whose winding course we traced till lost among the mountains of Hungery which bounded the view and which were scarcely discernible through the misty shroud which enveloped them. To our right and behind us rose a cluster of hills whose fir-clad summits were exposed to the violence of a boisterous wind. Indeed, this part of the scene would have had quite a November appearance had not the light green of the acacia and willow broken the savage harmony of the darker wood and attested by their freshness the presence of Spring. To the west, a deep and woody glen separated us from the opposite height where stood the dismantled ruins of an old castle. The sun was just setting—a partial ray of light burst from behind the sombre clouds and streaming through the Gothic casements sparkled for a moment on the leaves still dripping from the late shower—then lingered away, and evening resumed her former grayness. So picturesque a scene made me almost wish I had been a landscape painter: (a thing I never desired before) but I laughed at the idea when I caught the notes of the distant bell of Medling murmuring through the woods as I descended

Era giã l'ora che volge il disio
Ai naviganti, e'ntererisce 'l cuore
Lo di c'en detto a' dolci amici: A Dio;
E che lo nuovo peregrin, d'amore
Punge il ore squilla di conteno,
Che paia 'l giorno pianger che si muore.

[Note in red] Purg. Can. VIII.[151] Gray took the first line of his elegy from the last of these.

---

[151] Dante's *Purgatory*, canto viii. The last line of this unfinished verse: "Che paia 'l giorno pianger che si muore" is also the first line: "The curfew tolls the knell of parting day", of Thomas Gray's (1716–71) *Elegy written in a country churchyard* (1751).

Could Salvator Rosa have transported on this canvas the wind-beaten firs, the crumbling ruins, and the parting glare [?] of the setting sun? Yes. But the calm solemnity of the Ave Maria? and the whisper among the woods
"As if the first leaves were stirred with prayer?"
I threw away the pencil—and all I regretted was that you were not there to share the scene with me, and I had not had the pen of Walter Scott to describe it.
With best love to all at home. Believe me, dear Eliza, your affectionate Brother—John Elliott

PS. I <u>desire</u> one of you to write to me as late as the eight of June, so that it will arrive in time for me at Brussells. Do not forget. Tell my father I have drawn on him for five and thirty pounds. If he has any command for Hoch, he must write immediately. I hope to see the inside Metternich's cellars in less than a fortnight.[152]

---

[152] Prince Klemens Lothar Wenzel von Metternich (1773–1859), Austrian statesman, who dominated central European politics between 1814 and 1848.

6

Benevolent Favours

The twenty-two letters in this section, chronologically arranged, form a self-contained group and do not relate to any of the other correspondence in this volume. All the letters were loose when first seen by us. Their provenance is uncertain, but given the possible connection through Lettsom's sons-in-law, Philip and John Elliot, they may have been given or lent by Mrs. Jill Martin (see Introduction, p. 10). However, that would suggest they were available to Abraham and interestingly he quotes from none of them. The authors of the letters can be identified as four sisters named Elliot (sometimes spelled "Elliott"). There is only one letter from a C. Elliot in Islington (Letter 3) but the contents make it clear she was a sister.[1] Jane Elliot wrote from various addresses in London, M. C. Elliot wrote from Market Downham, a village in Norfolk (with one letter from Norwich, also in Norfolk), and Cordelia Pitter, the married sister, wrote from Brixton and Bedford Street, London.[2] Nearly all the letters relate to charitable assistance Lettsom gave to the three spinster sisters. True to English Enlightenment thinking, Lettsom saw organized philanthropy as the means of achieving social stability and progress, but he was also known for his benevolence to needy individuals. Famously, he assisted and redeemed a highwayman who had held him up with a pistol.[3]

It is probable the Elliot sisters were distant connections by marriage. Lettsom's daughter Mary Ann married Philip Elliot M.D. in 1794, and her sister Eliza married Philip's brother John Elliot F.R.S. in 1804.[4] It is possible that the relationship occurred through the Elliot sisters' father, unknown to us but clearly someone acquainted with Lettsom (Letter 1). The sisters seem to have been people of the middling orders. M. C. Elliot reported she was born on 5 February 1764, putting her in her forties for most of this correspondence. Cordelia was probably two years older (Letter 18). We do not know

---

[1] The letter is in a different hand from the others making it virtually certain that we have not simply misread the signature.

[2] Letter 3, from C. Elliot of Islington could not be from Cordelia before her marriage since Cordelia Pitter is referred to in it.

[3] James Johnston Abraham, *Lettsom: his life, times, friends and descendants*, London, William Heinemann Medical Books, 1933, pp. 268–9.

[4] There is a reference in Letter 6 to an unidentifiable Mary but the use of the past tense makes it unlikely this was Mary Ann Lettsom since she did not die until 1847.

Jane's age or that of C. Elliot. Jane Elliot knew Lettsom well enough for her to have "had the Pleasure of Drinking Tea with you and Mrs. Lettsom" (Letter 4). The three unmarried sisters were obviously in straightened circumstances and Lettsom helped them out with monetary gifts. Jane was forever looking for a "situation" and at one point found one "in Service" although as what we are not told (Letters 15 and 20). M. C. Elliot had aspirations to be a confectioner, although it seems she supported herself by gatekeeping and by needlework (Letters 14, 17 and 22). At times the letters are frankly begging (Letters 17 and 20). Cordelia, who seems to have been unpredictable and something of a tyrant, was in much better circumstances. She had a cook and probably other servants (Letter 9). Bedford Street, where she lived, was a fashionable area. Mr. Pitter paid C. Elliot an annual allowance of £30 (Letter 3). The poorer sisters seemed to live in some fear of Cordelia discovering that they were troubling Lettsom for money (Letter 15). Jane repeatedly promised to repay Lettsom's benevolent favours, and M. C. Elliot repaid them by sending turkeys, pheasants, hares, fowl, shallots and sausages on the coach from Norfolk. Lettsom frequently received such gifts from various people and on 4 January 1813 he reported that there had arrived since the beginning of the year "1 Goose, 2 Turkeys, 6 Hares, 2 Pheasants, 1 Dried tongue, 1 Welch Saddle of mutton, A Brace of Carp fish, 1 Large Pike or jack, A Breast of Venison, A large piece of ship beef."[5] Many of these gifts were from women. Lettsom was said to like female company, and his enemies branded him a seducer.[6]

The correspondence begins with a letter from Jane written in 1805 thanking Lettsom for a "benevolent favour" (Letter 1). From Letter 3 it is clear that C. Elliot had known Lettsom at least seven years previously and undoubtedly much longer. In 1810 Cordelia refers to a promise Lettsom had made seventeen years earlier (1773) (Letter 11). Philip Elliot had met Mary Anne Lettsom in 1793.[7] The letters make it plain that there was earlier correspondence that is now missing (Letter 3). The genteel aspirations of the ladies are obvious in many places, notably Letter 12 where M. C. Elliot thanks Lettsom for a pound note saying, "I have reserved it for a new gown". Her circumstances were then made plain by her revelation that "I have not had one these 4 years". Communication or mutual perceptions were not all they might have been. In January 1811, M. C. Elliot reports that she was pleased to have heard from Lettsom of her sisters' "prosperity" (Letter 14).

---

[5] Bound manuscript, untitled, diary of John Coakley Lettsom for 1813–1814, at the Medical Society of London. Also cited in Abraham, op. cit., note 3 above, p. 409.

[6] Abraham, op. cit., note 3 above, p. 437.

[7] Ibid., p. 456.

While in May of the same year, Jane wrote, "I am much distressed for Money" (Letter 15). But in December M. C. Elliot has heard from Lettsom that her sisters are "enjoying all the Blessings of this transitory life". For her own part she states, "My situation at this time is very miserable" and begs Lettsom for a "cast-off Great Coat" (Letter 17). The correspondence finishes abruptly with a letter from M. C. Elliot in March 1814. Presumably there were further letters but, like those known to precede these, they are lost.

1. [L]

Endorsed: From Jane Elliot, Oct. 15 1805, London. done

Dr. Lettsom, Basinghall Street, London

Dear Dr. Lettsom,

I received your kind and benevolent favour, which accompanied with a Heart overflowing with Gratitude, I return you my sincere thanks. I only regrett not being Mistress of Language, able to express myself in some degree adequate to your goodness. I stand lost, dear Sir, bewildered, not knowing how to express the Gratitude I feel and which you are so justly entitled to, but the Dear Dr. is good and I know he will Pardon every imperfection, knowing that I have no other Guide or Tutor than the Rough Hand of Nature. Well might (and with justice) did my Dear Father style you, good Sir, the Ornament of Mankind. I trust you will not think I flatter you, Worthy Sir; as mean thoughts seldom enter a Noble Breast. You do but remind me of our Blessed Saviour, but as he whent about doing good, healling the afflictions and infirmityes of others, so does the amiable Dr. I thank you, good Sir, for your Encomiums upon my conduct. I wish I was deserving of them, but I Blush at the recolection of my behaviour, when I had last the Pleasure of seeing you. I did not think that ever I should disgrace that inestimable Treasure, Female delicacy, but my distress was so Great I could almost have yealded to anything. I can only beg you, Dear Sir, to Pardon me and to think of me as I once deserved. I hope Mrs. Lettsom and all your Family are well. I will intrud no longer upon your Time, Blessed Sir, further than to beg you to except my sincere thanks for your abundant kindness, and to believe me, your thankful, obliged and Humble Servant,
Jane Elliott.

October 15 1805

2. [L]

Endorsed: From J. [*recte* M.][8] C. [E]lliot, Jan. 12 1807, Market Downham.[9] answered.

Dr. Lettsom, Sambrook Court, London.

9th Jan[ry.] 1807

Honoured Sir,
 sent you a Turkey and a Hare by the Market Downham Coach Tuesday the 23[d] of Dec[r.] Carriage paid and as I have not had the Honour of an answer I fear you have not Received it. Previous to the Parcel I sent a Letter to you that you might if you thought proper send a servant to the Coach. I did not mention the Hare in the Letter for I had not got it when I wrote the Letter. I am very unhappy lest it's lost but I had it Booked. The favour of an answer be duly acknowledged by yours with submission M-C Elliott

Please to address for Me to be left at Hewett's Confectioner, Market Downham.

3. [L]

Endorsed: From Miss Elliot, Febr. 12 1807, Islington. answered.

Dr. Lettsom

Feb:[y] 12th 1807

23 Britannia Row,
Islington

Sir,
 It is now seven years since I last took the liberty of writing to you for pecuniary assistance. I beg ten thousand pardons, for having done so. Had I had

---

[8] This does not appear to be an "M", but looks more like an "I" or "J". Lettsom has probably mistaken the writer for her sister, Jane, as he does in the endorsement of Letter 21. This letter is clearly signed M. C. Elliott.

[9] Downham Market in West Norfolk, East Anglia, is one of Norfolk's oldest market towns, dating from Saxon times. See *A history of Downham Market*, compiled by Downham Market and District Amenity Society, Totton, Downham Market and District Amenity Society, 1999.

the least intimation at that time how troublesome some of my relations had been to you upon the same subject I would not for the world have applied to you. My present reason for writing is to beg the favor of your opinion whether there is any certainty that the speculation of the Light and Heat Company may be encouraged by the public, and brought like the new River to the advantage of the shareholders.[10] The next question, and to me the most important to understand, is, whether any more money than the first 5 pound deposit will be demanded before any Dividends become due? I have got their printed Estimates and proposals, where it is promised that all the rest of the subscription (which I see will amount to fifty pounds) is to be deducted from the dividends. Now Good Sir I want better advice than my own head is capable of, whether I may safely <u>believe this</u>? Because if only five pounds is wanting, and all the rest deducted from shares, I will raise five pounds, some honest way or other; but if more is, or should be, required, I must give up the attempt. I am not, my good Sir, <u>aspiring</u>. The odd seventy pounds a year woud make me humbly blest, content, and happy. But if Heaven blest me with five hundred I wou'd spend it like a Christian, not in idle Vanities. I am allowed thirty pounds a year by Mr. P—r[11] which is my whole support and has been for six years ~~with~~ without incurring a shilling in Debt. Upon this I have set down quietly without ambition in the hope that it wou'd last for life. But Mr. P has himself inform'd me that the violence of my sister['s] Temper renders his life so completely miserable that he does not consider himself under any tie to do for his relations and that he shall withdraw my pension at Lady-day next. I hope it was written in some moment of resentment and may be overcome by and by. But as I am liable to these shocks again and again whenever they quarrel, I need not Sir to a man of your good sense and philanthropy expatiate upon the propriety of any endeavour to extricate myself from a situation so uneasy and precarious. This Sir I only tell you in confidence

---

[10] The German, Frederick Albert Winsor (1763–1830), came to Britain in 1799. He became interested in the technology of fuels. In 1804, he obtained the first patent in England for making gas and set up a gasworks. In 1807, he lit one side of Pall Mall with gas lamps. Miss Elliot was clearly thinking of taking out shares in Winsor's coal-gas lighting company, the National Light and Heat Company. Winsor's application to Parliament in 1809 for a Royal Charter for his company failed and he started a newspaper war on the issue. He subsequently moved to Paris, but his company made little progress and was liquidated in 1819. See 'To be sanctioned by act of Parliament: a National Light and Heat Company, for providing our streets and houses with hydrocarbonic gas-lights ... four tables of calculation ... prove the immense national profits and increase of revenue by the adoption of this plan, which is to be had at the National Light and Heat Company's office, no. 97, Pall Mall', London, printed for F. A. Winsor, the patentee, by Watts and Bridgewater [c. 1807]; 'Considerations on the nature and objects of the intended Light and Heat Company: published by authority of the committee', London, printed for James Ridgway by T. Davison, 1808.

[11] Mr. Pitter, who was married to the writer's sister, Cordelia.

as an apology for taking the liberty to ask your opinion, and believe me Sir
your obedient, able servant,
C. Elliott

4. [L]

Endorsed: From Jane Elliot, May 4 1808, Long Acre.[12] answered.

Dr. Lettsom
Sambrook Court
London

Most Worthy Sir,
   I have taken the liberty of addressing a line to you, begging Permission to
assure you that I have embraced the earliest opportunity of acknowledging
your kind favour of the Pound Note, which Mrs. Pitter informs me, good Sir,
you kindly sent for me, for which I return you my most Humble, and sincere,
Thanks, which I certainly should ~~have~~ immediately have done, but from
Mrs. Pitter having been very unwell, the same Cause which prevented
her returning you those thanks which, good Sir, she now with her best
Compliments, begs me to present to you, reactioned her not sending me a
line informing me to whom I stood so highly indebted. I am sorry to add that
I am still in Trouble from the dearness of every kind of Provision, slackness
of employment, and having things still in Pledge to the amount of 2 Pounds
10 Shillings, which sum Mrs. Pitter a few days back, Promised to advance
me to redeem them, since which she has observed, that I might do very well
with the Note she had given me, which dear Sir is your kind favour. This,
I am sorry to say, is Mrs. Pitter's constant unsteady Conduct. Her kind Promise
afforded me much comfort now I Plunged again in to Trouble. I do not speak
from the imports of ingratitude, as she is very good to me, but her being
Worldly, fond of dress, and Company, and never having known the distress
that I have sadly experienced, she does not, and can not, see into my situation as I could wish. I am much distressed in Mind, not knowing how to act,
or what to do. I have been very unfortunate in an advertisement, which I put
in to the Papers 3 weeks back. I did not receive one Letter in Answer. I mean
to venture once more ere the Familyes leave Town. Dear Dr. Lettsom I often

---

[12] Long Acre in Covent Garden, London derived its name from seven acres of land owned by
monks in the Middle Ages. The area was well known for its coach makers.

think of you, and should have done myself the Honour of calling since I had the Pleasure of Drinking Tea with you and Mrs. Lettsom, to whom, Dear Sir, I beg to be presented with Humble and respectful Compliments, but must deny myself that Pleasure, untill I can return the 4 Pounds you kindly favoured me with when I was in Trouble. When I reflect, most Worthy Sir, upon your condescending goodness, in having so often received my visits, and upon the delicate way in which you have ever been willing to relieve me, my Heart overflows towards you, with Love and Gratitude. Do not think I flatter you, good Sir; believe me I write you but the sentiments of my soul, and I much regret not being Mistress of Language, to express myself with more Propriety. I can only say that you are the Worthyest of the Worthy, in short, you are a Character which <u>none can equal</u>. With much justice did my dear Father style you the Ornament of [Eng?]land,[13] for you are Possessed of every Virtue that the allmighty can bestow. [Allow?][14] me to observe, good Sir, that I know your Heart and disposition to be a composition of Tenderness, benevolence and humanity, your Temper and Manners sweetly Mild and Placable, and you disposition, so emphatically expressed in your Countenance which is sweetness and Tranquillity, that it's Great consolation to any, particularly those in distress, to Look upon you. I speak from experience; I beg Pardon, good Sir, for intruding so long upon your Time. I must now with abundant thanks for past Favours, as for the Present, conclude, with beging you, kind Sir, to believe me, your very much obliged, and Humble, Servant Jane Elliott

5. [L]

Endorsed: From Jane Elliott, May 7 1808, Long Acre

Good Sir,

I received your kind and generous favour of the Pound Note, for which accompanied with the Tears of Gratitude, I return you, Sir, my sincere thanks, and I beg to assure you Sir, that I feel myself equally indebted to you for your kind intention of writing to Mrs. Pitter, in my behalf. Mr. Pitter has been kind enough to forgive me a debt of 5 Guineas which he lent me 5 years ago. I take the liberty to mention this sircumstance to you, Sir, least Mrs. Pitter should mention it as a favour very lately confered. I should then

---

[13] Covered by seal.
[14] Covered by seal.

appear deceptious. Dear Sir, I feel myself very unequal to the Task of answering you, my Mind being too deeply impressed with Gratitude to express myself. Therefore, kind Sir, I beg that you will Pardon the insufficiency of the attempt, and to believe me, your sincerely, respectful, obliged and very Humble Servant,
Jane Elliott

May 7 1808
46 Long Acre

my best Compliments to Mrs. Lettsom, Sir, if you Please

6. [L]

Endorsed: From M. C. Elliot, Dec. 19 1808, Market Downham

Dr. Lettsome
Sambrook Court
Basinghall Street
London

Honoured Sir

I have neglected writing so long I am almost ashamed to acknowledge I am still alive But God takes the good, too good on earth to stay and spares the bad, too bad to take away. I wish I had more wit or you dear Sir a great deal less to make any Epistles worth your attention. But Sir, I have long felt an ardent desire to hear from you and hope your goodness will pardon my freedom. Dear Sir I can never forget that by a Thousand obligations I am bound to pray that every watchful Angel may guard thy life for if a soul formed for the most exalted exercises can render a Person amiable Dr. Lettsome has a just claim to that epithet. Pray Sir give my love to poor Jane.[15] I often think of Her and wish to see her. I have an Humble Cot. But the Brown Loaf and sleep are sweet. I should be very happy to see her and would endeavour to make her as comfortable as my situation will allow. Poor Mary used to say I should not know if she proved unfortunate least I should retort But bless her, far be it from me, my Heart is too tender from its own distress. We have now no Parents and why stand in awe of each other?

---

[15] Her sister, Jane Elliot, who worked in service in London.

The best may slip and the most cautious fall. They are more than mortal never erred at all. Dear Sir, pardon this dull prolix Epistle. I must add it's a selfish motive makes me write you, my design being to extort an answer which condescention I have many times enjoyed and, dear Sir, fondly antic-ipateing the Hour, I beg leave with subscription and every good wish to subscribe my self your Devoted humble servant
M-C Elliott

19th. Dec$^{r.}$ 1808

Your favour addressed to me at Market Downham Toll Bar will be duly acknowledged and honoured.

7. [L]

Endorsed: From Cordelia Pitter, July 19 1809, Brixton[16]

[No address]

My Dear Sir I trust that you have long ere this seen my sister Jane. In that case, I hope my conduct is justified to you. I can never posses any other sen-sations than of esteem and gratitude when you are in question, and however appearance my favour for, or against, I have the faith to think that you never will think otherwise than well of me. I shall not say more, as I have occasion to call upon you in your profession. The Young Lady who you attended here two years ago is ~~not~~ much indisposed and requests me to send for Dr. Lettsom as she says he has saved her life three several times. I shall there-fore hope to have the satisfaction of seeing you today, or this evening, if this reaches in time—she has a most delic[ate] constitution and has frequent reaching now on her which are attended wi[th] great exertion and I think must be attended to. I am with the hope of an early visit.
yours most greatfully
Cordelia Pitter

We are at Brixton. I therefore hope it [will] not be inconvenient to you.

---

[16] London district to the south of the river Thames. Brixton was not developed significantly until after the construction of Vauxhall Bridge in 1816.

8. [L]

Endorsed: From M. C. Elliot, Aug. 8 1809, Downham. answered.

Dr. Lettsome
Sambrook Court
Basinghall Street
London

Dear Sir,

Depressed by grief at the appearance of having lost the most valuable correspondant I ever had, I do therefore, Sir, humbly entreat your goodness that you tell me, for I am quite unhappy at the thought of having incurred your displeasure. It has pleased the Devine Providence, dear Sir, to place me in a situation by which I can find myself Bread. But how long it may continue I am not able to say, for I am only by the week. Your goodness, dear Sir, I trust will pardon this bold address and impute it as the weakness of woman. There is a great quantity of mushrooms in this Country and if any Catchup would be acceptable to you, Sir, I will, with the greatest pleasure make and send you some. Your answer, good Sir, would be esteemed the greatest of favours and be ever duly Honoured by yours with submission
M-C Elliot

Downham 8th August 1809

My address Market Downham Toll Bar

9. [L]

Endorsed: From Mrs. Pitter, Dec. 3 1809, Bedford Street. answered.

I trust, my Dear Sir, that you will not think me presuming when I request the favour of your advice to a woman who has served me upwards of four years in the capacity of a Cook. She has long been afflicted with a Violent Cough and has had advice from several medical Gentelmen who have given her temporary relief, only she now becomes so ill from the constant agitation proceeding from the frequent fits of Coughing that attends her, that I fear she will not be able to do her Business—without relief—in that case, poor creature, I know not what she will do as she has only her situation to depend upon—I have ever been most tenatious in asking any favor that should occasion you any trouble—but I know the charity of your Heart too wel to think you will consider me an intruder. I hope to hear by Monday that you

and family are well to whom I beg to be remember'd and am dear Sir most
sincerely grateful your friend
Cordelia Pitter

Sunday night
Dec.ʳ 3ᵈ· 1809

10. [L]

Endorsed: From Jane Elliott, Dec. 21 1809, James [S]treet

Dr. Lettsom
Sambrook Court
Basinghall Street
London

Most respected Sir,
   I have taken the liberty of addressing a line to you to inform you that I still
exist, in this world of Trials and hardships. I often think of you, Dear Sir, with
gratitude. I shall ever carry the Grateful recolection of many Favours and kind-
nesses you have so emmiently conferred upon me. Never shall they be eraised
from my memory, and the estimation in which I hold them can only be sur-
passed by my Gratitude. Dear Sir, I should do myself the Pleasure of calling
but the Weather is Cold and I have not a Warm Spencer, nothing of the kind is
to be had under 2 Pounds. I hope Mrs. Lettsom, and all your Family are well.
Sir, I should wish, with your Permission, to be kindly remembered to her and
I remain, Dear Sir, your Grateful, obedient servant
Jane Elliott

Thursday, December 21 1809
James Street, Covent Garden

11. [L]

Endorsed: From Mrs. Pitter, Jan. 13 1810, Bedford Street. done

Dr. Lettsom
Sambrook Court
Basinghall Street
Private

I hope my dearest Sir you were not offended at the request I made the other
evening—I see you so seldom, and when we do meet it is in so confused

a way as to give me no time for a conversation of any kind. As it is decreed so by fate I can only lament it. You will forgive my fears but as I so seldom see you I am even afraid that every time should be the last. I hope you are better. Pray dear Sir take care of yourself. I do not want anything to make me think of you oftener as all your kind and Benevolent attentions to me so deeply impress on my heart as never to be erased. I wish something in the Trinket way that I may carry about me at <u>all</u> times—on my neck, fingers, or ears—which you best like. You need not be in a great haste about it, but I shall not be comfortable till you have performed your promise made 17 years ago although you did tell me I had your picture—pray do not mention a word to Jane of me when you see her.

Adieu dear Sir, believe me sincerely grat[eful]
your friend C: Pitter

Saturday morning

12. [L]

Endorsed: From M. C. Elliot, Jan. 21 1810, Downham.

Downham 21:ˢᵗ Jan.ʳʸ 1810

Dear Sir,

Your last favour enclosing a pound note I Received and duly acknowledge your goodness, dear Sir, in sending it. I have reserved it for a new gown. I have not had one these 4 years. But, good Sir, it was not my intention in writing, But a real and ardent desire to hear of your Health. Now, Dear Sir, I have to beg your acceptance of these 2 Fowls. They should have come at Christmas But I feind[17] was not fit. They are now not what I could wish them, but hope you will accept them as a small mark of gratitude for your many repeated favours. I rear'd them, for all sorts of meat is so dear. I am a stranger to the taste of Beef, and these are the last Fowls I can keep on account of their geting into a neighbouring Farm. Yes, Honoured Sir, wishing you the Compliments of the season, I beg leave with submission to subscribe myself Your Honourable Servant
M-C Elliot

---

[17] Find.

13. [L]

Endorsed: M. C. Elliot, Dec. 5 1810, Market Downham.

Dr. Lettsome
London

Dear Sir,
   Impressed with the highest sense of gratitude for your goodness to me, I have now, dear Sir, to beg the favour of your acceptance of this Hare and a Brace of Pheasants and wish I had any thing more worthy presenting you with. You can, if you think proper, Sir, return the frai[ght?][18] by the Nelson Coach[19] which ~~which~~ leaves the White Horse, Fetter Lane, every Monday, Wednesday and Friday Morning about 6 ~~o'Cl~~ o'Clock to Lynn[20] and this place. If, Sir, my Poultry would be acceptabl to you this Christmas, if you would let Me know I will endeavour to get some for you. And wishing every Earthly Blessing, I beg leave ~~leave~~ to subscribe Myself Your devoted and Humble servant,
M-C Elliot

Market Downham
Dec[r] 5[th.] 1810

14. [L]

Endorsed: From M. C. Elliot, Jan. 24 1811, Norwich.

24th. Jan[ry]
Dr. Lettsom
Sambrook Court
London
Post paid

Honoured Sir,
   I have received your kind Letter enclosing a 2 Pound Note. Your goodness, dear Sir, confounds Me as I was a great Debtor to your goodness

---

[18] The margin of the letter has been cut closely.

[19] In the first decade of the nineteenth century, the Lord Nelson coach was a Scottish service, bound on its northerly journey for Edinburgh. See Robert Trow Smith, *The history of Stevenage*, Stevenage, Stevenage Society, 1985, p. 62.

[20] King's Lynn.

before. Permit Me, Sir, to add I feel a secret Joy that I should be Honoured as one of the number of Dr. Lettsom's private Friends, with the acceptance of your instructive Writings, for which I beg you, good Sir, to accept my most greatful acknowledgements. I am much obliged to you, Dear Sir, for your inquiry after My Health and situation. After what I have suffered, Sir, I must endeavour to think any situation Comfortable by which I can get a piece of Bread, else I am very uncomfortably situated. The last great Tide which I believe was general, was 3 Feet deep in the House and is the fourth time it has been so since I have lived here.[21] We have got a new Bridge this summer[22] and are now worse than ever as it's so far to go to the gate, I have been forced to wear boots, Sir, all this Winter. At the expiration of my time, I sometimes think I shall come to London and put myself under the Confectioners to learn that art as I think I could get my Bread in that line. I am, Dear Sir, greatly obliged to you for your goodness in mentioning my sisters. I am happy to hear of their prosperity. I never offended either of them intentionally. Could they have seen my situation in late years they would have found it, Dear Sir, little short of your Morning's walk in the Metropolis. But I fear it would not have awakened such Godlike charity and sensibility for which may every watchful Angel guard thy life. I hope, Sir, you will like these Fowls But they are not according to promise. You will receive them by the Union Coach, Bull Inn, Bishopsgate Street, 25th.

I send this Letter, Sir, that if you chuse to send your servant it will save postage. I have paid the Carriage of it. I am quite unhapp that the Fowls are not what I wished and expected. We give 1 shilling per pound so I am yet in your debt. I should not mention the price, only that you may judge, Sir, whether it answers to send them. They are not old, and that's all I can say in praise of them,
and remain your obedient
Humble Servant
M-C Elliot

Downham 24 Jan.ry. 1811.

---

[21] Much of Norfolk is flat and various drainage projects, since the Middle Ages, have reclaimed areas of land from the sea. Norwich lies at the head of the navigable waters of the Norfolk Broads, at the confluence of the River Yare and its main tributary, the Wensum. The tides from the North Sea, some 47 kilometres away, reach the centre of the city.

[22] The Carrow Bascule Bridge, an iron bridge of fifty foot span, was opened in 1810. It joined Carrow Hill with the north-eastern end of Carrow Road and was replaced by a wooden structure in 1833.

15. [L]

Endorsed: From Jane Elliott, May 14 1811, James Street. done

Dr. Lettsom
Basinghall Street
London

Dear Sir,

I have taken the liberty of addressing a line to you that I have gained a situation in Service. I go at 10 o'clock on Thursday Morning. I hope the Blessing of the allmighty will attend me. Dear Sir, allow me once more to implore your kind assistance. I am much distressed for Money. I know, dear Sir, you will not deny me, nor be angry at my request, for I believe with many more, that you are one of the Allmighty's best beloved, whom he has sent to do good. I shall ever carry the most Grateful recollection of you. Dear Sir, adieu, and I remain
your ever respectful, and Obedient servant,
Jane Elliott,

Tuesday May 14 1811
James Street, Covent Garden

Dear Sir, do not let Mrs. Pitter know that I have again Troubled you. Adieu, Dear Sir

16. [L]

Endorsed: Miss [M. C.][23] Elliot, Dec. 23 1811, Downham. answered

Dr. Lettsom
Sambrook Court
London

Downham 23^d Decr. 1811

Honoured Sir,

I have been very unhappy ever since I send you that wretched looking Turkey. Dear Sir, there is not a regular Market here for Fowls, But there are

---

[23] The hand is that of M. C. Elliot.

those who make it a living to fat them for thos that bespeak them, and the Woman promised me it should be such a one as nobody could find fault with. I went to bespeak it but I unluckily sent for it and the Money. But, Dear Sir, when it was brought in My Heart died and I sent it back, but she would not take it again. She was a base Woman and imposed on me every way. She Charged 1s per lb and the general price is 10d. I have been wretched, good Sir, least you should feel yourself offended. But I trust your goodness will take it in its proper light. I would have sent, but was persuaded it would eat better than it looked. I have now, most worthy Sir, humbly to beg you to accept this Turkey which I hope will prove as good as the other was bad. You will receive it by the Nelson Coach, Sir, sets up at the White Horse, Fetter Lane. I take the liberty of sending this line that you may avoid the expense of portage by sending it on Tuesday 24, and I should esteem it a favour you will return the Baskets as I have bespoke an other for you on New Year's Day, and remain with much respect and every good
yours at Command
M-C Elliott

Pray Sir, is there any truth in a report I have heard that ~~Gold~~ a Guinea fetches five or six and twenty shillings in London?

17. [L]

Endorsed: From M. C. Elliot, Dec. 30 1811, Downham.

Dr. Lettsom
London

Sir, I have received no Baskets.

Honoured Sir,
    I received your kind Letter enclosing a 1 Pound Note which I am ashamed to accept ~~it~~ but beg you to believe Me truly greatful for it. I am happy, dear Sir, the Turkey met your approbation. I am particularly obliged to you, good Sir, for your mentioning My sisters, for I am happy to hear they are well and enjoying all the Blessings of this transitory life. I often think of them with an aching Heart as I never intentionally offended any of them, and if I had in the midst of judgment we should remember Mercy. My situation at this time is very miserable as I have to undergo all the severity of the Whether both by Night and Day for My Board only. I cannot stand it much longer for I feel

the effects of it now, and it gains on me Daily. Pray, good Sir, pardon this prolix Letter, for Blest is the Man whose softening Heart feels all another's woes, for while to him we open our distress the pains grow lighter and the sorrow less. Fate is too cruel in its harsh decree that I must live yet live in misery, for I can with truth say that I look only to the Grave for the end of my persecutions. Dear Sir, the reason of My mentioning the Gold is I have little by me, and as I gain'd it by industry I wish to improve it if I could. I wish to learn the Confectionary if it was not too high. I think it is very hard to rise from my Bed these sharp nights to attend the Gate for a piece of Bread only. Good Sir, pardon my freedom, But if you have such a thing as a cast-off Great Coat it would be very acceptable to make Me one, as I have nothing of the kind and I cannot afford such Cloth to fence the Whether as you wear, Sir and you the festivity of the Season, I remain, Dear Sir,
yours at Command
M-C Elliot

Downham
30th Decr. 1811

18. [L]

Endorsed: From C. Elliot, Jan. 20 1812, Downham. answered.

Honoured Sir,
    You will receive by the Nelson Coach the two Turkies as desired. I should have sent them before but could not get them at the same place but hope these will be as good. Your Letter, dear Sir, conveys the Balm of Life; you relieve like Heaven and like the Gods are kind. Good Sir, I am not particular in what occupation I am placed so that I could be a little comfortable and get an honest living except the care of Children which I beg to be excused as they are too much for My spirits. You ask My age Sir. I am within 2 years and few Weeks as old as My sister Pitter. But least you are not acquainted with her age. I was Born the fifth of February 1764.
    I hope Sir I have answer'd your questions to your satisfactio and remain with grate respect and every good wish your
humble servant at command
M. C. Elliott

Downham
20 Janry. 1812

19. [L]

Endorsed: From C. Elliot, Febr. 23 1812, Downham. answered.

Honoured Sir,
   You will receive by the Nelson Coach on Tuesday the 25th a Turkey and a few Sausages which ~~which~~ I beg you to accept. I fear the last two was not good ones. I had some trouble to get them. Chance threw 2 in my way the Day after I sent the last and I have been Fating them But had the misfortune to loose one by overfeeding it. I never fed any before but hope it will prove a fat one. Dear Sir, I never have received any Basket. The Hamper I sent the Turkey and the 2 Chickings in last year I had to pay for as it was borrowed with a promise of its being returned. I thank you good Sir for your caution of My Gold. I had 12 guineas and half and 2 seven shilling pieces and I made 15 Pounds of them and since I parted with them a Gentleman at the Gate has offered 24 for as many as I could get him. I remain Sir with much respect and every good wish yours at Command
M-C Elliott

Downham
23^{d.} Feb.^{ry} 1812

20. [L]

Endorsed: From Jane Elliott, Jan. 18 1813, Temple Bar.

Dr. Lettsom
Sambrook Court
London

Dear Dr. Lettsom,
   Pardon me, I have taken the liberty of addressing you, Humbly wishing to inform you that many situations now ofer but for the want of things I cannot embrace any of them. Dear kind Sir, if you will <u>once more condescend</u> to come and see me, and be a Friend, I will do any thing in the World to oblidge you. I neaver will trouble you again. Dear Dr. Lettsom, you once told me that you never would forsake me. A few shillings or a pound you will never miss. I will return it when I get in to situation. I think, Dear Dr, that I see your smiling Countenance and although Troublesome, hear you say that you can not turn your face from me. Sir, it is Christmas and the new year, which I wish

you a happy succession of, and every comfort that the present season can Possibly afford. I shall expect you, Dear Sir, some Time tomorrow, as such I will make myself and miserable place of abode as clean as I can. Dear Dear Dr. Lettsom, I ~~kindnes~~ know that your Heart and Mind is true, sweet and amiable for you to be offended. Therefore I shall keep up my Spirits and trust to your goodness and Generosity,
and I remain Dear Sir, your Truly
Grateful, respectful, and very
Humble Servant,
Jane Elliott

1813

21. [L]

Endorsed: From Jane [*recte* M. C.][24] Elliot, Febr. 20 1813, Downham.

Dr. Lettsom, Sambrook Court, London

Honoured Sir,

I received the Basket containing the Print and am very much obliged to you, Sir, the trouble you have given yourself about it. It is a very neat print and a better than I have had for years as I never go higher than 20 pence per yard. I am very glad, dear Sir, you approved the Game and the Fowls. I did not send them with a view of being paid as I must ever think myself indebted to you, Sir, for past favours and it is a yearly acknowledgement I wish to make. The shalots are of My own growing and I was persuaded they are highly esteemed by the gentry in London. I feard it was a disappointment to you my not sending at Christmas but they was scarce this season on account of the high price of Corn. I do not know the price in London. They was 1/6 per lb here and at this time 1/4. The Hares was not bought. They came from Gunton Hall, the Country seat of Lord Suffield.[25] I sent you Sir a Hare the 2^d. of Feb.^ry I hope it reached your Hand. Pardon Me, Sir, I do not properly comprehend you in saying My sister Jane has heard of a situation. I thought she was in one. I shall be destitute of one the 1.st of July as the time is out

---

[24] The docket reads "From Jane Elliot", but the letter is in the handwriting of, and is signed by, M. C. Elliot, Jane's sister. The docket is also clear that the letter was written from Downham (Jane Elliot lived in London). Lettsom clearly mixed up the sisters.

[25] Gunton Hall, Hanworth, in Norfolk.

then. I have many times wished to see Jane but fear I never shall. I remain, good Sir, with much respect and every good wish your
humble servant
M-C Elliott

Downham
20th Feb.^{ry} 1813

Good Sir I must be the six shillings for the gown in your Debt till some future Day. I some time back received a Parcle from you containing a spencer, 2 pair of stockings and 1 pair of Mens' Gloves which I am much obliged for. I did not write to acknowledge them least you should think my Lettrs troublesome.

22. [L]

Endorsed: From M. C. Elliot, Mar. 14 1814, Downham.

Honoured Sir,
     You will Receive by the Nelson Coach a Brace of Hares which I beg you to accept. I am sorry I could not get them earlier in the season, but it has been so hard a Winter. Dear Sir, I was very unhappy I could not send as usual at Christmas, but I have been sadly streightened ever since I left the gate. There was some advantages allowed me and now I am destitute, and it is hard to trust to the Needle only and I never have had any favours from my relations as in the scripture with Divers and Lazaras who beg'd the Crumbs from the rich Man's Table, so with my sister Pitter, for was she to consider me with a few old Cloaths, I could appear in credit. She is a severe Judge, if we have not more mercy from above. I hop they are well. It's in vain to say more. But must beg to subscribe Myself yours at command
M-C Elliot

Downham 14.th March 1814.

7

Pettigrew

The life of Thomas Joseph Pettigrew, Lettsom's biographer, has been described in the Introduction to this volume and will not be rehearsed here. As with John Fothergill, Anthony Fothergill and Lettsom himself, Pettigrew's papers are not to be found as a single undisturbed collection but are scattered, although a substantial number are housed at Yale University (see Introduction, note 13). He is a figure who merits a major study. The Medical Society of London holds nine letters to Pettigrew from Lettsom and one from Joshua Dixon. We have arranged them in chronological order.

1. [JCL]

Mr. Pettigrew,

I should sooner have ~~acknowledged~~ conveyed by letter, my acknowledgements for the honour conferred upon me by the Philosophical Society, in electing me an honorary member,[1] had I not been desirous of doing it personally; but, prevented as I have been by professional engagements, I request you to communicate to the Society, my gratifi[ed se]ntiments on the occasion, as well as to accept my thanks for the polite manner in which you have conveyed ~~to me~~ their resolution to yours respectively
J. C. Lettsom

Sambrook Court
Mar. 25 1812

---

[1] Pettigrew founded the Philosophical Society of London in 1810 at the age of only nineteen. Lettsom was elected President in October 1812. See James Johnston Abraham, *Lettsom: his life, times, friends and descendants*, London, William Heinemann, 1933, p. 407. Abraham says Lettsom became a member, not an honorary member, but Abraham would not have had access to this letter for reasons we describe in the Introduction. The Society met in Scot's Corporation Hall, Crane Court, Fleet Street.

2. [JCL]

To Mr. Pettigrew Junr
Fleet Street

Paper made from East India Gunny bags[2]

Dear Mr. Pettigrew
    Anxious as I am for the prosperity and dignity of the Philosophical Society
of London, I wish to refer to your consideration, whether or not it might be
advisable to admit honorary members by Diplomas. I send you a few specimens, out of about 30 I possess, which might direct the choice of the Society.
    Should not the admission of Honorary numbers be permanent? It is so in
other literary Societies.
I am respectfully
J. C. Lettsom

Sambrook Court
Nov. 16 1812

3. [JCL]

To
Mr. Pettigrew
Bolt Court
Fleet Street

Sambrook Court
June 25 1813

Dear Mr. Pettigrew,
    Grieved as I am on account of last night's conclusion, I look forwards with
hope (for pain and pleasure alternate; or as Mr. Bedder said, like waves of the
sea we advance and retrograde, and again advance) that we have learned that
experience which will advance and unite, instead of disuniting, the Society.[3]

---

[2] The paper is light brown in colour and of poor quality.
[3] In view of the subjects the letter describes being discussed at the 'Society', this was the
Philosophical Society rather than the Medical Society of London. A heated discussion over
perfectibility seems to have led to a dispute over procedural matters.

Goode was wrong in his mode of replication and censure. And perhaps Brown shewed some thing of asperity. Besides, after calling to order, he ought to have left the degree of censure to the Chairman, and not have addressed the company, and assumed a power not acknowledged in societies of discussion. The Chairman should have been addressed, and he alone, so that strictly Mr. Brown was not quite in order. But powerful minds are apt to be too strongly and quickly excited, and rise into flame when a weak mind would scarcely feel the warmth of animation. I know that the succession of Goode would hurt himself, as well as the Society. If he is to ~~apt~~ part, let it be in a friendly manner. We have been much obliged to him, and as to myself, I have been improved by him. Added to this, from the regard that you and Mr. Brown entertain for your president, you will permit me to prevail, with your aid, on Mr. Brown, to coalesce in cordiality with Mr. Goode. I like to see a little flame, as well as smoke, at the same time. I am sensible it may ascend too high and consume the noblest fabric; and this flame I hope to extinguish, ~~and~~ or ever after to blaze with animated, but chastened warmth, with vigour, but with scientific discretion.

I have prepared Goode's mind (for high-minded characters may burn but do not consume, and violence pause and descend to moderation) and I shall request you to persuade Mr. Brown, and whom else, you please to bring with you, to take Coffee in Sambrook Court at seven precisely next Thursday, to meet Mr. Goode and shake hands like philosophers and fellow labourers in a noble Society, and forbearance in sentiment is the sourse of amity in society. "How would you be,
If He, which is the top of judgement, should but judge you as you are?" says Shakespeare.[4]

By reconciliation between the powerful minds of our two excellent members, we shall unite the Society in closer ties, and disappoint the enemies of a nascent and growing society, if enemies there are. And whether there are or not, we shall promote science and fair philosophy. But should my endeavours prove abortive, we shall find censure upon the Society who whilst argyui[ng] upon perfectibility, had afforded the melancholy instance that civilization produces animosity, and instead of directing the passions to great ~~attain~~ pursuits and acquisition, it debases it to those who characterize the ferocity of unsubdued nature. Let me therefore find a focus in Sambrook Court of virtue ~~con~~ improved by experience, of friendships augmented by union of sentiment, of animation chastened by moderation, and thus add to the gratification of you friend,
J. C. Lettsom

---

[4] *Measure for Measure*, II. ii. 76.

4. [JCL]

To
Mr. Pettigrew
Bolt Court
Fleet Street

Floriferis ut apes in saltibus omnia limant Lucretius[5]

This, however, is I think frequently used.

Dear Mr. Pettigrew,
I leave with you the Seal and Diplomas of the Medical Society of London. The great Fothergillian Medal Dye is left with Mr. Paige of the Tower. I desire you to make Entries of these matters, that at my death, it may be ascertained where this Dye, my Donation to the Medical Society,[6] is deposited. My wish is that Fothergillian Medal may be annihilated only at the period when medical science shall be no longer cultivated.
I am sincerely etc.
J.C. Lettsom

Sambrook Court
Aug. 7 1813

5. [JCL]

To
Mr. Pettigrew
Bolt Court
Fleet S

Mr. Pettigrew,
I am very happy that I did not know that any professional gentlemen were present at the letter, prior to my delivering it, as I should have felt more embarrassment than I really did, for I was not myself pleased with it. But you give me much satisfaction in intimating that it did not disgrace a Society I wish to see eminent and respected, and which must in some measure depend upon the conduct of the President.

---

[5] "Just as bees in flowery meadows feed on all things", Lucretius, *De rerum natura*, 3.11.
[6] This was the dye of the original Fothergillian medal. See Introduction, p. 3.

I have been very much professionally engaged lately. Yesterday only I hade 15 new families,[7] so that besides the preparations for lecturing and other imperious calls, I have yet prepared nothing for the Medical Society. Nevertheless, you may let the letter pass as you have enclosed to me, and I will endeavour to meet the Society with some scraps.

I <u>walked</u> to Kingsland[8] after the Lecture last night, as I promised to see the patient before 12, who sent for me just as I was setting out for the Philosophical Society. In walking, I passed two gentlemen, and heard an encomium on the Lecture of last night, which I suppose they had attended.

I shall dispose of 50 cards for the 6th of October, which will probably introduce 50 visitors, but I hope the intrusion will not be improper, and that the discourse will not derogate from the laudable views of the Society.

When can Mrs Pettigrew and you take a family dinner in Sambrook Court? The more I see of the former, the more I see of her and remember

Trifles light as air

Are to the jealous confirmations strong

As proofs of holy writ[9]

Sunday next would suit me; but if you should so conclude, send me word tomor tomorrow morning, that I may ask Miss Warren[10] and then all jealousy will subside.

yours sincerely

J. C. Lettsom

Sambrook Court
Sept. 17 1813

6. [JCL]

Endorsed: Mr. Pettigrew

<u>Straw paper</u>

Dear Friend Dear Mr. Pettigrew,

I have addressed a letter to our friend, the Rev.d Mr. Maurice, and have enjoined him to do what you proposed. He should before have performed,

---

[7] Lettsom was an extremely well established physician with an excellent reputation by this stage. It is not surprising that he could attract fifteen new families in one day. Most practitioners wanted to attract families onto their books, because they not only expanded, creating more patients, but often stayed with the same physician throughout their lives.

[8] A northern suburb of London, between Islington and Hackney.

[9] William Shakespeare, *Othello*, III. iii. 322.

[10] Possibly a daughter of Richard Warren (1731–97), physician to George III, who was one of the three physicians who attended John Fothergill in his last illness. See Abraham, op. cit., note 1 above, pp. 205–6.

and which with your additional influence, ~~he~~ may ~~be~~ induced him to canter, if he do not gallop, upon Pegasus. He is not a genius that trots calmly along the lower regions of Helicon; he delights in boldness and elevation. The Eagle does not descend to rills and ponds to rest upon frogs and Mice like the blinked owl, but with a bold eye, in frenzy rolling, he pounces upon loftier objects, and takes his station on some prominent mount or bold crag.

After reading the enclosed, please to convey it when convenient to him, as I suppose you have the pleasure of seeing him, oftener than is the lot of your friend

J. C. Lettsom

Sambrook Court
Oct. 8 1813

As I was closing this, Dr. Hamilton[11] called upon me to visit his Lady. He told me some more curious anecdotes—and explained the Scotch girls' aqua pura ~~vi~~ id est originalis.[12]

7. [JCL]

Endorsed: From Dr. Lettsom, Jan. 1 1814.

Mr. Pettigrew
Bolt Court
Fleet Street

Dear Mr. Pettigrew

If the good women who are attentive to times and seasons see the days to lengthen, it is more than I do; for at nine this morning, I write this letter by candle light; nevertheless, I wish you the compliments of the season.

I think that in the life of Dr. Johnstone,[13] I introduce the opinion of Dr. Rush; but of this I am not certain.

I will try to call upon Mrs Hicks, if possible, at 12. I have a regard for her independently of fees, and therefore, that object will not determine me to

---

[11] Probably William Hamilton who had been secretary to the Medical Society of London. See Abraham, op. cit. note 1 above, pp. 225–6

[12] This probably means that Hamilton's method of using pure water in treatment was original.

[13] Probably James Johnstone of Worcester who first sent Lettsom Lady Huntingdon as a patient. See Abraham, op. cit., note 1 above, p. 273. The reference to the "life" is obscure, perhaps Lettsom wrote an obituary in a magazine.

suspend visiting a patient, who is liberally, though perhaps ineffectually disposed to confer them. There are characters exactly the reverse; and do not merit attention.

In wishing a medical man at this time a cheerful Xmas and a happy New Year, it must be appropriate now from the numerous calls upon his practice; so that in the depth of a fog, he is making hay. I think the Society of Arts have proposed a premium for making hay in such weather; the present affords an opportunity to apply to Dr. Taylor for the honourable medal. The candidates are certainly numerous, and the fallen grass, and particularly the tenderest (children) demand the most active haymakers.

J. C. Lettsom

Jan 1. 1814

8. [CF]

Paper made of East India gunny bags

Mr. Pettigrew
3 Bolt Court
Fleet Street

Dear Mr. Pettigrew,

I do not expect, nor wish you, to peruse my diffuse lecture;[14] but if you can possibly spare time to throw your eye over it, just to determine what you wish me to leave out, as you know the <u>taste</u> of the Philosophical Society better than I do, I should be obliged to you. As I have not read the lecture over since composed, perhaps you could let me have it again, on Monday or Tuesday, that I may take that trouble before it is rehearsed on Thursday. Mr. Brown who accompanied me on Thursday evening and took a cup of coffee with me, and to whom I read a few papers, flatters me with a favourable opinion of the whole, but as its reception depends upon the <u>taste</u> of our Society you are the best judge of that undefineable quality.

I request the Philosophical Society's acceptance of a work of no little importance—The Geographical, Historical and Political History of Europe,[15] as a work of great information and sterling merit.

---

[14] Lettsom gave two lectures at the Philosophical Society of London in 1815 on the 'Philosophy of youthful sports'. He was deeply involved with the Philosophical Society towards the end of his life. See Abraham, op. cit., note 1 above, p. 434.

[15] Possibly *A geographical, historical, and political description of the Empire of Germany, Holland, the Netherlands ... translated from the German of J. G. Boetticher*, London, printed for John Stockdale, 1800.

Dr. Penrose's letter may be communicated next Monday to the Medical Society. It is a well written document, and were a correspondence once adopted, I think much useful medical matter might be assimilated in a medical journal.

I am sincerely etc.

J C Lettsom

Sambrook Court
Apr. 8 1815

9. [JCL][16]

I called to say, that unless requisite, I fear my home patients will confine me later than the meeting of the Humane <u>Society</u>. I shall be in Sambrook Court from 3 till seven today. Should you have it in your possession, I should like to see the Exhibition of pictures (not yet having seen) from your Catalogue,[17] for which I could call in Bolt Court tomorrow, should I be able to visit Somerset <u>house</u>.

Should I not see you before, bring if you attend on Thursday at the Philosophical Society—the amount of what I owe you for Spurzheim[18] and I believe for some thing else, which I do not recollect. Should the Humane Society want £50 I will endeavour to answer it—July 15 this Dividend will be due the 3 per Cents.

Professor Duncan[19] of Edinburgh breakfasts with me at 9 o'clock tomorrow morning, and if you call you may have Tea, toast, bread and butter and eggs.

June 20 1815   J C Lettsom

A friend of mine wants an Human-skull, in what manner can I procure him one?

---

[16] There is no addressee but, as noted, Pettigrew lived in Bolt Court which is referred to in the letter.

[17] Not identified.

[18] Johann Gaspard Spurzheim (1776–1832) along with Franz Joseph Gall (1758–1828) one of the founders of cranioscopy or phrenology. Lettsom could be referring to any one of a number of works by Spurzheim. More interesting is that the work of Gall and Spurzheim was seen as materialist and atheist in some quarters yet, although a Quaker, Lettsom makes no comment.

[19] Probably Andrew Duncan senior. See 'Letters to Lettsom' section, note 99.

[JCL]

Endorsed: Dr. Dixon,[20] Oct[r.] 8/16.
T. J. Pettigrew, Esq[r].

Whitehaven, Oct. 8 1816

Sir,

I was duly favoured with your very acceptable Letter, and feel it a satisfaction to comply with your intimation, relative to my correspondence with Dr. Lettsom. Though I was not personally acquainted with him, yet I have long entertained sentiments of esteem and regard, which it was a gratification to express. The enclosed twenty Letters[21] may furnish you with a few observations, but in general they are brief and of trivial import. The one in reply to Dr. L—'s invaluable Letter dated Oct. 23 and written the day before his death, Oct. 31, was returned to me, by Mr. Steel,[22] and I have never felt myself equal to open it, till the afternoon, when I was preparing it for your inspection. You will please to add my name to the List of Subscribers, and also accept my publication. I shall be happy to receive, as usual, the Reports of the Royal Humane Society, or any Tract relative to that most beneficent Institution. The earliest private opportunity will convey this Packet to you, and the Letters,[+] when perfectly convenient, may be sent to Mr. Steel's, Surgeon, Tower Hill, or Mr. Denison, Surgeon, Store Street, No. 31 Bedford Square, or perhaps Messrs. Longman and Co. may transmit them, along with other articles, to our Booksellers.
I am, very respectfully,
Your obedient servant
Joshua Dixon

[+] upon which I place a justly merited high estimation. You will also have the goodness to return Dr. Rush's Letters and mine to Dr. L—, inclosing them.

---

[20] See 'Letters to Lettsom' section, note 75.

[21] Pettigrew includes thirteen letters between Joshua Dixon and Lettsom. Thomas Joseph Pettigrew, *Memoirs of the life and writings of the late John Coakley Lettsom, with a selection from his correspondence*, 3 vols, London, printed by Nichols, Son, and Bentley, for Longman, Hurst, Rees, Orme and Brown, 3 vols, 1817, vol. 3, pp. 353–85; and three from Benjamin Rush to Dixon, ibid., pp. 385–90.

[22] This is the surgeon referred to by Dr. Dixon in his first letter in the 'Letters to Lettsom' section.

Index

Lettsom's publications are indexed under their titles. All other publications are under authors, with the exception of anonymous works. Page numbers in *italics* refer to illustrations in the text.